Exiles in Sepharad

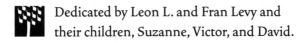

Dedicated by Leon L. and Fran Levy and their children, Suzanne, Victor, and David.

University of Nebraska Press

LINCOLN

Exiles in Sepharad

The Jewish Millennium in Spain

JEFFREY GORSKY

The Jewish Publication Society

PHILADELPHIA

A poem in chapter 6, "The mind is flawed...," is reproduced
from *Wine, Women, and Death* by Raymond P. Scheindlin by
permission of the University of Nebraska Press. © 1986 by
the Jewish Publication Society. A poem in chapter 7, "I weep
like an ostrich...," is reproduced from *Twilight of a Golden Age:
Selected Poems of Abraham Ibn Ezra* edited by Leon J. Weinberger
by permission of the University of Alabama Press. © 1997 by
the University of Alabama Press.

All rights reserved. Published by the University of Nebraska
Press as a Jewish Publication Society book. Manufactured in
the United States of America. ∞

Library of Congress Cataloging-in-Publication Data
Gorsky, Jeffrey, author.
Exiles in Sepharad: the Jewish millennium in Spain / Jeffrey
Gorsky.
pages   cm
"The dramatic one-thousand-year history of the Jews in Spain,
from their heyday under Muslim and then early Christian
rule—when Jewish culture was at its height, like nowhere
else in the world—to the late fourteenth century, when mass
riots against the Jews forced conversions and eventually led to
the horrific Spanish Inquisition and expulsion of the Jews"—
Provided by publisher.
Includes bibliographical references and index.
ISBN 978-0-8276-1251-8 (pbk.: alk. paper)
ISBN 978-0-8276-1239-6 (epub)
ISBN 978-0-8276-1240-2 (mobi)
ISBN 978-0-8276-1241-9 (pdf)
1. Jews—Spain—History—To 1500. 2. Spain—History—
711–1516. 3. Spain—Ethnic relations—History. I. Title.
DS135.S7G67 2015   946'.004924—dc23
2014042888

Set in Vendetta by Lindsey Auten.

To my wife, Renee;
my daughters, Laura and Adrianna;
and my parents, Lou and Rhoda.

Contents

Illustrations

Acknowledgments

This project, for many years, was my personal obsession. While I reached out to many people, few were aware of the compelling nature of Sephardic history, and as an outsider to this story I could not find anyone who had the time or interest to assist me. I was also neglected and eventually abandoned, serially, by two agents. For that reason I am extremely grateful to Rabbi Barry Schwartz with the Jewish Publication Society, who immediately recognized the importance of this subject, and to my editor at JPS, Carol Hupping. I am also grateful to the many scholars who shared my obsession and whose scholarship I relied on, and cribbed from, to tell this story. In particular David Raphael's *The Expulsion 1492 Chronicles*, an outstanding compilation and translation of primary source material, was an important resource for my research into this period. Finally, I thank Ira Shapiro for introducing me to my second agent, and Sharon Separ, who has long been my only reader and fan.

Chronology

711: Tariq ibn Ziyad leads a Muslim army and invades Spain

731–88: Abdul al-Rahman I establishes an emirate in Spain

929: Abdul al-Rahman III declares his kingdom
to be a caliphate

915–70 (c.): Hasdai ibn Shaprut

993–1056 (c.): Samuel ben Joseph Halevi ibn Nagrela,
grand vizier of Granada

1066: Massacre of Jews in Granada

1075–1141 (c.): Judah Halevi

1130–73 (c.): Benjamin of Tudela

1135–1204: Moses ben Maimon (Maimonides)

1252–84: Reign of Alfonso X (the Wise), king of Castile

1231: First Papal Inquisition established, to counter
the Cathar heresy

1263: Disputation of Barcelona

1350–69: Reign of Pedro (the Cruel), king of Castile

1356 (c.): Synagogue "El Transito" completed in Toledo

1391: Mass riots and forced conversions spread
throughout Castile and Aragon

1413–14: Disputation of Tortosa

1425–54: Reign of Juan II, king of Castile

1449: The Toledan rebellion

1454–74: Reign of Enrique IV, king of Castile

1474: Isabella ascends to throne of Castile

1480: Spanish Inquisition begins in Seville

1420–98: Tomás de Torquemada

1485: Assassination of Pedro Arbues

1490–91: Blood-libel trial in La Guardia

1492: Catholic monarchs sign expulsion decree for Castile/Aragon

1497: General conversion of Jews in Portugal

1498: Expulsion decree in Navarre

1506: Anti-Jewish riots in Portugal

1629: Dutch conquest of Pernambuco

1654: Dutch surrender of Pernambuco to Portugal

1654: Twenty-three Jews from Recife arrive in New Amsterdam

Exiles in Sepharad

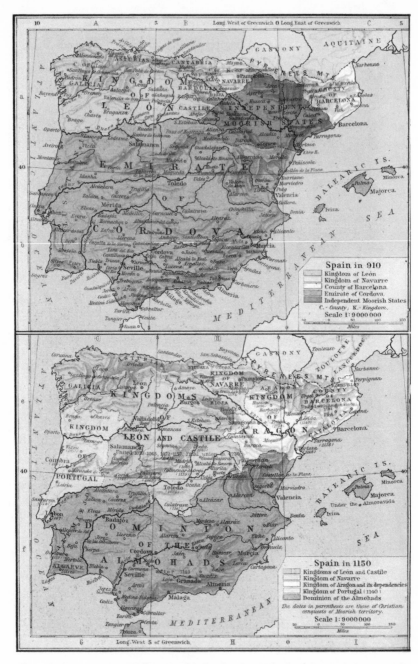

Fig. 1. Spain, 910–1492. William R. Shepherd, *Historical Atlas* (New York: Henry Holt,

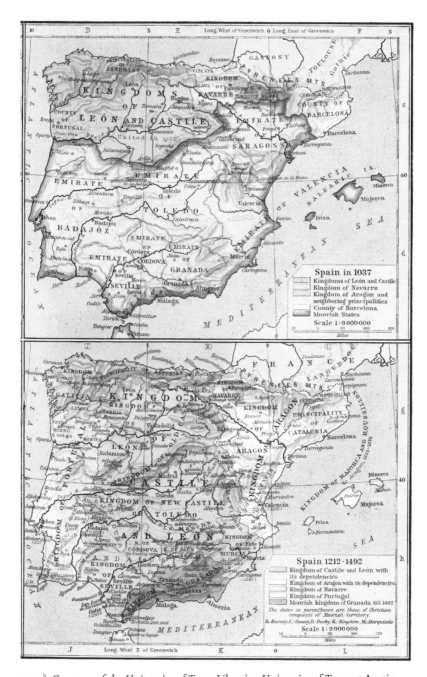

1923). Courtesy of the University of Texas Libraries, University of Texas at Austin.

Introduction

Chance brought me to Spain. In 1982 I came to the end of my first
U.S. Foreign Service tour in Colombia (Medellín and Bogotá), with
an onward assignment to Tokyo. A call from my assignments officer in
Washington "closed out" Tokyo, and Santiago loomed in my future. A
last-minute-assignment break brought me a new offer: Bilbao. In those
pre-Guggenheim days, I knew the place-name only from a song by Kurt
Weill and Berthold Brecht ("Der Bilbao Song"), but I needed no urging to accept a tour in Spain.

As a Jew in Bilbao, I was a statistical anomaly. Jews made up about
.0001 percent of the population, fewer than ten—all expatriates—in
a greater metropolitan area of about nine hundred thousand people.
The two years I spent in Bilbao gave me a few glimpses into Spain's
peculiar attitude toward Jews. The most revealing came after I attended
a lecture on the history of Jews in the Basque country, given by a priest
who served the expatriate community. Afterward, I introduced myself
to him, noting that I was one of the few Jews in the city. To my sur-
prise, he contradicted me: "There are a mountain of Jews in Bilbao."
He proceeded to recite a series of last names, none of which sounded
Jewish to me. I promised myself that I would look for this invisible
Jewish community.

A few weeks later, the priest called me to say that an Israeli ship had
put in at port, and the sailors on board wanted someone to host a traditional Jewish Sabbath dinner. I demurred, pointing out that I was
a bachelor who couldn't cook, and I was not very religious. He coun-
tered that I was the only one available to do it. I asked him about the
"mountain of Jews" he had mentioned before. "Oh," he said, "they are

all Catholics." The people he considered "Jews" had been practicing Catholics for five hundred years.

Bilbao also provided an education in the mechanics of ethnic conflict. Euskadi ta Askatasuna—a pro-separatist paramilitary group in the Basque country, better known as ETA—had diminished in size and activity since the Franco period but was still, back in the early 1980s, responsible for about thirty killings a year. The story of the Basques, whose revival of ethnic language and culture clashed, sometimes violently, with the non-Basque culture of the Spanish state, is a modern variation of the cultural and ethnic conflicts that sometimes overwhelmed the Jews in their thousand-year sojourn in Spain.

The Jewish community in Spain, living under Muslim and Christian domination and cultures, experienced both symbiosis and conflict, exemplifying both the potential for and the limits to coexistence between different cultures and religions. The ethnic and religious conflicts in medieval Spain and early modern Spain between the Muslims, the Christians, and the Jews are at the heart of this book.

These conflicts can seem strikingly relevant today in a world caught up in what seems now to be unending conflicts between tribes, religions, and ethnic identities. I started researching the story of the Iberian Jews at about the time of the quincentennial of the expulsion of 1492. In 1994, the Hutu massacre of the Tutsis brought the word "genocide" back into common use. The mid-1990s was also the period when Slobodan Milošević taught everyone the term "ethnic cleansing." The fall of the Soviet Union ended the Cold War and ideological conflict, while the world fell back on the same kind of ethnic and religious conflicts that drive the events in this book. Today one can see these kinds of conflicts in dozens of countries all over the world. The Jews forced to live as refugees after the Spanish expulsions have many modern parallels today.

There is a much-quoted assertion by the great Jewish historian Salo Wittmayer Baron that "lachrymose" accounts of the Jews—portrayals of Jews as perennial victims—distort the historical record. Such accounts, he says, both demean the Jews and ignore the often greater suffering of contemporary groups. I can be faulted for sometimes embracing a "lachrymose" approach to this period in Jewish history. Although I have attempted to do justice to the impressive and important achievements of the Spanish Jews, my primary motivation for writing this book was to document the injustices that they suffered. In an age of almost innumerable victims of ongoing ethnic and religious conflict, it is vital to document what happened to the innocent victims of these conflicts in the past.

One Thousand Years in Summary

In brief, this is the story of the Spanish Jews: After a period of early repression, the Jews of Spain found welcome in Islamic Spain. The Islamic rulers provided sponsorship in exchange for Jewish assistance and support. But the Jews maintained their separate identity and community, which left inherent tensions with the Muslim community. The Jews relied on the head of state (emir, caliph, or sultan) for protection.

This arrangement—a kind of marriage of convenience between the Jews and the central authority—allowed the Jews to prosper but left an inherent vulnerability. When the head of state could no longer protect the Jews, underlying tensions could flare up and lead to the destruction of the Jewish community. In Muslim Spain support failed when the breakup of the caliphate made it vulnerable to invasion by fundamentalist tribes from North Africa that were intolerant of Jews. The Jews were forced to flee to Christian Spain.

In the Christian lands Jews found a similar welcome as in Muslim Spain—support from the Crown in exchange for financial and other services. By the late fourteenth century, Spanish Jews enjoyed a level of prosperity and power unthinkable anywhere else in Europe. As in Muslim Spain, the Jews as a separate community relied on royal support to protect them from religious and popular resentment, making the Jews vulnerable when political instability undermined royal support.

This vulnerability manifested itself violently in 1391. A fanatic priest, exploiting a political vacuum, incited mobs against the Jews throughout Castile and Aragon with the slogan "convert or die." When the riots ended, a third to a half of the Spanish Jews had converted to Christianity, the greatest mass conversion in modern Jewish history.

These "conversos" became enormously successful. With the limits to advancement placed on Jews removed, they could marry into the aristocracy and obtain high positions in both the court and church. Their success fostered resentment, however, and some accused them of secretly practicing Judaism. During the political insurrection and civil wars in Castile under the reigns of Juan II and Enrique IV, the conversos, supporters of the kings, became scapegoats for the weak rulers, and in some cities battles broke out between the "Old" and the "New Christians."

When the joint reign of Queen Isabella and King Ferdinand restored stability to Spain, the monarchs decided to end the conflict between the Old and the New Christians by establishing an Inquisition, approved by the pope but under their control. The Inquisition focused on Christian conversos accused of Judaizing—it had little authority over the unconverted Jews. The Inquisition aggressively pursued conversos, trying thousands and burning many at the stake. It then lobbied for the expulsion of the Jews, arguing that the Jews undermined the converso Christian faith.

In 1492 the Spanish monarchs, accepting the Inquisition argument, ordered the expulsion of all Jews from Castile and Aragon. In 1497 the king of Portugal, at the urging of his bride, daughter of Ferdinand and Isabella, forcibly converted all the Jews. A similar forced conversion soon followed in Navarre. The Spanish Jewish community, the most populous and prosperous in Europe a century earlier, now ceased to exist in all of Iberia.

While it is important to memorialize the injustices suffered by these Jews, they were more than victims. The thriving if sometimes fragile world of the Jews in Spain made important contributions to Jewish and world culture and history. The Jews acted as conduits between Arab and Western cultures, contributing to and introducing to Europe Arab discoveries in mathematics and science and transmitting Greek and Roman works lost to the West but preserved in the Arab world. Jews produced important works of philosophy, religion, and poetry, including Maimonides's *Guide for the Perplexed*, and the seminal work of Jewish mysticism, the *Zohar*. Even after the expulsion, Spanish Jews continued to thrive in the diaspora in the Americas, Europe, and the Middle East. Today approximately 20 percent of Jews are descended from the Jews of Spain.

PART 1

La Convivencia

1

A Marriage of Convenience

The period in Spanish history beginning with the Muslim conquest in the eighth century is called by some the *convivencia*. The Spanish word literally means "living together." It is used to refer to a time in Spain when Christians, Muslims, and Jews coexisted in unparalleled harmony. For more than half a millennium, under either Muslim or Christian political control, the three cultures lived together, worked together, and explored new and old ideas together.

The *convivencia* was popularized—both as term and concept—by Américo Castro, a great Spanish historian of the twentieth century. Castro's work demonstrated the essential contributions of Muslims and Jews to Spanish culture, and he argued that these contributions played a pivotal role in forming the national character of Spain: "Between the tenth and the fifteenth centuries Spanish history was Christian-Islamic-Judaic; and during those centuries the definitive structure of Hispanic life was forged. It is not possible to break up this history into stagnant pools, or to divide it off into parallel, synchronous currents, because each one of the three groups was a part of the circumstances projected by the other two."[1]

Castro's *convivencia* has inspired numerous descriptions of a multi-cultured Spain. In her recent book *Ornament of the World*, María Rosa Menocal describes the *convivencia* as a multicultural Eden, and religious intolerance was the apple that brought exile from this paradise.[2] Islamic nationalists have cited the *convivencia* as proof that Islam is tolerant by nature, claiming that only Zionist distortions require Muslims to stray in self-defense from their natural tolerance of other faiths.

The *convivencia* provides a useful perspective on Jewish and Spanish history, highlighting the important contributions that Jews and Muslims in Spain made to Spanish and European culture. It also explains the basis for the great cultural accomplishments of the Spanish Jews and their economic and political achievements.

The exclusive focus on the *convivencia* and tolerance, however, distorts Jewish and Spanish history. While Jews participated in the Muslim and Christian kingdoms of Spain, they also largely lived apart from the other religious groups and maintained their autonomous culture. A focus exclusively on tolerance also makes it difficult to understand the bouts of anti-Jewish violence and repression that periodically erupted in both the Muslim and the Christian kingdoms.

In fact, Spaniards have traditionally presented the history of Jewish, Christian, and Muslim relations as a story of conflict, not cooperation. The *convivencia* was only popularized in the latter half of the twentieth century, by Américo Castro. Spaniards traditionally have focused instead on the *reconquista*, the lengthy war to reverse the Islamic invasion of Spain. This traditional Spanish narrative emphasizes devotion to Catholicism, a faith that led the Spanish to victory against the Muslim invaders, and which culminated in the Spanish expulsion of Jews and Moors from Spain. Jews, as well as Muslims, were foreign cultures that needed to be purged from Iberia to maintain Spanish Christian cultural purity.

This is the history told by conservative intellectuals such as the influential nineteenth-century scholar Marcelino Menéndez y Pelayo, whose basic views have been summarized by the British historian Henry Kamen: "[Menéndez y Pelayo] maintained the view that since earliest times there had been a genuine nation called Spain that drew its strength from the eternal values of Catholicism alone. All other cultures, whether Jewish or Arabic, were passing phases that only contributed distortions (or 'heresies') of the true essence."[3]

Castro's work contradicted the traditional focus of conservative Spanish historians on the purity of Catholic Spain, an image that also lay at the heart of Franco's nationalist ideology. As Isabelle Rohr notes in *The Spanish Right and the Jews*: "The myth of the *Reconquista* was not only central to Nationalist thinking [within Spain], it was also the lens through which [Nationalist Spain] perceived the external world. Thus,

Hitler's anti-Semitic campaign was labeled a crusade to save Christian Europe."[4] The victory of Franco's nationalists in 1939 forced Américo Castro, along with his liberal ideas, into exile.

Castro became extremely influential outside Spain, but Spanish scholars, at least during the Franco years, rejected the *convivencia* for the ideal of the reconquest and instead focused on religious conflict, not cooperation. For example, in his book *Understanding Spain*, the twentieth-century Spanish philosopher Julián Marías, who had supported the republic, at the end of the Franco period still criticized Castro and defended the idea of Catholic Spain: "To speak of 'Christians, Moors, and Jews' as homogenous and comparable elements means exercising very great violence on the reality of medieval Spain and disfiguring its structure; above all, its projective, that is to say, historical, character. What we understand by Spain … is the Christian Spain that did not accept its Islamization and struggled against it, with more or less success, with enthusiasm or with apathy, from early in the eighth century to the end of the fifteenth, without a single interruption of that constitutive project."[5]

Tolerance or Conflict?

Was the history of the Spanish Jews a story of religious tolerance or of religious conflict? From the Jewish perspective the period of the *convivencia* has a mixed legacy. It was, in some ways, a golden age. During this period Jews enjoyed over five hundred years of relative stability. During much of this period, up until the fourteenth century, more Jews lived in Spain than in all the European countries combined.[6] And Jews prospered. Some Jews, rich and powerful, under both Muslim and Christian rulers even became governmental ministers. Intellectually, the period opened the Jews to new ideas: They tried to reconcile their religion with the Hellenistic ideas that they had struggled with since the Maccabean rebellion. They built on Muslim advances to become world leaders in philosophy, medicine, and science. They explored new forms of mystical spiritualism, creating the canon of religious works known collectively as the Kabbalah.

Yet even at the best of times, Jews never were fully safe and secure under the *convivencia*. This so-called golden age was marked by outbreaks of repression, including the murders of prominent Jews and pogroms targeting entire communities. The *convivencia*—first under Muslim, then Christian rule—ended in violence and repression that matched or exceeded anything else in Europe.

Many people are struck by these extremes. How could Spain go from being the most tolerant to the most intolerant society toward the Jews? How could Spain foster intolerance after it had prospered as a multicultural society?

These are natural questions to ask, but they are the wrong questions. What made Spain unusual was its level of tolerance, not its repression. There was nothing unusual about intolerance; repression of Jews was endemic in the Muslim and Catholic worlds. Jews had been expelled from England and France. Rumors of ritual killings and well poisonings, as well as fears that Jews had been fomenting the plague, were all common reasons for anti-Jewish persecution. The Crusades often became a vehicle for anti-Jewish violence. What happened in Spain was different only in degree, not in kind. The interesting question is not why Spain turned intolerant, but why Spanish Jews were granted so much freedom and access to power in the first place.

A Marriage of Convenience

Muslims and Christians showed Jews tolerance because specific circumstances made Jews valuable to the rulers of Muslim and Christian Spain. To the Muslims the Jews were allies they could use to bolster their minority rule over a majority Christian population. To the Christians Jews were important cultural and political envoys to the Muslim world. Jews under the Muslims learned administrative skills later needed by the Christian rulers trained in warfare, not governance. As skilled artisans, Jews dominated the productive sector of the economy and made up much of the tax base. The *convivencia* was a marriage of convenience.

Richard Fletcher, a British historian who specializes in medieval Spain, describes the pragmatic basis for Spanish tolerance: "It is a myth of the modern imagination that medieval Islamic Spain was, in any sense that we should recognize today, a tolerant society. Much the same could be said of the fortunes of the Mudejars [Muslims] and Jews under Christian rule. They were reluctantly tolerated, not out of principle but out of pragmatism: because they could be useful."[7]

Even Américo Castro recognized the practical motivations for embracing the tolerant practices known as the *convivencia*. "That the three religions coexisted is due less to tolerance than to vital weakness."[8]

This marriage of convenience was maintained by the Muslim and the Christian rulers only with difficulty, in the face of strong, popular anti-Jewish pressures. In Muslim Spain the Jews suffered from the religious intolerance of fundamentalist Muslim sects. In Christian Spain motives for intolerance included resentment against the Jewish moneylenders and tax collectors for the Crown. The Jews came under almost constant attack from the church, particularly from the mendicant friars who had taken up the mission of converting the Jews.

This underlying antagonism to the Jewish presence created inevitable tensions even in the best of times in the Jews' relations with their Muslim and Christian neighbors. Strong, stable government could suppress anti-Jewish pressures. But when the government lacked the power or the will to protect the Jews, the result could be tragic—either for individuals or, on occasion, for entire communities. This happened repeatedly to Jews under both their Muslim and their Christian patrons. Significant anti-Jewish measures almost always came at periods of unusual political instability.

The expulsion decree of 1492 was an exception because it came at a time of both political stability and an exceptionally strong monarchy. But Ferdinand and Isabella could sign such a decree because, by 1492, the practical incentives for tolerance had largely disappeared. Converts from Judaism—controlled through the repressive apparatus of the Spanish Inquisition—could perform almost all the services that the Jews had provided in the past.

The end to the practical considerations that fostered tolerance in Spain would end the *convivencia* forever and lead to the eradication of Judaism from Iberia for nearly five hundred years.

2

The Visigoth Persecution of the Jews

It is not known when Jews first settled in Iberia. Medieval legends have it that the city of Toledo in central Spain was founded by Jews, following the destruction of the first temple in Jerusalem and the Babylonian captivity.[1] Some Sephardic families claimed descent from the time of King David. Jews may have joined early Phoenician or Carthaginian trading settlements. It is known that Jews had accompanied the Romans into the area and had joined settlements in the Roman provinces of Hispania and Lusitania. The oldest known synagogue remains that have been discovered, in Elche (near the Mediterranean), date from between the third and the fifth century.

But before the turn of the first millennium, the Visigoths almost brought an end to the Jewish presence in Iberia. The Visigoths were Germanic mercenaries who, after sacking Rome, wandered west to pick off the remains of the defunct empire. By the end of the fifth century, they controlled most of the Iberian Peninsula. Theirs was a weak kind of control, a series of unstable reigns rocked by wars of succession and local revolts. The original royal line died out in 507 AD. Only eight of the twenty-three Visigoth kings succeeded their fathers, some of them only very briefly.[2] Religious differences stoked instability: the Visigoths initially were Arians, who believed that Jesus had an existence distinct from God, while most Iberians followed the Roman Catholic belief in the Trinity.

Culturally, the most prominent intellectual figure during the Visigoth period was Isidore of Seville, the archbishop of that city, who was later canonized by the Catholic Church. His *Etymologiae* was meant to be an exhaustive encyclopedia of all learning known to humankind. It demonstrated how much Greek and Roman knowledge was lost to Europe, and why, given this loss of classical learning, these years would be called the "Dark Ages." Isidore also wrote *De fide catholica ex Veteriet Novo Testamento, contra Judaeos*, which was to become one of the most popular anti-Jewish books of the Middle Ages.

At first the Jews were treated under the Visigoths much as they had been under Roman rule. They were permitted to hold senatorial rank and were recruited to important fortresses for garrison duty. Jews were permitted their own courts and allowed to perform their religious observances.[3] But the Visigoth king Reccared, who converted his people to the Roman faith in 589 to conform with Spanish practice, enacted a few laws unfavorable to the Jews. Serious troubles began with King Sisebut, who ascended to the throne in 612. He freed all Christian slaves owned by Jews and forbade Jews from hiring Christian workers. Violators had half of their property confiscated. Sisebut also instituted the death penalty for Jews convicted of proselytizing. Jews married to Christians had to convert or leave the kingdom, and Jews were prohibited from holding any office with power over Christians.

Either these laws proved ineffective, or King Sisebut lost patience with them. He subsequently instituted forced conversions, including the conversions of several prominent rabbis. Jews fled en masse into exile. Even Bishop Isidore, who had penned his great tract against the Jews, protested the severity of these measures.

Sisebut's far-reaching measures were the first in a series of cycles of repression and tolerance. Kings favorable toward the Jews alternated with others who passed ever more repressive—even genocidal—anti-Jewish laws. Ultimately, the Visigoths promulgated some of the most repressive anti-Jewish laws in European history. As noted by the historian Norman Roth: "The Visigothic period produced the most vile polemic and the harshest legislation against Jews encountered at any time in medieval Europe."[4]

King Chintila, whose reign began in 636, required all Jews to convert or to leave the Visigoth territory. Any convert deemed insincere was subject to death by stoning. Reccesuinth, who reigned from 649 to 672, made the practice of Jewish rites a capital offense. Erwig, king after 680, promulgated twenty-eight anti-Jewish laws, including a penalty of death for refusal to eat pork. King Egica, Erwig's successor, copied King Reccesuinth's description of the Jews as a "contagious pestilence" by coining the Latin phrase *judaeorum pestis*, or the "Jewish plague."[5] Under Egica Jews were stripped of all they possessed and ordered into slavery.

Politics—rather than religious fanaticism—seem the most likely cause for these actions. Repressive measures of kings from Chintila to Egica were often suspended by succeeding monarchs like Wamba and Witiza. These changes of policy might have reflected efforts by successive kings to appease their most powerful bases of support. Anti-Jewish laws pleased the Spanish bishops (who held considerable secular power beyond their religious authority), while the more tolerant kings traditionally looked to the Jews and their aristocratic allies for support.

Bishop Julian of Toledo articulated the anti-Jewish opinion of clerics in the late 600s: the Jews "had to be cut off... like the cancerous part of the body, before this harmful disease could be passed on to the healthy parts."[6] The royal anti-Jewish policies of the seventh century imply a reliance on the support of the bishops, since almost all the anti-Jewish legislation came from those kings (Reccared, Sisebut, Chintila, Reccesuinth, Erwig, and Egica) in close alliance with—or under the thumb of—the clerical party.[7]

The fact that each new set of anti-Jewish laws remained valid for generations and became more draconian over time indicates that the rulers who imposed them were too weak to effectively implement them. Otherwise, it would not make sense to implement a law enslaving Jews a generation after all Jews faced an order of death or conversion. As noted by the historian Eliyah Ashtor: "The very severity of these enactments is proof that they were not fully executed, and despite the decrees of kings and councils many Jews remained in Spain. Indeed, from the decisions of the councils we learn that Jews bribed the nobles who held the reins of government, and even the clergy themselves, not to enforce these laws strictly. Nevertheless their plight worsened and they looked for a source of deliverance."[8]

For Jews relief from Visigoth persecution would come with the Muslim invasion of the Iberian Peninsula. But the legacy of the Visigoths continued to poison the lives of the Jews. The Visigoth experiment in forced conversions was cited by advocates of anti-Jewish measures in the later medieval period as a precedent for the much larger forced conversions of the fourteenth and fifteenth centuries. The false legend that the Jews had played an important role in the betrayal of the Visigoths to the invading Muslims would become standard fodder for anti-Jewish propaganda in Spain.

3

Muslim Rule

Al-Andalus

The memory of al-Andalus—Muslim rule in Spain—which brought the greatest Muslim culture ever to flourish in what is now Christian Europe, still resonates in the modern world half a millennium after its disappearance. In the past few years, the dream of al-Andalus transformed into a nightmare, as al-Qaeda called for its restoration. Al-Qaeda leader Aymanal-Zawahiri called al-Andalus "a promised land that one day would revert to Islamic rule."[1] After the 2004 al-Qaeda-inspired train bombings in Madrid, one Spanish parliamentarian pointed to allegiance to the memory of al-Andalus as a motivation for the attacks: "They have a grander vision, which is an obsession with the demise of al-Andalus. We hear this in the sermons of the militant Islamic sheikhs."[2] One hundred and ninety-one people were killed in these attacks.

The memory of al-Andalus persists in part due to the striking physical legacy the Moors left in Spain. These architectural remnants include great Islamic structures such as the Córdoban Mosque, with its dark, indoor forest of striped marble arches—recycled stone from a Christian cathedral that in turn had been built on the ruins of a Roman temple; the Alcázar palace in Seville, refurbished by Pedro the Cruel in the fourteenth century in the Moorish style, and used as a residence by Queen Isabella at the beginning of her reign; and the most famous palatial complex in Spain, the Alhambra in Granada, finished in the fifteenth century shortly before the end of Muslim rule in Spain.

This physical legacy of al-Andalus extends throughout Spain. The builders and artisans of Islamic Spain, both *mudejar* (Islamic) and *mozárabe* (Christian and raised in the Moorish kingdoms), were valued throughout Iberia, and they erected buildings from Córdoba to

Toledo, including Moorish-style churches and synagogues. This architectural legacy is only a small portion of the extensive wealth and cultural achievements of al-Andalus at its height, which transformed Jewish life. Islamic intellectual discoveries and achievements exposed Jews to the most advanced scientific, mathematical, and philosophical ideas. Two of the greatest medieval Jewish works, Maimonides's *Guide for the Perplexed* and Halevi's *Book of the Kuzari*, were written during this period, and in Arabic, not in Hebrew. In exchange for Jewish support, Moorish leaders provided the Jews with unparalleled opportunities for wealth and power. The most successful Jews became courtiers, fully assimilated (except for religion) in the life of the Islamic court.

But for all its achievements and longevity—there was a Muslim state in Spain for over seven hundred years—al-Andalus began as an accidental kingdom and remained always fragile. Only the strongest leaders could cope with the great physical and cultural diversity that always threatened to fragment the kingdom. In the end these internal tensions, rather than external enemies, led to the shattering of the caliphate. The fragmentation of al-Andalus weakened the sponsorship that Jews received from the kingdom's leaders in exchange for Jewish support. Al-Andalus became vulnerable to invasion by tribes from North Africa that saw nothing to be gained by dealing with the Jews. Yet while life in al-Andalus became increasingly intolerable for Jews, the benefits they had received from the Moors in the form of wealth, administrative experience, and cultural knowledge made them valuable and welcome guests to their next "hosts," the newly risen Christian kingdoms of the North.

Invasion

The al-Andalus that sheltered and nourished the Spanish Jews for several centuries started as an accidental kingdom. In 710 a Berber tribesman named Tarif ibn Malik led four hundred men on a successful raiding party into southern Spain. The raid gave him immortality—he became the namesake of the city Tarifa—and encouraged a larger incursion. The very next year, in 711, an army of Moors from North Africa, led by the governor of Tangiers, Tariq ibn Ziyad, invaded southern Spain. According to legend, Julián, the Goth governor of Ceuta, incited the invasion in order to avenge the rape of his daughter by Roderic, the Visigoth king. More likely Julián used the invasion to advance his own claims to the Visigoth throne.

Invasion expeditions crossing the narrow strait separating Africa from Spain were frequent. A common (although disputed) explanation for the origin of the Arab name for southern Spain, al-Andalus, is that it comes from the Vandals, a Germanic tribe that invaded North Africa after being pushed out from Iberia by the Visigoths. From the perspective of the North Africans, Spain was the land of the Vandals.

Tariq found little resistance: King Roderick was engaged in the north, fighting off a Basque revolt. He reinforced his raiding party with an army of seven thousand—mainly Berbers—and built a fortress called Jabal Tariq, which gave its name to the nearby rocky hill, Gibraltar.[3] Tariq then conquered Toledo, where he was joined by Musa ibn Nusayr, his superior as governor of North Africa, who took over the expedition. Musa eventually led his armies to the Picos de Europa, mountains near the Atlantic coast. There he was stopped by a resurgent Spanish force that had been able to take shelter in the mountains. Geography as much as military resistance preserved the north from Muslim rule.

Neither Musa nor Tariq in the end profited from this great conquest. Summoned by the caliph Walid ibn Abd al-Malik to report to Damascus, Musa left his son, Abd al-Aziz, in charge of the newly conquered territory. In Damascus Tariq found Walid on his deathbed. According to a different version of this legend, Walid's heir, Sulayman, ordered Musa and Tariq to delay their trip to Damascus until after Walid's death, so that Sulayman could claim all the booty himself. Instead, Musa brought his treasure to the ailing caliph.

Sulayman accused Musa of embezzling the treasure, fined him, and had him imprisoned and tortured until he could pay.[4] Tariq was thrashed and demoted; he died in obscurity.[5] Musa's son, Aziz, was assassinated by one of his own men at Sulayman's orders.[6] Sulayman, as an Arab ruling over a geographically vast and ethnically diverse caliphate, could not afford to encourage independence among his far-flung subjects, some of whom had only recently converted to Islam. He gave similar treatment to the conquerors of Turkestan and India.

A Prince of Islam

The new Muslim province started out as unstable and provincial as its Visigothic predecessors. This large and ethnically diverse province, with a Christian majority, needed a strong leader to become a coherent and vibrant kingdom. It would receive one with the entry of Prince Abd al-Rahman ibn Mu'awiya ibn Hisham, the last surviving heir to the Umayyad kingdom. Abd al-Rahman came to Spain because of a revolt in the heart of the young Islamic caliphate. After the death of Muhammad, Islam was ruled by four successor caliphs, all contemporaries of the Prophet. The last, Ali, was assassinated in 661. His successor, Muawiyah I, claimed a common ancestor with the Prophet. Muawiyah I founded the Umayyad dynasty and moved the capital of Islam from Medina to Damascus.

The Umayyads were defeated in a revolt by the Abbasid clan, which claimed descent from one of Muhammad's uncles. The Abbasids proceeded to obliterate any trace of their predecessors. They searched out and killed every member of the Umayyad family, even destroying Umayyad grave sites. But one Umayyad escaped. Abd al-Rahman, grandson of Caliph Hisham ibn Abd al-Malik, fled as soldiers surrounded his house and murdered his family. From Syria he escaped first to Palestine, then Egypt and the Maghreb. There he found allies in Spain. With this support he defeated the Abbasid governor. Abd al-Rahman established himself as a semi-independent emir. As an aristocrat with a family connection to the Prophet, he had a royal claim to leadership. As the son of a Berber mother, he could exploit his ethnic connections to the North African tribesmen who had conquered al-Andalus. Abd al-Rahman ruled for thirty years, establishing a dynasty that would last for almost three hundred years. He and his successors built this emirate into one of the richest provinces in the world.

The Caliphate

Only the strongest leader could fully unify Muslim Spain. The first to successfully meet this challenge was Abd al-Rahman III, who in the tenth century converted Spain to a fully independent caliphate. Up until the tenth century, the Umayyad rulers had failed to establish a strong central government because the country's diversity, both ethnically and geographically, worked against it. The Umayyad Arabs ruled over distinct ethnic groups, including Berbers, Spanish Muslims, Christians, Jews, and Slavs imported as slaves. Moreover, the widely dispersed cities and mountainous terrain had always made Spain a difficult land to control. Historian Richard Fletcher observes "that geography encouraged the political fragmentation of the peninsula; that Roman and Visigothic centralism had depended upon the active and benevolent role of local magnates; and that the imposition of Umayyad rule after the chaotic years of the mid-eighth century had been slow."[7]

All this changed in the year 912, when Abd al-Rahman III assumed control of the emirate, a succession surrounded by violent political intrigue. Abd al-Rahman had been groomed for succession by his grandfather, after an uncle had beaten Abd al-Rahman's father to death. Once in power Abd al-Rahman executed one of his own sons for disloyalty, after his son criticized his father's cruelty. He is said to have cut his own grandfather's throat during the Festival of the Sacrifice on the open-air oratory, where Muslims were slaughtering animals for the ritual sacrifice.[8]

These political struggles were exacerbated by the absence of clear rights to succeed by primogeniture. Multiple marriages—each emir was allowed four wives and unlimited concubines—created multiple claimants to the throne. Abd al-Rahman himself was the son of a Christian concubine. Due to frequent intermarriage, the Arab leaders were Arabs more by culture and tradition than by ethnic descent. Abd al-Rahman's father was also born of a Christian concubine, and Abd al-Rahman was probably three-quarters native Iberian. He had blue eyes, light skin, and reddish hair and was said to have dyed his hair black in order to make himself look more like an Arab.[9]

The new leader immediately set about taking control of his country. From 912 to 929, he engaged in almost continuous warfare with rebellious regions. He also faced potential enemies in North Africa and on his northern border with the Christian kingdoms, but he focused on his own kingdom. The seventeen years it took him to consolidate control of his country demonstrates the enormous diversity of interests that fractured Muslim society. On January 16, 929, al-Rahman felt secure enough to proclaim himself caliph, head of an independent caliphate no longer subordinate to Abbasid rule in Baghdad. This title has a religious as well as a political significance. As caliph (*khalifa*) he acted as God's representative on earth through the inheritance of the Prophet Muhammad, since the Prophet had acted both as the religious and the political leader (imam) of the community of believers established by him in Medina.[10]

In addition to Abd al-Rahman's domestic successes, foreign considerations may have prompted him to proclaim an independent caliphate in Spain. Abbasid rule was weak: al-Muqtadir, leader of the Abbasids in Baghdad from 908 until 932, was deposed twice during his reign by rival Abbasid candidates. His successors were little more than puppets in the hands of Turkish troops, and their reigns were short.[11]

Abd al-Rahman also had a new foreign rival to worry about. In Morocco a new dynasty called the Fatimids was founded, which claimed descent from Muhammad though the Prophet's daughter, Fatima. Its ruler, Idris ibn Abd Allah, was Shiite (the Abbasids and the Umayyads were Sunni). In 909 Abd Allah named Morocco a caliphate and took on the messianic title of al-Mahdi. Abd al-Rahman may have claimed title to the caliphate to challenge the legitimacy of the Fatimids, his closest Muslim rivals. The Fatimid caliphate founded by al-Mahdi eventually moved into Egypt, where it founded Cairo as its capital and became the most powerful force in the Muslim world.

To commemorate the founding of his new kingdom, Abd al-Rahman began the construction of a huge palace outside Córdoba called Madinat al-Zahra, to serve both as his residence and the seat of government. It may have been meant to rival the Abbasid palace of Samarra. He spent as much as a third of the country's annual income on the building.[12] When completed by his son Al-Hakem II, the Madinat was one of the most luxurious buildings in the world. According to possibly legendary descriptions, the magnificent throne rooms included the most important, the "Hall of the Caliphs." It was constructed from thin sheets of variously tinted translucent marble. In the center of the room, a large bowl containing mercury acted as a mirror that could be tilted to shoot light all around the room. A colossal pearl, a gift to Abd al-Rahman III from Leo, emperor of Constantinople, hung in the center of the room.[13] The palace included a menagerie, an aviary, and fishponds so extensive that the daily allowance of bread for their fish is said to have been twelve thousand loaves.[14] The magnificence of the palace demonstrates why the tenth-century Saxon nun Hroswitha, upon hearing descriptions of the caliphate, called it "the brilliant ornament of the world."[15] But this palace, like the caliphate that erected it, proved incredibly fragile: only seventy years after its completion, it would be sacked and abandoned. The caliphate itself lasted only a few years longer.

It appears that Abd al-Rahman's triumphs brought him little personal satisfaction. In her biography of the caliph, Maribel Fierro relates that al-Rahman "was said to have kept a daily written record of his forty-nine year's reign. It revealed, after his death, that he had only fourteen days of happiness. He did not say which ones they were."[16]

Abd al-Rahman's son and successor, Al-Hakem II, focused on culture and made Córdoba into a world center of learning. It was Al-Hakem who built up the collections of the Córdoba library. Ibn Hazm, a scholar of the eleventh century, described the catalog of the Córdoba library as consisting of over forty volumes, each of them containing more than fifty folios. Richard Fletcher puts the number of books at possibly over one hundred thousand, adding: "Incredible though we may choose to find these figures, we have reliable evidence that books were acquired for the caliph from as far afield as Persia and that he maintained a team of copyists in Córdoba for their rapid multiplication."[17]

The Fall of the Caliphate

Although the Caliph Al-Hakem died at the relatively advanced age of sixty-one, he left only one heir, eleven-year-old Hisham II. Al-Hakem's apparent infertility has been attributed to his homosexuality. It is said that he only consorted with men, and that he could only procreate when they dressed a female concubine in male clothing and gave her the masculine name of Jafar.[18]

Hisham's youth required the creation of a three-man regency. One of these men, Abu Amir Muhammad ibn Abi Amir al-Ma'afari, took control of the caliphate while Hisham was still a child. In the West al-Ma'afari became known as Almanzor.[19] Like an evil *wazir* in the *Arabian Nights*, he deliberately pushed the young caliph toward a life of debauchery, so that Almanzor could remain in control of the state.

Almanzor's reign was marked by continuous warfare against his Christian neighbors. The constant battles were aimed less at territorial expansion than at loot. Profit from raids helped finance Almanzor's expenses, including the construction of his own palace complex outside Córdoba, called al-Madina al-Zahira. The raids, driven by Almanzor's greed, would in the future create two significant deleterious consequences for the Muslim kingdom. First, in order to maintain these expeditions, Almanzor imported manpower from northern Africa. Thousands of Berbers were ferried across the straits to al-Andalus, where, still in their tribal units under their own tribal commanders, they became the private armies of Almanzor and his son.[20] Al-Andalus always suffered from ethnic conflict, and the introduction of a large Berber military force introduced a threat to the Arab control of the government. These Berbers would play a major role in the destruction of the caliphate.

The second effect of the raids carried out under Almanzor, with Berber support, was to spread anger among Christians over the caliphate's deliberate symbolic attacks on the Christian religion. In 997 his troops invaded the town of Santiago de Compostela in far northwest Spain, the legendary resting place of the apostle James. His men carried the bells of the church dedicated to Saint James to Córdoba. News of this theft raised the renown of the town, helping to establish it as the principal pilgrimage site in Europe. The raid on Santiago prompted the transformation of the apostle into "Santiago Matamoros," or Saint James the Moor-Slayer. Santiago Matamoros became the patron saint of the *reconquista*, inspiring generations of Christians in battles against the Moors. When Córdoba finally fell to King Fernando of Castile in 1236, the bells were returned to the church.

While Almanzor controlled the caliphate, he ruled as *hajib*, or chamberlain, and maintained the fiction that the line of rule from the Umayyad founder remained unbroken. Almanzor's son and heir, Abd al-Rahman ibn Abi Amir—known as Shanjul—was less discrete. He made the caliph, whom Almanzor had maintained as a puppet ruler, appoint him as heir. Shanjul's bald power grab and his ties to his Berber supporters were too much for the Umayyad Arabs. When the *hajib* left Córdoba for another campaign against the Christians, Umayyad supporters attacked and destroyed his palace. Shanjul was captured and killed. His body was stuck up on a gibbet in his former capital. His police chief and drinking companion, Ibn al-Rassan, was ordered to stand beneath the gibbet and to curse both his dead master and himself.[21]

The coup against the *hajib* set off a twenty-two-year-long civil war for control of Córdoba. The war became a struggle between the Arabs and the Berbers, many of the latter imported as mercenaries by Almanzor. Christian mercenaries and Slavs also participated in the conflict. The unending warfare destroyed much of Córdoba, and the home of the caliph was razed so thoroughly that the ruins would not be recognized as the former palace until 1911. In the end the Berbers triumphed, and the caliphate was destroyed.

4

Jews of Muslim Spain

Jewish Life in al-Andalus

Jews were welcome in this new Muslim state. Many achieved high office under the Muslim rulers, and others grew rich through trade, including trade in slaves obtained from the Vikings.[1] By the tenth century, Spanish Jews were so proud of their status and achievements that they viewed themselves as the exiles and inheritors of Jerusalem: the name they gave to their province, Sepharad, comes from the book of Obadiah: "The exiles of Jerusalem who are in Sepharad will inherit the cities of the Negev."[2] The Jewish success transcended the normal limits in Islam for minority religions. Legally, the status of Jews within Islam was one of limited tolerance. Jews and Christians were *dhimmis*, or protected persons.

The nature of Muslim-Jewish relations goes back to the earliest history of Islam. The Prophet knew of Judaism and built his religion on the foundation of Judaic/Christian belief. The Prophet also dealt with Jewish communities. He initially regarded Jews as potential followers, but when they resisted his teachings, he came to see them instead as rivals. Beginning in 624 he attacked Jewish tribes that refused to recognize his mission. He first attacked the tribe of Qaynuqa in Medina; he ultimately spared their lives but expelled them from the city and confiscated their property. He followed this with similar attacks on the Jewish Nadir tribe. In 627 he attacked the Jewish Qurayza tribe in Medina, slaughtered six to nine hundred of the men, and divided the women, children, and property among his Muslim followers.

When he besieged the Jews in the oasis of Khaybar, he settled the conflict with a treaty known as the *dhimma*. The treaty allowed the Jews to continue to live and cultivate in the area under the sufferance of the Muslims, provided that they ceded to the Prophet half their produce.

Eventually all the Jews and Christians in Arabia submitted to a similar *dhimma*. The *dhimma* pattern of treating other religions and conquered peoples as subordinates forced to pay tribute to Islam would form the basis for Islamic relations with Jews, Christians, Zoroastrians, and Hindus in all Muslim-dominated lands.[3]

Status under *dhimma* would be governed by the terms under the "Pact of Umar," purportedly the peace treaty that Umar, the second caliph, had signed with the Christians of Syria—although it is generally considered to have been written later. The pact allowed *dhimmis* to worship in their faith but precluded them from building new houses of worship or repairing old ones. It banned public displays of religion and required non-Muslims to dress differently from Muslims in order to set them apart as nonbelievers. This practice was later adopted by the Christian Church, starting a tradition that eventually led to the Nazi yellow star for Jews.

Jews could not hold public offices with authority over Muslims, and in commercial partnerships, Jews could not have control over Muslims. Jews were also required to pay a poll tax, or *jizya*, from which Muslims were exempt. As *dhimmis*, Jews could worship but only invisibly, in old, dilapidated synagogues, and quietly, without public display. This last rule was a particular hardship for Jews when it came to funerals, which perforce required groups to gather in public around the grave site. The ban on exercising authority over Muslims included a ban on holding Muslim slaves, at a time when slavery was common.

Jews would never have prospered under these conditions. Fortunately, the value of the Jews to the emirate meant that until the end of the *convivencia* these rules were applied lightly or ignored. Jews were valuable allies because the Muslims ruled over a majority Christian population and were surrounded by potentially hostile Christian states. Jews had no incentive to betray the emir to Christian rivals. The hostility that the Jews faced under the Visigoths had alienated them from the Christians and given them a strong incentive to seek Muslim patronage. Jews could be trusted even more than Muslims, since they could not find sufficient popular support to compete for power in a Muslim state.

Jewish success, then, was built on Muslim tolerance and recognition of the practical advantages of fostering a Jewish alliance. Meanwhile, the wealth and cultural attainments of the Muslim state in Spain gave the Jews unprecedented opportunities for material and intellectual advancement. The most successful Jews became sophisticated in the manners of the court. Some even practiced polygamy, which had been banned by the Jews of northern Europe. Many of these Jewish courtiers were what we consider Renaissance men: they were polymaths and part of a court life that was, in many ways, on a level with that of Renaissance Europe—both Renaissance Europe and al-Andalus advanced culturally by reviving and expanding on classical learning.

Jews in Muslim Spain were also artisans, engaged in dyeing, metalwork, weaving, baking, wine making, glassmaking, tailoring, tanning, cheese production, sugar manufacture, and silk work. Unlike Jews in Christian Europe, Spanish Jews could own land and engage in agriculture, and some owned vineyards and orchards.[4] The skills they acquired in Muslim Spain would provide a trade—and value to the Crown—when they moved to Christian lands.

Absorbing Arab Arts and Science

The greatest advances by Jews under Muslim rule, however, were intellectual. At the time of the Muslim conquest of Spain, Islam was by far the most advanced culture in the West. The Islamic conquests extended across much of the former Hellenic world and Roman Empire. Muslim leaders and intellectuals actively collected and assimilated this classical knowledge. The caliph's library in Córdoba was said to be one of the three greatest libraries in the Islamic world, supposedly holding four hundred thousand books, at a time when the greatest library in Europe, in the monastery of Saint Gall, in Switzerland, held only six hundred books.[5] This cultural flowering was possible in part because Arabs had learned the Chinese technology for manufacturing paper out of cloth rags. A paper factory in the Spanish town of Játiva made possible cheaper books than could be produced on the vellum used in Christian Europe.[6]

Muslims led the world in other ways. They adopted the Indian place value decimal system, incorporating the zero, which is essential to modern arithmetic. The word "algorithm" comes from the name of a Persian mathematician, al-Kwarizmi. The word "algebra" comes from his book, *Al-Jabr-wa-al-Muqabilah*. In medicine Ibn Sina, known in the West as Avicenna, wrote the *Canon*, largely a restatement of the great ancient Greek physician Galen, which became one of the principal medical texts in Europe. In the fourteenth century, it was the main textbook in the famous medical schools at Montpellier and Bologna.[7]

As one modern scholar has noted: "Between 800 and 1400 A.D., scientists in the Islamic world had invented algebra, taken the idea of the sine and developed trigonometry, transformed mathematical notation from the awkward Roman numerals to the forms we use today, and incorporated zero into counting systems. Al-Farbi calculated the circumference of the earth (close to its modern measurement), and other scientists created sophisticated instruments of astronomical observation from earlier primitive devices."[8]

Jews took full advantage of this learning. In philosophy the Jews, who had been conquered by and had struggled against both the Hellenic and the Roman Empires, made their first major efforts to reconcile classical thought with Jewish tradition. There were numerous attempts, working with both Platonic and Aristotelian models, to balance these ancient ideas with Jewish doctrine: much of Jewish philosophy in the Middle Ages involved attempts to reconcile philosophy (or a system of rationalist thought) and scripture.[9]

One of the most important fields of Islamic culture for the Jews was medicine. Classical medicine, restated by Avicenna, was a complex, logical system that explained all functions and malfunctions of the human body. The primary focus was on "complexion," or the balance of the four elements: hot, cold, wet, and dry. The proper complexion varied with the individual; for example, youth was dominated by heat and wetness, while old age tended toward the cold and dry. Complexion was determined by the balance of the four humors, or bodily fluids: blood, phlegm (any colorless substance), bile or choler, and black bile.

These humors were produced in the liver from the digestion of foods.[10] Doctors diagnosed the patient partly by examining excreta. Urine was especially important, and the urine flask was an essential medical tool. Treatments included bloodletting, cauterization and cupping (to draw out the humors), diet, and herbal medication.

Jews took the lead in this profession. The Catholic Church often associated disease with sin, for which the proper treatment was repentance, not medicine. Judaism, however, had always stressed the importance of health and proper care of the body. There was no conflict between medicine and religion. In fact, many physicians were also prominent rabbis, with Maimonides the most famous example.

Another reason why medicine became an important profession among Jews was the stigma attached to teaching the Torah for money. In the words of Rabbi Hillel, "Whosoever derives a profit for himself from the words of the Torah is helping in his own destruction."[11] Medicine provided a moral and intellectually stimulating profession to support scholars who continued religious study in their spare time. The value that Judaism attributed to healing—the biblical dictum of *pikuahnefesh*, or the value of saving a life—was reflected in the fact that even those rabbis who banned the study of secular classical philosophy did not oppose the study of medicine.[12]

The Wandering Jew

The Jews in Muslim Spain did not live in isolation from other Jews in the Diaspora. They stayed in contact with their fellow Jews in both the Christian and the Muslim world and used those contacts to further their intellectual development and as the basis for a widespread trading network. The widespread Jewish communities and web of contacts supported important Jewish trading networks in Muslim Spain. The rise of the Muslim kingdoms in the Mediterranean cut the Christian world off from trade with the East, but the Jews could still move and trade from East to West. Jews could exploit contacts with the Jewish Diaspora over much of the world, including both Christian and Muslim lands. Hebrew gave them a common language with Jews all over the world. Trade was also assisted by a Jewish system of letters of credit (called *suftaja*). The Talmud provided a commonly accepted legal system for resolving commercial disputes.

One Jewish commercial house, the Radhanites, kept records of trade routes through Europe via Prague, Bulgaria, and the land of the Khazars, along the Mediterranean to Iran and Iraq, and by sea extending as far as China. The historian Eliyah Ashton provides a sample of the impressive trade itinerary available to Spanish Jews of the caliphate:

> At times they would travel by sea to a place near Antioch, transfer their merchandise overland to the Euphrates, sail on that river to the vicinity of Bagdad, continue from there on the Tigris to the city of al-Ubulla, and from there would sail by sea to Oman, India, and China.
>
> At times they would travel on land. Departing from Spain or the land of the Franks from Morocco, they would then travel in caravans to Tunisia, and thence to Egypt, to Ramleh in Palestine, and then to Damascus and Iraq; from there they traveled by way of the southern provinces of Persia to India and China. A fourth approach to the Far East was to cross over the country of the Slavs to Khamlij, a Khazar city, sail the Caspian Sea, and then go to Khurasan and the lands of the Turks.[13]

Nothing better illustrates the state of the Jewish world at the time than the famous travel journal of Benjamin ben Jonah, aka Benjamin of Tudela, sometimes called the Jewish Marco Polo. Benjamin set out about 1160 for what became almost a thirteen-year journey through much of the world known at that time in the West; he did not return to Spain until around 1173. Other than the notes he left of his voyage, which appear to have been complied by someone else into book form, nothing is known about him, including his motives for spending much of his life on this trip.

Benjamin started his trip from his native city of Tudela, in the southern part of the Christian kingdom of Navarre. He proceeded along the south of France (probably traveling by foot or mule) to Marseille. From there he took a boat to Genoa, then went north to visit Pisa and Rome. Returning south, he followed the coastline of Italy to the Adriatic city of Otranto; from there he embarked to cross the Greek isles to Constantinople, the capital of Byzantium. He then went by sea back to Cypress and across to the Levantine coast, near Antioch, and down to Israel. After traveling extensively in Israel, he went north to Damascus and Aleppo and then to Baghdad. He traveled throughout much of what is now Iraq and from there to Khuzestan, in western Iran. His subsequent itinerary is somewhat unclear as he mentions, without describing (other than by stating the length of the voyage), places such as India and China that he probably did not visit. He eventually ended up in Egypt, where he visited Cairo and Alexandria before returning to Europe and Spain.

The record he left is a complete journal of the trip. Some of it reflects only cursory notes of where he traveled, how long it took to get there, and, if Jews lived there, a description of the Jewish community. The larger cities receive lengthier descriptions, and the journal includes a number of "firsts": he was the first European to mention China, the first to describe the Islamic sect known as the Assassins (the source of the English word), and the first to describe the Druze sect, an offshoot of Islam whose followers today reside primarily in Syria, Lebanon, Jordan, and Israel.

He also demonstrated that a twelfth-century Spanish Jew in a famous foreign city is capable of acting like any modern tourist. In the larger cities he visited the famous sites, including ancient monuments, churches, and mosques. In Rome, for example, he describes his visit to the Coliseum.[14] He also repeats tales he had heard that are clearly legendary. For example, he tells of a giant bird called the griffin, which could fly away with sailors, a tale found in the *Arabian Nights* and repeated, a century later, by Marco Polo. Two of the longest sections relate to the two regions of most importance to Jews of that time: Israel and Iraq.

Benjamin traveled extensively in Israel, visiting Acre, Haifa, Caesarea, Jerusalem, Bethlehem, Hebron, Jaffa, Askalon, Tiberias, and smaller towns. Wherever he went, he noted the state of the Jews. Despite Israel's great religious and historical importance, at that time it had few significant Jewish communities—by the mid-twelfth century, only a few Jews remained in Israel. The Jews suffered from the invasion of the Christian crusaders, who burned synagogues and killed or forcibly converted some Jews. Many towns no longer had Jews, but there were a number of small communities left, ranging from twenty to two hundred families. There were about two hundred families in Jerusalem, and Benjamin described Jews praying at the Wailing Wall.

He also tells an Indiana Jones–type story he had heard in Jerusalem from a rabbi. Two workmen, part of a crew hired to move stones from Jewish ruins to repair a church on Mount Zion, tarried into the night, and while moving a large stone, they discovered a cave filled with treasure including the graves of David, Solomon, and the other ancient kings of Judah. When they tried to enter the chamber, a fierce wind from the entrance of the cave smote them to the ground, where they lay until evening. A wind like a man's voice cried out: "Arise and go forth from this place!" They rushed away in terror and ran to tell their story to the Christian patriarch. When the patriarch sought their assistance to uncover the graves, he found them lying in their beds in terror. They refused to help, saying: "We will not enter there, for the Lord doth not desire to show it to any man." The patriarch then ordered the area to be closed off and hidden.[15]

Iraq was, like Israel, important to the Jews for religious, historical, and social reasons. It was here, in the third to fifth century, that the Babylonian Talmud was compiled. Two important Jewish academies, in Sura and Pumbedita, remained respected sources of talmudic interpretation. Jews from all over the world, including Spain, used the academies as a kind of supreme court, writing to them to resolve issues of talmudic interpretation.

Iraq also had one of the largest, if not the largest, Jewish communities in the world. Benjamin counted twenty-eight synagogues in Baghdad and Al-Khorkh on the opposite side of the Tigris. According to Benjamin, there were ten Jewish academies in Baghdad, and the principle rabbi, known as the exilarch, had an almost royal status in the Jewish world. Benjamin described how every five days, the exilarch made an official visit to the caliph, received an official escort to the caliph's palace, and was seated on a throne opposite the caliph.[16] (It should be noted that one modern scholar suggests that Benjamin exaggerated the status of the exilarch in order to embellish the status of the Jews in Iraq. The scholar notes that by the eleventh century the exilarch had become a figurehead whose authority was limited to passing out honorific titles.)[17]

Benjamin also provides an elaborate description of the life and palace of the caliph. He says that the caliph was confined to the palace complex, which he left only once a year, to visit the great mosque. Benjamin describes at length the elaborate ceremony that accompanied that short pilgrimage.[18]

In the city of Susa, now part of Iran, Benjamin visited the synagogue said to hold the remains of the prophet Daniel. Two towns on either side of the Tigris feuded over the right to host the tomb, each believing that the tomb would bring the town good fortune, while the other town would fall into poverty. The towns agreed to share the tomb, exchanging it on alternate years. The Persian king, believing that this practice dishonored the prophet, ordered the tomb to be suspended in a glass coffin on the underside of a bridge connecting both towns.[19]

Benjamin also describes various Jewish sects. The most important of these were the Karaites, who rejected the authority of the oral law found in the Talmud and only followed the precepts in the Torah. He also found in Nablus, Israel, and Damascus, communities of Samaritans, the sect mentioned in the New Testament.

These elaborate descriptions and fanciful stories are why Benjamin's account became popular and widely translated when rediscovered in the sixteenth century. Yet the book is principally an inventory of the Jewish world visited by Benjamin. He carefully describes the Jewish communities everywhere he visited, providing a rough estimate of the Jewish population, naming the most prominent Jews, and including other details, such as the number of congregations and the Jews' specialized occupations.

The great question relating to this book is why Benjamin undertook his trip of over a decade and took the care to record it. The trip seems too long and circuitous to have been merely a personal voyage, made for trade or religious pilgrimage. The journal may have been meant as a guide for Jewish traders. Benjamin notes the important commercial products of the areas he visited, from dyestuffs to pearls, and the book would have been a valuable map for Jewish merchants.

Another possibility is that he had been commissioned to map out escape routes from Spain. By the mid-eleventh century, Jews had largely lost their sanctuaries of centuries in Muslim Spain, and even without Muslim repression the *reconquista* was converting the country to Christian domination. Tudela itself had passed into Christian hands several decades before Benjamin set off on his trip.[20] While Jews were welcomed in Christian Spain, it was too early to consider this new shelter a stable home, particularly in light of the repression that European Jews had suffered from Christian forces in the First and Second Crusades. Benjamin's extensive account of Jewish life outside Spain could have been used as a map of possible refuge. If that was his motivation, the trip proved unnecessary, or at least premature—expulsion was over three hundred years away.

5

Judah Halevi and *The Kuzari*

Hasdai ibn Shaprut

For all their success, the Jews of Muslim Spain remained *dhimmis* and experienced anxiety over their inferior status. This anxiety is reflected in their fascination with Khazars, a Tatar kingdom whose people briefly existed as a Jewish state, embracing Judaism as a buffering compromise to separate itself politically from its Islamic and Byzantine neighbors.

Jews prospered under the strong leadership of the caliphate. They were protected by the most influential Jew of his time, Hasdai ibn Shaprut (915–70), the first Spanish Jew to be mentioned by name in the Arab records of the day.[1] Hasdai served Caliph Abd al-Rahman III as court physician. He became the caliph's confidant, entrusted with diplomatic responsibilities. As a Jew he was an invaluable envoy to the Christian world, for Muslim-Christian frictions made direct contact extremely difficult. His taskings included trips to the lands of the Byzantines, the Franks, and the Germans. Some of Hasdai's missions included his medical training. Abd al-Rahman sent him to assist the Prince of Navarre, who suffered from extreme obesity. Hasdai helped the prince lose enough weight to mount his horse with dignity.[2] Hasdai became the leader of the Jewish community, which gave him the title of *nasi*, or prince. As the leader of what may have been the most important Jewish community in the world, his fame spread beyond Spain. He corresponded with and provided assistance to Jews in both Muslim and Christian lands.

Despite Hasdai's importance, he felt insecure with his minority status in al-Andalus and the need he and other Jews had to seek protection and support from the Muslim leadership. He longed for Jewish autonomy and became obsessed with the story of the Khazars, whose purported Jewish political power and independence stood in contrast to the vulnerability he felt as a Jew in an Islamic kingdom.

Hasdai and his contemporaries' interest in the Khazars had been sparked by stories told by the ninth-century charlatan Eldad ha-Dani, an Iraqi Jew who traveled throughout the Jewish communities of northern Africa and Spain. Eldad claimed to be from the lost tribe of Dan and told stories of independent Jewish kingdoms in Ethiopia and other places led by the descendants of the ten lost tribes. Hasdai's attraction to the idea of an independent Jewish nation was also fueled by his awareness of the precarious status of the stateless Jew. As a close confidant of the caliph and the leader of his Jewish community, Hasdai was approached by Jews from both Muslim and Christian lands. He learned of the oppression suffered by Jews in places like Otranto in southern Italy, where under the Byzantines Jewish books had been banned and soldiers had tried to force conversions. He had also been approached by the Jews of Toulouse in Provence, who complained of repressive actions by local clergy.[3]

While Jews in Muslim Spain were generally supported and protected by the caliph, the community's growth was fueled by Jewish emigration from lands outside al-Andalus, prompted by Muslim oppression and political instability. Jews from Morocco immigrated to Spain, fleeing the military campaigns of the Fatimids and repression from Berber tribesmen. Jews leaving Egypt in the tenth century sought escape from internal strife, drought, famine, and pestilence.[4] In Palestine and Syria, too, it was increasingly difficult for Jews to live in security, as the region became the central battleground of the Crusades.

In Iraq conflict between the Sunnis and the Shiites, repression from the military, and Bedouin raids caused damage to irrigation, agriculture, and industry. One effect of these troubles was to unsettle two important talmudic academies in the towns of Sura and Pumbedita.[5] Hasdai, as the leader of one of the most important Jewish communities, corresponded with other Jews outside the caliphate, and his knowledge of Jewish vulnerability in the Islamic and Christian worlds increased his fascination with the Khazars, who he believed had formed an independent Jewish state. Hasdai made numerous efforts to contact the

Khazars' ruler to learn more about the nature of Jewish nation, about which he had few if any confirmed reports.

He first attempted to send an envoy via the Byzantine Empire and Constantinople. The Byzantine emperor, however, wanted to isolate Khazaria and refused access. Hasdai's envoy did meet one Jew who claimed to have come from the Khazar kingdom, and the stranger provided the envoy with a written report about the nation.[6] Hasdai then attempted to contact the kingdom through Germany. Two Jewish envoys to the caliph from Otto I, the Holy Roman emperor, proposed bringing back a response to a letter that they could send to the Khazars using Hungarian Jews, who could pass the letter to the Khazars via the Bulgars. While there is no record of such a response, Hasdai's letter has been preserved and reflects his longing for a Jewish State:

> If I knew that the thing is surely so [namely, the account regarding the kingdom], I would reject my honor, leave my high office and forsake my family, and I would go over hill and mountain, on the sea and over dry land to reach the place where my lord, the king, dwells, to behold his greatness and the glory of his majesty, the abode of his servants and the attendance of his ministers, and the repose of the survivors of Israel.
>
> We have been cast down from our glory and have nothing to reply when they say daily unto us, "Every other people has its kingdom, but of yours there is no memorial on the earth."[7]

Judah Halevi

Over a century later, Judah Halevi (c. 1075–1141) would return to the theme of the Khazars. Another polymath physician, Halevi was one of the greatest Hebrew poets as well as a philosopher, who, in the end, rejected classical philosophy for religious faith. He was also a transitional figure, caught in an awkward epoch when the Jews were losing their place in al-Andalus but had not yet found a stable, prosperous refuge in Christian Spain. His life reflects his rootlessness, cut off from al-Andalus and unable to feel at home in Christian Spain.

Halevi was born on the border between Muslim and Christian Spain, possibly in Toledo or Tudela. He was still a small boy when Toledo fell to Christian rule. As a youth he moved south to be educated in what remained of Muslim Spain. He became an associate of Moses ben Ezra and became a respected and prolific poet—he left the largest collection of poetry of any of the golden age poets.[8] Much of that was traditional poetry of the court—panegyrics to friends or important people (probably the most common genre of Arab/Hebrew poetry), and poems about love and wine.[9] His sacred poems, which mix secular and biblical images with strong emotional force, remain particularly striking, as in this poem, which references Psalm 55:78, "O that I had the wings of a dove," with the dove representing the Jews:

The dove, afar, she flew about the forests;
She stumbles, she cannot shake herself free.
Flying, flitting, fluttering,
Round about her beloved she swirled, she stormed
She deemed a thousand years would be the limit of her set time,
But she is ashamed of all whereon she counted.
Her Beloved who had afflicted her with long years of separation
Hath poured out her soul to the grave.
"Lo," she said, "I will not make mention any more of His name";
But it is within her heart like a burning fire.
Why will Thou be as an enemy to her, since she
Opened wide her mouth for the rain of thy salvation?
And she made her soul believe and despaired not,
Whether she win honour in His name or whether she be brought low.
Our God shall come and shall not keep silence;
All round about Him is fire; it storms exceedingly.[10]

Throughout Halevi's life, he remained primarily a product of Muslim-Jewish culture; his best known book, *The Kuzari*, was written in Arabic. Yet he lived at a time when life for Jews in Muslim Spain was becoming difficult, if not impossible. Jews were massacred in Granada in 1066. The Almoravid takeover of Muslim Spain beginning in 1190 would force Jews out of court positions and impose stricter Islamic conditions. The Almohads, who would eventually take over Muslim Spain and drive out most of the Jews, were already operating in North Africa. Halevi also lived and worked in Christian Spain, but he never settled down in one place there. In Christian Spain, too, there were problems; anti-Jewish riots broke out in 1109 after the death of Alfonso VI, conqueror of Toledo.[11]

Halevi's awkward position between sometimes hostile Muslim and Christian worlds led him both to embrace his Jewish identity and to long for a Jewish homeland. He expresses this longing in a famous poem, "My Heart Is in the East," written around 1130:

> My heart is in the East and I am in the uttermost West.
> How can I find savor in food? How shall it be sweet to me?
> How shall I render my vows and my bonds while yet
> Zion lieth beneath the fetter of Edom [Christianity], and I in Arab
>   chains?
> A light thing it would seem to me to leave behind all the good
>   things of Spain—
> Seeing how precious in mine eyes to behold the dust of the deso-
>   late sanctuary.[12]

"My vows and my bonds" refers to his vow to leave for Israel. By "the fetter of Edom," he is referring to Christian sovereignty over Israel.

The Book of the Kuzari

Halevi's longing for Jewish autonomy probably attracted him to the story of the Khazars, just as it had for Hasdai. His book *The Kuzari*, now recognized as a classic Jewish text, opens with the legend of how the Khazars converted to Judaism after a debate among all the religions. The Kuzari king calls for the debate after seeing an angel in a dream, who tells him: "Thy way of thinking is pleasing to God, but not thy way of acting."[13] The king then calls before him a philosopher, a Muslim, and a Christian to explore their beliefs. He does not invite a Jew, saying, "As regards the Jews, I am satisfied that they are of low station, few in number, and generally despised."[14] But when he discovers that the other faiths emerged from Judaism, he invites a rabbi, too, to speak about his faith.

In the book Halevi quickly abandons the premise of a debate between the philosopher and the leaders of the different faiths. Once the rabbi is called in, the book becomes a dialogue between the rabbi and the king. The king converts to Judaism at the end of the first of five books and, for the rest of the book, seeks guidance from the rabbi, who is now his spiritual advisor. Halevi relates this story as though it had occurred centuries earlier. While Hasdai saw the Khazars as a possible ally, for Halevi the Jewish Khazars are a legend to use as a platform for espousing religious and philosophical beliefs. He shows no interest in the true history of the Khazar nation nor in the ideal of a strong Jewish state outside of Israel.

Halevi instead sees the Diaspora as God's way of preparing the Jews for the Messiah and for the return to a religious kingdom in Israel. He compares this process to the preparation of soil for the planting of a vineyard. For Halevi there is no permanent place for the Jews outside Israel. Even in its fallen state, Israel should still be a present goal for the Jews.

After hearing Halevi's rabbi praise Israel, the Khazari king concludes: "If this be so, thou fallest short of the duty laid down in thy law, by not endeavoring to reach that place, and making it thy abode in life and death."[15] The rabbi agrees. He notes that God was ready to restore Israel to greatness after the destruction of the second temple, and that only the failure of the Jews to return from a comfortable exile in Babylon had prevented the creation of a Jewish state.

For Halevi the diaspora, even if it provides prosperity to the Jews, is only a distraction from the Jewish mission to reestablish a Jewish kingdom in Zion. The book ends with the rabbi's decision to break off his teaching and risk the dangerous trip to Israel.

The rabbi's decision to return was more than a fictional device. Shortly after finishing the book, Halevi determined to leave Spain for Israel. He rejected the non-Jewish influences that had fertilized the burst of intellectual creativity at the height of the *convivencia*. He wrote to a North African scholar: "Greece and its wisdom have drowned me in mucky grease; Islam and its language have painted me dark, and Christendom has dissected and destroyed me!"[16] In a poem, he condemns the Jewish life in exile:

Were it well to be happy
For a man simple and upright,
Like a bird that is bound
In the hand of little boys—
In slavery to Philistines,
And Hagrites and Hittites,
Alluring his heart
With other gods
To seek their favor
And forsake God's will[17]

In *The Kuzari* and another work, *Treatise on Hebrew Meters*, he condemned the use of Arab techniques in Hebrew poetry: "In truth, Arabicizing Hebrew prosody is objectionable for it corrupts the articulation of Hebrew speech."[18] Yet he continued to write poetry in this style, included strikingly original poems focused on his intent to return to Israel.

To Zion

Halevi became obsessed with the idea of Jerusalem. Poems of his late period include "Zion poems" on Jerusalem, some of which were written as answers to friends, describing why he was motivated to abandon Spain and leave his family behind, including at least a daughter and a grandson (both mentioned in one poem). The best known of the "Zion poems," his "Ode to Jerusalem" (too long to quote here), became part of the liturgy for the fast day of the Ninth of Av, which commemorates the destruction of the second temple by the Romans.[19]

He also wrote "sea poems" that dramatically describe his voyage and real or imagined hardships at sea on his pilgrimage:

Hath the flood come again and made the world a waste
So that one cannot see the face of the dry land,
And no man is there and no beast and no bird?
Have they all come to an end and lain down in sorrow?
To see even mountain or marsh would be a rest for me,
And the desert itself would be sweet.
But I look on every side and there is nothing
But only water and sky and ark,
And Leviathan making the abyss to boil,
So that one deemed the deep to be hoary.
And the heart of the sea concealed the ship
As though she were a stolen thing in the sea's hand.
And the sea raged and my soul exalted—
For to the sanctuary of her God she draweth near.[20]

He departed Spain in 1140, at the age of sixty-five. He left despite the danger of the trip and his knowledge that the Crusader masters of Jerusalem were unfriendly toward Jews. He arrived first in Egypt and remained in Cairo and Alexandria for approximately eight months. Documents found in the Cairo *geniza* (a trove of hundreds of thousands of discarded papers) reveal that he was welcomed in Egypt as a celebrity, and prominent Jews competed to host him and listen to his poetry. In May 1141, he sailed from Alexandria for Israel. He was never heard from again.

A Renaissance Italian Jewish scholar left an account of Halevi's death that was probably imaginary but would be passed down in Jewish tradition. He wrote that when Halevi arrived at the Temple Mount, he tore his clothes and crawled in his devotion. An Arab, angered by this sign of Jewish piety, ran him down on a horse and trampled him to death.[21] The German poet Heinrich Heine, himself of Jewish origin, used this legend for a poem and called Halevi "the fiery pillar of sweet song."[22]

6

A Golden Age of Poetry

A New Hebrew Poesy

The exposure to Muslim culture fostered the emergence of great Jewish poets. The confluence of a rich Arab poetic tradition with biblical Hebrew and the Sephardic experience produced a poetry that was both reflective of Arab tradition and a unique record of the Spanish Jews at their intellectual zenith. The late Muslim period, the eleventh and twelfth centuries, produced five great poets—and extraordinary men: Solomon ibn Gabirol, Samuel ibn Nagrela, Moses ben Ezra, Judah Halevi, and Abraham ben Ezra.

There had been a long Arab tradition of writing and reciting poetry. Even though Muhammad had denounced secular poetry, he was said to have personally enjoyed and encouraged some poets. This tradition was adopted by Islamic society, maintaining the pre-Islamic themes of wine, women, and song. It became accepted that Islamic courtiers would have a sophisticated knowledge of poesy.[1] This poetic tradition, often accompanied by music, passed into Europe through the Provencal troubadours and became one basis for secular European poetry and music.[2]

By the time of the caliphate in Spain, centuries of Arab poetic practice had developed into a highly formalized and sophisticated poetic tradition. It employed stock imagery and generic subjects, emphasizing technical facility over original description or personal expression. The poetry formed an essential part of the court social life. Many of the poems were written as entertainments to be recited, often at long evening wine parties where the men would sit in the patios of formal gardens while a *sáki*, a boy or young man wine steward, passed watered wine into the guests' goblets.

The first Jew to adopt and use this Arab art form was the tenth-century scholar Dunash ben Labrat. A Moroccan Jew (with a Berber name), Dunash came to the court in Cordoba after studying in Baghdad under one of the greatest Jewish scholars, S'adia ben Yosef al Fayummi, the *gaon*, or leader, of the Sura talmudic academy. Under the patronage of Hasdai ibn Shaprut, he applied the metric forms and poetic structures of Arabic poetry for the first time to Hebrew.

Jews had a long tradition of religious poetry, called *piyyut*, a type of hymn, written to be used as part of the Jewish religious service. Now, for the first time since the biblical period, Jews wrote secular poetry, adopting Arab forms and themes of wine, women, and song.[3] While Jews were fluent in and normally wrote in Arabic—the language of Maimonides's *Guide for the Perplexed*—they composed poetry in Hebrew, using classical Hebrew as the Islamic court used classical Arabic. The result was an unprecedented body of Jewish secular poetry that would be matched only in the twentieth century.

The use of Hebrew in place of Arabic would in itself shape the poetry. Hebrew, of course, was the language of the Bible, and Jews learned the language in the course of religious study, which was the foundation of study, for all religions, in the medieval period. The poetry—sacred and secular—would be replete with biblical references, which the poet could confidently expect his readers to recognize. An analogy would be how English poetry would have developed if the English writers knew the language only through study of the King James Bible.

The secular Hebrew poems used the same traditional subjects and stock imagery as Arab poetry and like the Arab poems, were often written to be recited at wine parties. As with the Arab poets, technical virtuosity was valued over originality of description or themes. The poets often used acrostics and word games. The Sephardic poet Judah Alharizi, for example, wrote a ten-verse poem in which every word contained the Hebrew letter resh, and followed by a poem omitting the same letter. Many of these poems were essentially word games; about 20 percent of the secular poetry of Abraham ben Ezra consisted of riddles or puzzles.[4]

This Arab tradition included homoerotic poetry. Love poems to boys or young men—called in Arabic *mu'adhdār* poems and addressed to boys before they developed facial hair—were common.[5] Many may have been exercises in an established literary convention rather than expressions of homosexual desire, but some, including poems by the sybaritic Abu Nuwas, contain explicit homoerotic imagery. The Jews adopted this tradition. Approximately half the love poems they left—including works by all the major poets—were addressed to boys or young men, often to the *sáki*, or wine server.[6] As with the male-directed love poems among Shakespeare's sonnets, it is not clear what significance to ascribe to these poems about male desire. They do not appear to reflect tolerance for homosexual conduct in the Jewish society of that time. As Maimonides would later note in his Mishnah Torah, the Talmud made homosexual intercourse a capital offense.[7] Alharizi in his book *Tahkemoni* (written in approximately 1220), told of a Jewish acquaintance who wrote a poetic response to the prohibition against homosexual conduct in Leviticus 20:13: "Had Moses seen how my friend's face blushes when he is drunk, and his beautiful curls and wonderful hands, he would not have written in his Torah: do not lie with a man." Alharizi claimed that ten Jewish poets who heard these words rose up to refute this claim and defend the biblical ban.[8]

Since many of the poems use standard Arab themes and motifs as a platform to highlight the poet's skills, some scholars argue that the homoerotic elements in these poems do not reflect homosexual desire but rather represent a convention adopted from the Arabic.[9] Not all, however, agree with this conclusion.[10] Solomon ibn Gabirol wrote what might have been a satirical reference to this type of poem:

All in red, and come from Edom
settle down and be still:
By God, I love you well—
But not like the men of Sodom.[11]

The revolution in Hebrew poetics extended to sacred as well as secular themes. Their sacred poems, some of which are still used in the liturgy, radically transformed a tradition that had remained largely unchanged for five hundred years.[12] The Sephardic sacred poems incorporated Arab meter and rhymes. They also used the Arab stock descriptions and sub-jects, including (with the biblical book Song of Songs as a model) erotic images, so that it is sometimes difficult to tell if these poems have a secular or a religious subject. Judah Halevi, for example, wrote a litur-gical poem that was a translation of an Arab love poem with only the last lines changed to give it a religious meaning.[13]

Another innovation was to write poems in the first person, making them personal expressions of piety or religious doubt. This contrasts with traditional *piyyut*, told from the viewpoint of the Jewish people on the whole or in the voice of the congregation.[14]

Solomon ibn Gabirol

The first poet to incorporate Arab techniques and secular themes into religious poetry was Solomon ibn Gabirol.[15] A poet and a philosopher (born 1022), Gabirol led a difficult life. Orphaned at a young age, he suffered most of his life from a skin disease, possibly from tuberculosis of the skin, which left him often debilitated and made him subject to pus-filled sores that isolated him socially. He also characterized himself as small and ugly, and his appearance added to his social isolation. As a young man he benefited from the patronage of Yekutiel ibn Hassan, who was prominent in the court of Gabirol's home city of Saragossa. Unfortunately, Yekutiel was assassinated when Gabirol was only sev-enteen. Soon after Yekutiel's death Gabirol wrote a poem, "On Leav-ing Saragossa," complaining about his isolation in that city, in which he complained that he lived there like a hated stranger, where people inferior to him, "impostors and fools," pretended to respect him while poisoning his life.[16]

He spent the rest of his life in search of patronage, which required him to travel to the courts of Granada and Valencia. His principal sponsor became the poet and courtier Samuel ibn Nagrela, but Nagrela sometimes broke off with him, and Gabirol several times had to work to repair the breach. Rivalries with other poets and Gabirol's own difficult personal-ity contributed to these breaks. While the Arab and the Jewish poetic traditions favored both boasting and poetic rivalries, Gabirol could be considered arrogant. He wrote at the age of seventeen that his fame was known in all the lands of East and West. He wrote satirical poems attacking his rivals.[17] The poet Moses ben Ezra criticized Gabirol for his lack of discretion in launching these sarcastic attacks on prominent and respected Jewish figures.[18]

Gabirol's physical travails may have influenced his philosophic thought. A Neoplatonist, he believed that the soul belongs to the spiritual world and is imprisoned in a nature it longs to escape. It was a philosophy he laid out in one of the most pessimistic of the Sephardic poems:

> The mind is flawed, the way to wisdom blocked;
> The body alone is seen, the soul is hid,
> And those who seek the world find only ill;
> The servant rises up and kills his lord,
> And serving girls attack their mistresses.
> Sons are raising hands against their parent's will.
> My friend, from what I've seen of life I'd say
> The best that one can hope is to go mad.
> However long you live you suffer toil,
> And in the end you suffer rot and worms.
> Then finally the clay goes back to clay;
> At last the soul ascends to join the Soul.[19]

His philosophic work *Mekor Hayyim*, or *Fountain of Life*, is one of the few medieval philosophical works of any religion not concerned with the conflict between philosophy and religion, and it makes no reference to Jewish scripture. Perhaps for this reason his influence on later Jewish writers was limited. However, his book, translated into Latin under the title *Fons Vitae* in the twelfth century, became an important source for Christian philosophers like Duns Scotus, who believed that the work was by a Christian or Arab philosopher named Avicebron or Avencebrol. The real authorship of this book was not discovered until 1846, based on the research of the German Jewish scholar Salomon Munk.

Gabirol's religious poetry often was written as love poetry, as in this poem, where the speaker turns out to be the Jewish people and the love object the awaited Messiah:

Come to me at early dawn,
Come up to me, for I am drawn,
Beloved, by my spirit's spell,
To see the sons of Israel.
For thee, my darling, I will spread
Within my court a golden bed,
And I will set a table there
And bread for thee I will prepare,
For thee my goblet I will fill
With juices that my vines distil;
And thou shalt drink to heart's delight,
Of all my flavours day and night.
The joy in thee I will evince
With which a people greets its prince
O son of Jesse, holy stem,
God's servant, born of Bethlehem![20]

Gabirol's longest and most ambitious poem, "Keter Malchut," "The Royal Crown," is both a poem of praise of God and a meshing of his Neoplatonic ideas with Jewish faith. He talks of the Jewish soul as female and in one passage describes the soul as a menstruating (unclean) woman.[21] Gabirol died in Valencia in 1057 at the age of thirty-six.

The relatively late flowering of Jewish poetry in the Muslim period—the greatest poets all lived after the breakup of the caliphate, and several were forced into exile—gives some of this poetry an elegiac quality. Moses ben Ezra, for example, lived through several forced exiles, and exile formed the subject of some of his most powerful poems.

Moses ben Ezra

Moses ben Ezra (1055–1138) was considered the most technically accomplished of the Sephardic poets, and he left a treatise that discussed the art of poetry. Born in Granada to a family of courtiers, he fled the city during the anti-Jewish massacres of 1066. His family resettled and prospered, but the invasion of the fundamentalist Almoravids in 1090 made his life increasingly difficult. He remained in Granada with his family after his brothers and other Jews fled Muslim repression. He came to complain about his isolation, acknowledging that he had stayed too long in his native city: "I remain in Granada, a city of declining bustle and splendor, like a stranger in the land, like a sparrow strayed from its nest, like a bird banished and driven; and amongst this generation, wayward and corrupt, there is no refuge for me; there remains no one to remember me and inquire after my welfare."[22]

Ben Ezra managed to escape from Granada in 1095, and he spent the rest of his life wandering about Christian Spain, where he complained about the loss of the cultural richness he had experienced in al-Andalus, as in this poem:

> Fortune has hurled me to a land where the lights of my under-
>   standing dimmed ...
> I have come to the iniquitous domain of a people scorned by God
>   and accursed by man,
> Amongst savages who love corruption and set an ambush for the
>   blood of the righteous and innocent.[23]

Exile became the subject of several of his poems:

> I am weary of roaming about the world, measuring its expanse;
>   and I am not yet done ...
> I walk with the beasts of the forest and I hover like a bird of prey
>   over the peaks of mountains.
> My feet run about like lightning to the far ends of the earth, and I
>   move from sea to sea.
> Journey follows journey, but I find no resting-place, no calm repose.[24]

Exile probably colored this religious poem, one of his best known, which opens as a love poem but deals with the love of the Jewish people in exile for their God:

> Why is my loved one wroth—
> That he should be disdainful of me,

While my heart, in its yearning for him
Is shaken like a reed?
When, joyously, I followed him into the wilderness;
Else how should I cry this day,
And he not answer?

Yet verily, though he slay me
Still will I trust in him;
And if he hide his face,
I will bethink me of his tenderness, and turn thereto,
The loving-kindness of the Lord will not fail his servant
For pure gold changes not nor dims.[25]

Abraham ben Ezra

Another poet whose life was marked by exile was the last of the great
Sephardic poets, Abraham ben Ezra (1093–1167, no relation to Moses).
He was a friend to Judah Halevi. Although Abraham was twenty years
younger than Halevi, his son married Halevi's daughter. Like Solomon
Gabirol, Abraham was a Neoplatonist, and this view influenced some
of his poems, such as this one, which uses Gabirol's phrase "fountain
of life":

Sent down from a luminous fountain of life, . . .
Why were you ushered into the world
and then in the dark of the body imprisoned?[26]

His poems include a moving memorial to Jewish life in Muslim Spain,
lost to the intolerance of Islamic fundamentalism, the "Lament for
Andalusian Jewry," which begins: "Calamity came upon Spain from
the skies / and my eyes pour forth their stream of tears."[27]

Abraham left Spain in 1140 for Rome, noting in one commentary,
"Oppressors have driven me out of Spain."[28] He spent the rest of his life
wandering about Europe, living in Italy, France, and England, where he
called himself Avraham HaSefaradi, taking his Spanish heritage as his

name. His sojourn in Italy started a tradition of Hebrew poetry there that would bloom again during the Renaissance, fertilized in part by a new round of exiles from Spain in 1492. The first sonnets written in a language other than Italian were in Hebrew.

Abraham also became an important conduit to the West of Arab advances in science and math. He wrote three works on mathematics, in which he correctly attributed the concept of "zero" as a placeholder to India.[29] He translated into Hebrew an important commentary on astronomical tables, and he supported himself in Europe in part by adopting standard Arabic-style astronomical tables to the local meridians.[30] Abraham also wrote important religious commentaries on most of the books of the Bible, as well as several works on Hebrew grammar.

The nineteenth-century British poet and playwright Robert Browning may have heard of Abraham's stay in England when he made Abraham the narrator of the famous dramatic monologue *Rabbi ben Ezra*, which opens:

Grow old along with me
The best is yet to be
The last of life for which the first was made.

7

The End of the Caliphate

The Party States

When the Umayyad dynasty came to an end, power quickly devolved to small city-states called *taifas*, or party states. At one point there were some thirty-eight separate political divisions. There were also smaller enclaves, some no more than a castle and the territory in its immediate vicinity.[1] The downfall of the caliphate did not bode well for the Jews, who traditionally relied on a strong leader to provide them security and support. In the short term, however, the Jews prospered from the breakup of the caliphate, working with the leaders of the smaller states, particularly in Granada. But over the long term the loss of the caliphate was disastrous for the Jews: the small states could not provide sufficient security to protect the Jews against Muslim resentment of Jewish success, nor could the weakened smaller states defend against incursions from fundamentalists who saw no value in working with the Jews. Life for the Jews of Muslim Spain eventually became intolerable.

While the Jews suffered from the privations of the civil war, the destruction of the caliphate had one advantage: it broke up the Arab monopoly on positions of authority. The end of the Arab lock on power and the multiplicity of small states, some run by Berbers with no previous experience in administration, opened up opportunities for all, including Jews.

A Jewish Grand Vizier

The most successful Jewish courtier was Samuel ben Joseph Halevi ibn Nagrela, who became grand vizier of Granada. Samuel was born in Córdoba in 993, from a family of Levite Jews (he later claimed descent from King David). He received the education of a Jewish courtier: fluency in

Hebrew and Arabic, training in Jewish law, expertise in trading and business, and, like most Arab courtiers, facility in reading and writing poetry. When Berber Muslims raided and sacked Córdoba in 1013, Samuel's family fled and settled in Mérida. From there Samuel moved to Granada, to the court of Sultan Hubbus. He may have been invited to go there by a Muslim official of the Granada court who also kept a house in Mérida.

In the early eleventh century, Granada was a new city. After the breakup of the caliphate, the town of Elvira had been named provincial capital. When a family of Sinhadja Berber soldiers took control of the region in the 1020s, they founded the new capital, Granada, in a more defensible position at the foothills of the Sierra Nevada. One modern historian has described the problems that these new officials faced with their complete inexperience in governance: "When Samuel ha-levi arrived, the Sinhadja had not yet established their own governmental apparatus and had no organized administration. The sole function of the native officers whom they appointed was to collect taxes as high as they could get away with."[2]

Samuel pursued work, both as a tax collector and as a scribe. In 1020 he was arrested and charged with embezzlement but released after payment of a heavy fine.[3] He worked himself back into the good graces of the court and was appointed to collect taxes from all the Jews in the province. According to the twelfth-century writer Abraham ibn Daud, Samuel worked as the anonymous scribe for the vizier, who claimed credit for his work, but Samuel's skills in Arabic were so striking that the sultan soon discovered his talents.[4] More likely, Samuel's promotion by the sultan was a reward for Samuel's support in 1037 and 1038, when he backed the sultan's son Badis against his brother Bullugin as they struggled for the right to succession.[5] Whatever the reason, when the local vizier died, Samuel replaced him. Then Sultan Badis appointed him as grand vizier. While not unprecedented—at least six other Jews served as viziers in *taifa* states—Samuel was the most respected and prominent Jewish leader in the Muslim period.[6] Not only was Samuel now chief administrator, but he was also charged with negotiating with the neighboring Islamic and Christian kingdoms and was made head of the military.

At first Samuel had to receive training in warfare from the sultan, but authority over campaigns eventually fell to him alone. This function was an essential part of his job. The small states vied against one another for territory, and Seville in particular was a major rival. Fighting raged continuously between these rival regions. Samuel as chief vizier went to war almost every year of his administration.[7] For twenty years Samuel led the army of Granada. He waged war against other *taifas*, beginning with Almería at the battle of Alfuente, and he later put down an internal revolt from the sultan's cousin Yadir. His generalship led to an almost unbroken series of victories over rival Muslim city-states. At least one modern scholar, however, noting that there is no mention of Samuel in any Muslim source, has suggested that Samuel may have exaggerated his success and involvement in military engagements.[8]

The sultan also made Samuel head of the Jewish community, for which he took the title of *nagid*, or "exalted." Granada had a community of about six thousand Jews, almost equal in number to the Muslim population, which earned it the designation of Gharnatat al-Yahud, or "Granada of the Jews."[9] In his position as *nagid*, Samuel acted as chief rabbi, resolving community disputes through a thorough knowledge of talmudic law.

Samuel called himself a modern David, referring both to his lyrical gifts and to his military successes. His contemporaries recognized him as the first great Sephardic poet. According to the twelfth-century writer Abraham ibn Daud: "In the days of R. Hasdai the Nasi, the bards began to twitter, and in the days of R. Samuel the Nagid, they burst into song."[10] The poet Moses ben Ezra also noted Samuel's fame as a poet: "His poems ... are various and full of color, powerful in their contents, fine in their form, original in their ideas, and clear in their rhetoric. All that pertains to his compositions and works and letters is known to the uttermost edges of east and west and across the land and sea, and up to the leaders of the Babylonian community and the sages of Syria and the scholars of Egypt and the nagids of [North] Africa and the lords of the West and the Spanish nobility."[11]

His poetry was unique in Hebrew literature, because in addition to poems of love, pleasure, and religious devotion, he wrote about warfare and left forty-one war poems. Some of these poems, which are based on a classical Arab genre, reflected his role in specific battles, including his campaigns against the city-states of Almería and Seville, and his role in suppressing an attempted coup against the sultan.[12] Not all these poems are glorifications of battle:

> War at first is like a young girl
> With whom every man desires to flirt.
> And at the last it is an old woman
> All who meet her feel grieved and hurt.[13]

Samuel's son put together three anthologies, or *diwan*, of his poems. One, *Ben Tchillim* (After Psalms), contains poems on love and wine, as well as elegies on the death of his brother. Many of the love poems are homoerotic in theme, as was common at the time. For example, the poem "In Fact I Love That Fawn" even acknowledges the transgressive nature of this kind of passion. When the male object of the poet's passion rejects the offer of passion angrily, saying that this kind of passion would be a sin, the poet responds that he would take the sin upon himself.[14]

Ben Mishle (After Proverbs) contains reflections on life, and *Ben Qohelet* (After Ecclesiastes) contains poems on mortality. Most of Samuel's poems—nearly two thousand in total—were lost for almost a millennium, only to be rediscovered by chance in 1924 in a crate of manuscripts.[15]

Many of the poems are aphoristic, maxims on society, politics, or mortality, little longer than haiku. For example, the poem "Could Kings Right a People Gone Bad" asks how a society can end corruption when the leaders themselves are false.[16] Another short poem, "Earth to Man," reflects Solomon ibn Gabirol's Neoplatonist view that the soul is trapped in a mortal frame, describing earth as a prison without escape.[17]

Even one of his Muslim enemies acknowledged Samuel's character and brilliance:

> This cursed man, even though Allah did not let him know the only true religion, was nevertheless a superior man, possessed of excellent knowledge, suffering with patience stupid conduct, of a lucid spirit notable for his vivaciousness, of pleasant and ami-

able manner, combining a firm, capable and shrewd character. Always of exquisite courtesy, he knew to take advantage of all circumstances, disarm their hatred by his pleasant ways. What an extraordinary man! He wrote in the two languages [Hebrew and Arabic] and studied the literature of the two nations, was proficient in the principles of the Arabic language and was familiar with the writings of the best grammarians.... He was outstanding, furthermore, in the sciences of the ancients—in the exact sciences—and excelled those who consecrated themselves to these [sciences] in his knowledge of astronomy, which he studied with scrupulous attention. He ... was superior in dialectic, and on that ground he always defeated his adversaries. Notwithstanding the vivacity of his spirit, he spoke little and thought much.[18]

The End of "Jewish Granada"

Samuel ben Joseph Halevi ibn Nagrela's success, however, came at a terrible price. He broke the Islamic law of *dhimmi* subservience, breeding resentment that would rebound on his son. After his death he passed his position to his son, Joseph. A popular Muslim poet voiced the community's resentment of this Jew's position:

[The King] has chosen an infidel as his secretary when
    He could, had he wished, have chosen a Believer.
Through him, the Jews have become great and proud and arrogant—
    They, who were among the most abject,
And have gained their desires, and attained the utmost,
And this happened suddenly, before even they realized it.
And how many a worthy Moslem humbly obeys the vilest ape
    Among these miscreants? ...[19]

Their chief ape has marbled his house
And led the finest spring water to it.
Our affairs are now in his hands
And we stand at his door,

He laughs at us and at our religion
And we return to our God....
Hasten to slaughter him as an offering,
Sacrifice him, for he is a fat ram
And do not spare his people
For they have amassed every precious thing.
Break loose their grip and take their money
For you have a better right to what they collect.
Do not consider it a breach of faith to kill them
—the breach of faith would be to let them carry on.[20]

These verses helped to incite a slaughter. As later described by the sultan's grandson, Abdallah: "Both the common people and the nobles were disgusted by the cunning of the Jews, the notorious changes which they had brought about in the order of things, and the positions which they occupied, in violation of their pact. God decreed their destruction on Saturday, . . . The Jew [Joseph] fled into the interior of the palace, but the mob pursued him there, seized him, and killed him. They then put every Jew in the city to the sword and took vast quantities of their property."[21]

There was no other pogrom like this in the history of Islamic Spain. And yet neither was the 1066 attack on the Jews of Granada a complete aberration. Rather, the pogrom was a violent expression of the tensions that had existed throughout the Islamic period, when Jews had been required to acknowledge their own essential inferiority as mere *dhimmis* in an Islamic world.

Soon after the pogrom in Granada, the world of Jewish culture in Islamic Spain effectively ended. The armies of the Berber Almoravid kingdom, invading Spain from Morocco, temporarily united al-Andalus. Almoravid is the Westernized form of *al-murabi-tun*, meaning "united for holy war." In his history of Moorish Spain, Richard Fletcher describes the Almoravids as "outsiders, peoples of the *bled*, unsophisticated tribesmen, materially and culturally impoverished," whose military leader "dressed in skins, reeked of camels and spoke Arabic only with difficulty.... The Almoravid leadership were puritans, ascetics, zealots. They saw their role as one of purifying religious observance by the reimposition where necessary of the strictest canons of Islamic orthodoxy."[22]

In North Africa the Almoravids subjected Jewish communities to brutal repression. Now they spread this policy to Spain. The result was a wave of exile and forced conversion. Eventually, the Almoravid rulers were replaced by the even more intolerant Almohads, Berbers from the Atlas Mountains. The name they took for themselves, Almohad, is derived from *al-muwahhidum*, or "asserters of religious unity."

The trauma they wrought in the lives of the Jews, who had prospered in—and assimilated to—Muslim Spanish society, was described by the poet Abraham ibn Ezra, who left the following lament for the end of Jewish life in Muslim Spain:

> I weep like an ostrich for Lucena,
> Her remnant dwelt innocent and secure,
> Unchanged for a thousand and seventy years;
> Then came her day and her people were exiled and she a widow
> Forbidden to study the Torah, the Prophets and the Mishnah;
> Even the Talmud was lonely, its glory departed;
> The killers took over and fugitives sought shelter;
> The house of prayer and praise became a mosque.
> For this I weep and smite hand against hand in lament without
> respite;
>> I cannot keep silent; Oh, that my head were a spring of water.
>
> I will shave my head and cry bitterly over the exiles from Seville,
> Over its noble men who were slain and their sons enslaved,
> Over refined daughters converted to the foreign faith.
> Alas, the city of Cordoba is forsaken; its ruin as vast as the sea!
> Her sages and learned men perished from hunger and thirst.
> Not a single Jew was left in Jaen or Almeria,
> Majorca and Málaga struggle to survive,
> The Jews who remained are a beaten, bleeding wound.
> For this I mourn and learn a dirge and wail in bitter lamentation;
>> I shout in my distress; They have vanished like water.[23]

8

Maimonides

At about the same time that Abraham ibn Ezra bemoaned the exile of Jews from al-Andalus, the greatest Jewish intellectual of the *convivencia* was born: Moses ben Maimon, known in the West by the Hellenized form of his name, Maimonides, and in Hebrew by an acronym of his name in Hebrew letters, the RaMBaM. Although Maimonides left Spain at an early age and spent his adult years in what is now Cairo, he is traditionally featured in histories of the Spanish Jews, and for good reasons. He remained closely tied culturally to Spain. His training, both religious and philosophical, came out of Spanish traditions. It is no coincidence that his Islamic counterpart, the great Islamic philosopher Averroës, was his near contemporary and a fellow native of Córdoba. Although Maimonides never returned to Spain, neither did he forget his Sephardic heritage. He signed letters as Moses ben Maimon ha-Sefardi (the Sephardic Jew).[1] In his biography, Joel Kraemer describes Maimonides as "Andalusian to the core of his being, and [he] followed Andalusian models in law, medicine, and philosophy."[2]

Even if Maimonides was not tied to Spain through residence or culture, the Spanish Jews who followed him were tied to Maimonides, whom they recognized as their most important religious and intellectual figure. At least until the expulsion, he was the most important religious authority other than the works considered to be of divine inspiration. As a thinker he was a touchstone for the later Spanish Jewish writers. It was not that everyone revered Maimonides. There was a strong reaction against his rationalism and reliance on classical philosophers, which inspired a countermovement toward religion and faith. But to a large degree, every subsequent Spanish Jewish thinker would be judged in part on the extent to which he either followed or dissented from the writings of Maimonides.

Moses ben Maimon was born in Córdoba in 1135. The city was an important intellectual center of Muslim Spain, as well as a fertile agricultural base, irrigated by the Guadalquivir River. Arab chroniclers called Córdoba "the bride of al Andalus" and "the most beautiful jewel of al-andalus."[3] The city's Jewish quarter lay in the shadow of the great mosque and the royal palace. The nearby town of Lucena had a Jewish academy then considered the foremost institution of higher rabbinic learning in the West.[4] Almoravid repression had closed the academy before Maimonides could study there, but he benefited from it indirectly: his father, who became his teacher, had studied under the head of the academy, Rabbi Joseph ibn Migash, and Maimonides later acknowledged the influence on his own thought of Migash and of another Lucena master, Isaac Alfasi.[5]

In Exile

Maimonides's father, a rabbi-businessman, fled Córdoba, with its Almohad oppression, in 1148, when his son was thirteen. After wandering through Muslim Spain and witnessing the repression suffered by the Jews, they escaped when Maimonides was twenty-two years old to North Africa, where they settled in Fez, Morocco—Almohad territory. Despite these misfortunes, the young Maimonides continued his religious studies. He wrote several commentaries on the Bible, a book on logic, and an essay on the Jewish calendar involving complicated mathematical and astronomical formulas (astronomical calculations to regulate the Jewish calendar, which is based on a lunar cycle, are crucial in determining days of worship).

Under Almohad domination, Fez was only marginally safer for Jews than was Spain. The Maimonides family might, instead, have gone to Christian territory. Other Jews from Córdoba had fled to France, including Judah ibn Tibbon, whose son would produce the authorized translation from Arabic to Hebrew of Maimonides's greatest work, *The Guide for the Perplexed*. Maimonides, however, was fluent in Arabic and acculturated to Muslim society. His philosophic investigations flourished with access to sophisticated Muslim libraries containing translations of major Hellenic works and related commentaries still mostly unknown in the Christian world. When Maimonides finally settled in Cairo, he had access the library of the rich merchant and counselor to Saladin, al-Qadi al-Fadil, which contained one hundred thousand bound volumes.[6] There was nothing like it in the whole Christian world: had he settled in Provence, Maimonides would have lacked the resources he needed to write *The Guide for the Perplexed*.

Maimonides and his family arrived in Fez at a relatively peaceful time, but conditions soon worsened. The Almohad ruler had just put down a rebellion in Granada supported by forced Jewish converts to Islam, and he now retaliated by repressing the Jews and converts of Fez. It is possible that Maimonides's family was forced to convert to Islam while in Fez. Maimonides lived in Fez under the Arabic name Abu Imran Musa ibn Maimon. Many families in the city had been forced to convert under the tyrannies of two local caliphs, Abd al-Mumin and Abu Yakub Yusuf. The leading rabbi of the city, Judah ibn Shoshan, was himself an involuntary convert who secretly practiced Judaism. In 1165 he was arrested, tortured, and killed for this crime.[7] Reports of Maimonides's conversion to Islam were widely circulated in both Muslim and Jewish sources.[8]

In 1160, in response to his experience of the oppression Jews suffered in Spain and North Africa, Maimonides wrote his *Epistle on Forced Conversion*. The widespread forced conversions under the Almohads had opened a debate on whether it was permissible to convert under duress, or whether martyrdom was the only acceptable option. One widely circulated opinion by an anonymous rabbi compelled martyrdom: "Whoever attests the mission of Mohammad thereby renounces the Lord God of Israel. One should rather be killed than profess the *shahada* [the Islamic creed], even if remaining alive would prevent one's children from becoming Muslims."[9] Maimonides, perhaps with his recent forced conversion in mind, wrote that compelled conversion was allowable, as long as the convert remained inwardly faithful to Judaism. "Belief," he writes in this epistle, "is not the notion that is uttered, but the notion that is represented in the soul."[10] The letter distinguished between laws that must always be obeyed and those that could be violated if necessary. He did, however, urge converts to immigrate as soon as possible to a place where they could again live openly as Jews.

Maimonides's *Epistle on Forced Conversion* would again become relevant and resonate with Jews in Christian Spain. After the forced conversions of the Jews in Spain in 1391 and later both in Spain and Portugal, this epistle would be used by converts both for consolation and to rationalize and defend their decision to convert. As Kraemer notes: "His solution of dissimulation, semblance, and a double life became an existential norm for Jews from the late medieval period, during the Inquisition and its aftermath, until the modern period. Indeed, in Europe it became the Jewish symptom par excellence."[11]

Maimonides finally fled Almohad rule for Acre, the crusader city on Israel's Mediterranean coast, under Christian rule. There he experienced little anti-Jewish repression, but the Jewish community in Israel had diminished significantly in size. Maimonides needed a larger community for support. His family resettled in Alexandria, under Fatimid control. It was not until Sultan Selah ad-Din, known in the West as Saladin, took control of Egypt in 1169 that Maimonides would find a politically stable home. He eventually became Saladin's official court physician, though it is possible that he never met his royal patient, who was off fighting crusaders in Jerusalem.

The Religious Writings

In 1158 Maimonides began ten years of study, which would produce one of his three major projects, his *Commentary on the Mishnah*. The Mishnah is a compilation of what is believed to be oral law maintained by the priests of the temple in Jerusalem. Ascribed to Rabbi Judah the Nasi, it was written down sometime after the second century AD. The Mishnah is at least as long as the Old and New Testaments combined.

About three centuries later two academies of religious study—one in Israel, and the other in Babylon—produced works of explication and commentary on the Mishnah known as the Talmud. The Talmud is many times longer than the Mishnah (the Babylonian Talmud is 2.5 million words) and is discursive in nature. It tries to fully reflect and explain the reasoning behind the interpretations. All these works became canonic, an essential part of rabbinical Judaism.

Maimonides's *Commentary* provided a clear and organized précis of the oral law in the Mishnah and was a pioneering work that became a standard reference source for Jewish religious law. It was also novel in its use of Aristotelian logic. Where logic conflicted with the canon, he tried to reconcile the conflict, explaining that parts of the Torah (the first five books of the Bible) and the Talmud were allegorical and did not have to be read literally. He also produced an unprecedented (for Judaism) basic Jewish creed, the Thirteen Principles of Faith.

All this time Maimonides was supported in his studies by his younger brother, David, who traveled widely as a gem dealer. In 1174 David made the arduous journey from Cairo to the Red Sea port of Aydhab in what is now Sudan, over three hundred miles of rough mountain and desert territory. He had brought part of the family savings along with him as business capital. But when he arrived at the port, he found little worth trading and decided to push on by sea to India. His ship went down in the Indian Ocean. David's death was a terrible blow. Maimonides later described the devastating effect this loss had on him: "For nearly a year after I received the sad news, I lay on my bed struggling with fever and despair. Eight years have since passed, and I still mourn, for there is no consolation. What can console me? . . . My one joy was to see him. Now my joy has been changed into darkness. He has gone to his eternal home, and has left me prostrated in a strange land. . . . Were not the study of the Torah my delight, and did not the study of philosophy divert me from grief, I should have succumbed in my affliction."[12]

The loss was also financial. Maimonides lost savings and his brother's financial support and was now responsible for his brother's wife and daughter. Religious principles barred him from making a living from religious teaching. Maimonides considered someone whose Torah was his profession as a person who does no work at all and wrote: "It is better to strip hides off animal carcasses than to say to other people, 'I am a great sage, I am a priest, provide me therefore with maintenance.' So did the Sages command us. Among the great Sages there were hewers of wood, carriers of beams, drawers of water to irrigate gardens, and workers in iron and charcoal. They did not ask for public assistance, nor did they accept it when offered to them."[13] Instead he turned to medicine, in which he was already widely read, since the study of medicine had been part of his general education. Many of the rabbis and philosophers whom Maimonides studied, such as Averroës, also wrote medical papers, most of them drawing on Galen and other classical medical sources. Maimonides had already attained prominence as a physician, but now medicine was to take up much of his daily routine.

Despite this financial calamity, he undertook the writing of the work for which he would become best known in Judaism, the *Mishneh Torah*. This work was the first comprehensive, organized restatement of the whole corpus of Jewish law. It was the one work that Maimonides wrote in Hebrew (rather than in Arabic, with Hebrew characters); he wished to make the *Mishneh Torah* accessible to readers throughout the Jewish world. It eventually became accepted as an essential Jewish text, leading to a common adage playing on Maimonides's first name: "From Moses to Moses there was no one like Moses." It would be two centuries until Joseph Caro, another Spanish exile—one of the victims of the Spanish expulsion of the Jews in 1492—could improve upon Maimonides's work to produce another digest of Jewish law of similar stature.

Although the *Mishneh Torah* dealt with religious law, Maimonides did not abandon philosophy. He placed in the work a proof for the existence of God derived from the Hellenic philosophers. As Kraemer notes: "Maimonides combined a rabbinic *Midrash* with an Aristotelian argument, and as a result the God of Abraham is identified with Aristotle's first mover. By transforming Abraham and then Moses into philosophers, Maimonides succeeded in naturalizing philosophy and the sciences within Judaism."[14]

Maimonides's prominence—both as a religious scholar and in the Jewish community—required him at times to take on leadership responsibilities. He earned the title "the Great Rav in Israel," effectively "Head of the Jews."[15] This title reflected the respect others held for him. Rivalry for position, as well as his own lack of ambition for power, kept Maimonides from seeking a position of any formal or appointed authority.

His prominence meant that he was frequently requested to write responsas, formal opinions on religious questions. Jewish religious law applied to issues now seen as secular, such as domestic relations and property disputes, and Maimonides was often called on to act as a judge. At such times his opinions leaned toward achieving a just, merciful, and commonsense result rather than strict or severe adherence to the letter of the law. For example, when a congregation asked him to sanction the banishment of an elder who had shouted in the middle of a sermon: "How long will you go on with this senseless jabber?" Maimonides acknowledged that the elder had transgressed, but he respected him as a pious scholar and empathized with his impatience while listening to a tedious sermon.[16] In other cases he defended women's rights and found legal ways for allowing widows to remarry despite technical legal impediments.[17]

Dr. Maimonides

While writing his religious works, Maimonides became a prominent physician whose services were so much in demand that his practice became burdensome. He complains in one letter that on a typical day he would start at sunrise with a medical visit to court. In the afternoon he would return to find his house filled with patients, both Jews and Muslims. As he describes in another letter: "The yoke of the gentiles is on my neck regarding medical matters, which have sapped my strength, and have not left me one hour, neither day or night. But what can I do now that my reputation has reached most countries?"[18]

Maimonides wrote ten medical treatises, most of them on specific conditions. He is certainly the only famous philosopher or theologian to have written a book on hemorrhoids. He also wrote a book on sexual intercourse—probably at the request of Saladin's nephew, Al Muzaffar Umar ibn Nur ad Din, a sultan in Syria—in which he prescribed various herbs and foods, as well as certain massages.

His best known medical work is the five-hundred-page book that became known as the *Medical Aphorisms of Moses*. A compilation from Galen and other Hellenic works, it had five Latin publications in Europe.

None of Maimonides's medical works contains original information, but his style was unusually clear and concise for the period. The only medically related work for which he is still cited today, the "Prayer of Maimonides" (still posted in many doctor's offices), is spurious, the work of Marcus Herz, an eighteenth-century German physician.[19]

The Guide for the Perplexed

Despite his busy practice, Maimonides was able to produce the work for which he is best known outside Judaism: *The Guide for the Perplexed*. At the age of forty-seven, he began working on this book at the request of a pupil, Joseph ben Judah ibn Simon, to provide him instruction after he moved to Aleppo and to clarify questions raised by this student.

The first issue Maimonides addresses in *The Guide* is one that had plagued both Jews and Muslims: the anthropomorphic descriptions of God in the Bible. As Kraemer explains, the "mythopoetic language" of the Hebrew Bible had presented a God with "human features and emotions, even anger, jealousy, regret, and disappointment. God sees; he descends and ascends; he sits on a throne; he passes through the land; he dwells in Zion."[20] These descriptions were problematic for both Judaism and Islam, which had placed the incorporeal, omnipresent nature of the deity at the center of their religions. Christians saw no conflict, given their belief that God had assumed a physical form in the body of Christ.

Maimonides could reconcile this apparent anthropomorphism with his core belief in an incorporeal God by expanding on an idea that he had touched on in his religious works: the notion that some religious texts were allegories. If the text seemed to conflict with reason, then the text was not meant to be taken literally. Only where there could be no reconciliation would faith trump reason. *The Guide* also attempted to reconcile the principles of logic and classical philosophy—primarily the thought of Aristotle—with Judaism. Maimonides held that Aristotle's insights into the nature of reality had been surpassed only by the biblical prophets.[21] This reverence for Aristotle and classical texts led Maimonides to redefine the Jewish God using terms from Hellenic philosophy: intellect is the primary force of the universe; God is the first mover; divine will is divine wisdom; angels are intelligences of the spheres; holy spirit is Agent Intellect; divine inspiration is the uniting with Agent Intellect.[22]

The Guide departs from the clarity of his other works. He states in the book that it is deliberately difficult, written for Jews familiar with philosophical speculation: "It is not here intended to explain all these expressions to the unlettered or to mere tyros, a previous knowledge of Logic and Natural Philosophy being indispensible."[23] As Kraemer notes: "The Guide is an encoded text, containing hints and deliberate contradictions, drawing the reader into an amazing labyrinth, a dark forest."[24]

The Guide proved controversial. The difficulty of the book and the replacement of traditional religious interpretations with Hellenic philosophy laid Maimonides open to charges of apostasy; he was accused of having rejected religion after his forced conversion. *The Guide* did, however, continue to find defenders. A century later it would inspire the Christian scholastics: Thomas Aquinas, Roger Bacon, Albertus Magnus, and Duns Scotus. While they criticized aspects of the work, it was an essential predecessor of this new Catholic school of rationalism.

It is unlikely that Maimonides was an apostate. He devoted much of his life to religion. Aside from his work on the *Commentary* and the *Mishneh Torah*, he was spiritual leader to all the Jews in Saladin's domain; he was formally named chief rabbi—*nagid*—in 1187; and he was called on continually to write letters resolving religious disputes. He took on the onerous, voluntary obligation of copying a Torah scroll, which required utter exactitude; unrolling and reading the scroll of the Torah over the calendar year is the central focus of the Jewish religious service, and any error renders the scroll impure. At the end of his life, Maimonides planned to write a book on the Jerusalem Talmud. These are not the actions of an apostate.

Moreover, *The Guide* does eventually lead Maimonides to God. Maimonides even recommends in it a form of religious meditation that used rational thought to reach revelation. A later Spanish follower of the Kabbalah, Abraham Abulafia, drew inspiration from Maimonides to develop a method of ecstatic meditation as a mystical path to the divine.[25] Maimonides describes his path to the divine through rational thought in his *Guide*:

> When you are alone by yourself, when you are awake on your couch, be careful to meditate in such precious moments on nothing but the intellectual worship of God, viz., to approach Him and to minister before Him in the true manner which I have described to you—not in hollow emotions. This I consider as the highest perfection wise men can attain by the above training. When we have acquired a true knowledge of God, and rejoice in that knowledge in such a manner, that whilst speaking with others, or attending to our bodily wants, our mind is all that time with God; when we are with our heart constantly near God.... Then we have attained not only the height of ordinary prophets, but of Moses, our Teacher.[26]

The Guide can sometimes seem very modern. In discussing the nature of evil—by which he meant ill fortune, as well as the wrong actions of men—Maimonides said that our misfortunes will appear much smaller when seen in the context of an enormous universe, "for an ignorant man believes that the whole universe only exists for him; as if nothing else required any consideration.... If, however, he would take into consideration the whole universe, form an idea of it, and comprehend what a small portion he is of the Universe, he will find the truth.... What we have, in truth to consider is this: the whole mankind at present in existence and a fortiori, every other species of animals, form an infinitesimal portion of the permanent universe."[27]

Secrecy and hidden meanings are a common reaction to repression, and it may be that the obscurity of *The Guide* was Maimonides's late reaction to a lifetime of witnessing and experiencing repression. As we will see, secrecy and hidden meanings were to become a part of the house style of Spanish conversos and Jews.

Maimonides witnessed and documented some of the worst episodes of Islamic religious repression. In one letter, addressed to the French Jews, he writes: "In Maghreb, as we know, a heavy doom weighs upon the Jews."[28] In the *Mishneh Torah*, he adds: "In our days, severe vicissitudes prevail, and all feel the pressure of hard times. The wisdom of our wise men has disappeared; the understanding of our prudent men is hidden.... Since we went into exile, the persecutions have not stopped. I have known affliction since childhood, since the womb."

Maimonides was the last important Spanish Jew to work in the Muslim world. The future of the Spanish Jews now lay in Christian Spain.

9

Christian Rule

A New Home for the Jews

Repressive actions by the fundamentalist Berbers who took control of Muslim Spain forced most Jews (as well as many resident Christians, who also suffered persecution) to flee to the Christian kingdoms. Other Jews saw their Muslim towns converted to Christian rule by the Christian *reconquista*. Fortunately, the Jews found themselves welcomed in Christian Spain, both as allies and as valuable assets to the ruling kings. By the twelfth century, the Jews of Spain lived almost entirely under Christian rule.

In his chronicle *Sefer ha-Qabbalah*, Abraham ibn Daud wrote his account of the difficult exile that he and other Jews faced as they fled the Muslim kingdoms—their home for centuries—and of the welcome they received from their new Christian hosts. Abraham ibn Daud, one of the first Jews to write about Aristotle, was born in Córdoba around 1110, and after fleeing the Almohads, took refuge in Christian Toledo.[1] As Ibn Daud recorded, in statements seeded with biblical quotations: "The rebels [Almohads] against the Berber kingdom had crossed the sea to Spain after having wiped out every remnant of Jews from Tangiers to al-Mahdiya. 'Turn again thy hand as a grape-gatherer upon the roots.' They tried to do the same thing in all the cities of the Ishmaelite kingdom in Spain, 'if it had not been the Lord who was for us,' let Israel now say."[2]

The chronicle goes on to depict the arduous journey of the escaping refugees and the suffering of those who were unable to flee. Those who fled northward into Christian Castile were welcomed at the frontier castle of Calatrava, on behalf of Alfonso VII, by his Jewish representative, Judah the Nasi. Ibn Daud added: "Now when this great Nasi,

R. Judah, was appointed over Calatrava, he supervised the passage of the refugees, released those bound in chains and let the oppressed go free by breaking their yoke and undoing their bonds.... When all the nation had finished passing over [the border] by means of his help, the King sent him and appointed him lord of all his household and ruler over all his possessions."[3]

Spanish Christians held radically conflicting attitudes toward Jews. On the one hand, Spain's Christian kingdoms offered Jews the most tolerant refuge in Europe. At a time when England and France were expelling their Jews, Spanish Jews prospered, and some held important positions in the different kingdoms. But Iberia also fostered extreme intolerance. A constant anti-Jewish campaign by elements of the church, social conflicts, and traditional anti-Jewish attitudes all periodically became manifest in outbreaks of violence against individuals or the community. As noted by the historian Yitzhak Baer: "Christian Spain stood out among the Christian states of Europe as at once a land of religious fanaticism and religious tolerance."[4]

The Development of Christian Spain

Iberia had been transformed since the fall of the Visigoths. It was now divided into four kingdoms. Portugal took up the westernmost region. Castile, which had merged with León, took up the center, eventually spreading from the Basque country on the Atlantic Coast to Seville and the Mediterranean. The small, land-locked kingdom of Navarre straddled the Pyrenees. In the southeast, Aragon had merged with Catalonia and its emerging mercantile center in Barcelona. Most of the Spanish Jews would eventually reside in the larger kingdoms of Castile and Aragon.

As the Muslim kingdom broke apart, the Christian kingdoms took advantage of the Muslim weakness. In the conflict called the *reconquista*, they gradually regained the territory lost to the Moors. Alfonso VI conquered Toledo (and with it a substantial Jewish community) in 1082. The battle of Las Navas de Tolosa in 1212—in which all four kingdoms managed briefly to fight in unity—ended in a huge defeat for the Almohad military. King Fernando III (1217–32) conquered the major cities of al-Andalus: Córdoba, Murcia, and Seville. The Aragonese king

Alfonso the Battler managed to expand his kingdom westward to Saragossa with the help of French crusaders. In the single generation that separated the victory at Las Navas from the fall of Seville in 1248, the Christian kingdoms reclaimed almost half the peninsula from Muslim control.[5] By the mid-thirteenth century, the emirate of Granada was the last sizable Muslim territory in Iberia.

The *reconquista* was sometimes considered a part of the crusade to regain the Holy Lands. Even before the First Crusade, the pope had offered indulgences to knights who would assist in the Aragonese campaign against the Muslims. The crusading orders of the Knights Templar and the Hospitalers established a presence in the peninsula. The Spanish had their own crusading orders in the Knights of Calatrava, the Order of Alcántara, and the Order of Santiago.[6] The *reconquista*, however, was not a continuous war. As José Ortega y Gasset has observed, "Something which lasted for eight centuries can hardly be called a reconquest."[7] The two societies shared the same land mass for close to a millennium, during which time it was often in the Christian kingdoms' interest to work with the Muslims.

The Muslim *taifas* were very wealthy. Even after their territory was reduced by the *reconquista*, income generated by irrigated agriculture and trading in manufactures like silk gave the Taifa of Granada the wealth to finish the Alhambra in the mid-fifteenth century. The Muslim states had long taken on a client status to the Christians and were the source of substantial tribute payments to the Christian kingdoms, a major incentive toward continued peace. The tribute payments, called *parias*, were so substantial that they provoked a real estate bubble in Aragon that collapsed in the late eleventh century, when the Christian reconquest had dried up the tributes by conquering much of the territory that had paid the tribute.[8] The Christian states would also sometimes ally with the Muslims, even against other Christians, to achieve short-term goals. For example, the kingdom of León formed an alliance in the twelfth century with the Almohads to fight against their rival, Castile.[9] This pragmatic attitude toward the Muslim states is exemplified in the life of Rodrigo Diaz de Vivar, the legendary hero "El Cid." Although he is remembered as a fighter against the Muslims, he fought on both sides. When a quarrel arose with King Alfonso VI, El Cid took up service with the emir of Saragossa, fighting on the side of the Moors.

Jews in the Christian Kingdoms

From the beginning of the Jewish move from Muslim to Christian territory, the Christian kings of Iberia recognized the Jews as valuable—even indispensable—subjects. The reconquest presented Christian rulers with the same dilemma once faced by Muslims after their conquest of Spanish territory: the need to establish control over a population largely of another religion. In 1270, for example, about thirty thousand Christians were living in the kingdom of Valencia (controlled by Aragon) but four times as many Muslims.[10] Jews could provide administrative support in consolidating Christian authority over the newly conquered Muslim territories.

Moreover, the Christian conquests led to widespread emigration of resident Muslims, particularly in Mallorca. This vacated land needed to be resettled. Jews were offered substantial incentives to move to the new territory, including tax incentives, land grants, and writs of safe conduct.[11] Eventually some of the largest Jewish communities developed in cities like Seville and Córdoba, areas reconquered from the Muslims. It is estimated that by the early thirteenth century approximately eighty thousand Jews lived in Christian Iberia, about forty thousand in Castile, and the rest in Aragon, Portugal, and Navarre, in a population of about two million Christians and a million Muslims.[12] The population of Seville by the late fourteenth century has been estimated at seven thousand.[13]

Legally Jews held the status of slaves or vassals to the king, although the Jews did not consider themselves slaves. This legal status could have real consequences. For example, in the case of an unlawful killing of a Jew, the wergild, or blood-money payment, would go not to the family of the Jew but to the king. In cases of anti-Jewish riots, the king exacted his blood payment. Jewish communities derived some protection from the fact that these killings had financial consequences for the perpetrator.

While Jews in medieval Spain were commonly associated with money lending, only a minority of Jews were actually engaged with finance in the Christian kingdoms. Instead, most of the Jews were artisans, doing work that today would be considered "blue collar" labor: they were tailors, cloth makers, shoemakers, bakers, and smiths of iron, gold, and silver and thus represented the manufacturing base of Spain. This gave them enormous economic importance. While the Jews made up only about 5 percent of the population, they provided over 20 percent of all tax revenues to the state.[14]

The most controversial role filled by Jews was that of tax farmer. Jews in this position would advance the king estimated tax revenues and in exchange received the right to collect and keep the taxes. This practice made some Jews enormously wealthy. It gave the Jews some political protection, since tax farming provided a valuable service to the monarch. It also contributed to the unpopularity of Jews in general, even though the king was ultimately responsible for the imposition of taxes, and many Christians also engaged in the practice.

Ironically, although the Jews paid a disproportionate share of the taxes, they were blamed for the unfairness of the tax system. Taxes were also a frequent source of dissent within the Jewish communities, where less prosperous Jews complained that the well-connected and wealthy Jewish tax collectors were using their influence to obtain tax exemptions, thus placing an unfair burden on the less prosperous Jews. While tax collectors participated at court and had high public profiles, most Jews involved in money lending probably worked on a smaller scale, by providing credit for goods or services. The economic value of the Jews made them the kingdoms' piggy bank. Their relative wealth tempted each king to smash the bank open and grab the short-term profit by extorting money from the Jews. This temptation repeatedly proved disastrous to the Jews.

Another important occupation for the Jews was that of physician. Jews, who had learned Hellenistic medical traditions from the Muslims, would have a near monopoly on the practice of medicine in Christian Spain. On paper numerous religious and secular decrees prohibited or limited the ability of Jewish physicians to treat Christians. Alfonso X's civil code, the Siete Partitas, stated that no Christian "shall take any medicine or cathartic made by a Jew."[15] One Franciscan monk, as late as 1460, complained about the Jewish hold on medicine: "The temporal lords, nay—and that is the thing to weep over—the ecclesiastical prelates set great store by them, to such an extent that hardly one of them is to be found who does not harbor some devil of a Jew doctor."[16]

These proscriptions and objections were largely ignored. Even the pope had Jewish physicians—there are records of six during the papal residence in Avignon.[17] Jewish physicians treated kings, aristocrats, churchmen, and commoners. The close access that Jewish physicians had to the court, as well as royal gratitude for their dedication, often created close personal relations, even friendships. The trust generated from medical services frequently led to important court positions. Even Alfonso X likely used Jewish physicians, and a number of them held prominent positions in his court.[18]

Evidence of the gratitude that this medical dedication could engender can be found today in the city of Vitoria, in northern Spain. At the end of two streets called Olaguibel and Carlos VII in the northern part of the city, there is a public park called Judizmendi, the former site of Vitoria's Jewish cemetery. There on a plaque, it is written that at the time of the expulsion of the Jews in 1492, the residents of Vitoria agreed to leave the site undeveloped, out of respect for the assistance provided by Jewish physicians during an attack of the plague. Vitoria's residents kept this promise for over five hundred years.

The New Jewish Focus on Religion

The transition from life in Muslim lands to life in Christian territory had more than an economic effect on the Jews: it also led to a shift in cultural and intellectual attitudes. The Jewish interest in exploring the philosophy of Aristotle and in reconciling logic with religious tradition culminated, and largely ended, with Maimonides. Jews in Christian Spain instead explored new aspects of Judaism, including the radically new body of mystical thought known as the Kabbalah.

The neglect of philosophy did not mean a rejection of rationalism and science. In Christian Spain Jews remained prominent in the fields of science, including medicine, astronomy, astrology, alchemy, cartography, horology, and instrument making. They were even more prominent in these fields than they had been in Muslim Spain, since these traditions had been developed in Islamic lands and had not yet been understood in—or embraced by—Christian Europe.

This rejection of philosophy—except for Platonism and Neoplatonism, which figured into religion—and a move toward faith may have been a reaction to the increased attacks that Jews suffered in Christian Spain at the hands of the church. Anti-Jewish pressures were increasing in most of Christian Europe. In Germany and northern France, the ascetic movement of Hasidism (not related to the modern Hasidic movement) had emerged in the eleventh and twelfth centuries, partly in reaction to the oppression suffered by Jews during the Crusades.[19] The Hasids of northern Europe, who themselves had been influenced by Franciscan asceticism, stimulated pietism in Spain—both directly, through German Jews like Rabbi Asher of Cologne, who became a leader of the community in Toledo, and indirectly, through pietists like Jonah Gerondi.

One of the most important European influences on the increasing Jewish religiosity in Christian Spain came from nearby France, from followers of the great eleventh-century rabbi Shlomo ben Yitzchak, known as Rashi. He founded a school called the Tosafists, and his followers went beyond the traditional focus on interpreting specific passages in the Talmud to focus instead on general issues using multiple talmudic sources.

As Spanish Jews joined in the religious life of other European Jews, the philosophical brand of Jewish thought pioneered by Maimonides, and especially his *Guide for the Perplexed*, came increasingly under attack. Anti-rationalist Jews in fourteenth-century Provence declared a ban on the book and excommunicated as heretics anyone who followed its precepts. A fierce debate concerning the danger of Maimonides's rationalism erupted and continued throughout much of the thirteenth century. There were even accusations that opponents of Maimonides tried to enlist support among the Dominicans and the Inquisition.[20]

Some of the most prominent of these opponents were followers of the Kabbalah.[21] The mysticism of the Kabbalists was diametrically opposed to the rationalism of Maimonides. Although followers of the Kabbalah saw themselves as defenders of traditional Judaism, in fact they were proposing a radical reinterpretation of Jewish tradition.

The attempt to limit Maimonides's influence in Saragossa in 1232 led supporters of Maimonides to propose a counterban on anyone who spoke out against the great sage.[22] The controversy was fanned by the church, which hoped to promote dissension among the Jews on the premise that poor Jewish morale would encourage conversion to Christianity. Public argument over Maimonides was largely limited to Aragon and Catalonia and had lost most of its force by the end of the thirteenth century. However, the new religious ideas, derived from Rashi, the Kabbalah, and other sources, would supplant philosophy as a focus of Jewish religious thought in Spain.

....

10

Jews in Castile and Aragon

Castile

The kingdom of Castile grew out of the kingdom of Asturias, the strip of land between the Atlantic and the mountain chain called the Picos de Europa, which had withstood the Muslim invasion. The kingdom eventually spread south. King Alfonso el Magno (866–911) moved the capital to León, south of the mountains, and the kingdom took on that name. The territory to the east of León—including modern-day Santander, Burgos, and Álava—became known as Castile, or "Castle," for its many fortifications. The military prowess of Castile eventually led to its regional dominance, although the tendency of kings to split their dominions among their heirs resulted in several splintered successions after the initial unification of Castile and León. It was not until 1230, in the reign of King San Fernando III, that the kingdoms became permanently united.

From 1252 until 1284, the policies of Alfonso X, known as "the Wise," son of King San Fernando III, exemplified the contradictory Spanish attitudes of tolerance and intolerance toward Jewish subjects. The king made frequent use of Jews, both in his many cultural projects and to support his regime. But his works also reflects a distrust of the Jewish religion, and at the end of his reign, King Alfonso turned on the Jews as he suffered the downfall of his own regime.

Alfonso was given his nickname, El Sabio, or "the Wise," in part because he understood the value of the Muslim advances in the arts and sciences, and he underwrote numerous translations. Spain had become an enormous repository of Hellenistic writings and Arab discoveries in math and science, whose value would soon be recognized across Europe. One modern historian has described the central role

Spain played in transmitting classical learning from Islam to Christian Europe:

> The creative role of Islamic Spain in the shaping of European intellectual culture is still not widely enough appreciated.... The scientific and philosophical learning of Greek and Persian antiquity was inherited by the Arabs in the Middle East. Translated, codified, elaborated by Arabic scholars, the corpus was diffused throughout the culturally unified world of classical Islam in the ninth and tenth centuries until it reached the limits of the known world in the west. And there, in Spain, it was discovered by the scholars of the Christian west, translated in Latin mainly between 1150 and 1250, and channeled off to irrigate the dry pastures of European intellectual life.[1]

Alfonso was deeply involved in the revival of classical thought, as well as in the promotion of Muslim advances in science, and he used the Jews of his kingdom to assist him in translating and interpreting these works of science and philosophy. He promoted the use of the vernacular Castilian over Latin, codified a series of laws based on Roman principles that would become a basis for modern legal codes in Europe and Latin America, and helped to compile many books on subjects ranging from history to philosophy, religious devotion, and chess.

Although Alfonso's intellectual achievements are universally admired, his regime has been judged largely as a political failure. In his *Historia general de España*, seventeenth-century historian Juan de Mariana marked him with the epitaph: "While he was contemplating the heavens and looking at the stars he lost the earth and his kingdom."[2] This comment accurately reflects the conflict between Alfonso's intellectual successes and his political failures but unfairly blames those failures on intellectual distractions. It was instead a misplaced political ambition that helped to destroy his regime. Alfonso wasted much of his time (and his country's treasury) on a fruitless quest for the crown of the Holy Roman Empire, a distinction that he claimed was his as the grandson of Frederick Barbarossa.[3]

The Jews played an important role in the success of Alfonso's reign. They were essential intermediaries between Muslim culture and territory and the West. They were fluent in Arabic, as well as in the new Spanish vernacular that Alfonso was beginning to promote over Latin. Since they had collaborated with the Muslims in their scientific discoveries, many Jews were experts in these fields. For example, one of the most important works to come out of Alfonso's court was the set of astronomical observations collected in the "Alfonsin Tables." This work, which would become the standard reference work for navigators until the invention of the telescope, was not a translation but the work of two Jews, identified as Yehuda and Rabbi Çag.[4]

Astronomy always had a particular prominence in Jewish intellectual circles because of its religious and secular significance. As the historian Abraham Neuman has noted, astronomy was of critical importance in the adjustment of the Jewish calendar, since "the central problem in Jewish calendrical calculation was the adjustment of the solar year with the lunar months; or the proper arrangement of a calendar whose months were lunar while its cycle of festivals was agrarian and necessarily based on the solar seasons."[5]

Numerous Jews held prominent positions in Alfonso's court. Don Solomon ibn Zadok served as chief collector of tax revenues and as ambassador. Jews took on diplomatic missions to the Muslim courts. Rabbi Todros ben Joseph Halevi Abulafia, who may have been a physician, once accompanied Alfonso and his consort Violante on a diplomatic mission to France. Jews dominated the treasury and collected revenue as tax farmers.

Although Jews were entrusted with important positions by Alfonso, his writings reveal his ambivalent attitude toward his Jewish subjects. His Siete Partitas, for example, was an important and pioneering effort to write a comprehensive modern legal code. Too radical for its time, it would not be implemented for another century.

The Siete Partitas contained a number of protections for the Jews. The code punished breaking into a synagogue, "for a synagogue is a house where the name of God is praised."[6] It forbade forced conversions and ordered that Jewish holidays be respected. It also contained, however, a ban on the treatment of Christian patients by Jewish doctors. It barred Jews from public office and from exercising authority over Christians. Moreover, it set the procedures for prosecuting blood-libel crimes, which the king appeared to believe was a problem. Blood libel— stories of ritual murder of Christians by Jews—first became current in 1144.[7] A blood-libel story (the death of Hugh of Lincoln) had been one of the causes of the expulsion of the Jews from England in 1290, and the Hugh of Lincoln story provided the basis for "The Prioress's Tale" in Chaucer's *Canterbury Tales*. Blood-libel stories had been denounced by Pope Innocent IV before the writing of the Siete Partitas.

Alfonso also compiled a set of illustrated songs praising the Virgin Mary, called *Cantigas de Santa Maria*. Many contained anti-Jewish stories. *Cantiga* 3 relates how a Jew helped a Christian sell his soul to the devil. In *cantiga* 4, a young Jewish boy tells his father that he has been inspired to convert, whereupon the father locks the boy in a burning furnace, and the Virgin appears to save him from the flames. In *cantiga* 6, a Jew is irritated by a child's songs in praise of the Virgin and kills the child. Chaucer's "The Prioress's Tale" gives the same motivation for the ritual murder: the child is killed by Jews angered at hearing the child's songs to the Virgin.

These anti-Jewish sentiments would erupt into violence at the end of Alfonso's reign. A revolt against the king broke out in 1254, when some of the most prominent aristocrats in Castile, joined by Alfonso's brother Enrique, foreswore their loyalty to the king, instead aligning themselves with the Muslim ruler in Granada. The rationale for this revolt was excessive taxes and the recent attempt at juridical reforms. Alfonso had continually imposed large taxes on a perennially weak and overtaxed economy, in the interest of supporting his futile quest to be named Holy Roman emperor. One historian has called him "a notorious spender.[8] And he antagonized the nobles with his proposed legal reform, which would have centralized power in the hands of the king and eliminated the powers and privileges enjoyed by the aristocracy and local officials.

Alfonso settled this initial revolt by making concessions both to the rebels and to Granada's ruler. But in 1277 the king had his brother

Fadique strangled and then had Fadique's ally, Simón Ruiz de los Cameros, burned at the stake. No explanation was given for these executions. The men may have been caught in a conspiracy. More recently it has been speculated that Fadique and his ally were killed after their homosexual relationship was discovered.[9] Alfonso's judgment may also have been clouded by illness; he suffered frequent bouts of bad health (possibly the result of maxillary cancer).[10] His features were so distorted that he had been called a leper, and his left eye was pushed out of its socket. But these seemingly arbitrary executions of prominent figures—Fadique often led the king's army—further antagonized the aristocracy.

In 1278 the chief (Jewish) tax administrator, Don Çag de la Malaha, was ordered to finance the armies besieging Muslim forces in Algeciras. Instead, the money was diverted by the prince, Sancho. Alfonso reacted by imprisoning all the Jewish tax farmers. Çag de la Malaha was hung. Another Jewish tax farmer was dragged to his death through the streets of Seville. One Jew converted to avert death. These Jews were probably executed merely to discipline Alfonso's son, Sancho, and to prevent further diversions of treasury funds.

Two years later, on a Sabbath, King Alfonso imprisoned all the Jews until they could pay him a ransom equal to two years' annual tribute (the king of France had done something similar one hundred years before). Some Jewish leaders were imprisoned for months and then subjected to torture in an attempt to convert them. The Toledo *aljama*, the Jewish quarter, was demolished.[11] By 1282 the king's actions had driven much of the aristocracy, many church officials, and Prince Sancho into open revolt. The king, isolated, turned to Muslim forces in North Africa for support, and the country was plunged into civil war that ended with Alfonso's death in 1284.

After the death of Alfonso X, the Jews were restored to their old positions at court. They continued to prove indispensable to the Crown because of their ability to raise taxes and to administer finances. Yet they remained under constant attack, from members of the church and rivals in the aristocracy and from the common burghers. As Yitzak Baer has noted: "The fomenters of the religious agitation made common cause with the estates, the knights and the municipalities, and all, as one man, demanded the removal of the Jews from the service of the state."[12]

Aragon/Catalonia

What became Catalonia began as the French province known as the Spanish Marches, or mark, because it was a buffer zone between the Frankish and the Spanish provinces. Barcelona became the principal city of this region after Charlemagne's son recaptured it from the Muslims in 801, whereupon the region was dominated by the counts of Barcelona. Aragon consisted of rural provinces west of the Pyrenees, too remote to come fully under Muslim control. King Ramiro I of Aragon (1035–63) built up a military force strong enough to require tribute from the wealthy *taifa* of Saragossa. In 1137 King Ramiro, concerned about the territorial ambitions of Castile, turned for help to Count Ramon Berenguer IV of Barcelona. The arranged marriage of the count to the king's infant daughter created the joint kingdom of Aragon-Catalonia, which would have a single ruler but nevertheless would maintain separate institutions and laws.

Jews were initially favored in Aragon. Major territorial expansion during the reconquest created a need to repopulate after Muslim flight or expulsion, and Jews were ideal settlers; their reliance on royal protection ensured their loyalty, and they made significant contributions to the economy. Ultimately, however, the Jews faced as much or more repression in Aragon as in Castile. Two factors undermined their status in the newly incorporated territories of Aragon: the proximity of the pope in Avignon and the Inquisition led to greater, church-led anti-Jewish lobbying and propaganda; and the rise of Catalan mercantilism, manufacturing, and banking led to economic competition with Christians that did not exist in Castile.

Jaume I "the Conqueror" (1208–76), a contemporary of Alfonso the Wise (whom he served as father-in-law and mentor), occupies an equally prominent place in Spanish history and can also be viewed as an exemplar of royal attitudes toward the Jews. His reign was not weakened by inflated ambition, as Alfonso's had been. Jaume ruled for fifty-three years, during which he expanded the territory controlled by his kingdom by 50 percent through the successful conquest of Valencia and the Balearic Islands.

If, like Alfonso, Jaume's policies toward the Jews could be a mixture of tolerance and repression, in Jaume's case other forces required him at times to take repressive measures against the Jews. He himself valued Jewish contributions to his kingdom and provided the Jews with rewards and opportunities. But Jaume also assisted the Dominicans, who, particularly at the urging of Raymond de Penyafort, saw the Jews as targets for conversion; thus the king was forced to accommodate their anti-Jewish demands, in spite of his own reservations.

Jaume earned his title—"the Conqueror"—at an early age. Orphaned at the age of five, he was first taken in by his father's slayer, Simon de Montfort, then rescued by Pope Innocent III, who placed him in the care of the Knights Templar. Jaume led his first battle at the age of ten and began a successful campaign to conquer the Balearic Islands at the age of twenty-one.

Jaume found the Jews to be important allies for several reasons. After his father's defeat and early death in the battle of Muret, the kingdom was heavily in debt, and Jews became an important source of revenue and credit. Before Jaume's rule, the kingdom had relied primarily on royal incomes for revenue. Jaume began instead using taxation as a major source of revenue, and the Jews assisted him in the administration and collection of new taxes.[13]

The need to administer the newly conquered territory opened another role for the Jews. Jaume encouraged Jewish resettlement of these areas, through grants of land, privileges, and promises of royal protection. He exempted the *aljamas*, the Jewish quarters, from inland custom payments. He even compromised Christian principles to help the Jews: when Jews complained that they were losing Muslim slaves through Christian conversion efforts—Jews could not legally enslave Christians—Jaume placed legal disincentives in the way of Muslim-to-Christian conversion to accommodate his Jewish subjects. At the same time, the church, including the pope, the Dominicans, and the Inquisition that had been formed to deal with the Cathars, continued to call for repressive measures against the Jews. Anti-Jewish propaganda included the first Jewish blood libel to appear in Spain, an accusation that Jews had killed a Christian boy in Saragossa in 1250.[14]

Allied with these efforts were attempts by municipalities to limit the power of the Jews. Some of these attempts were influenced by the ambitions of the new burgher class in Catalonia, which resented competition from the Jews. These efforts to restrict the Jews also reflected resentment by Christians in general against their Jewish creditors. The Cortes (local council) of Gerona passed legislation in 1241 limiting the rights of Jews to charge interest to Christians, legislation that, according to Yitzak Baer, was anti-Jewish to the core: "The language of this legislation breathes hatred and mistrust of the Jews and repeatedly charges them with avarice."[15] King Jaume acceded to some of this pressure by passing a law limiting interest rates. In 1254, when the French king Louis IX expelled the Jews and canceled all debts owed to them, Jaume also confiscated for the Crown all Jewish debts.

In general Jaume tried to mediate between the Jews and their enemies. He recognized the importance of the Jews' economic contribution to his kingdom. For example, after the Disputation of Barcelona (a debate over the Talmud that will be described in detail in a later chapter), Jaume acceded to pressure from the church to force the Jews to hear Christian sermons. He subsequently tempered this measure by decreeing that the Jews had the freedom to decide whether to attend these sermons, which canceled their effectiveness.[16]

King Jaume's support, however, could come at a great price. One Jew wrote a letter to his rabbi complaining of the "large expenditures made by the communities in the interests of public welfare and safety, namely, protection money paid during the Christian festivals and like items, municipal improvements, expenses in connection with the king's order to wear a broad badge, and to return to the Christian debtors the interest collected above the legal rate and suffer forfeiture of the principal upon investigation by two Christians. The community made large expenditures to obtain mitigation of such measures."[17]

Jaume's contributions to the advancement of intellectual and cultural pursuits did not match those of Alfonso the Wise, but they were still substantial. He revived the medical university at Montpellier, founded a university at Valencia, and published the first generally applicable Roman law code in Europe, the Furs of Valencia.[18] His kingdom produced a number of important intellectuals, including Ramon Llull, one of the greatest of the medieval philosophers. The autobiography that Jaume authorized for publication in Catalan, the *Llibre del Sfeyts*, is unique in the medieval period, covering both his military and romantic conquests—he was married three times and had numerous mistresses and concubines. The strong personal voice expressed in the *Llibre* can be seen in the line: "We kings take no more from this world than a single shroud, except that it is of better cloth than those of other people."[19]

Jewish culture, benefiting from the support of a strong, stable king, also flourished. The town of Gerona became a center for the radically new mystical ideas that would become known as the Kabbalah. The Jews of the kingdom of Aragon—exposed to the disparate techniques and ideas passed down through Maimonides's rationalism, the commentaries of Rashi, and the still secret lore of the Kabbalists—produced a number of famous Jewish leaders.[20]

Jaume's son, Pedro III, experimented with an even greater reliance on Jewish administrative support. He saw Jews as a loyal force completely dependent on the Crown, whom he could use to restrict aristocratic power at home by replacing officials loyal to other nobles with Jews. This reliance on Jewish support led to a revolt by the nobility, who refused to supply the king with troops to fight a French invasion unless Pedro dismissed his Jewish officials.[21]

The Jews faced other difficulties. The church actively proselytized against the Jews and sometimes fomented anti-Jewish riots. In Calatayud mobs tore down the gates of the *judería*, the Jewish quarter, and in Huesca Jewish rites were parodied in the streets. The municipal *cortes* passed numerous anti-Jewish laws, such as the requirement of an anti-Jewish oath, a ban on Jewish appointments to official positions, and the imposition of a special costume. Pedro ultimately affirmed some of the demands of the *cortes* but did restrain church proselytizing to protect the Jews.

Pedro had a pressing need for funds to pay for his suppression of a revolt of Catalan nobles, as well as for his campaign in Sicily. The Jews had to pay a large percentage of this cost in taxes and other impositions. Toward the end of his reign, Pedro imposed a system of taxes on the Jews that, as Yitzak Baer has noted, "even by the standards of that day, was nothing less than a predatory raid upon Jewish wealth."[22] At the same time, he took steps to prevent any Jewish flight to Castile to evade the tax burden. At one point he had the richest Jews in Saragossa arrested and held hostage. All these policies came close to destroying the economic base of the *aljamas* in Aragon.

After Pedro's rule Jews ceased to hold significant public office in Aragon, although some, particularly during the relatively permissive reign of Pedro IV, had important responsibilities amounting to de facto political offices. As previously they continued to bear a heavy financial burden for royal protection, and that protection continued to be vitally needed. This was to be the model of Jewish life in Aragon—survival on the basis of royal support, ensured only by continual bribes sometimes amounting to extortion. As Yitzak Baer has described it: "From now on the Jews [became] primarily a sponge to be squeezed dry for taxes."[23]

....

11

Book of Splendor and Kabbalah Mysticism

Moses de León

In the last half of the thirteenth century, an inhabitant of León, in Castile, claimed to have made a remarkable discovery. He said that he had found a hitherto unknown collection of works by the famous third-century rabbi Simeon ben Yohai that revealed secrets of the hidden mystical meanings found in the Torah. This man, Moses de León, sold these pamphlets throughout Spain. They were eventually collected in a work called the *Zohar*, or *Book of Splendor*. The *Zohar* has now become a canonical work of Judaism, probably the best known work of the group of mystical texts known collectively as the Kabbalah.

The *Zohar* is also one of history's great literary frauds.

Some religious followers (including the New Age Kabbalah Centre, with which Madonna is affiliated) still believe that Simeon ben Yohai wrote the *Zohar*. But most scholars and rabbis accept Moses de León as the true author. Not much is known about his life. He was born Moses ben Shemtob in León in northern Spain, around 1250. He lived in Guadalajara (a center of Kabbalah study), Valladolid, and in Ávila. He died at Arévalo in 1305, while traveling home to Ávila from the royal court of Valladolid. It is known that he had a copy of Maimonides's *Guide for the Perplexed* transcribed for him in 1264. That, and the philosophical references in his early works, demonstrates Moses de León's initial interest in Hellenistic philosophy, before he turned to the mystical thinking of the Kabbalah.

In order to strengthen his claim that the *Zohar* was the ancient work of Rabbi Simeon ben Yohai, Moses de León wrote it in the language of the Talmud, Aramaic, despite his limited fluency in that language.

He carried this deception further still by continuously citing fictional sources, including the Book of Adam, the Book of Enoch, the Book of King Solomon, and others. These false attributions have led some followers to believe that the Kabbalah was based on lost books—ancient sources of mysticism. The use of fictional sources, however, is consistent with the use of bogus quotations throughout the book.[1]

There is a well-known story about Moses de León told by a later Kabbalist, Isaac of Acre, who visited Ávila after Moses's death. While in Ávila, Isaac heard that a rich man in town, Joseph de Ávila, had hoped to acquire the original ancient *Zohar* manuscript from the widow of Moses de León. As payment Joseph offered to marry his son to the widow's daughter. But the widow would not admit to Joseph that such a manuscript, penned by her deceased husband, existed. She said that her husband had told her, "If I told people that I am the author, they would pay no attention nor spend a farthing on the book, for they would say that these are but the workings of my own imagination. But now that they hear that I am copying from the book Zohar which Simeon ben Yohai wrote under the inspiration of the holy spirit, they are paying a high price for it as you know."[2]

On the basis of this story, Moses de León has been called a mountebank, a traveling salesman who supported his family by selling his fraudulent pamphlets all over Castile. There, are, however, good reasons for believing in his sincerity, both as author and mystic. First, he was not alone among Kabbalists in his "pseudepigraphy"; it was not uncommon for Kabbalists to falsely attribute their works to ancient sources.[3] "Kabbalah" means "tradition," and the use of this term for what was basically a new set of doctrines reflected the Kabbalists' belief that they were following an old tradition, one that could not be documented because it had been passed down secretly. Kabbalah was seen as a kind of mirror to the Talmud; like the Talmud it was believed to have been divinely revealed to Moses and passed down through an oral tradition, but unlike the Talmud, because of its esoteric nature, this tradition was kept secret and known only to Kabbalah masters.[4]

Moreover, the *Zohar* reflects a deep understanding of concepts being developed by thirteenth-century Kabbalists. Moses de León may have invented his sources, but he did not make up the ideas at the heart of the book. The ideas behind the Kabbalah originated in twelfth-century Provence and later spread first to Gerona and then across the rest of Spain. This birth date and place correspond with the high point of the sect known as the Cathars, condemned by the church as the Albigensian heresy.

The Kabbalists absorbed some of the Cathars' ideas—elements of gnosticism, as well as the doctrine of reincarnation and the transmigration of souls.[5] The Kabbalists also incorporated into their beliefs elements of Neoplatonism and were probably familiar with some Christian mystical thinkers—particular Scotus Eriguena—and with the Islamic Sufi mystical writings.

Kabbalah Teachings

The result was a new interpretation of Judaism that took the opposite approach from Maimonides's rationalism. In traditional Judaism the Torah laid out God's commandments and his guidance to humankind. The religious treatises on the Torah, the texts of the Mishnah and the Talmud, and the various commentaries and responsa were all designed to clarify God's laws. The Kabbalists, however, believed that the Torah was not meant to be understood in its straightforward, literal meaning. Rather, it is a coded text containing secret meanings not decipherable by traditional rational analysis.[6] Thus, in the Kabbalist tradition, the *Zohar* makes the case against an analytical reading of the Torah: "Rabbi Simenon said: If a man looks upon the Torah as merely a book presenting narratives and everyday matters, alas for him! Such a Torah, one treating with everyday concerns, and indeed a more excellent one, we too, even we, could compile.... But the Torah, in all of its words, holds supernal truths and sublime secrets."[7]

The Kabbalists believed that the true nature of reality was essentially unknowable. The essence of God, the En-Sof, was hidden and unapproachable. God, however, had ten outward manifestations, called the Sefirot, the contemplation of which would provide mystic revelations and an approach to the divine. The idea of the Sefirot was embraced in part as a solution to the same great Jewish problem of the Middle Ages that Maimonides approached in the beginning of his *Guide*: anthropomorphism in the Torah. Maimonides solved this problem by deeming these descriptions merely allegorical, but this answer bothered Jews who believed in the literal truth of the Torah. The Kabbalah takes a more literal interpretation. The Sefirot represent the mystical, incorporeal, body of God.[8]

From the modern perspective, one of the strangest ideas in the Kabbalah is the Shekhinah, the feminine aspect of God. The Talmud and the Midrash both mention a Shekhinah, but only in Kabbalah does it appear as a feminine attribute. The recognition of a feminine aspect of God, however, was not a protofeminist idea. All the Kabbalists were men—there was no equivalent to the female Catholic mystics like Saint Catherine of Siena or Saint Clare of Assisi.

The female aspect of the Shekhinah sometimes seems to mirror the use of the Virgin Mary in the Catholic Church and may have been influenced by Marian veneration. As Gershom Scholem, a renowned twentieth-century expert on Jewish mysticism, explains: "She is the true 'Rachel weeping for her children,' and in a magnificent misinterpretation of a Zoharic passage, the Shekhinah weeping in her exile becomes for later Kabbalism 'the beauty who no longer has eyes.'"[9] In 1571 one Kabbalist, in a Virgin Mary–like description, "saw her at the Wailing Wall in Jerusalem as a woman dressed in black and weeping for the husband of her youth."[10] The Kabbalah text *Sefer Hameshiv*, the 1470 "Book of the Responder," makes the Shekhinah/Virgin Mary parallel even more explicit, predicting that the Shekhinah will engender the Messiah through a virgin birth.[11]

The Kabbalah's description of divine attributes led to accusations that the Kabbalah advocated polytheism, violating Judaism's fundamental principle of the unity of God. The Kabbalists were sensitive to this problem and took pains to reconcile their vision of a multifaceted deity with the proclamation found in the most fundamental prayer in Judaism, the Shema (from Deuteronomy 6:4–9): "The Lord is one."

The Kabbalah also describes methods of achieving mystical revelation. The most common of these is the contemplative prayer, or *kawwanah*. The thirteenth-century mystic Abraham Abulafia prescribed meditation on Hebrew letters. This practice originated in the belief that every aspect of the Torah, including the Hebrew lettering, shares in divinity. Abulafia proposed that meditation on Hebrew words and letters would assist in untying the knots that bound the soul to the material world, and would lead to mystical revelations of the divine. This meditation method was called the *Hokhmath ha-Tseruf*, or "science of the combination of letters."

The Jewish theologian Moshe Idel sees Moses de León and Abulafia as representing the two different approaches to the divine by followers of the Kabbalah. While the *Zohar* tries to describe the nature of the divine, Abulafia represents the ecstatic Kabbalah, which searches for a means of personal revelation.[12] This search for revelation can involve an inward search: since the soul is of divine origin, self-revelation can lead to the divine.[13]

The popularity of these new ideas reflected significant changes in the Jewish communities in Spain. There had been schools of Jewish mystics incorporating esoteric interpretations of the Torah previously, but never had such a movement obtained such widespread and long-lasting acceptance among the Jews. This focus on mysticism among the Spanish Jews reflected the general changes they faced in adapting to life in Christian Europe. The transition from the Muslim to the Christian world led to a shift in cultural and intellectual focus for them. The interest in exploring the philosophy of Aristotle and reconciling logic with religious tradition culminated, and largely ended, with Maimonides. Jews in Christian Spain instead explored new aspects of Judaism, including the Kabbalah.

This rejection of rationalist philosophy and the shift toward faith may have been a reaction to the increased oppression that the Jews suffered in Christian Spain. This reflected repression against the Jews in all of Christian Europe starting with the Crusades. It may also be that the oppression and persecution to which Jews were subject in Christian Europe made them more ready to embrace an esoteric and secret interpretation of their faith. In the midst of persecution by the church, it may have been a relief to the Kabbalists to see themselves as adepts in a powerful faith that could lead to secret revelations of the divine. Moreover, there was a magical aspect to the Kabbalah: the path to revelation could provide magical power. Most Kabbalists condemned the use of the Kabbalah for magical purposes, but the fact that it needed to be condemned indicates that some believed in its magic potential.

The repression suffered by the Jews is directly reflected in the Kabbalah. The *Temunah*, written around 1250, describes the doctrine of the Shemitah, the idea that the world passes through cycles of periodic creation and destruction. Thirteenth-century Jewish mystics believed themselves to be in a period of stern judgment, dominated by rigor, commandments, and prohibitions; in the next period the power of evil would be curbed, opening a utopian age. Another work, the *Raya Mehemna*, as Scholem describes it, contains "pointed social criticism in an apocalyptical vein . . . whose burning hate of the oppressive groups in contemporary Jewish society is unmistakable."[14]

The *Zohar's* popularity may have resulted in part from the fact that the very same qualities that make it fraudulent gave it a tone of authority. Although other Kabbalists had ascribed their work to false sources, none had taken it to this extreme. Moses de León adopted the voice and style of an ancient sage. The *Zohar* is filled with the homilies and anecdotes of a second-century rabbi as he wanders through ancient Israel. The language is generally simple, probably because of Moses's limited Aramaic (he was more florid when he wrote in Hebrew).

Finally, the *Zohar* acquired its authority in part because of the comparative reticence of other writers. While numerous writings make up the Kabbalah, there are many more works that went unpublished or were never written down. The Kabbalist "tradition" was a secret doctrine, considered too dangerous for exploration by unprepared souls. The great rabbi Nahmanides, for example, was a leader of the Gerona Kabbalah School. Yet while he left many writings behind, he approached kabbalistic concepts with circumspection. There was nothing circumspect about Moses de León's approach: the published volumes of the *Zohar* run about 2,500 pages.[15]

During the first century after its publication, the *Zohar* remained an obscure book, known only to kabbalistic adepts. By the nineteenth century, though, it had entered the canon of religious authority, along with the Bible and the Talmud.[16] While Maimonides is much better known, few now read his *Guide*, whereas the *Zohar* and the Kabbalah still have a following. The *Zohar* may be the most enduring legacy of the Jews in Spain.

PART 2

The End of Tolerance

12

Toward 1391

Jews and the Early Church

From the beginning Christianity struggled with Judaism. The two faiths arose out of the same tradition, but early Christians saw themselves as the sole legitimate inheritors of this tradition, and this required Christians to prove the illegitimacy of their Jewish rivals' beliefs. Christians also resented the Jewish resistance to accepting Christ's teachings.

The Gospels whitewashed the role of Pontius Pilate in Jesus's death, instead placing blame on the Jews. The fairness of Pilate and his Roman administration that is displayed in the Christian Bible is not supported by the nonbiblical historical accounts. As Elaine Pagels has noted in *The Origin of Satan*: "Even Josephus, despite his Roman sympathies, says that the governor displayed contempt for his Jewish subjects, illegally appropriated funds from the Temple treasury, and brutally suppressed unruly crowds. The Jewish Greek historian Philo describes Pilate as a man of 'ruthless, stubborn and cruel disposition,' famous for, among other things, ordering 'frequent executions without trial.'"[1]

The parables that Christ tells the Pharisees reflect Christian resentment of the Jews' refusal to accept Christianity. As Pagels notes, Luke "relegates Israel's greatness to the past, and confidently claims its present legacy for his own—predominantly Gentile—community. In both Luke and John . . . Jesus himself identifies his Jewish opponents with Satan."[2] As James Carroll points out in *Constantine's Sword*, the Emperor Constantine's decision to have the church adopt the cross as its principal symbol meant that Christ's death would always be the central focus of the faith.[3] The church's view that the Jews were guilty of the death of Christ would guarantee that Jews be considered enemies of Christendom in the popular imagination.

The stigma of deicide would be for centuries the font of anti-Jewish violence. Even church pleas for clemency could never overcome the message at the center of the Christian faith: that the Jews bore responsibility for Christ's death. In the opinion of James Carroll: "To label a group the most heinous of enemies and then to demand for them tolerance (albeit limited) and safety … is probably to make demands that the human psyche, over the long run, must have difficulty in meeting."[4]

Saint Augustine established the church's official position toward the Jews in the fifth century by declaring that the Jews had a legitimate role in Christendom: since Jews and Christians shared a belief in the Old Testament, the Jews could testify to the history and validity of this shared tradition. For Augustine the primary value of the Old Testament was that it contained prophecies that Christ fulfilled. The Jews, by upholding the old traditions, involuntarily corroborated the old prophecies, thereby testifying to the truth of Christianity.

Augustine also believed that Christian triumphs demonstrated the truth of Christianity. While Christendom succeeded and prospered, the Jews had been scattered by the Diaspora and had the lowly status of slaves in many of the lands in which they resided. Moreover, the purpose of the Diaspora had been precisely to scatter the Jews all over the world, so that they could fulfill this role of witness everywhere they lived: "For if they lived with that testimony of the Scriptures only in their own land, and not everywhere, the obvious result would be that the church, which is everywhere, would not have them available among all nations as witnesses to the prophecies which were given beforehand concerning Christ."[5]

Although Augustine did not advocate repression of the Jews, by his logic the worse the Jews fared, the better they demonstrated the superiority of the church. Moreover, he considered Jews themselves to be responsible for their own failures, for their stubborn refusal to accept Christ. While this position seems oppressive, it was the basis for the toleration of a Jewish presence in Christendom. The church's position on pagans was simpler: conversion, exile, or death. There were no remaining communities that worshipped Jupiter or Odin. Only the Jews were allowed to live and to worship separate from the church. As the eighteenth-century Jewish philosopher Moses Mendelssohn put it, but for Augustine's "lovely brainwave, we would have been exterminated long ago."[6]

Starting around the twelfth century, the church developed a significantly more aggressive attitude toward the Jews. There are numerous reasons for the change, including the church's militant response to what it perceived as the Islamic threat during the Crusades. Three factors in particular contributed to greater church militance against the Jews, which would later have a major impact on the Spanish Jews in particular: a shift within the church to more uniformity and greater intolerance of dissent; the rise of the orders of preaching friars; and the church's exploration of heresy in the Talmud and other postbiblical works of rabbinical Judaism.

Conformity and the Lateran Council

The shift to more-centralized control of church institutions reflected a general transition among European institutions toward more powerful governance by civil and church authorities and toward greater order and uniformity. As the Yale historian John Boswell observes: "Probably nothing so exemplifies the later medieval fascination with order and uniformity as the astronomical increase in the amount of legislation of all sorts enacted from the thirteenth century on. The total of royal edicts and enactments for all the ruling houses of Europe during the twelfth century would probably come to not more than 100 volumes. By the fourteenth century the output from a single monarch in a small kingdom might run to 3,000–4,000 registers of documents."[7]

The church move toward institutionalization was reflected through the promulgation of many new laws; it set forth more legal pronouncements in the twelfth century than in all prior centuries put together.[8] The twelfth-century *Decretum Gratiani*, put together by the Italian lawyer Gratian, would become the principal basis for church canon law until it was revised in the twentieth century. This trend led to a general decrease in social tolerance. As Boswell notes: "During the decades surrounding the opening of the fourteenth century, the Jews were expelled from England and France; the order of the Templars dissolved on charges of sorcery and deviant sexuality; Edward II of England, the last openly gay medieval monarch, deposed and murdered; lending at interest equated with heresy and those who supported it subjected to the Inquisition; and lepers all over France imprisoned and prosecuted on charges of poisoning wells and being in league with Jews and witches."[9]

The church's move toward uniformity spurred a series of four ecumenical councils, known as the Lateran Councils, between 1123 and 1215. There have only been twenty-one ecumenical councils in the history of the church: that four councils were held in the space of one century is extraordinary and reflects the degree to which the church perceived Islam, heretics, and resident Jews as a threat.

The Third Lateran Council prohibited Jews and Muslims from having Christian servants. It required judges to trust the testimony of Christian witnesses over Jewish ones and protected the property of Christian converts from Judaism. But it was the Fourth Lateran Council—called the "Great Council" because it was the largest convened in the history of the church to date—that most affected the Jews. It promulgated crucial church resolutions designed to isolate, restrict, and denigrate Jews.[10]

The Great Council introduced into Christendom the Muslim concept of *dhimma*, calling for Jews and "Saracens" (Muslims) to wear special clothing, to set them apart from and to prevent "damnable mixing" with Christians, and particularly with Christian women. While this may have been conceived as retaliation against Muslims for previously imposing *dhimma* on Christians (Christians resided in Muslim-controlled communities not only in Spain but in Africa and the Middle East), it now mainly affected Jews; outside Spain there were few Muslim communities living under Christian rule. The council decreed:

> In some provinces a difference in dress distinguishes the Jews or Saracens from the Christians, but in certain others such a confusion has grown up that they cannot be distinguished by any difference. Thus it happens at times that through error Christians have relations with the women of Jews or Saracens, and Jews and Saracens with Christian women. Therefore, that they may not, under pretext of error of this sort, excuse themselves in the future for

the excesses of such prohibited intercourse, we decree that such Jews and Saracens of both sexes in every Christian province and at all times shall be marked off in the eyes of the public from other peoples through the character of their dress. Particularly, since it may be read in the writings of Moses [Numbers 15:37–41], that this very law has been enjoined upon them.

Moreover, during the last three days before Easter and especially on Good Friday, they shall not go forth in public at all, for the reason that some of them on these very days, as we hear, do not blush to go forth better dressed and are not afraid to mock the Christians who maintain the memory of the most holy Passion by wearing signs of mourning.

Other provisions forbade Jews from holding public office over Christians "since it [was] absurd that a blasphemer of Christ exercise authority over Christians." It condemned excessive interest and called on Jews who had acquired Christian property to continue paying church contributions that would have been due on the property. Finally, it forbade converts from reverting to Judaism.[11]

The prominent modern Catholic theologian Han Kung has remarked on the major impact this council had on the lives of the Jews: "It was not the riots in connection with the First Crusade in 1096, but this council which fundamentally changed the situation of the Jews, both legally and theologically."[12]

The church did not have jurisdiction over Jews and therefore could not enforce the changes recommended by the councils. As a matter of law, the Jews belonged to the monarchs and, in some cases, to local aristocrats. However, special costumes for Jews did become widespread throughout Europe, which was consistent with the medieval practice of marking class and status by clothing—colored hats or caps but most commonly a badge sewn on to the garment. In Spain, where the Jews were at the height of their value to the Christian kings as administrators and go-betweens with the Moorish lands, these rules were largely ignored.[13] Only in Catalonia was a conspicuous costume required: a long, round cape topped by a monk-like hood.[14]

The Rise of the Friars

Another significant factor that increased pressure on the Jews was the rise of the mendicant orders of preaching friars, the Dominicans and the Franciscans. The Dominicans in particular were to become leaders in the campaign against the Jews.

Saint Dominic probably never imagined that his order would initiate the Spanish Inquisition and oversee the public immolation of heretics. The only torment he advocated was self-directed. According to a history of the order by the Dominican Benedict Ashley, Saint Dominic "was merciless on himself with regard to fasting (in Lent on bread and water), and even sick never ate meat. He wore a hair shirt, a chain, and frequently used the discipline to blood when praying at night for those he hoped to convert."[15]

The future saint was born in Caleruega, Spain, on a small estate in Old Castile between Burgos and Madrid. His parents had the financial means to keep him in school; for ten years he studied liberal arts and theology at Palencia. He then joined the Cathedral Chapter in Osma and became a protégé of the Bishop Diego de Azevedo. Dominic found his mission by chance. Alfonso VIII had selected Bishop Diego for a diplomatic mission to Denmark, where he was expected to arrange the marriage of the king's son to the Danish princess. While traveling through southern France, the bishop and his subprior discovered the Cathars and began preaching to them, hoping to lead them away from their heretical ideas. They made two trips to Denmark. During these journeys they continued preaching in Cathar territory.

The Cathars embraced the gnostic tradition, holding that the world was created by the demiurge, which they identified with Satan. They opposed the corruption within the Catholic Church and followed religious adepts they called the good men or women—called "perfecti" by the Roman Church—who alone were initiated into the deeper mysteries of their faith. It was probably Diego who made the decision to turn his back on material wealth and instead adopt the style of mendicant preaching. He embraced poverty in imitation of the Cathar "perfecti." He wanted to demonstrate that church representatives were as capable of virtue as the leaders of the heretics.

After the death of Diego in 1207, Dominic expanded his order and began to preach more widely. He obtained permission from Cardinal Ugolino (who would become Pope Gregory IX) to found the Order of Preachers and establish a base in Bologna. Dominic dedicated himself to church orthodoxy rather than to the personal vision that inspired his contemporary, Saint Francis of Assisi.

Saint Dominic himself did not oppose the Jews. There are recorded stories of early Dominicans assisting Jews in England. Friars protected Jews against the blood-libel murder charges in which Jews were falsely accused of the ritual murder of a young child, Hugh of Lincoln, in 1255. The Dominican archbishop of Canterbury several years later sought the king's clemency on behalf of a particular Jew.[16]

Dominicans and the Inquisition

The order took a significantly more militant stand after the death of their founder. Saint Dominic's vision of converting heretics—particularly the Cathars—through sermons and by leading an exemplary life proved too slow for the church. In 1231 Pope Gregory IX issued a bull condemning heretics, calling on secular authorities to punish them with the "appropriate penalty." At the same time, the Holy Roman emperor Frederick II announced that the appropriate penalty for heretics was "to be burned alive in the sight of the people." Inquisitors were soon appointed to carry out the papal edict, and an inquisitorial commission was constituted in 1231, directed against the Cathar heresy.[17] Dominicans would take up important posts in the administration of the Inquisition.

The Inquisition opened with extreme severity against Cathar followers, burning hundreds alive in public spectacles. The two lead inquisitors, Conrad of Marburg and Robert le Bougre in Northern France, have been called by one historian "untypically savage, even perhaps insane."[18] Conrad eventually was murdered and was not replaced. Robert was disgraced and imprisoned.

The Inquisition, established in the province of Languedoc in the mid-Pyrenees, watched the Jews in nearby Aragon closely. While the church technically had no legal authority over the Jews, it could investigate and order punishment whenever Jews were accused of helping

Christians convert to Judaism or of fomenting attacks on Christianity. There were also Inquisition trials of Jews accused of black magic and heresies that violated principles common to Christians and Jews.

Allegations that Jews assisted in Christian conversions to Judaism centered on French refugees in Spain who converted to Christianity to escape repressive anti-Jewish policies in France and had subsequently tried to revert to Judaism. One such allegation forced Jews in Majorca to pay a large royal fine in order to evade confiscation of all their property. Jews from Tarragona were tried for conversion charges, despite the opposition of the king. The Inquisition tried to arrest Jews in Lérida on similar charges. Some individuals were jailed or tortured, and some suffered confiscations. Worse punishments were prevented by royal protection in exchange for the payment of large fines to the royal treasury.

The Inquisition descended on the Jewish community of Saragossa in 1324. Although the basis for its investigation is not clear from the historical record, there is evidence that it led to the financial ruin of the Jewish community.[19]

The Franciscans competed with the Dominicans in their zeal to preach against the Jews. Most friars, both Dominican and Franciscan, were sons of small landowners and tradesmen. Many of their families competed with or were indebted to Jews, which accounted for some of their anti-Jewish passion. Aristocrats, in contrast, including some prominent churchmen, benefited from services by Jews and were therefore more likely to protect them.

A published sermon by the Franciscan friar Giordano da Rivalto, delivered in Florence in 1304 (when the city had few, if any, Jews), gives an extreme example of the kind of message the friars were spreading. The sermon is a compilation of almost every anti-Jewish legend of the time. The Jews kidnap and crucify Christian children. Jews buy Christian children to circumcise and convert them. They steal and desecrate the host. Giordano claimed that after one incident involving desecration of the host by Jews, he witnessed the boy Jesus miraculously appear on the scene and rally the local Christian population to slaughter twenty-four thousand Jews in punishment for their evil deed. He claimed that Jews abused drawings and carvings of Jesus. One tortured icon, he asserted, responded with real blood, causing forty thousand Jews to convert.[20] Another Franciscan, Pedro Olligoyen, instigated a massacre of the Jews of Estella, in the Spanish kingdom of Navarre, in 1308. He led a mob to burn down the entire *aljama* and kill most of the resident Jews.

Discovery of the Talmud

Jews had been insulated from official church criticism for centuries by the church's ignorance of Jewish practice and belief. As long as the church associated Jewish belief with the Old Testament, the church's acknowledgment of the text as sacred protected Jews from charges of blasphemy. Yet much of Jewish belief is based on the Talmud and on other postbibical, rabbinic works that also postdate Christianity, therefore requiring no deference from church officials.

The first major criticism of the Talmud came from a French apostate, Nicholas Donin. He appears to have been a Franciscan monk, who may have been excommunicated from Judaism before his conversion.[21] Apostates were to become a major resource in the church's attacks on the Jews. They were valuable both because of their fervor to demonstrate their new loyalty to the church and because of their knowledge of Judaism. In 1236 Donin presented Pope Gregory IX with a list of thirty-five specific charges against the Talmud and other post-Christian liturgical writings that Jews considered sacred. These charges consisted of three claims: Jews had abandoned their Old Testament beliefs for the false teachings of the Talmud and other rabbinical texts; rabbinical teaching was inimical to Christians; and the Talmud contained anti-Christian blasphemy.

"The rabbis," Donin held, "called Jesus' mother an adulteress; they speak obscenely of Jesus, the pope, the Church, and Christianity; and they curse the Church daily in their prayers, believing that Christians are condemned to perpetual damnation, while sinful Jews suffer a maximum of only one year in hell or in purgatory."[22]

It took the pope three years to respond to these charges. In 1239 he issued a directive to the bishop of Paris that the archbishops and kings of France, England, and Iberia be instructed to confiscate all Jewish books, which were to be transferred to the Dominicans and the Franciscans while the Jews were attending services on the Sabbath. These offensive books would be burned at the stake. Only the king of France, Louis IX, responded, and he demanded that the Jews first be given a chance to defend themselves. A debate was organized in Paris, followed by an inquisitorial hearing. The Talmud was determined to be blasphemous and condemned to the stake. Over ten thousand books were burned in Paris over a two-day period.[23]

Pope Gregory IX endorsed the accusations of Nicolas Donin:

> If what is said about the Jews of France and of the other lands is true, no punishment would be sufficiently great or sufficiently worthy of their crime. For they, so we have heard, are not content with the Old Law which God gave to Moses in writing; they even ignore it completely, and affirm that God gave another Law which is called "Talmud." ... In this is contained matter so abusive and so unspeakable that it arouses shame in those who mention it and horror in those who hear it. Wherefore ... this is said to be the chief cause that holds the Jews obstinate in their perfidy.[24]

Several decades later his words about the Talmud were echoed by Pope Innocent IV: "The wicked perfidy of the Jews ... commits such grave sins as are stupefying to those who hear of them and horrible to those who tell of them. ... They ... throw away and despise the law of Moses and the prophets, and follow some tradition of their elders. ... In it are found blasphemies against God and His Christ, and obviously entangled fables about the Blessed Virgin, and abusive errors, and unheard-of follies."[25]

Disputation of Barcelona

The debate over the Talmud in Paris led to other debates. The most famous took place in the Royal Palace in Barcelona, on July 20, 1263, arranged by Raymond de Peñaforte, a Barcelona native, now master-general of the Dominican order. Pope Urban IV and King Jaume I (the Conqueror) of Aragon attended. The church adopted a novel strategy for this event. Instead of attacking the Talmud, as it had in Paris, the church sought to demonstrate that the Talmud and other rabbinical sources supported Christian principles. This tactic did not reflect any church deference to these Jewish texts; the church continued to press for the burning or censorship of the Talmud. Instead, the idea was to demoralize the Jews by demonstrating their own leaders' acceptance of Christian principles. This tactic would soften the Jews up for later missionary assaults. As the church account of the dispute later stated, the purpose was "to destroy the Jews' errors and to shake the confidence of many Jews."[26]

Taking the side of the church was Pablo Christiani. Another apostate Jew, born Saul, he did not convert until he was a married man in his twenties. His Jewish education gave him the ability to quote from an extensive range of Jewish sources. After his conversion he devoted his life to proselytizing among the Jews.

One of the greatest Jewish scholars of the Middle Ages was present to defend the Jews (defense is the appropriate term, since this was more a trial than a debate). Rabbi Moses ben Nahman was so famous that like Moses ben Maimon before him he became known by a Hellenized version of his name in the West, and a Hebrew acronym among the Jews: Maimon had become Maimonides and the RaMBaM; Nahman is remembered as Nahmanides and also the Ramban.

Nahmanides came from a prosperous family in Gerona, a town between Barcelona and what is now the French border. He was a product of a diverse background, incorporating aspects of Spanish culture, French Talmudism, German pietism, the mysticism of the Kabbalah, and an acquaintance with Christian theological writings.[27] This diversity of influence may have given him an instinct for compromise. When anti-Maimonists in France condemned the works of Maimonides, Nahmanides attempted unsuccessfully to mediate. As a mystic he objected to Maimonides's rationalism, but he respected the master's learning. He suggested that the works be criticized but still be made available for study, and he even wrote to Maimonides's son in Egypt to enlist his support.

The center of kabbalistic studies had shifted from Provence, where it had originated, to Gerona. As the leader of the Gerona Jews, Nahmanides probably played a major role in the development of kabbalistic ideas. The Kabbalah, however, was still considered a secret movement that only adepts could properly understand. As a result, while there are traces of mystical ideas in his works, Nahmanides himself wrote little directly addressing the Kabbalah.

It was probably King Jaume who urged Nahmanides to participate in the Barcelona disputation of 1263. The king had once sought his guidance in the past, to settle a dispute over the status of the wealthy Jews of Barcelona. This time, choice of a respected, sixty-eight-year-old rabbi would, the king hoped, prevent the Jews from complaining that they had no proper chance to respond to the church.

Pablo Christiani began, on behalf of the church, by setting out to demonstrate that Jewish texts recognized four basic Christian principles: (1) that the Messiah had already come; (2) that the Messiah was both divine and human; (3) that he suffered and was killed for man's salvation; and (4) that the old Jewish laws and ceremonies should have been abandoned after the coming of the Messiah.[28]

Nahmanides, in response, was not allowed to criticize Christianity. Any open challenge to church doctrine would be considered heresy, though the church could freely condemn all aspects of Judaism. He was therefore limited to challenging the accuracy of Pablo's accusations. Nahmanides held his ground by showing that the friar continually misunderstood or misconstrued the Hebrew sources, which Nahmanides said did not, in fact, refer to Christ.

The dispute lasted only four days. On the last day Nahmanides pleaded with the king to end the debate. The Christian account later claimed that the rabbi fled in defeat and confusion: "Since he was unable to respond and was often publicly confused and since both Jews and Christians insulted him, he persistently claimed before all that he would in no way respond.... Whence it is clear that he tried to escape the disputation by lies."[29]

Nahmanides said he had asked the king for permission to end the debate out of fear that it would raise crowds against the Jews, and because he felt he had succeeded, by the fourth day, in rebutting the church's claims. A later royal payment made to the rabbi adds credence to Nahmanides's claim that he departed with royal permission. Scholars still debate who may have "won" the disputation. The church published an account of the dispute that drily laid out Pablo's accusations, giving little credit to Nahmanides's responses.

Nahmanides published a full dramatization of the affair. He showed himself holding off the attacks of Christiani, who was supported by the other church officials. The king was portrayed as a monarch who deferred to the church but who tried to treat Nahmanides justly, and whom Nahmanides always addressed with deference and respect. Through the affair Nahmanides claimed to have successfully answered all charges, always having the last word, thanks to his superior erudition, intelligence, and knowledge of both Jewish and Christian sources. Nahmanides's book was frequently copied and circulated. It may be the most widely translated of either medieval Hebrew narratives or polemical writings. It was translated into Latin, Catalan, French, German, and English—the latter no less than four separate times.[30] In the eyes of posterity, Nahmanides clearly won the contest.

The book is short, about fifty pages in the modern edition. Although Nahmanides portrays himself as readily able to fend off any attack, his description of the constant barrage of questions from various parties, including his king, makes it clear that he faced real peril and creates genuine dramatic tension. The work also reflects Nahmanides's personality. While respectful to the king and deferential to the church officials, he was openly contemptuous of his apostate opponent. "I speak words of wisdom with [Christiani], who neither knows nor understands, and it would be appropriate that he be judged by fools."[31] He is often sarcastic, answering Christiani "scoffingly" or "mockingly."[32]

The book proved enormously costly to the rabbi. He said something that he probably had not dared to say in the real debate, when the king, pope, and leader of the Dominicans presided as witnesses. Breaking the church established rules, he openly criticized Christianity:

> The prophet says concerning the messiah: "He shall rule from sea to sea, from the river to the ends of the earth." But he [Jesus] exercised no rule. Rather, during his lifetime he was pursued by his enemies and hid from them. Eventually, he fell into their hands and was unable to save himself. How then could he save all of

Israel?... Now the adherents of Muhammad exercise greater rule than they [the Christians] do.

Similarly, the prophet says that... "They shall beat their swords [into plowshares and their spears into pruning hooks]; nation shall not take up sword against nation; they shall never again know war." Now, from the days of Jesus till now all the earth is full of violence and plunder. Indeed, the Christians spill blood more than the rest of the nations. They are also lustful. How difficult it would be for you, my lord the King, and for those nobles of yours if they could no longer learn war.[33]

This belief "that the Creator of heaven and earth returned into the womb of a certain Jewess and grew in it for seven months and was then born tiny. Subsequently, he grew and was then turned over into the hands of his enemies, who judged him to death and killed him." These notions "cannot be borne by the thinking of a Jew or of any person."[34]

Nahmanides may have been motivated to violate the terms of the debate and openly criticize Christianity in order to raise Jewish morale or out of frustration at having to bear so many Christian attacks on his own religion. But the remarks proved to be costly. The Dominican leader and other friars, including Pablo Christiani, lodged a formal complaint with the king, and an ecclesiastical tribunal examined his book for heresy. After consulting with the tribunal, the king agreed to a punishment of two years in exile and the burning of all copies of Nahmanides's book. The church rejected this sentence as unacceptably lax, and the punishment was never imposed.

Nonetheless, after this incident the rabbi decided, at the age of seventy-two, to leave his homeland and make a pilgrimage to Jerusalem, following the example of Judah Halevi over a century before him. He arrived in a city ruined by generations of wars between Christians and Muslims. He wrote: "O Jerusalem that art destroyed, and its towns that were the appointed cities for instruction and for testimony! ... Happy is he who has not seen these ruins, for today I have seen in you, O holy city, a grievous vision."[35]

Despite his advanced age, Nahmanides continued his writing, completing his best known commentary on the Torah. He established first a synagogue and then a yeshiva. He died in Haifa at the age of seventy-six. Zionists still cite his actions as evidence of the continuity of Jewish life in Israel after the Diaspora.

Anti-Jewish Writings

The church continued its campaign against the Jews after the disputation. Shortly afterward the king, along with Friar Paul and the Dominican master-general, visited the principal synagogue of Barcelona, where they delivered sermons to the Jews. In August 1263 a royal decree required that the Jews of Aragon assemble in their temples to listen to sermons given by the Dominicans. Around the same time the king ordered that all Jewish texts containing anti-Christian passages be censored by the Dominicans, and a similar edict was issued involving the works of Maimonides. Probably as a result of Jewish lobbying, the king curtailed these orders, clarifying that Jewish attendance at Dominican sermons would be strictly voluntary.

The Dominican leader Raymond de Peñaforte sponsored the production of a massive work by his fellow Dominican Raymond Martini, titled *Pugio Fidei*, or *Dagger of Faith*. A compendium of perceived errors in non-Christian religions, its main focus was Judaism, and it became an important source for anti-Jewish writings. *Dagger of Faith* is filled with anti-Jewish invective: "To believe this, that God gave Moses all that is in the Talmud, should be deemed—on account of the absurdities which it contains—nothing other than the insanity of a ruined mind." The book literally demonizes the Jews. It claims that at the time of Jesus the Jews ignored the Christian nullification of old laws and adhered to the Mosaic Code, not only rejecting Christ, but transferring their allegiance to the devil: "The devil Bentamalyon ... restored to them circumcision, the Sabbath, and the other rituals which God removed through the agency of the Romans? The devil undoubtedly ... misled them and deprived them of a sense of understanding the truth, so that they are less intelligent than asses as regards divine scriptures." Raymond de Peñaforte claimed that a "demonic" insanity had led the Jews to reject Jesus and caused them to ascribe his miracles to "Beelzebub, the prince of the demons."

"The legendary *bat qol* or voice of God, described in rabbinic homilies, was, according to Peñaforte, not a heavenly voice but a satanic one."[36]

Peñaforte's production and other writings and sermons by the friars of the preaching orders both reflected and intensified a general increase in anti-Jewish sentiment throughout Europe in the thirteenth century, as has been described by the historian Jeremy Cohen:

> From the thirteenth century onward, anti-Jewish violence increased throughout Europe. Only from this period were Jews portrayed as real, active agents of Satan, charged with innumerable forms of hostility toward Christianity, Christendom, (and individual murder) and charges of host desecration first appeared in medieval Europe during the thirteenth century. In this century, the representation of Jews in Christian art became noticeably more hostile and demeaning, with the first examples of the infamous *Judensau* (portrayals of Jews sucking at the teats of a sow) and the frequent juxtaposition of the Jews and the devil. No longer were the Jews depicted like their Christian neighbors or as mere symbols in the drama of religious history; they had become pernicious enemies of Christians and the Church, and pictorially they have often come to represent the archetypal heretics. Permanent expulsion of European Jewries began in 1290. By the middle of the next century, it was almost inevitable that Jews were blamed for the Black Death and many of their communities in Germany completely and permanently exterminated. And by the mid-1500s, most of Western Europe contained no Jews at all.[37]

The questioning of the Talmud and attribution of Jewish beliefs to the devil brought into question even the limited acceptance granted to the Jews by Saint Augustine. Jews could be witness to the validity of Christianity only as a people that shared some Christian beliefs. If, since the time of Christ, Jews had been tempted by the devil to embrace beliefs opposed to Christianity, then they had become undeniable enemies of Christendom, and no legitimate role for them in the Christian world remained.

This attitude is reflected in the writings of the Catalan theologian, philosopher, and mystic Raymond Llull. His *Libre del Gentil e los tres savis*, *The Book of the Gentile and the Three Wise Men*, is structured as a debate, in which a Christian, a Jewish, and a Muslim sage explain their religions to a gentile without faith. Probably inspired by Halevi's *Book of the Khuzari*, it presents a relatively impartial account of the different religions, though it is clearly told from a Christian viewpoint.

Yet Llull eventually concluded that there was only one solution to the "Jewish question": conversion or exile from Christendom. He envisioned a training program that would lead Jews to Christian belief. When such training failed, he demanded that those Jews who did not convert to Christianity be expelled from Christendom forever. Christians who permitted Jews to live in their community would be acting contrary to the precepts of the Christian faith.[38]

Soon a minor prelate in Seville was to come up with an even more drastic choice for the Jews than conversion or exile: conversion or death.

One last note: David Nirenberg, in his much-cited book *Communities of Violence*, examined some of the specific examples of clashes and cooperation between Jews, Christians, and Muslims, principally in fourteenth-century Aragon, to counter the idea that the downfall of the Jewish community in Spain was the result of a deterministic crescendo in anti-Jewish hatred and violence. In regard to the shifts in church attitudes described in this chapter, he warned against viewing it as a "linear march toward intolerance," adding: "While it may be true that the style of Christian anti-Jewish polemic changed between the twelfth and fourteenth centuries, we should be cautious about over-schematizing Christian-Jewish relations on the basis of such evidence."[39]

This chapter is not meant to suggest that the change of attitudes by the church inevitably led to the end of the Jewish community in Iberia. However, it was a major factor in what transpired. While it is possible to imagine ways in which the Jews could have survived in Spain despite the conditions described in this chapter, it is almost certain that without this shift in attitudes, and in particular, without the development of the mendicant orders and their mission to convert or oppose the Jews, the Spanish Inquisition—led by these friars—and the expulsion that the Inquisition campaigned for, would never have taken place.

Fig. 2. Coat of arms, Synagogue of Samuel Halevi (Sinagoga del Transito), Toledo. Courtesy of Spanish National Heritage.

13

Seeds of Destruction

Disunity in the Royal Family

In 1391 mobs raged across the Spanish kingdoms, compelling large-scale conversions of the Spanish Jews. This campaign was partly inspired by an anti-Jewish campaign three decades earlier, when Enrique II of Castile deliberately exploited anti-Jewish feelings to further his own political ambitions during a war to seize the throne from his half brother, Pedro. Enrique's actions during this civil war significantly undermined Jewish security and were the first step toward the end of *convivencia*.

The immediate cause of the civil war was domestic, not political. The royal household was a nuclear family in the explosive sense of the word. The drama generated by their political ambition and sexual conflict was suitable material for Italian opera and would, in fact, be exploited by the composer Donizetti in his 1841 opera *Maria Padilla*. Because these domestic problems festered into a civil war that targeted the Jews, the problems have a direct relevance to Jewish history.

The family issues began with Pedro the Cruel's father King Alfonso XI (1311–50), great-grandson of Alfonso the Wise. King Alfonso married Maria of Portugal at a time when he was already romantically involved with Leonor de Guzmán. When Queen Maria gave birth to Pedro, Alfonso recognized his only legitimate son's right to succession but ceased to live with Pedro's mother, Queen Maria. He instead consorted openly with his mistress, who advised him at court. He also acknowledged and favored his illegitimate children with Leonor. It was said at the time that Alfonso had given everything he could "except the Crown" to his bastard sons.[1] The king's acknowledgment of a second family would drive the next generation into war. Alfonso had also alienated much of the nobility by trying to centralize authority with the Crown, a policy that his son Pedro would continue, and which would fuel his half brother's rebellion.

Alfonso, like his namesake Alfonso the Wise, had a mixed record toward the Jews. Initially, Jews occupied a considerable number of prominent posts in his administration. He appointed as his *almoxarife mayor*, or treasurer, Con Yucaf de Ecija and gave him a seat on the privy council. Another Jew, Don Samuel ibn Wakar, a physician, obtained the concession to the mint, and R. Moses Abzaradiel, the king's scribe, had substantial tax-farming responsibilities. The position of the Jews in King Alfonso's court was compromised by the rise of a Christian courtier, Gonzalo Martínez de Oviedo. According to a contemporary Jewish account, Gonzalo offered the king ingots of silver for the lives of the Jewish courtiers.[2] Yucaf and Samuel were imprisoned, Samuel was tortured, and both died.

Gonzalo then proposed the seizure of all Jewish assets and the expulsion of the Jews from the kingdom, patterned after the expulsions from England and France. This plan, opposed by some prominent Christians, led to the arrests of some Jews. Taxation of the Jews became extortionate. Restrictions were placed on religious practices, as Jews became subject to an anti-Jewish campaign led by an apostate, Abner of Burgos. Fortunately for the Jews, Gonzalo had a falling-out with the brother of the king's mistress. Gonzalo was executed for high treason. Alfonso succumbed to the plague, and his son Pedro inherited not only the kingdom but also a domestic rivalry that would lead the kingdom to civil war. This war created tensions that would destroy *convivencia* and ravage the Jews.

Up until this point, anti-Jewish measures had been ad hoc, near-random expressions of temporary royal displeasure. In contrast King Pedro's rival and half brother Enrique during the civil war systematically and successfully exploited anti-Jewish popular sentiment for political gain. His actions set the stage for the massacres that would take place in 1391. His political success would be emulated in future attacks against Spain's Jews and conversos, particularly in the Toledo revolt of 1449. Enrique's commitment to gaining aristocratic allies would mire Castile in economic and political instability for another century, further undermining the security of conversos and Jews.

Pedro earned his nickname "the Cruel" by losing the civil war against his illegitimate half brother, and with it, the support of the main chronicler of the era, Pedro López de Ayala, who deserted Pedro for Enrique and granted Pedro his cruel nickname. Pedro "the Cruel" could be unstable and vindictive, but not more so than many kings of his time. His contemporary, King Pere of Aragon, for example, gained a reputation for being "extremely suspicious, subtle, vindictive and inventively cruel."[3] In 1348, after crushing the Unionists of Valencia, Pere had the town bell melted down. Proclaiming it was only right that those who had rung the bell should "taste of its liqueur," he ordered that the molten lead be poured down the throats of rebel leaders.[4] Despite such behavior Pere was known merely as "the Ceremonious."

Pedro's illegitimate older half brother, Enrique de Trastamara, rebelled against Pedro almost from the start of Pedro's reign. The civil war that resulted was fueled by the Hundred Years' War, in which the English Crown battled for control of France; the armies fighting that war in France hired themselves out as mercenaries to the Spanish rivals and carried their battles on in Spain. The rebels, led by Enrique, had the support of France, along with the kingdom of Aragon (which was fighting a losing territorial war with Pedro), and the pope in Avignon lent at least covert support to Enrique's cause. England's Edward the "Black Prince," with his long-bow archers who would later triumph at Agincourt, backed Pedro.

A Jewish Treasurer

Pedro had appointed as his chief treasurer Don Samuel Halevi of Toledo, who may have been the most powerful court Jew in the history of Christian Spain. Halevi came from a prominent Jewish family in Toledo and began his career as the protégée of Pedro's chief minister, Juan Alfonso de Albuquerque. He had become a tax collector for the king in 1351 and the king's treasurer in 1353. In addition to his fiscal responsibilities, Halevi was entrusted with an important diplomatic mission to Portugal and defended the king's interest against ambitious noblemen.

Halevi owed his prominence in part to Pedro's break with his cousin Albuquerque. Pedro wanted a supporter independent from his mother and her allies and his illegitimate brothers and rivals. Halevi was an official who would be loyal only to the king.

Thanks to Don Samuel Halevi we have the greatest physical remnant of the Jewish presence in Spain, one of the few Jewish buildings that remains half a millennium after the expulsion of the Spanish Jews: the beautiful synagogue in Toledo known as El Transito. The synagogue he commissioned was built in the Mozarabic style, in imitation of the great buildings of Muslim Spain. Inside the hall of worship is a long, rectangular room, with a high ceiling of slanted wood beams. The windows, with arches and filigree frames, are close to the roof, high enough to be protected from rocks or bricks thrown by attackers. The walls are divided into large panels of ornamental plasterwork, each with alternating designs of diamond-shaped fields or pomegranates. Every inch of the panels is covered in designs: cusped arches, tendrils and leaves, heraldic shields, branches and cockle shells, and intricate script in Hebrew and Arabic—more Arabic than Hebrew. An engraved inscription in tribute to Don Samuel reads: "Since the day of Ariel's exile, none like unto him has arisen in Israel. . . . He appears before kings to stand in the breach. . . . Unto him people come from the ends of the earth. . . . The king exalted him and set him on high, above all his princes. . . . Into his hands he entrusted all that he had . . . and since the day of our Exile no son of Israel has attained to such exalted estate."[5]

In 1360 Don Samuel and all his kinsmen were arrested and imprisoned in Seville. He was accused of embezzlement of state funds, but the real basis for these charges is unknown. Embezzlement had little meaning in an era when government positions were considered sinecures. As one modern biographer of Pedro writes: "Most functionaries tended to regard their positions as symbols of status and sources of patronage, delegating, sometimes negligently, the duties of their office."[6] Halevi was an effective and efficient treasurer, who kept the king's coffers full.

The king may have been tempted by Halevi's personal fortune. The charges against Halevi also coincided with a difficult period in Pedro's reign. The Aragonese aristocrat Ferran had just betrayed Pedro to King Pere of Aragon and led him to suspect and lash out against other of his allies. At the same time, suspecting that two of his officials, Gutier Fernández de Toledo and Gómez Carillo, had engaged in conversations with the rebels, Pedro sentenced them to death. He also exiled to Portugal the archbishop of Toledo, Don Vasco, brother of Gutier Fernández.[7] Pedro may also have been anxious to demonstrate his independence from his most important Jewish advisor in reaction to his half brother's claims that Pedro was too close to the Jews.

Don Samuel died in prison after being tortured. His riches were confiscated by King Pedro. But the king did not implement further anti-Jewish policies, and other Jews continued to hold prominent positions in his court.

The Anti-Jewish Campaign

Pedro's half brother Enrique took a much more antagonistic position toward the Jews. In 1355 Enrique and his brothers took the city of Toledo and in the course of their invasion ransacked and destroyed the Jewish quarter. This attack on the Jews was the start of a pattern of anti-Jewish actions by Enrique and his forces. Enrique was heavily in debt to the foreign mercenaries who made up the majority of his forces, and the Jews proved to be a rich source of funding. Moreover, he discovered that he could enlist the support of the nobles by attacking the Jews. Pedro was addressed as "King of the Jews," though his policy toward the Jews was no more favorable than that of most of his predecessors.[8] Enrique even spread the rumor that Pedro was the son of a Jewess, exchanged at birth for the king's daughter.[9]

In 1366 Enrique and his French knights massacred the Jewish community in the town of Briviesca, about two hundred families in all. He then took the Jews of Burgos hostage for an immense sum of money. Those who did not pay were sold into slavery. He extorted the Jews of Toledo in a similar fashion. Pedro retrenched, with English assistance. Enrique, in his next assault, destroyed synagogues in Valladolid and other communities. Burgos was once again held for ransom, as were the Jews in Palencia. The contemporary Jewish chronicler Samuel Zarza described the attack mounted by Enrique's troops on the Jewish community of Valladolid: "They shouted, 'Long live King Enrique!' They attacked the Jews who lived among them and destroyed their houses. Among them they destroyed eight synagogues, exclaiming 'Aru, aru,' and they took away all the silver crowns and garlands, tore the scrolls of law and threw them on the streets. Even the destruction of the Temple [of Jerusalem] did not equal it."[10]

At the same time, Pedro's English allies began attacking other Jewish communities. To obtain assistance from the Muslims in Granada, Pedro also let the Muslims seize and sell into slavery the Jews of Jaen. The war became truly fratricidal in 1358. Enrique's brother Fadrique had, until then, stayed in Pedro's camp. Pedro, however, remained suspicious of Fadrique's loyalty. He called Fadrique to an interview at his court in Seville and first had Fadrique captured and beaten, then executed. In 1359 Pedro sentenced to death two of his remaining younger half brothers: Juan, who was nineteen, and the fourteen-year-old Pedro.

King Pedro eventually broke with England's Black Prince. The prince had demanded an unacceptably high price in territory and money to maintain the alliance. With the English no longer supporting Pedro, Enrique now had the advantage. In 1369 Enrique cornered Pedro in the fortress of Montiel. Pedro offered to pay off Enrique's French allies. When he entered the French quarters to close the deal, he was confronted by Enrique, who outbid his brother for the French mercenaries' loyalty.

There are two contemporary versions of the story of Pedro's death. According to the chronicle of Pedro López de Ayala, Enrique confronted his brother at the French tent, took out his dagger, and stabbed Pedro to death. The French chronicler Jean Froissart gives Pedro a more elaborate finish: "When Enrique entered the tent, he demanded to know 'Where's that Jewish son of a whore who calls himself King of Castile?' to which Pedro replied, 'You're the son of a whore. I'm the son of good King Alfonso.'" After this exchange the two brothers came to blows; Pedro wrestled Enrique to the ground and was on the verge of killing him when the viscount of Rocaberti intervened. Pedro lost his advantage, was knocked over, and Enrique finished him off. Froissart ends the account with the following words: "So ended King Peter of Castile, who once had reigned in great prosperity. Those who had killed him left him lying on the ground for three days, which in my opinion was an inhumane thing to do. And the Spaniards came and mocked him."[11]

Pedro's death was memorialized by Chaucer in "The Monk's Tale" from *The Canterbury Tales*:

O noble Pedro, glory once of Spain,
Whom Fortune held so high in majesty,
Well ought men read thy piteous death with pain!
Out of thy land thy brother made thee flee;
And later, at a siege, by scheme crafty,
Thou wert betrayed, and led into his tent,
Where he then, and with his own hand, slew thee,
Succeeding to thy realm and government.

Once in power, Enrique II brought Jews into his court, and they resumed their duties in the administration of the treasury. His anti-Jewish campaign, a cynical attempt to gain public support, now ended. But the damage was done; some communities had been completely destroyed. The anti-Jewish propaganda continued—the prominent historian and poet Pedro López de Ayala wrote about Jews coming "ready to drink the blood of the poor Christians, flaunting the contracts made with them and promising gifts and jewels to the king's favorites."[12]

The attacks on the Jews carried out under Enrique's command during the civil war legitimized and popularized anti-Jewish violence, laying the groundwork for the horrible violence soon to follow. Clara Estoy, in her biography of Pedro the Cruel, notes: "The raid of the Alcana [by Enrique's forces] was the first of several focused attacks on Castile's Jewish populations; Pedro's apparent defense of 'his Jews' offered his opponents, especially Enrique, a powerful ideological tool with which to undermine the king's authority and garner wider support for his growing political ambitions. As an overt and violent expression of resentment against Castilian Jews, this episode also marked the beginning of a new stage in Christian-Jewish relations that reached its climax in the persecutions of 1391."[13]

Enrique's successful exploitation of anti-Jewish feelings set a precedent that would be repeated in Castile throughout the fifteenth century. The rebels of Toledo in 1449, for example, cynically used anti-Jewish propaganda to scapegoat the conversos and build support for their rebellion.

Finally, Enrique built up a new and powerful aristocracy by purchasing alliances with promises of hereditary grants. While this helped Enrique in the short term and at little cost, it mired his successors in debt. Enrique's strategy of buying political friends also drained the Crown's treasury and gave new aristocrats enough wealth to enter into competition with the Crown. The loss of revenue created by these permanent grants fostered economic and political instability that would undermine the safety and security of Jews and converts throughout the following century. Enrique became an extraordinarily successful monarch. His descendants would control all the Spanish kingdoms and eventually unite them under Ferdinand and Isabella. But for the Jews and converts, Enrique left a poisoned legacy that brought an end to Spanish tolerance and the age of *convivencia*.

14

The Conversion of the Jews

Ferrand Martínez's Anti-Jewish Mission

The anti-Jewish riots of 1391 and the massacres and forced conversions that the riots engendered would change Jewish, Spanish, and world history. The riots were fueled by the anti-Jewish campaigns of both political and church leaders. The responsibility for instigating these riots, however, lay almost entirely in the hands of one man: Ferrand Martínez, archdeacon of Écija. For over a decade, Martínez led a virulent and tireless anti-Jewish campaign. He maintained his campaign despite the express opposition of the Crown, the nobility, and the organized church. As the nineteenth-century Spanish historian Amador de los Ríos has noted: "The cause of this attack was something else: the tinder was already at hand, only awaiting the application of fire. The sermons of the archdeacon of Ecija ... caused this horrible firestorm."[1]

Martínez started his campaign in 1378, soon after Enrique II ended his exploitation of anti-Jewish sentiment during his war against Pedro. Martínez, in addition to responsibilities in Écija (a town about halfway between Seville and Córdoba), held several posts in Seville, including that of diocesan judge. In the latter capacity, he insisted that he had the authority to preside over judicial disputes involving Jews. The Jews appealed to the king, who had abandoned his fight against the Jews once he had obtained the throne and now needed Jewish assistance in his administration. The king sent Martínez a clear order: "Do not dare to interfere in judging any dispute which involves any Jew in any manner."[2]

There is little biographical information on Martínez to explain the basis for his obsessive, passionate, and tireless persecution of the Jews. Unlike King Enrique, Martínez hated the Jews based on conviction, not convenience, and Enrique's order did nothing to abate his vehemence. He continued to harangue against the Jews in sermons, only fragments of which still exist.

Martínez soon took up a campaign to convince towns to eject all Jews from their territories. With the support of other episcopal officials, he went personally to visit towns in an unsuccessful eviction campaign. In response Enrique wrote to all the officials in Seville's archbishopric, ordering them to "refuse to enforce any sentence" that Martínez might impose on the Jews. The town councils were ordered to refrain from making any move against the Jews or causing "their degradation in anything in any manner" and were enjoined "not to place any restriction upon the Jews with respect to their dwelling places, their shops, or their offices."[3] When the officials supporting Martínez ignored this letter, the Jews petitioned for and received bulls of protection from Rome.[4]

After Enrique died in 1379, at the age of forty-six, Martínez began testing his successor, Juan I. He resumed judging disputes between Christians and Jews. The Jews complained to the Crown, and King Juan reaffirmed his father's orders: he forbade the priest from using in "preaching or other utterances any words that [might] harm or prejudice the Jews or raise a tumult against them." He expressly barred Martínez from adjudicating disputes involving Jews: "Any dispute relating to the Church which may be against a Jew or Jewess shall be handled from now on by the Archbishop, or by anyone the latter may assign for the task, and not by you."[5]

Martínez continued his campaign in face of royal opposition. He now openly encouraged anti-Jewish violence and assured his audiences that he personally knew that if any Christian killed or injured a Jew, the king and queen would be pleased with his deed and, on issuing judgment, would pardon him. Martínez guaranteed that such a man would suffer no harm at all.[6] This claim by Martínez resulted in another directive from the king, including his amazement that Martínez would attribute anti-Jewish sentiments to the royal couple: "Since when have you been on such intimate terms with us that you may know our intention and that of the Queen?"[7]

In 1388 the Jews of Seville summoned Martínez to appear before the highest court in Seville. They also summoned him to appear before the town officials and had all the royal letters read to him. Once again Martínez responded with defiance. He called the Jews criminals and defrauders of the Crown. He cited the Bible as evidence that Jews should be viewed as enemies and sons of the devil. He then called for the separation of Jews from Christians. He advocated the destruction of synagogues, including twenty-three in Seville, since they had been built in violation of laws prohibiting the construction of new temples; only repairs to old buildings were allowed.

Now the Jews turned to the church for protection. Martínez had claimed that not even the pope could authorize Jews to build more synagogues. Archbishop Pedro Gómez Barroso called Martínez before an assembly of laymen and ecclesiastics, where he was questioned about whether he doubted the pope's authority. Martínez continued to maintain that the pope had no right to allow the Jews to build new synagogues. He offered to justify his position before the "people," demonstrating his willingness to stir up a mob. As a result on August 2, 1389, the archbishop suspended Martínez from office until he could be tried for heresy, ordering him not to preach or to act as judge or official until a final determination was made in his case. Martínez's defiance of church authority implies that something other than religious fervor fueled his anti-Jewish campaign.

Instability and Danger

The death of the archbishop in July of 1390 gave Martínez a reprieve; it meant that Seville lacked a strong church figure to restrain him. The king himself died only a few months later, on October 9, 1389, leaving behind an eleven-year-old heir, Enrique III, known as El Doliente, or "the invalid." A weak and divided committee held royal power as the regency, limiting the Crown's ability to assist the Jews.

Now the Jews were extraordinarily vulnerable. The contract that held the *convivencia* together required a strong and stable government to provide protection for the Jews in exchange for Jewish support and services. Not only were there weak monarchies in both Castile and Aragon, but decades of war, natural disaster, and economic mismanagement had created a tremendous reservoir of public discontent, which Martínez could call on and direct against the Jews.

Jewish vulnerability came first from Spain's exhaustion from civil conflict. Spain—including Aragon but particularly Castile—had suffered decades of almost continuous, draining warfare. In Castile the civil war waged by Enrique II did not end with the death of his half brother. It took several more years for Enrique to subdue his entire kingdom. He fought the Muslim ruler Mohammad V of Granada for control of Algeciras and the Straits of Gibraltar. King Fernando of Portugal challenged him, too, by occupying Galicia in the northwest and blockading Seville.

Pedro the Cruel's alliance with England had stirred the ambitions of King Edward III's son, the Duke of Lancaster, aka John of Gaunt. (Gaunt refers to his birthplace, Ghent. Gaunt appears as a character in Shakespeare's *Richard II*.) John of Gaunt was one of the great kingmakers: although his own royal ambitions failed, his children succeeded. His son, Henry Bolingbroke, overthrew Richard II to become England's King Henry IV; his daughter, Katherine of Lancaster, was to obtain the throne of Castile as Queen Catalina.

Lancaster married Pedro's daughter, Doña Constanza, and then conspired with Portugal against Castile and Juan I. Juan, for his part, married the Portuguese heiress and attempted to have her proclaimed queen of Portugal. His invasion of Portugal ended in the defeat of Castile in the battle of Aljubarrota, where Castile fell to superior tactics and the English longbow. Lancaster followed up with a Portuguese invasion of Castile that was not settled until 1388. Aragon was locked in the same civil war, a territorial conflict between Pedro of Castile and Aragon's Pedro IV. Wars fought by Aragon for territory in the Balearics, Sardinia, and Sicily proved draining and largely unrewarding. Barcelona, the economic powerhouse of the kingdom of Aragon, had grown to be a mercantile rival of Venice but suffered a permanent decline after a financial crash in 1381–83.

All this warfare and instability had drained Spain's treasuries. Attempts to pay for troops by debasing the currency in Castile had resulted in bouts of inflation. Taxes increased, which placed a double burden on the Jews; since many were tax administrators, they were blamed for the rise in taxes, most of which they paid themselves. The hard times forced Spaniards to seek loans or credit for goods and services. The Jews had a lock on lending, and they produced most of the nonagricultural goods and services. Their prominence as creditors added to the Jews' unpopularity.

The wars, fought mainly by mercenaries, left Spanish cities full of troublesome men, trained for violence and killing. The chronicler López de Ayala, in his *Rimado* (written around 1385) depicted an exhausted country, plundered by unpaid soldiery and newly ennobled beggars on horseback.[8] One nineteenth-century scholar described Valencia at that period as a "meeting point for all the vagabonds, roughnecks, gamblers and adventurers of the kingdom, enemies of all work, who expected to find in it a field and opportunity to dedicate themselves to their perverse inclinations.... saloons and gambling dens were established without shame in the streets, in the market places and even in the square of the Bishop's place." From here "emerged all the broils and quarrels that stained the city's streets with blood. The chief of the vigilants and his agents could not guarantee personal security or the inviolability of the domicile."[9]

The man-made woes were compounded by natural disaster. Plague broke out in 1362, 1374, and 1384. Parts of the country were depopulated. Jews suffered from these outbreaks on two counts, since they dwelled mainly in the urban areas most susceptible to the plague, and because they were widely blamed for spreading the disease. Political instability made public discontent potentially explosive. To survive Jews needed protection from the monarch or, if the king was not available, from local nobles or even from the church, though assistance was often purchased with hefty bribes.

The Anti-Jewish Riots—Castile

Martínez quickly exploited the political vacuum that followed the deaths of the king and the archbishop and took advantage of the popular discontent created by war, economic decline, and plague. After the death of the archbishop, he successfully petitioned the Seville chapter of the church to reinstate him in his positions and, additionally, to appoint him as a provisor. On December 8, 1390, he sent orders throughout his diocese to raze the town synagogues, threatening excommunication for noncompliance. Several towns, including Écija, where Martínez was archdeacon, obeyed.

The Jews immediately appealed to the regency, which quickly responded in the Jews' favor. In a letter signed by the full committee, it informed the dean and members of the Seville church that they would be held responsible for Martínez's actions. It ordered the chapter to suspend Martínez from the office of provisor—the post that had given him the authority to order the destruction of the synagogues—and also to place him under ecclesiastic censure, to prevent him from preaching against the Jews, and to repair all damages to the destroyed synagogues. On January 15, 1391, the chapter assembled and agreed to comply with the regency's instructions. Martínez reacted, as always, with defiance. He claimed that his actions were legal, and that neither the king nor the chapter had the authority to administer these orders. He turned back to the people and continued to preach against the Jews.

In order to suppress the anti-Jewish disturbances stirred up by Ferrand Martínez's preaching, two noble officials decided, as an example, to punish select members of the mob he had incited. The provincial governor (*adelantado*) was Juan Alonso de Guzmán, the Count of Niebla, the most powerful noble of Andalusia; his kinsman Alvar Pérez de Guzmán was *alguazil mayor* (chief of the royal police) and *alcalde mayor* (chief mayor) of Seville. They ordered two men from the Martínez mob flogged and jailed. This order incited a mob insurrection. The rioters freed the prisoners, in the process capturing Pérez de Guzmán. The *alguazil* was released on the orders of Martínez.

The Jews again appealed to the regency, whose members were themselves divided, and who were preparing to defend themselves from opponents to their authority led by the archbishop of Toledo, who threatened civil war. There were no troops available to aid the Jews. Instead, the regency sent letters to all the town councils, ordering them to keep the peace. They also replaced Alvar Pérez de Guzmán as *alguazil* with the nobleman Pero Ponce de León, Lord of Marchena. Unfortunately, instead of increasing the *alguazil's* authority to protect the Jews, Ponce broke with Juan Alonso de Guzmán, the governor, splitting the local authorities into factions. Meanwhile, tensions only increased. As the contemporary chronicler Ayala noted: "The people were so aroused that they now had no fear of any one, and the desire to rob the Jews was increasing from day to day."[10]

The destruction began on June 2, 1391. Before dawn rioters attacked several points along the fortified wall enclosing the Jewish quarter. No support from Spanish troops arrived, and the Jewish defenses were quickly surmounted. The Jews—men, women, and children—were massacred without mercy. Others were captured and sold into slavery. The only defense was to submit to conversion. Thousands of Jews were herded into churches and to the baptismal fonts. They returned to find their homes looted, ravished, or burned. One seventeenth-century historian said that after the riots, the *judería*—Jewish quarter—looked like a wasteland.[11] The community was so reduced in size that two out of the three synagogues were converted to churches.

The anti-Jewish riots spread from Seville like the plague. Mobs first attacked outlying towns, including Martínez's area of responsibility, Écija. The wave of attacks then spread to Córdoba and Jerez, leaving thousands dead. The disorders quickly moved northward. Toledo fell to the mob on June 20. In Cuenca town officials joined with the mobs to loot, kill, and forcibly convert Jews.

The regency, now in Segovia, issued another proclamation, blaming the destruction and mass conversions on Martínez and the "little people." It stated that the kings had always protected the Jews and would not tolerate this violence.[12] The proclamation was not backed up with troops, however, and therefore had no effect. A few days after it was issued, rioters attacked the Jews of Burgos. Although the Jewish quarter was well fortified, the Jews, possibly intimidated by the fates of the other towns, fled to the homes of the nobility. In the end most Jews probably opted for conversion. In Madrid, where most of the Jews were killed or converted, looting continued for a year. Even Segovia, the seat of the regency, did not escape the anti-Jewish riots. By summer's end mobs had decimated the Jewish communities in almost all the major towns of Castile. The next target for the mobs would be Aragon.

Unlike Castile, Aragon had a functioning monarch. In 1388 Juan I was crowned king of Aragon. Unfortunately for the Jews, he was not a forceful ruler like his father, who had earned the nickname "Man of the Dagger" for the small knife he always wore at his belt. His son's nicknames were "the hunter" and "the lover of gentility." Juan was less interested in ruling than he was in pursuing the pleasures of the court. He left many decisions to his wife, who in turned relied on an unpopular confidant, Carroza de Vilagut.

Aragon's anti-Jewish riots started in the port city of Valencia in early July. The city was filled with soldiers preparing to accompany the king's brother, Don Martin, Duke of Montblanch, on an expedition to Sicily. Bands of rioters attempted to incite the troops to join the mob. Local officials, aware of the troubles in neighboring Castile, had been urged by the Jews and the Crown to take precautions. They placed gallows on the streets adjacent to the Jewish quarter as a warning to potential rioters and had guards patrol the area at night. The Jewish quarter was surrounded by a newly completed wall.

On June 9 a small group of men approached the main gate of Valencia's Jewish quarter, shouting that archdeacon Martínez was coming, and that the Jews must choose between conversion and death. As the gates to the *judería* were being closed to prevent an invasion, several of the men pushed their way inside. Those left outside the gates began to scream that their trapped companions would be murdered and demanded their release. They attracted a large mob, some of whom may have been soldiers of Don Martin. The duke and the magistrates demanded that the gates be opened and the men released, claiming that they would provide protection to the Jews. Outside the gates was a raging mob that the duke did nothing to pacify: the Jews chose to keep the gates shut.

The mob succeeded in scaling the wall and overcoming the Jews' defenses. Several hundred Jews were murdered. Some fled the city by sea. Thousands more succumbed to forced conversion. So many Jews converted that a story arose that the baptismal fonts had miraculously filled with holy anointing oil, but even this miraculous oil was eventually exhausted by the number of baptisms.[13] The mobs also attacked the Moorish quarter. The king's troops rescued the Moors, and Don Martin had one of the rioters publicly hanged. The Moorish quarter needed to be protected because armies of the neighboring Moorish kingdoms could retaliate against any attack on the Moors. The Jews did not necessitate this kind of protection from the king.

Joseph Abraham, a Jew from Valencia, later left this testimony with a notary describing his experiences during the riots:

> At noon of the ninth of July past, the plaintiff being in his house they closed the gates of the juderia with great noise and shouts from the Jews and he shut his door. Before the hour of three, the people of the town assaulted the wall by the Old Valladar and even though he had his gate secured by great and strong nails, they forced it down with a battering ram and his house was assaulted by twenty men armed with swords, sticks and knives, some with blackened faces and hoods. They immediately broke and splintered boxes, desks, wardrobe. They even took the little mattresses off the beds without leaving a nail on the wall . . . all assessed as three thousand gold florins. They also stabbed his brother Nahor in the neck while he was trying to repel their attack . . . Because the plaintiff complained about the damage . . . the head of the criminals hit him, wounding his arm and also behind his ear . . . Asked whether he knew . . . the perpetrators of the assault and those who raped the women, he said that by certain words and a golden earring which one of those with a blackened face wore he suspects a man of estate but he cannot be sure.[14]

Even the king of Aragon criticized his brother for his failure to protect the Jews: "Had you acted with the strictness and severity called for by the nature of the crime and the contempt showed from our chastisement—especially when so abominable a crime was committed in front of you who represent our person . . . you would have put to the sword or hanged 300 or 400 men during these riots against the Jews."[15]

A month later riots spread throughout Aragon. On the island of Majorca, the governor evacuated all the Jews to the capital city of Palma for their protection. Anti-Jewish mobs rose up on August 2, probably with the assistance or forbearance of local bailiffs, and killed hundreds. The governor, who later executed one of the negligent bailiffs, tried to prevent Jews from escaping by sea to North Africa, fearing the loss of Jewish revenues.

In Barcelona the riots broke out on August 5. As in Valencia the port was filled with troops headed for Sicily. About fifty Castilian followers of Martínez were also in the city. The riots were inspired by the success of anti-Jewish violence in Majorca. After rioters killed about one hundred Jews in Barcelona, other Jews took refuge in the city's new fortifications. For days rioters looted the Jewish quarter, taking care to burn the *escribanías*—written IOUs—that recorded Christian debt to the Jews.

Local authorities fortified the defenses protecting the Jews and arrested some of the rioters. The mob, enraged at these actions, attacked local officials and freed anti-Jewish prisoners, many of whom were Castilians. Their slogan was "Long live the King and the people! The fat ones wish to destroy the little people."[16] One of the burghers, Mosen Pons de la Sala, turned the mob aside by persuading the people to attack Jews rather than the Christian officials who had been protecting the Jews.[17] Throughout the days and nights, the mob besieged the Jewish fortifications. Some Jews escaped to Christian homes. Hundreds were murdered. The rest—the majority—succumbed to baptism.

Anti-Jewish rioters soon followed suit in Gerona. Those who escaped these riots sought shelter with the Count of Ampurias in the castle of Geronella, which was then besieged and overrun by the peasants. Jews suffered similar fates in the towns of Lérida, Tortosa, and Perpignan. In Perpignan even the governor profited from the looting.

The most prominent Jew in Spain at the time of the riots, both because of his influence with his fellows Jews and the Aragon court and because of his intellectual ability, was the philosopher and rabbinical authority Hasdai Crescas. Born in 1340, he had become a leader of the Jewish community in Barcelona by 1367, when he was briefly imprisoned with other important Jews on false charges involving desecration of hosts. In 1390 he was appointed supreme judge of all cases involving accusations by informants, and the appointment letter cited him as unsurpassed "not only in knowledge of the laws of Moses, but in power of reasoning."[18]

Hasdai was close to King Juan I and his wife, Violante, and his contacts with the court probably motivated his move to Saragossa, where he became the chief rabbi. When the riots broke out, the queen personally wrote to Barcelona, requesting protection for his family. When Hasdai left in August to raise funds to help the Jews, the Queen called him back out of concern for his safety. Despite the royal favor, Hasdai's only son was killed in the Barcelona riots. The rabbi wrote: "Many sanctified the Holy Name, my only son among them, an innocent lamb; him have I offered up as a burnt offering, I shall vindicate God's judgment against me, and I shall be comforted with the goodliness of his portion and the sweetness of his fate."[19]

The rabbi continued his work for years after the riots, both by leading the efforts at reconstruction and in his own research and writing. His philosophical work, *Or Adonai, The Light of God*, was the first Jewish work to attempt a critique of Aristotle, but its main purpose was probably to defend Judaism against rationalist attacks by followers of Averroës and Maimonides.[20] Rationalism was viewed as a force that sapped religious fervor and made Jews vulnerable to conversion. Hasdai also wrote the *Refutation of Christian Dogmas*. It may be that his inability to defend the Jews from physical attack drove him instead to produce works defending the Jews from intellectual attacks.

In 1393 Hasdai Crescas wrote to the king, asking for permission to take a second wife. While this request reflects continued Moorish influence on the Jews (Jews had elsewhere long abandoned the practice of polygamy), it was primarily an effort to make up for the loss of his son after the riots: "Sire, I have lost my only son. My wife is an old woman who can no longer conceive. Unless I am blessed with a second son, my family name will not continue." But a later letter implies concern, not only that his own line would not continue, but that the Jews, themselves, might not survive in Spain: "Each night I hear the beating of the wings of the angel of death. Shall not my seed yet continue in this land?"[21]

Why Did the Jews Convert?

There has been some debate about why the Jews of Spain accepted conversion so quickly and in such large numbers. During the first crusade of 1096, most German Jews had chosen death rather than conversion. Yitzak Baer has blamed the Jewish victims, attributing the Spanish conversions to their lack of sufficient religious devotion: "The large and leading communities, like those of Seville, Toledo and Burgos, were destroyed not only by the violence of their enemies, but chiefly by their own moral deterioration."[22]

The historian Norman Cantor has taken the opposite view, that the Jews were to blame for their excessive religiosity: "If during the thirteenth century the rabbis had not withdrawn into the theosophic, astrological, and mystical shell of the Kabbalah; if they had remained loyal to the high intellectual road taken by Maimonides in the twelfth century, that of liberal rationalism and the effort to integrate Judaism with contemporary science, the way in fact taken by secular humanistic Judaism today, would that have made a difference? ... Would there have been less tendency for Christians to make scapegoats out of the Jews ... and unleash horrible pogroms on them?"[23]

Both these arguments unfairly blame the victim. The responsibility for the massacres lies with intolerant Christians, not Jews. Martínez would not have been mollified had he thought that the Jews were more dedicated to Torah study or more proficient in Aristotelian philosophy. He saw only one solution to the "Jewish problem": conversion. And as the Spanish Inquisition would later demonstrate, even conversion would not provide complete protection from intolerance.

One difference between the massacres during the crusades and the riots of 1391 is that the Spanish killings were led by a priest who openly pressed for conversion. Martínez, for all his hatred of the Jews, could not justify a deliberate program of mass murder. By calling for conversion, Martínez gave at least some religious justification to persecution, although forced conversion violated church doctrine.[24] Maimonides had already provided a religious argument justifying insincere conversion for those facing the threat of death. With Jews being killed by the thousands throughout Spain, mass conversion—not just to save one's own life but also to save one's family, including small children—could seem justified and understandable.

Many may have thought that they could save their lives and their families by insincere conversion and then revert to Judaism once the danger had passed. If that was their plan, they proved to be mistaken. Martínez's pogrom would change their world forever.

15

The Church Campaign against the Jews, Postconversion

Jews and Converts after the Riots

As with smoldering embers after a massive firestorm, anti-Jewish passions flared up into sporadic riots for years after the massacres of 1391. The sway of Ferrand Martínez, however, had ended. When in 1392 a friar, nephew to Ferrand Martínez, tried to renew the "holy war" against the Jews in Saragossa, King Juan I had him arrested and remarked: "Such persons must not be allowed to live." If Ferrand Martínez himself should show up, he added: "Arrest him and send him to me; or else throw him in the river."[1] When Enrique III of Castile reached the age of majority, in 1395, he went to Seville and had Martínez arrested. There is no record of the punishment imposed. Upon his death in 1404, Martínez reportedly had a substantial estate, which he bequeathed to the Hospital of Santa Maria.

While Martínez was now under control, this did not put a stop to repressive acts against the Jews. Although the church had played no direct role in the riots, Ferrand Martínez provided some church leaders with something that they had long sought: widespread conversions of the Jews. Now church leaders began to plan a campaign to complete this unforeseen victory and to bring all Spanish Jews into the church. Four clergy took the lead in this project: two apostate converts, a Dominican, and Benedict XII, the "Avignon pope," a man now known as the "Antipope."

Immediately after the riots, the authorities in both Castile and Aragon took steps to bring the country back into order. Some culprits were punished. In Valencia five were hanged and twenty banished from the kingdom. Twenty-six men were condemned in Barcelona. The authorities in

Castile established missions of inquiries to investigate the culpability for the riots. Too many people had been involved in the riots for all to be punished, and some were too influential to prosecute. Both Castile and Aragon largely limited their punishment of the instigators and rioter to fines. This policy in part reflected the governments' main concern, that the devastation wrought by the riots to the Jewish communities hit the Crown's main source of income. Government officials even sought compensation from the Jews themselves. The Crown confiscated Jewish communal property from the now-deserted communities, including synagogue buildings and ornaments. Jews who chose martyrdom over conversion were considered suicides, so that their property devolved to the state.[2]

In an attempt to repair the damage from the riots, the king of Aragon—with assistance from Hasdai Crescas, the most prominent Jewish leader and scholar of the time—attempted to rebuild the Jewish settlements in Barcelona and Valencia. He allotted a new quarter for the Jews, and offered benefits like tax exemptions for Jews who were willing to resettle the *judería*. Few Jews were willing to return. The local Christians opposed any new settlement, and in 1401 they persuaded King Martin to forbid the settlement of Jews in Barcelona.

At the time of the riots, Barcelona had one of the oldest Jewish communities in all of Europe. One of the principal neighborhoods of the city today—also a major tourist attraction—is still called Montjuich, the "hill of the Jews" (probably because it was the site of the Jewish cemetery). After the riots, however, Jews ceased to live in Barcelona for almost six hundred years.

One of the most pressing issues for the church and Spanish authorities was whether to recognize the conversions. Officially, the church condemned forced conversions and could have allowed Jews subjected to forced conversion to revert to Judaism. King João of Portugal adopted this position, openly embracing a kind of "don't ask, don't tell" policy. He encouraged resettlement and did not investigate cases of reversion to Judaism. In contrast the authorities of Castile and Aragon determined, with church support, that while forced conversion was improper, once the sacraments of conversion were completed, converts would be recognized Christians and could not revert to Judaism. Returning to

Judaism after conversion, even an involuntary conversion, would be considered heresy, potentially punishable by death.

For most of the Spanish converts, the only path to open practice of Judaism was exile. A small number made a pilgrimage to Israel. More, particularly the converts in Majorca, fled to North Africa and some to Portugal. These exiles helped to form communities that would be joined, a century later, by much larger numbers of expelled Jews.

Most converts remained in their old homes. Authorities took measures to prevent converts from fleeing to areas where they could revert to Judaism, both to defend the faith and to preserve the converts' economic resources for the state. As early as 1391, the king of Aragon mandated separation of converts from the remaining Jews, in order to prevent "New Christians" from the temptation to practice their old faith. Economic necessity also compelled many Jews to accept conversion. The widespread looting and destruction of the riots had left many converts destitute. To earn a living as Christians in the Christian world would require compliance with Christian dress and customs.

In some cases the riots of 1391 led to intrafamilial strife, leaving spouses and children on different sides of the religious divide. One physician, weeping over the conversions of his father and brothers, wrote to a friend: "Look about you! Everywhere brother is divided against brother and kin against kin. Be strong, then, my brother, for the land is swept with violence.... As for your poor, regal mother, I can inform you that she is living in bitterness in her husband's house and continues to abide by the Law and act decorously; and although many are her tormentors and would-be converters, her one reply is that she would die before going over."[3]

Some converts exploited this split as an opportunity for extortion. Converso husbands demanded money from their Jewish wives in exchange for divorce, so that the wives could remarry in the faith. These cases were sufficiently common that the king of Portugal, protective of the Jewish community, published a law requiring such converts to grant their wives a Jewish divorce.[4] In another case a convert had to be ordered by Aragon's queen to free his brother's widow, who otherwise was bound to remarry him by the Jewish custom of "levirate."

The Jews of Castile and Aragon had to deal with the loss of a third or more of their community to death and conversion, as well as the widespread destruction of homes and property. The Jewish poet Solomon de Piera left a testament to the sadness of the years following the 1391 riots in a poem written after his own home was destroyed and his children lost to an unknown fate:

> That day death's angels ransacked my home.... My sons sought
>   the safety of the stony cliff, and fled
> without a blessing on their head.... I know not where
> They rest tonight; nor whether they are
> Not somewhere sold or slaughtered; nor on what pyre
> Their bodies' flesh is broiled by fire.[5]

He later wrote: "We can inherit no portion of comfort, only think of the favor of those who have been lost and cast out by the fury of the oppressor. He has subdued the best among our faith, he has brought the youth of Israel to its knees. Nor did the first days last long, and they are best off who have been killed and murdered by the sword, and especially God's martyrs."[6]

The New Anti-Jewish Campaign: Vincent Ferrer

Soon after the riots subsided, church leaders took advantage of Jewish despair to push for further conversions. The first prominent church leader to exploit this "opportunity" was the Dominican friar Vincent Ferrer, born in 1350 in Valencia. His English or Scottish father had been knighted for fighting (probably as a mercenary) in the reconquest of Valencia from the Moors. Ferrer's was a religious family—his brother would become general of the Carthusian order. Ferrer became a Dominican monk at the age of seventeen. He studied in Barcelona and at the Catalan university in Lérida. In his late twenties he took up studies in Toulouse. Cardinal Pedro de Luna gave him his doctoral cap, and Ferrer became an important backer of the cardinal after Luna took the disputed papal seat in Avignon. The alliance between Ferrer and Luna would extend to this new anti-Jewish campaign.

Ferrer was in Valencia when the anti-Jewish riots first broke out. He condemned forced conversion. He was, however, the most famous sermonizer of his day and the strong proconversion message of his oratory probably added significantly to the anti-Jewish passions of the rioters. Ferrer's opposition to forced conversion did not prevent him from accepting the conversions, once performed, as sacrosanct. Ferrer's preaching was heard throughout western Europe, including Switzerland, Italy, and England. Since he spoke only Catalan, his popularity is hard to understand. It was claimed that people could miraculously understand the sermons, and that the further one stood from him, the better one could hear. The huge crowds that followed him everywhere probably played a large part in his popularity. His sermons had the electric emotional appeal of a revival meeting. The modern scholar Howard Sachar describes Ferrer: "Over the years, as he traveled from town to town, a miracle-hungry rabble thronged after him in solemn procession, carrying banners, crosses, icons of saints, and other holy relics, and chanting religious and penitential hymns. His sermons were delivered in public squares or fields, and usually at night when people were returning home from work. Great flambeaux were lit, creating an unearthly effect among crowds that grew to eight or ten thousands. As Ferrer preached, threatening to whirl away a corrupt society in an instantaneous dance of death, he reduced his audience to weeping, babbling, pleading for salvation."[7]

The *Catholic Encyclopedia* says: "He was followed by an army of penitents drawn from every rank of society.... This strange assemblage ... numbered at times 10,000."[8] These followers included a band of flagellants, as one modern popular historian describes: "After him in later years followed his Flagellants, men and women in white and black robes like himself, sleeping on the hard ground, living from unasked alms. They came singing the hymn he had written for them, and when they reached the church porch of a town they would kneel—up to three hundred of them, their faces veiled, their backs and shoulder bared—and as silent thousands, hardly breathing, waited, the Flagellants would begin the rhythmic scourging of their bodies with a 'noise as of heavy rain.'"[9]

For much of his career, Ferrer had focused on converting the Jews. After the riots, as part of his campaign to increase conversions, he obtained orders from Spanish authorities requiring Jewish congregations to attend his sermons. His fiery orations, supported by mobs of anti-Jewish supporters, became much more intimidating after the riots and massacres of 1391. According to Yitzak Baer, "The bands of flagellants who accompanied him, scourging themselves as they walked, so terrified the Jews that they fled for their lives at their approach."[10] His sermons were often followed by anti-Jewish riots. One anonymous chronicler wrote around 1500 that his grandfather told him that Ferrer's preaching brought on the slaughter of nineteen of Toledo's most eminent Jews, men, women, and children, who were beheaded in a mill run: it was "a thing sad to see, the wheel turned human blood instead of water."[11]

The New Anti-Jewish Campaign: Pablo de Burgos

Whether by inspiration or intimidation, Ferrer was said to have converted thousands of Jews. One Jew he reportedly influenced in his decision to convert was Solomon ha-Levi, who took the Christian name Pablo de Santa Maria. Santa Maria, better known as Pablo de Burgos, would become another of the prominent clerics who worked to bring about more Jewish conversions. Solomon ha-Levi probably converted sometime before the anti-Jewish riots reached Burgos. If he converted after the Seville riots, there may have been an element of coercion involved. But he may have converted a year before the riots, possibly as part of a group. Even if some coercion was involved, ha-Levi characterized his conversion as fully voluntary, and he became a fervently devout Christian.

The apparently voluntary and enthusiastic embrace of Christianity by one of Spain's most successful Jews shocked the community even at a time when thousands more were submitting to the baptismal font. Solomon ha-Levi had come from a wealthy family, had received an extensive education (including a familiarity with Latin unusual for Spanish Jews), and, prior to his conversion, had become chief rabbi of Burgos, one of the richest cities in the country. Burgos also served as an occasional residence for the Castilian king, in whose court ha-Levi also served.

The shock of ha-Levi's apparently genuine religious conversion led one of his former students, Joshua ha-Lorki, to write him a long letter, puzzling over why so prominent a Jew would turn to Christianity. The letter is notable because it demonstrates what some Jews of the late fourteenth century might have considered tempting about the prospect of conversion to Christianity.[12]

In the letter the student Joshua ha-Lorki speculated that four factors could have led ha-Levi, now Pablo of Burgos, to convert: material temptation and ambition; philosophy and rationalism; despair over the eternal suffering of the Jewish people; and belief in the truth of Christianity. It is strange that ha-Lorki would place religious belief last among the various reasons for religious conversion, but that can perhaps be explained by the fact that the letter dates to a time when Jews were being forced to convert throughout Spain. Ha-Lorki's long letter examined these four temptations and rejected most of them, based in part on his personal knowledge of Pablo of Burgos. The letter hinted at ha-Lorki's own doubt in his faith, as he acknowledged that Pablo's knowledge of Latin may have exposed him to Christian truths unknown to ha-Lorki.[13] The doubt hinted at in this letter took a long time to mature. Twenty years later, under the influence of Vincent Ferrer, ha-Lorki, too, converted, transforming himself into Geronimo de Santa Fe. He joined Pablo de Burgos as one of the apostate former Jews leading the church's campaign against their abandoned religion.

Pablo of Burgos only briefly replied to the young ha-Lorki's letter. He made it clear that he had moved away from his old Jewish life and Jewish friends to a life in his new religion, identifying himself as "Formerly in Israel when he did not know God, Solomon of the House of Levi, and now since his eyes have beheld God, he is called Paulo de Burgos."[14]

The newly converted Pablo of Burgos, no longer a rabbi, quickly took up another profession: the priesthood. He had a potentially disqualifying attribute for a priest: he was married with children. But because he had not been married in the church, the marriage was not recognized, allowing Pablo to enter a celibate profession. Pablo de Burgos took up studies at the famed University of Paris, where Thomas Aquinas had studied and taught over a century before him. There he spent three years, obtaining a master's of theology and then entering the priesthood.

The New Anti-Jewish Campaign: Pedro de Luna

Pablo de Burgos also allied himself with the most prominent Spanish clergyman of the time, Pedro de Luna—then cardinal of Aragon and one of the leaders in the new church campaign against the Spanish Jews. Luna came from a prominent Aragonese family, said to be descendants of Said ben-Alhakam, the Muslim king of Majorca baptized after his capture by the Spanish. Luna studied law at the university in Montpelier, where he himself later taught canon law. He served Pope Gregory XI in Avignon as a counselor and administrator for seven years. It was this service that led, in 1375, to Luna's promotion to cardinal.

As cardinal Luna became a central figure in one of the worst crises in the history of the church: the Great Western Schism. This schism split the church apart for forty years. It would also figure in the history of the Spanish Jews, who would be prosecuted as part of the campaign for rights to the papacy. The Jews of Aragon in particular became victims of the political machinations created by this church conflict: once Luna became pope, he would campaign against the Spanish Jews, exploiting anti-Jewish prejudice to gain popularity in his quest to solidify his claim to the papacy. While the schism threatened to tear the church apart, it had almost nothing to do with religion. The church split over politics, geography, and personal ambition, the most important factor being ambition.

The schism began by chance. The pope moved from Rome to Avignon in 1309. Pope Clement V had been archbishop of Bordeaux and chose Lyons as the site of his coronation. Rome was rife with sectarian strife and feuds. A move to Avignon was justified by security concerns. In November 1377 Pope Gregory, in Rome exploring the feasibility of moving the papacy back, died at the age of forty-six. Mobs surrounded the Vatican, demanding an Italian pope. The cardinals acquiesced and elected the archbishop of Bari, who took the name Urban VI. Whether the cardinals made their choice voluntarily or under coercion is not known.

With an Italian pope in charge, the largely French coalition of cardinals, which included the Spaniard de Luna, fled Rome as soon as possible. They met again in Fondi, a town between Rome and Naples.

Claiming that their earlier choice of Bari was coerced and invalid, in September 1378 they instead elected as pope Robert of Geneva, knows as the "Butcher of Cesena" due to his brutality in putting down a riot in an Italian town near Ravenna. Robert of Geneva became Pope Clement VII: his election split the church in two. Pedro de Luna had cautioned against choosing a second pope, but once the decision was made, he proved a loyal advisor to the "Clementine" side.

In 1394 Pope Clement died at the age of fifty-two. By this time no one was happy with the split in the church. One proposed solution was the "Way of Cession," where both popes would abdicate in expectation of another uncontested election. Pedro de Luna was a long-standing supporter of cession. In October 1394, he was elected Pope Benedict XIII on the expectation that he would reach an agreement for mutual abdication and bring an end to the schism. Pope Benedict instead soon demonstrated that he believed in only one solution to the schism: making himself the only recognized pope. For the rest of his long life, he made many feints toward compromise but never surrendered his claim to being the only proper leader of the faith.

Pablo of Burgos became acquainted with Cardinal Pedro de Luna while studying in Paris and was invited to work with the new pope in Avignon. Pablo, as a new convert, made it his mission to convert the Jews. In 1394, only a few years after the great massacres in Spain, the French king expelled all the Jews from his kingdom. Pablo preached to the exiles in Perpignan, where he reportedly succeeded in making many converts. He moved on to promote repressive anti-Jewish measures. These were blocked by the cardinal of Pamplona, but Pablo convinced Aragon to adopt some less onerous anti-Jewish laws.[15]

In 1398 Luna—now Pope Benedict—sent Pablo to Castile, appointing him archdeacon of Trevino, in the Burgos diocese. Castilian support was vital to the pope, and this appointment made Pablo an important representative to the Castilian court. Pablo succeeded in becoming the royal chaplain. In 1406 the king made him one of the three executors of his will, major chancellor, and tutor to his son.[16]

That year King Enrique III of Castile died at the age of twenty-seven. His son Juan was then only a year old. Juan's mother, Catalina, ruled with the regent, the late king's nephew, Fernando. In 1410 King Martin of Aragon died with no surviving male issue. The consequence of all this was that in the absence of a strong leader, the state was far more receptive to demands by church officials for repressive measures to be taken against Jews to encourage more conversions.

Toward the end of Enrique's reign, Castile passed important anti-Jewish legislation. These laws restricted money lending between Jews and Christians and limited Jewish eligibility to work as tax farmers. Another law reaffirmed the rules requiring Jews to wear an identifying badge. Given Pablo's prominence in Castile, it is likely that he played a significant role in passing—if not writing—this legislation.

Anti-Jewish demonstrations continued. In Segovia around 1410, rumors spread that Jews had "tortured" a host. In retaliation the Jewish former chief physician to King Enrique III was arrested and tortured. Accusations of crimes against a host were extended to charges that he had poisoned and killed his former patient, the king, despite the fact that the king's early death had never been a mystery—a lifetime of infirmity had earned him the nickname El Doliente, "the Invalid." Still, the king's physician, Don Meir Alguades, was hanged, drawn, and quartered, and other Jews suffered similar fates. The bishop then claimed that Jews had bribed his cook to poison him, and more tortures and executions followed.[17]

At this point both Pablo and his patron, Pope Benedict, embroiled in the church crisis caused by the schism, had other priorities besides the persecution of the Jews. Christendom was tired of the split in the church, and it had become clear that Benedict (Luna) would support no solution that diminished his authority. In 1398 France withdrew its support of his papacy. A mission was sent to Benedict to demand his resignation. He responded: "I will never resign nor submit myself to any King, Duke, or Count, nor agree to any treaty that shall include my resignation from the Popedom."[18] A French army besieged the Palace of the Popes in Avignon, but it proved impregnable. Benedict held fast for five years and finally escaped in 1403.

Pablo was vital in obtaining Spanish support for the literally besieged pope. In 1402 Pablo succeeded in getting Castile, which had sided with the French, to reaffirm its loyalty to Benedict. His service to the pope earned him an appointment as bishop of Cartagena in southern Spain, as well as the post of official ambassador of the pope to the Castilian court.

Benedict's escape from Avignon earned him only a brief reprieve. The Way of the Cession had proven futile, due to the tenacity of the sitting popes. Cardinals on both sides agreed on another solution: they would convene a general council to resolve the split. This council met at Pisa in 1409. Both popes refused to attend—instead, they called rival councils. Benedict stood alone against his cardinals in refusing to send delegates to the council, saying that because of his refusal, the recommendation to have representation "was not the unanimous opinion of [his] Council."

"'Holy Father,' the remnant answered, 'there is but one man here who is of a different opinion.'

'Well,' said Benedict, 'that one man is right.'"[19]

A council without papal authority was contrary to canon law. In order to justify its authority, the council began by convicting both sitting popes of heresy. The accusations against Benedict included charges that he was friendly to Jews.[20] Both popes were convicted on flimsy charges of heresy. An elderly Franciscan, Petros Philargos, elected pope by the council, became Alexander V, and the church now had three popes. Pope Benedict was now in Spain. There he and Pablo de Burgos used their authority to unleash a new campaign against the Jews.

The New Anti-Jewish Campaign: The Laws of Catalina

Although Vincent Ferrer had earned worldwide fame for his ability to convert Jews, most Spanish Jews resisted his sermonizing. In frustration he now sponsored a new plan, one of the most repressive laws ever proposed against the Jew, laws likely drafted by Pablo de Burgos. Known as the "Laws of Catalina," after the Spanish queen (née Catherine of Lancaster, daughter of John of Gaunt) who endorsed them, this legislation required the ghettoization of the Jews, who were to be removed from their homes near Christians and segregated in ramshackle housing. They were forced out of their old homes even if no other dwelling place was available, and otherwise were assigned filthy and unsanitary quarters.[21] In each town once local authorities applied the law, Jews had eight days to move out and find new quarters. Those who failed to comply were subject to loss of all possessions and corporal punishment.[22]

The segregation legislated by Ferrer's Laws of Catalina also banned interreligious social and commercial contact. Jews could not visit Christians during their illnesses, give them medicines, talk idly to them, or send them presents of dried herbs, spices, or any articles of food. They could not attend Christian weddings and funerals or take part in any ceremony in which Christians were honored.[23] Worse, Jews were banned from any commerce with Christians, when many Jews relied on such trade for support. Jewish physicians could not treat Christian patients. Jewish apothecaries could not sell drugs to Christians. Jewish artisans could not serve Christian customers.

Vincent Ferrer never endorsed Ferrand Martínez's campaign of "conversion or death." Now he embraced, instead, extreme coercion. The Laws of Catalina gave most Jews the choice between conversion and privation. According to the nineteenth-century Spanish historian Amador de los Rios, the fundamental target of the new laws was precisely "the legal annulment of the Jewish people as such; all of it [the ordinance] was designed to reduce that people to a state of the greatest misery and impotence and put forever an end to the influence which it had gained."[24] One of Ferrer's justifications for this new legislation was that new converts needed to be protected from Jewish influence, which could lead New Christians back to Judaism. This argument would be used as a justification for the Spanish Inquisition, as well as for the expulsion of the Jews. The Laws of Catalina were first promulgated in Valladolid in 1412. Although these laws applied throughout Castile, they required local enforcement. The laws also prohibited Jews from any travel outside the realm of jurisdiction.

Soon after Ferrer's laws were passed, a succession crisis in Aragon that started with the death of King Martin in 1410 ended. Ferrer joined Pablo de Burgos and Pope Benedict in supporting the newly crowned king of Aragon, Infante Fernando in 1412. In exchange for this support, Fernando made Pablo de Burgos one of four representatives chosen to carry out the king's former duties as joint regent in Castile. Fernando then promulgated less extreme versions of the Laws of Catalina in Aragon.

The Disputation of Tortosa

These various severe laws constituted only the first phase of the new anti-Jewish campaign. The next phase would be led by Pablo de Burgos's old correspondent, Joshua ha-Lorki. After receiving a visit from Vincent Ferrer, Joshua ha-Lorki resolved the religious doubts that he had expressed previously in his letter to Pablo de Burgos: in 1412 he embraced Christianity, taking as his new identity the Christian name Hieronymus de Sancta Fide. Jews gave him another name, using the letters of the Spanish spelling of Mestre Geronimo de Santa Fe: *megadef*, Hebrew for "the blasphemer."[25] One of Hieronymus de Sancta Fide's first acts was to write a derivative treatise attacking Judaism, called *Contra Perfidiam Judaeorum*, which he presented to Pope Benedict.

The treatise inspired Benedict to resurrect an old idea. He would sponsor a public debate, like the Disputation of Barcelona but on an even larger scale. In February 1413 Benedict opened the debate at the papal court in Tortosa in Aragon. Hieronymus de Sancta Fide, like the earlier apostate Pablo Christiani, led the Christian side. For the Jews there was a problem: since the death of Hasdai Crescas in 1410, no Jew had achieved the authority that Nahmanides had wielded in the Barcelona debate. Instead of one representative, the pope invited each major Jewish community to send several representatives. The wording of the invitation made clear that this would be no impartial debate but rather a forum that would use the Talmud to prove the tenets of Christianity.[26]

Any illusion of papal objectivity must have been dispelled by the pope's opening statement: "You, the Jewish sages, ought to bear in mind that I am not here, nor have I sent for you to come to this place, in order to discuss which of the two religions is true. For I know that my faith is the only true one; yours had once been true but it has since been superseded. You have come here only on account of Geronimo who has promised to prove, through the very Talmud of your masters who are wiser than yourselves, that the Messiah has already come. You shall debate before me this topic exclusively."[27]

The debate was held with great ceremony and was attended by dignitaries of both the papal and the royal courts. The Jews who attended left accounts describing their dismay at seeing the forces that the church had recruited in its support: "We found the whole large court arrayed in embroideries . . . and there were seventy seats for the dignitaries called cardinals and archbishops and bishops, all garbed in golden vestments. And all the great ones of Rome (the papal court) were there, and men from the city and princes, near unto a thousand men."[28] "Our hearts melted and turned to water."[29]

Why did Pope Benedict take on this project and devote so much of his time and resources to it, at a time when he was under political attack throughout Europe, which now viewed him as one of the primary obstacles to resolving the split in the church? He may have hoped that by successfully accomplishing the conversion of the Spanish Jews, he could win recognition as pope. His advocacy of increasing Jewish conversions to Christianity while in residence at Aragon raised his political profile in Spain, now his main base of support. Finally, he would at last put to rest the charge made against him in Pisa: no one could again accuse him of being a friend to the Jews.

The thirteenth-century debate at Barcelona formed the blueprint for the Tortosa disputation. As before, much attention was paid to a section of the Palestinian Talmud that stated that the Messiah was born on the day of the destruction of the temple. The intention behind this emphasis was to convince the Jews of the contradictions in their own faith, since the passage could be interpreted to mean that the Messiah had already come, and hence, that continuing to wait for a Messiah held little purpose.

The Jewish debaters referred to the response earlier given by Nahmanides: that only some of the Talmud represents Halakha, or religious law. Other passages are Aggadah, or homilies and parables that are not to be taken in the narrow, literal manner in which these passages were now being used by church debaters. The Jews argued that while the Messiah may have been born on the day that the temple was destroyed, he could still be alive and "held in reserve" by God until the proper time. The Christians responded that to deny some passages of the Talmud a literal meaning undermined the respectability of the Talmud as a basis of faith.

In the debate Hieronymus regularly cited arguments in Martini's *Pugio Fidei*. Martini's knowledge of the Talmud was limited, however, and he had used incorrect citations that Hieronymus repeated as the basis for his argument. At one point the Jewish debater Astruc Halevi pointed out that one of these passages was false and produced a copy of the correct text. Hieronymus grabbed the manuscript and pretended to read the false version from it. The next day the Jews challenged him to show them a section of the Talmud containing the passage he had quoted. Hieronymus refused, saying that the Jews themselves were responsible for finding the passage. He later promised to produce evidence that his quotation had been authentic but never did.[30]

At the end of February 1413, the head of the Dominican order summed up the Christian argument. The Jews, he said, would either have to concede that Hieronymus had proven all his points or come up with new arguments. The pope concluded that the debate would continue, but that from now on, all arguments would be presented in writing and read aloud to the audience.

The debate dragged on until the end of August and then resumed at the end of November. On January 8, 1414, almost a year after the start of the debate, the pope gave an address in which he blamed the Jews for prolonging the session. At this point most of the Jews were ready to end the debate. Astruc Halevi composed a memorandum in February describing the hardships that the debate had imposed on the Jewish participants: "They had been far away from their homes for ten months.... Their possessions had decreased and had been almost entirely destroyed. Their absence from their communities has caused the latter immeasurable harm. They had lost their wives and children on account of the debates. The needs of many of the delegates at Tortosa and of their families at home had not been adequately provided for; and here, in Tortosa, they were put to great expense."[31]

Early in the course of the debate, Jews began coming to Tortosa, announcing their decision to convert. Conversions followed all over Spain. Some prominent court Jews renounced their religion and in exchange were rewarded with important court responsibilities. Bonafos de la Cavalleria, who had belonged to an important Jewish family, was renamed Fernando under his new faith. He was then named "counselor and treasurer of the King of Aragon," a position not open to Jews.[32] One of the Jewish leaders participating in the debate, Don Vidal de la Cavalleria, also converted, in March 1414.

By May 1414, over a year after it had begun, the debate was closed, and a new debate opened. Now the Talmud was put on trial. The charges were "the errors, heresies, abuses and revilings of the Christian religion in the Talmud."[33] Hieronymus read out numerous passages from the Talmud that he claimed involved heresy or defamation of Christianity. By July the exhausted Jews concluded that further argument was futile. Instead, they sought the mercy and compassion of the pope: "The Jews here assembled ... declare that, because of their ignorance and lack of enlightenment, they are unable to rebut the arguments of Hieronymus against the talmudic sayings cited by him, and do not know how to defend those sayings. They are, nevertheless, firmly convinced that, were the authors of those sayings now alive, they would have known how to defend them because, as wise and good men, they could not have uttered any unseemly statements."[34] They then petitioned to be allowed to go home. They had now been away for almost a year and a half.

Hieronymus summed up his arguments in September. He called for the condemnation of the Talmud, as well as for a trial of the Jewish representatives for heresy. Yet another debate was held in November. It was not until December that the Jews were finally released and allowed to return home after an absence of nearly two full years. The verdict was issued jointly by the pope and King Fernando in May and June 1415: it reaffirmed the sanctions of the Laws of Catalina. The Talmud was condemned. Jews were ordered to surrender all copies, so that they could be cleansed of offensive passages.

During this long debate, Jewish communities in Castile and Aragon were continually subject to repression actions, in conjunction with the debate's attack on Jewish morale. Vincent Ferrer tirelessly pursued his sermons, which Jews were forced to attend. The Laws of Catalina, enforced haphazardly, struck selected communities in which they were enforced with great harshness. Other communities invented their own anti-Jewish measures. The town of Daroca, for example, subjected Jews to arbitrary arrests and property confiscations, until most of the community fled under cover of night.[35]

The combination of repressive laws, a lengthy debate that kept as virtual prisoners many of the leaders of the Jewish community, and the tireless sermonizing of Ferrer with his large group of followers in attendance succeeded in gaining a new wave of converts. Some of the Tortosa delegates returned to their homes as Christians. Wealthier Jews were particularly vulnerable to the temptations of conversion. One contemporary, Solomon Alami, described the devastation these measures had visited upon his fellow Jews:

And of late we have been beset by evil up and down the provinces of Castile and Catalonia in 1391, where many communities were destroyed, both small and large. And twenty-two years thereafter those that still remained in Castile were a byword and a mockery... for they were forced to change their manner of dress and to refrain from commerce, tax-farming and handicraft.... They who had abode securely in their homes were driven out from their pleasant palaces to dwell in tombs and places of concealment. O worm of Jacob! They who were brought up in scarlet now embrace dunghills! Summer and winter, all Israel's citizens shelter in tabernacles, in everlasting contempt. As for our oppressing tax-gatherers, no sooner were they deprived of farming the taxes than the majority of them left their religion, for none was master of a handicraft by which to earn his livelihood. And in the face of ruin, hardship and confinement, many artisans, too, left the fold, for when they saw the mischance and the travail they could no longer stand in the presence of vicissitude. Such, too, was the case with the remaining communities in the Kingdom of Aragon, where a new king arose to issue new decrees. Who hath heard the like! Suckling at their mothers' breasts cry for hunger and thirst and barebodied children perish in snow and frost.[36]

Fortunately for the Jews, this anti-Jewish campaign would soon end. The pope's authority had dwindled almost to nothing. The European powers, tired of dissension within the church, finally united to impose a solution to the Great Western Schism. The Council of Constance convened in November 1414, while Pope Benedict was still engaged in the Disputation of Tortosa. Sigismund, the Holy Roman emperor and king of Hungary, led the Council of Constance and had the power to ensure that its decisions were enforced. Pope John, the former Baldassare Cossa, was the first to be brought to submission. Gregory, the Roman pope, agreed to abdicate in July 1415.

Benedict, now eighty-seven years old, was the only holdout. Sigismund met him in Perpignan, but Benedict insisted on full recognition as the lawful pontiff. In a final attempt to establish his legitimacy, Benedict brought in Vincent Ferrer to speak for his cause. Even Ferrer, however, by now had enough, and he repudiated Benedict's claims. Benedict fled to the coast, where he met with King Fernando of Aragon, who owed his throne in part to Benedict's support. Through an emissary, Fernando pleaded with him to abdicate. Benedict responded: "Tell your King this from me. You send me into the wasteland, and I made you King."[37]

The Council of Constance did not wait for Benedict. On November 11, 1417, it elected a new pope, Martin V. Martin was almost universally recognized as the one legitimate pope. Benedict retreated to the castle of Peniscola near Valencia. He was formally deposed by the council. Almost all his supporters had abandoned him. One of the few who remained was his personal physician, the former Jew Joshua ha-Lorki, who as Hieronymus de Sancta Fide led the debate in Tortosa. Benedict died in 1423, at the age of ninety-five. He has now been labeled an "antipope" by the church. His name was recycled and used by another pope in 1724. King Fernando of Aragon died in April 1416. With the death of the king and the isolation of Benedict, political support for Jewish repression had largely ended.

These events sapped the authority of Pablo de Burgos. Pablo had endorsed Fernando over the claims of Queen Catalina's son. When Fernando died, Catalina removed Pablo as regent, and his political influence ended. He turned to writing and produced a polemic on Christianity and Judaism, *Scrutinium Scripturarum*. It describes the Jews as "greater criminals than the people of Sodom." He even defended Ferrand Martínez, who he said was understandably motivated by his desire to "avenge the blood of Christ," even though Pablo himself could have ended up as one of Martínez's victims.[38] Vincent Ferrer spent the last years of his life in France. He died in Brittany in 1419. He was canonized in 1455. His feast day is April 5.

The campaign against the Jews that followed the riots of 1391 had ended. Now Spain would face a more complicated problem that for a century or more would obsess the Spanish kingdoms and lead to open armed conflicts in Castile: what to do about the converts.

PART 3

The Age of the Converts

16

New Christians

The rapid creation between 1391 and approximately 1415 of a converso (convert) or "New Christian" population completely changed the social structure of Spain. Never before in Europe had so many Jews been assimilated into a Christian nation. While imperfect statistics make it impossible to accurately gauge the numbers of converts, estimates range from tens of thousands to over 600,000.[1] Some modern estimates range between 225,000 and 400,000.[2] Any of these figures constitutes a huge number of people to absorb into a new social status.

The converts quickly rose to prominence in almost all ranks of Spanish society. As Jews many had been well educated, wealthy, and highly skilled in finance and government administration. Now as Christians all social restraints that had applied to Jews were lifted. Nothing prevented them from competing as equals with other Christians. But their rapid rise to prominence put them at the center of controversy in fifteenth-century Spain. In Castile in particular, suspicion that conversos remained Jews, and as such heretics and enemies of Christianity, would fuel armed civil conflict and lead to the establishment of the Spanish Inquisition in 1480.

Convert success was particularly striking in two realms completely closed to Jews: marriage with Christians and careers in the church. While many conversos married among themselves, others were not slow to use marriage to develop political and economic alliances with the most powerful families in Spain. As early as 1449, a petition submitted to Lope de Barrientes, bishop of Cuenca, by the "Conversos of Toledo" listed all the noblest families of Spain as being of Jewish blood.[3]

As for the church, the two leading Spanish prelates in this period were converts themselves or descended from converts. The mother of

Juan de Torquemada, 1388–1468 (uncle to the future inquisitor general, Tomás de Torquemada), was probably a converso. Juan was named "Defender of the Faith," promoted to the rank of cardinal-bishop and, according to the historian Benzion Netanyahu, very nearly elected to the papacy following the death of Pius II.[4] Paul of Burgos's son, Alonso de Cartagena, 1384–1456, converted at the age of six with his father. He served as a Castilian delegate to the Council of Basel (convened to deal with the issues of papal supremacy and the Hussite heresy) and replaced his father as bishop of Burgos. He also took up important diplomatic duties on behalf of Castile. His failure to rise further may have been due to church reluctance to include a second converso in the College of Cardinals.[5]

Converso ubiquity can be measured by the number of racial epithets used to describe them. In addition to "converso" and "New Christian," they were known as *confesos, Judeochristianos,* or as worshippers of *Dio* (a singular God, instead of what was seen as the plural word *Dios* representing the Trinity, although *Dios* actually derives from the singular Latin noun, *deus*). *Marrano* may have originally derived from the Hebrew *mumar-anus,* or convert. It became a common term of insult, as well as another word for "swine."[6] Among Jews converts were called *anusim,* "forced convert," or *meshumad,* "willful converts." Jews disagreed about who fell into which category; some felt that even children of conversos raised in the church should be considered *anusim* because they had not chosen their upbringing.

Who Were the Conversos—What Did They Really Believe?

Shortly after the initial conversions, in 1391–1412, most new converts probably knew little about Christianity, and the church of the time had little interest in general in promoting education. But the conversos lived as Christians throughout the fifteenth century for several generations, and by 1480 and the reign of Ferdinand and Isabella the conversos lived outwardly like any other Christian, attending church and engaging in christenings and other church rituals.

Nonetheless, in 1480 Ferdinand and Isabella established an Inquisition with the mission to ferret out Jewish practices among the conversos, which was perceived as heresy. The persecution of conversos, the almost sole initial focus of the Spanish Inquisition, was based on the belief that many or most conversos were "secret Jews"—in other words, converts in bad faith, who continued to practice Judaism behind closed doors.

Was the Inquisition right in 1480 to suspect the conversos of crypto-Judaism? There is a large body of evidence demonstrating that Judaizing was common among the New Christians. However, most of that evidence consisted of accusations against and confessions of conversos compiled by the Inquisition itself. Traditionally historians have largely accepted this evidence at face value, although much of this evidence was obtained under compulsion or even torture.

Even Jewish historians such as Yitzak Baer have made use of the Inquisition's evidence. To Baer the accusations that the Inquisition brought against conversos illustrates the latter's heroic efforts to defend their old religious beliefs and customs in the face of threats of torture and capital punishment. "The story of the conversos is not one of racial 'remnants' which had lost their Jewish characteristics," Baer argues, "but of a large population-group, the majority of whose members adhered, consciously and by conviction, to the living Jewish tradition."[7]

More recently Benzion Netanyahu has taken the position that by the time of the Inquisition almost all the converts were "sincere Catholics." The historian Norman Roth goes further, claiming that most New Christians had willingly converted. These arguments rely in part on Jewish legal decisions, the responsas, which determined that New Christians should be considered Christians, not Jews or *anusim*, forced converts. They also point to the anti-Jewish writings of prominent conversos.

This conclusion—that conversos were, in fact, "sincere Catholics"—would eventually influence the work of Henry Kamen, the prominent authority on Spanish history, in his assessment of the Spanish Inquisition. In 1965, prior to the publication of the best-known works of Netanyahu, he concluded: "Of the thousands of Jews who in the course of the preceding century had been forced by execution and massacre to accept baptism, very few embraced Catholicism sincerely. Many, if not most, of them continued to practice the Jewish rites in secret."[8] By 1997, acknowledging the influence of Netanyahu, he had changed his views on the conversos, as reflected in his *Spanish Inquisition: A Historical Revision*: "Were thousands of converso Christians all over Spain secretly observing Jewish practice? There is, as we shall see, good reason to doubt it."[9]

Heresy or Custom and Tradition?

Leaving aside for the moment the question of the nature of the conversos' beliefs, much of the evidence collected by the Inquisition to show that conversos were secret Jews did not establish what the church would now consider as heresy. The evidence they found was related to customs and traditions that were only indirectly connected to religious faith.

It is clear that the lives of many of the Jews and New Christians remained intertwined. The forced conversions of 1391 had arbitrarily split families, households, even marriages, into two religious camps. Even several generations after the conversions of 1391, conversos still had close family and social ties to Jews. They lived in the same neighborhoods and maintained professional and business contacts with one another. As David Gitlitz, in his study of the conversos, notes: "From the earliest wave of forced conversion in 1391 until the Expulsion in 1492 Iberian conversos continued to live in close proximity to their Jewish neighbors despite sporadic attempts to formally segregate the city neighborhoods according to religion. ... In their professional lives, whether buying or selling, signing contracts or borrowing money, engaging in manufacture or collecting taxes, the two groups mingled."[10]

These social connections drew New Christians to Jewish family and social events, where religious rituals were included as a matter of course. Generations of marriage within the Jewish community meant that Jews and New Christians continued to have multiple family and social ties, and family events—births, circumcisions (or baptisms), weddings, illnesses, funerals—would continue to bring the groups together.[11]

The same blurring of the boundary between religious and nonreligious practices occurred even during overtly religious occasions, because these were generally understood to be family events. According to Gitlitz:

Major Jewish festivals sparked family gatherings; in fact prior to the coming of the Inquisition it was commonplace for new-christians to celebrate the festivals with their Jewish friends, especially the holidays whose observance involved family feasting (such as Passover and Sukkot) or communal home ritual (such as Purim). . . . Among Jews, these holidays were occasions for gathering together the extended family, which frequently included members who had converted. . . . The most common festival, of course, was the Sabbath, and the documentary record overflows with evidence of conversos who continued to celebrate it with their Jewish friends and family, often sharing their Sabbath meals.[12]

In the eyes of the Inquisition, attendance at these celebrations and rituals constituted heretical behavior, even though the motivation for attendance may only have been to respect personal and family ties.

Lack of Religious Education

The Inquisition also made accusations against conversos without accounting for the New Christians' general ignorance of Catholic doctrine. After the mass conversions, the church paid little attention to teaching the new congregation about its new religion.[13] The church's general neglect in promoting religious education resulted in many conversos being forced to follow a religion they only half understood. Complicated concepts such as the Trinity or transubstantiation were mysteries held by the clergy and not properly explained to the congregations (New or Old Christians), who were also uneducated in the prayers and ceremonies of Catholicism.[14]

The lack of Christian education provided to conversos was due, in part, to the focus of church leaders like Archbishop Carrillo on personal ambition rather than pastoral obligations. It also reflected a church policy of suppressing religious dissent by giving the church leadership a monopoly on knowledge of the faith. The church had good reason to fear religious dissent: in 1517, only a few years after the institution of the Spanish Inquisition, Martin Luther would nail his Ninety-Five Theses to the door of the Wittenberg church.

The church was already taking steps to repress dissent by church reformers. The Council of Constance, held in 1418 to heal the divisions caused by the Great Western Schism, took time out to try and condemn Jan Hus, the Czech religious reformer, to death at the stake. John Wycliffe's Bible led the Oxford Convocation of 1408 to vote that no translation of the Bible could be made again without prior approval from the church. When the Inquisition began publishing lists of prohibited books in 1547, translations of the Bible were among the first books to be banned, reflecting the church officials fear that the popular spread of knowledge of religion would loosen the church's control of doctrine and encourage the development of heretical ideas.[15]

The conversos' doctrinal ignorance was shared by the general population. As Henry Kamen notes: "In the mid-sixteenth century a friar lamented the ignorance and unbelief he had found throughout Castile, 'not only in small hamlets and villages but even in cities and populous towns.' 'Out of three hundred residents,' he affirmed, 'you will find barely thirty who know what any ordinary Christian is obliged to know.' ... It was a situation that Church leaders did very little to remedy."[16] But while both Old and New Christians were ignorant of religious doctrine, only the New Christians would be required to prove their familiarity with doctrine and the purity of their faith before an Inquisition tribunal.

Above all, the conversos clung to the rituals and traditions of Jewish life, ones that were neither reflective of Jewish religious doctrine nor antithetical to Christianity. These customs, including dietary and burial customs, were repositories of personal and familial identity and therefore extraordinarily long-lived. Customs, rather than religious doctrine, became important indicators of "heresy" for the Spanish Inquisition. The Inquisition's focus on customs over belief derived partly from practical reasons: it was much easier to obtain testimony about physical acts than to elicit confessions of private belief. But the prosecution of conversos for the practice of habits and rituals that were cultural rather than religious in nature also reflected the inquisitors' own lack of understanding of the Jewish religion.[17]

Inquisition Preconceptions

In their fanaticism various detractors of converts confused faith and custom. Some of this confusion is found in the writings of Andrés Bernáldez, a priest sympathetic to the Spanish Inquisition whose history of the reigns of Ferdinand and Isabella is one of the most important contemporary sources of the period. Bernáldez, for example, relates that some converts washed infants after baptism, implying that the converts were attempting to erase the baptismal marks, rather than washing the baby in accordance with tradition.[18]

The modern Spanish historian Joseph Pérez, describing the confusion between belief and custom at that time, states: "It is absurd to regard culinary or other indifferent cultural practices as if they were religious or claim that they indicate one faith or another. Bernáldez knew that perfectly well: 'Changing customs is like dying.' It is easier to renounce religious beliefs or philosophical or political opinions than ancestral customs learned from childhood that have become part of one's personal day-to-day lifestyle. It is important to emphasize that these were precisely the accusations Bernáldez's contemporaries frequently made against converts."[19]

The Inquisition would institute proceedings in each new town with a reading of the Edict of Faith, a list of Jewish customs that constituted heresy and had to be repented from in order to avoid condemnation. The edict became a detailed description of practices that the Inquisition considered "Jewish," many of them customs and rituals that today would not be considered contrary to church doctrine. In a list published by the Inquisition in 1624, the proscribed activities included "putting on clean personal linen" during the Jewish Sabbath, as well as one's "best or festival clothing, placing clean linen on their tables and throwing clean sheets on their bed."

Kosher food preparation techniques, or the avoidance of pork and lard, were viewed with equal suspicion. Other practices cited as evidence of heresy by the Inquisition included women waiting forty days after childbirth to go into the temple (presumably, the "temple" here meant the church, since this practice was cited after the expulsion of the Jews in 1492); putting a baby, seven days after its birth, in a basin of water into which was placed gold, silver, pearls, wheat, barley, and other things, and then washing the child in that water, saying "May you be as well supplied with the goods of this world as is this basis";

when kneading dough, taking a piece from the dough and throwing it into the fire as a sacrifice; and when some person was at the point of death, turning him toward the wall to die.[20]

Because the Inquisition focused on customs, rather than religious observance, women were accused of heresy as often—or more often—than men. In Judaism men were educated in Jewish law and were responsible for carrying on the synagogue services. Women could receive only a rudimentary Jewish education, but they were principally responsible for the home rituals essential to Jewish life. As the historian Renee Levine Malammed observes: "Time after time, there was a sense of passivity on the part of many of the men, who were often accused of 'allowing' or 'permitting' their wives to perform Jewish rites. The wives, on the other hand, were more likely accused of actively judaizing.... It is important to note here that even the prosecution was aware of the strong and unusual role of the women in crypto-Judaism."[21] Contemporary Jews who witnessed the persecution of the conversos claimed that only a few of them died as Jews, and of these most were women.[22]

The Inquisition's persecution of so many women for what were essentially long-standing habits of family life in Spain provoked the criticism of Hernando de Pulgar, personal secretary to Queen Isabella (and a converso himself): "In Andalusia there are at least ten thousand young women who have never left their parents' home. They observe the ways of their fathers and learn from them. To burn them all is an extremely cruel and difficult act and will force them to flee to places where their correction will be impossible."[23]

Inquisition methods contributed to the mistaken prosecution of conversos. Most inquisitors assumed guilt on the part of conversos. They accepted weak evidence and abused their almost unlimited authority to elicit confessions of this presumptive guilt. The historian David Gitlitz succinctly describes the biased nature of Inquisition evidence:

They tended to report the truth as they saw it, but the lenses through which they perceived their truth induced an astigmatism of bias. For most Inquisitors, Judaizing was Devil-induced heresy, pernicious and dangerous. They were predisposed to react to it emotionally and with severity. They interpreted what they saw and heard against a template of preconceptions about crypto-Judaism.... They were much less likely to write down objective observations than they were to record statements that corroborated their preconceptions.... On the whole the Inquisitors were inclined to see in the testimony more guilt rather than less. For the more serious the menace of Judaizing was, the more their own profession was justified. And the more convictions the Inquisition obtained, the greater were its confiscations of property.[24]

The Inquisition also inspired tremendous fear, which often led to false accusations and false confessions. Accused persons whose confession was deemed "incomplete" could be subject to torture, sometimes lengthy imprisonment, and might be burned at the stake. An acceptable confession had to be to all heretical acts and also had to name any others "known" to have committed heresy; omitting an act that the Inquisition would consider heresy could lead to further prosecution, prompting confessors to inflate their list of known transgressions. Because the accused was not presented with a list of charges nor allowed to know who had testified against her or him, he or she felt pressured to list any potential sins, whether committed or not, and to accuse other innocent conversos.

In summary the conversos by the middle of the fifteenth century were a mix. Some were devout Christians, including prominent figures in the church. Some were secret Jews. But many, if not most, were practicing Christians who by reason of family ties, customs, or rituals, followed some of the traditions and rituals of Jews or participated in family ceremonies with Jewish relatives associated with Jewish festivals. Because the Inquisition would associate these rituals with heresy, there is a large and biased body of evidence greatly inflating the incidence of Jewish practice among the conversos.

One of the most interesting reflections on the nature of converso identity comes from an anonymous attack on the conversos written between 1467 and the early 1480s called *El Libro del Alboraique*. The Alboraique was the mythological animal that carried Muhammad to heaven. Smaller than a horse and larger than a mule, it mixed the characteristics of different breeds, resembling nothing in nature. The book similarly states that the conversos are a mix of different characteristics, as Netanyahu describes: "In their intentions they are Jews although they 'do not keep the Talmud, nor all the ceremonies of the Jew'; nor do they treat any better Christian Law, in which they do not believe. Hence, they are neither Moors nor Jews, and Christians in name only."[25] As a vicious attack on the conversos, the book is not fair in its assessment of converso faith in Christianity, but it does reflect one apparent truth: that the conversos were a mix of Christian practice and faith with Jewish habits and customs, a unique kind of creature not seen before in nature or culture.

17

....

Converts and Castile

Juan II and Conversos

In Castile the mid-fifteenth century proved to be a critical and difficult period, both for the nation and for the "New Christian" converso community. Two weak monarchs in a row plunged the country into constant rebellion and civil warfare. At the same time, the conversos became the targets for popular resentment as a riff opened between New and Old Christians that sometimes erupted into armed warfare.

The failings of the Castilian monarchs Juan II (who reigned 1425–54) and his son Enrique IV (1454–74) contributed significantly to the unpopularity of the conversos. The Jewish habit of supporting the Crown in exchange for Crown protection carried over to the conversos. Unfortunately, for much of the fifteenth century the monarchy in Castile could not provide the political stability and support they needed to fully incorporate themselves into Spanish society. Converso success made them important allies with the kings, but this alliance also made them easy targets, scapegoats, for popular resentment against the monarchs.

This was particularly true during the reign of Juan II. Conversos became close supporters of the most powerful politician of the century, Juan II's chief minister, Álvaro de Luna (often referred to by one of his titles, "the Constable"). This alliance facilitated converso success—Luna awarded conversos with important government positions—but it also marked them as Luna's men. As Luna's numerous enemies plotted his destruction, conversos became targeted for indirect attacks on the Constable. Exploiting centuries of anti-Jewish propaganda, the ills of Castile were all blamed on distrust of the New Christians.

The troubles of these two monarchs, therefore, also impacted the conversos. Conversos become targets of popular resentment, discrimination, even mass attacks and murders. The resentment generated against the conversos in this time of political instability provided the popular support for the Spanish Inquisition, and the Inquisition in turn tirelessly and successfully lobbied for the expulsion of the Jews from Spain.

The critical role that the royal drama in Castile played on the fate of conversos and Jews in Spain is apparent when the fate of the Castilian conversos is compared with the conversos in Aragon. Aragon had a large converso population, like Castile, and its conversos had a similar success rate and close association with the Crown. Moreover, Aragon was as instable as Castile. But while Aragon conversos complained of discrimination, they never experienced the level of discrimination and resentment seen in Castile. Moreover, the Spanish Inquisition faced popular opposition when it attempted to extend the Inquisition from Castile into Aragon. The kingdoms differed mainly because conversos were not scapegoated for the failures of the Aragon Crown. None of the enormous political problems faced in Aragon—territorial conflicts in Italy, a peasant revolt, and a Catalan war of independence—could be blamed on the conversos.

While converso success and controversy place them at the center of this period, the Jews in the mid-fifteenth century also began to regroup and recover from the difficulties they had faced in the early 1400s. The large-scale conversions did not put an end to Jewish life in Spain, but Jewish life had been permanently transformed by the conversions and the more than two decades of repression, beginning with the riots of 1391. The Jewish population had declined by a third or more. Most Jews had fled the bigger cities to small towns and villages, finding shelter in more isolated and less conspicuous communities. Jews who had not converted generally continued to prosper, but in new, smaller, communities where they kept a lower public profile. The deserted old Jewish neighborhoods, *juderías* or *aljamas*, were renamed—many were called simply *barrionuevos*, or "new neighborhoods"—and repopulated by the New Christians.

As indicated earlier, the political problems facing conversos in Castile began when they allied themselves with Juan II's chief minister, Álvaro de Luna, the Constable.

Álvaro de Luna and King Juan II forged one of the closest political alliances in history. The alliance was close in a literal sense—the duties of page including sharing a bedroom, and possibly a bed, with the prince, a practice that continued on occasion even when the prince reached manhood. This was not considered unusual at the time. Some nobles complained about the practice, not because of impropriety but because they coveted Luna's access to the king.[1] Based on this constant access, from childhood Juan looked to Luna as his closest advisor— perhaps as a surrogate father—and delegated to him all the responsibilities of the Crown.

This bond led to accusations that Luna had bewitched the king. A 1440 proclamation of grievances published by the king's aristocratic enemies went further, claiming that the king had been seduced: "He has brought to your most distinguished and blameless court the filthiest of all vices, that thing most detestable to both God and nature, which has always been condemned most in Spain, especially among the people of your own realms, and whose repulsiveness is such that we cannot bring ourselves to name it."[2]

The relationship, however, can be explained without resorting to witchcraft or sexual attraction. Juan had little interest in the responsibilities of kingship. He loved jousting, music, history, and poetry. He may have been the most cultured king of Castile since Alfonso the Wise. With Luna in charge, Juan could freely delegate all responsibilities of rule. Luna was not selfless; his devotion enabled him to accumulate his own wealth and power, and he made himself the richest man in the kingdom. But his loyalty was beyond question, and he shared a common goal with the king: to centralize power in the Crown and to resist the consolidation of a powerful and demanding aristocracy.

The challenges to the task of transferring power from nobles to the king were enormous. Fifteen families controlled most of the land in Castile. These were not ancient houses. Most had obtained their power and positions as a reward for loyalty to King Enrique II in his war against his brother, Pedro the Cruel. Enrique had instituted a practice of awarding his allies with hereditary grants called *mercedes*. These grants were supplemented by subsequent kings and regents; between 1406 and

1426, *mercedes* increased by twenty million *maravedis*.[3] By the reign of Juan, they amounted to an enormous drain on the Spanish treasury. This transfer of revenue to the nobles both weakened the Crown and enriched the king's rivals, who were largely exempt from taxes.

Luna tried to deal with this problem by printing money. The inflation only weakened the economy and increased public unrest, much of which would take the form of attacks on conversos. The greatest immediate threat to the Crown came from the king's cousins. Juan's uncle Fernando, who served as his regent and became king of Aragon, had four sons. All these cousins of Juan were princes of Aragon, but they were also of Castilian origin, possessed tremendous wealth and land in Castile, and would not abandon their ambitions to dominate that land.

Juan took power on March 7, 1419. On July 12, 1420, the infante Enrique placed the king and his entourage under arrest. He used a pretext that would henceforward be used to justify all subsequent actions against the king: he was acting in the king's best interest, in order to free him from the influence of bad advisors. In particular, Enrique and his supporters cited the need to free King Juan from the influence of the Jew Abraham Benveniste. Álvaro de Luna had not yet become a figure of prominence and so was allowed to remain with the king. In the future he and his converso supporters would become the focus of all these accusations.

The king, with Luna's assistance, escaped, and while under siege managed to politically outmaneuver Enrique. After only a little over a week, Enrique was forced to relinquish his attack and restore Juan to the throne. During the following year, Luna entered into negotiations with Enrique and obtained concessions that undermined Enrique's support and led both to his arrest in 1422 and to the seizure of some of his estate. This pattern would be repeated throughout Juan's reign. The infantes continued to invade Castile. They succeeded several time in forcing Luna into exile, only to see him return with even greater power and authority. For two years Juan of Navarre ruled Castile. But the infantes could not depose Juan, and ultimately, Luna returned to his position of power as King Juan's closest adviser.

These struggles for power left Castile in a continuous state of civil war, but one with little actual fighting. Only one major battle took place, at Olmedo in 1445. There Infante Enrique was killed. Luna was granted Enrique's position as master of the Order of Santiago, a capacity in which he also presided over the order's enormous wealth. With Enrique's death the infantes' power in Castile had ended, but now Juan's son—also named Enrique—emerged as a new rival, with prompting from his advisor and Luna's new competitor, Don Juan Pacheco.

Faced with all this factional plotting, Luna staffed his government with men who owed loyalty only to himself and the king. To do this he relied to a significant degree on support from conversos. Many of these men, both New and Old Christians, were highly educated students of the law and were known as *letratos*, or men of letters. Luna's reliance on professional administrators, rather than patrons of the fifteen most powerful families, was a practice that would be continued by the "Catholic Monarchs" (Ferdinand and Isabella) and which would form the beginning of modern governance in Europe.

Fernán Díaz de Toledo was the most prominent of these *letratos*. Born to a Jewish family, he converted as a young child. He received a degree from the university at Valladolid, where he studied canon, civil, and Roman law. He became one of the period's greatest legal experts. He began service with King Juan in 1420, and within a few years he had attained multiple offices, the most important of which was *relator*, a kind of chief of staff to the king. He also served on the Royal Council and was second in office only to Luna.

Fernán Díaz was known for his honesty and probity, immune to bribery at a time when bribery was considered a normal perk of holding office. Fifteenth-century historian Alvar García notes: "[Although] he could have earned as much money as could have made ten *Escribanos de Camara* rich and opulent, he is not known to have taken a single penny; nor did he get anything for his reports on litigations, nor for any of the other matters for which people customarily earn large sums of money, even though on many occasions he was entrusted with their settlements."[4]

Although honest, Fernán Díaz did not embrace poverty. He received substantial remuneration from the Crown and arranged for important marriages and positions for his family, including his own children—both legitimate and illegitimate. He could, however, have made himself much richer. By contrast, Fernán Díaz's cousin Alfonso Álvarez de Toledo, who served as a treasury official, became immensely rich: as a modern biographer of Luna, Nicholas Round, notes, Alfonso Álvarez de Toledo owned "no fewer than 380 houses in various parts of Castile. In 1447 he had a personal income from royal sources of more than 274,000 *maravedis*; the total sum which he shared with his most immediate family came to well over 400,000."[5]

The political prominence of Fernán Díaz and the other conversos made them politically vulnerable. It set them against the grandees of Spain, who coveted their positions as sources of patronage and influence. It also set the converts up to become scapegoats for enemies of Luna. These vulnerabilities would make conversos into the principal targets during the rebellion of Toledo in 1449. Luna also revived the position of the court rabbi. Abraham Benveniste, appointed chief rabbi by King Juan, acted as chief tax collector for Castile. The infante Enrique, exploiting anti-Jewish prejudice, cited this appointment of Benveniste as one pretext for his attempted coup.

Benveniste honored his responsibilities as Castile's Jewish leader. He brought the most important Jewish leaders together in Vallodolid in 1432. There they drew up communal statutes to reform and regularize the governing of the local Jewish communities, in light of postconversion realities. In postconversion Castile all the Jewish communities were small. There were no longer leading communities that imposed their authority on neighboring localities, and these new rules helped the Jews deal with their new role in Castilian society.[6]

The Toledan Rebellion

In 1449 mobs in the city of Toledo rioted over a new tax impost. The riots grew into a citywide insurrection. This rebellion would become a major event in converso history, the first to target conversos and pit the

Old Christians against the New. Conversos became the primary victims of the rebellion as local grievances against Luna were subsumed into what would cynically be converted into a racial campaign, with conversos representing the powerful Constable. The rebels' decision to attack conversos initiated what would become a racist movement, converting a minor local incident into a watershed event. As Netanyahu has written, "it marked the opening of a drive that was to culminate in the founding of the Spanish Inquisition and emerge, through its agency, as a force that affected the course of world history."[7]

Toledo had been under the control of the López de Ayala family since 1398. In the thirty years preceding the revolt, Pero López de Ayala ran the city. He was a harsh ruler; one contemporary chronicler accused him of having "committed great outrages."[8] Ayala's biggest political error, however, was to side with the infantes of Aragon. He aligned himself on several occasions with the Aragonese prince Enrique. During the battle of Olmedo, he formally sided with the king but failed to provide the Crown with significant support. After the battle of Olmedo and the defeat of the Aragonese forces, the local administrators of Toledo appeared before the king to complain about Ayala's abuses, saying: "He expelled from Toledo many nobles (of both low and middle rank) who disagreed with his antiroyal acts, robbed many of his opponents of their possessions, and even put some of them to the torture."[9]

The victory in Olmedo gave the Crown the freedom to impose change on Toledo. Ayala was removed from office and replaced by another nobleman, Pero Sarmiento. Sarmiento had belonged to the king's court. He had held the royal office of *repostero mayor*, or majordomo, and was a member of the Royal Council. His loyalty was soon tested. Ayala turned for support to the man who was now the king's chief rival: his son, Prince Enrique. At the prince's intercession, Ayala was returned to one of his offices, the chief judge of appeals.

Sarmiento, who had until his appointment in Toledo been poorly compensated for his service, rebelled against this move.[10] He refused to allow the king's order to be published and blocked Ayala from taking office. This led to two years of negotiations with the king. Not until the end of 1448 was the matter resolved, with Ayala being removed from his post and granted a lesser position. Sarmiento was also punished for his intransigence: he was stripped of all offices except for command of the city fortress, the Alcazar. Luna took control of the rest.

The rebellion began six weeks later. On January 25, 1449, Luna visited Toledo and demanded a loan of one million *maravedis*. The loan was to be used for defense of the Crown. There was need for the money. The victory at Olmedo had left the king in debt, without having resolved the Crown's political problems. Now threats came in from all ends of Castile. Juan of Navarre began a new offensive and captured several fortresses along the northeastern border. In the south the Muslim *tarifa* of Grenada began new raids into Castile. The southern grandee Rodrigo Manrique, who coveted Luna's claim to his title (and huge purse) as leader of the Order of Santiago, aligned himself with the Muslim forces in order to expand his base in Murcia.

Luna reacted to this opposition by arresting many of the nobles who opposed him. Several important nobles, however, evaded arrest and joined the Aragonese forces. One of them, the Count of Benavente, escaped from prison and started a revolt in his castle near the Portuguese border. Luna's monetary demands, even if justified, were not popular. The council sent a delegation to Luna, rejecting his request, but he insisted on obtaining the money. The council then instructed their converso treasurer, Alonso Cota, to proceed with the collection. Only two days after Luna had made his demand of a one-million-*maravedi* loan from Toledo, the townspeople began to actively resist payment. When one artisan refused to pay his share and cried out raucously while being dragged to prison, the whole town broke into an uproar.[11] A mob gathered and set off after Cota, but he escaped. In retaliation the mob looted his houses and set them on fire.

One man emerged as leader of the rebels. Marcos García de Mora had come from local peasant stock but managed to cobble together enough education to call himself a bachelor of law. The relator described him as "a liar and infamous for his evil ways, and accused of many crimes and transgressions."[12] García de Mora became the architect of the anti-converso campaign, and in that role, he can be considered a pioneer of Spanish anti-Jewish racism. The movement against the generally wealthy conversos was also a class war, and García's peasant background fostered in him a hatred of the privileged conversos.

Alonso de Cartagena, the bishop of Burgos (and the converso son of Pablo de Burgos), attributed García's hatred of the conversos to envy:

> It doesn't surprise me that you would be eaten away with envy, especially because you descend from ignoble country people, as some say, and the scripture tells us that "envy kills those of low birth." It is nothing more than human weakness that awakens when we see people we believe our inferiors, or even our equals, gaining honors and riches when we remain in our poverty and obscurity. If Marcos is tormented this way, we must respond with understanding and compassion. However, not all is lost if he learns to moderate his ambition. But if he persists in persecuting his Catholic brothers [conversos], he will learn that he has gone beyond the limits of human zeal, and is mortally wounded by hellish envy.[13]

The mob quickly obtained control of the city gates. Now Sarmiento (who may previously have conspired with the mob leaders) met with the mob and agreed to support the revolt, on the condition that the mob recognize his authority over the city. The leaders ceded control to him, and he quickly granted himself the title that the king had withheld: chief judge of appeals.

On taking control of the city, Sarmiento announced that he was compelled to act by "the need to remove Alvaro de Luna from the Court and his other positions, of the privileges of the city which the Constable had violated, and of the need to secure the city of Toledo against further such encroachments on its rights."[14] No mention was made of the town's conversos, whose supposed misdeeds would later become the principal justification for the revolt. Enemies, or supporters of Luna, were jailed. Sarmiento suppressed the city council and other city administrators. One of the most important fifteenth-century histories, the

Chronical of the Halconero, states: "Whether out of love or out of fear, there was not a man in the city who dared utter a single word against the will of Pero Sarmiento."[15]

Possibly at the urging of García, Sarmiento soon turned on the converso community. The conversos could initially have been targeted for their alliance with Luna. Greed made wealthy conversos a tempting target: they were among the richest men in Toledo, and Sarmiento and his followers used the revolt as a pretext to confiscate their belongings.[16] Sarmiento ordered the leaders of the converso community arrested. He had them tortured until they admitted to conspiring with Luna against the city government. Those judged guilty were, in the words of a contemporary chronicler, "cut to pieces."[17] Sarmiento sent his mob out against the conversos. Some conversos resisted, but their leader, Juan de la Cibdad, was killed and hung upside down in the main city plaza. The conversos, outnumbered by the mob, ended their resistance. Arrests, banishments, and expropriations followed in rapid succession.

Up to this point, all accusations made against conversos had been purely political: they were accused of working with Luna against the interests of the city. But in order to justify the looting and appropriations of converso property, rumors and accusations were soon floated that they were also heretics—secret Jews working against the interests of the church. Sarmiento formed a commission of inquiry to investigate these religious charges. The commission concluded that most conversos were, indeed, secret Jews, and it published a list of twenty-two non-Christian practices that had been discovered. Based on this report, Sarmiento formed an Inquisition, in order to punish heretical conversos. As a matter of law, a religious Inquisition should have been established by church authorities. However, the leading cleric—the archbishop of Toledo—was away from the city, accompanying the king. In his absence, without the proper legal authority, the proceedings were approved by the cathedral's vicar, Pero Lope Galvez, an ally of García.

The tribunal began its trials. Those judged guilty—and it is likely that few, if any, were acquitted—were publicly burned. All their goods and estates were confiscated by the religious court. These proceedings were soon cut short. At the time of the rebellion, the king had been near the Portuguese border, besieging the Count of Benavente. This left the rebels free to operate without fear of reprisal. By May, however, the king and his army had set up camp only a few miles from Toledo, and the rebels now had to explain their actions to the king.

With the army approaching, Sarmiento and his ally García produced a petition to the king, justifying their actions and outlining their demands. The initial part of this petition presented a standard set of grievances against Luna. The Toledan upstarts claimed that Luna was a "tyrant" and "usurper" of the king's authority, insatiably greedy; he cut off the access of loyal grandees to the king, trampled on the rights of the cities, and imposed on the country "unjust and illegal" tributes; he stole for himself much of the revenue he collected.[18]

The petition then did something that was new and significant: it turned on the conversos. Conversos had complained of discrimination before, in both Castile and Aragon. But this was the first written attack on conversos as something like a race, the first to tie them to the centuries of prejudice against the Jews: attacking the conversos expressly because of their "lineage" as descendants of Jews and condemning them as a group for having the same hated characteristics normally found in anti-Jewish writings of the time. Netanyahu claims that "by so presenting the converso question, the Petition not only brought it into the open, but also placed it in the forefront of Spain's internal politics. In that position it was to remain for decades—and in some respects for centuries—to come; and it is this fact, and this fact alone that lends this manifesto of the Toledan rebels historical significance."[19]

According to the petition, Luna's greatest crime had been to entrust the government of Castile to converso officials. These officials, Sarmiento and García wrote, had been charged with the responsibility of protecting the subjects of the kingdom: "under the guise of doing so, and with the power of the offices entrusted to them, [they] robbed and destroyed the whole land. . . . These people have usurped, with the power of the offices, the lordship which belongs to the great of our kingdom, and have applied their powers to the possession of the Old Christians and all their estates. . . . The conversos from the lineage of the Jews . . . in their majority have been found to be infidels and heretics."[20]

The petition claimed that conversos were secret Jews, still practicing their old rites and ceremonies. The baptismal water had "touched [only] their skins, but neither their hearts nor their wills."[21] They had converted to Christianity only as part of a conspiracy to obtain power as Christians (and not, as in fact happened in most cases, to avoid being put to death by angry mobs). Their real aim was to "squeeze the souls and bodies and possessions of the Christians who are old in the Catholic faith," and that is what the conversos had "been doing and [were] doing."[22]

The petition may have been drafted by Marcos García based on his genuine detestation of conversos, but Sarmiento likely agreed to it out of political calculation. There was a precedent for political exploitation of anti-Jewish prejudice: Enrique II cynically had exploited anti-Jewish prejudice in his battle against his half brother Pedro the Cruel. Just as Enrique's campaign had paved the way for the pogroms of 1391, the new anti-converso campaign would have enormous long-term repercussions for both conversos and Jews in both Castile and Aragon.

The king ignored Sarmiento's petition entirely and lay siege to the city. Sarmiento then began to seek allies in his struggle against the king. He wrote first to Juan of Navarre. When Navarre failed to come forward with support, Sarmiento turned to the king's son, Prince Enrique, offering Enrique control of the city. Enrique's advisor, Juan Pacheco, ambitious and ruthless, encouraged Prince Enrique to oppose his royal father, while Pacheco positioned himself as a rival in power to the king's chief advisor, Luna. Enrique asked his father for permission to enter the city. The king and Luna turned him down. The prince then marched to the city with an army larger than his father's. The king retreated, and his son entered Toledo.

Sarmiento retained control of some of the city's fortifications. He obtained several concessions from the prince; these included assurances that Sarmiento could keep any property he had seized during the rebellion, and that he would not be punished for harm his orders had caused to individuals or their property. He also obtained a promise from the prince that exiled conversos should not be allowed to come back, and that those removed from office would not be returned to their posts.

Purity of Blood

Next Sarmiento took a step that was to have enormous long-term consequences: on June 5, 1449, he proclaimed a set of rules known as the Sentencia-Estatuto, effectively the first comprehensive racial exclusion laws in modern European history. They barred conversos, regardless of whether they were sincere Christians, from holding private or public office or church benefices. Conversos were also denied the right to testify in court. These restrictions applied to all conversos, unless a family could prove four generations of Christian affiliation. By discriminating against a group based on lineage as opposed to religious belief, these rules were functionally equivalent to modern racial discrimination.

The text of the Sentencia-Estatuto provided various justifications for the restrictions it imposed. It claimed that the exclusions complied with earlier decrees, some dating from the Visigoths. It cited anti-converso accusations made by the commission and tribunal established by Sarmiento to judge conversos. Some of these accusations were inconsistent with the allegation that the conversos were secret Jews. For example, conversos were accused of worshipping idols and of believing that there was both a God and a Goddess in heaven. Both concepts are contrary to Judaism, and it is logically inconsistent to accuse the conversos both of clinging to their old Jewish beliefs and, at the same time, of fundamentally violating Jewish doctrine.

The Sentencia repeated the list of converso crimes enumerated in the earlier petition issued by Sarmiento and García to the king. The conversos had conspired to control offices throughout the land, so as to control all the material goods and ruin the faithful Christians: "All the goods and honors of the fatherland are being wasted and destroyed, while they become lords in order to destroy the Holy Catholic Faith and the Old Christians who believe in it."[23]

The most pernicious aspect of the Sentencia was its introduction of racial principles into Spain. Conversos, it claimed, committed their crimes because they came from the "perverse lineage of the Jews" and thus were of a race that brought the "same harms, evils and wars which the Jews, the enemies of our Holy Catholic faith, [had] always brought, and [were] still bringing about, since the passion of our Savior Jesus Christ."[24] The four-generation stipulation in the Sentencia suggests that Sarmiento crafted it based on political calculation as opposed to racial hatred. No religious or legal precedent existed to support a bar extending back four generations. The only rational basis for this limit is mathematical: almost all conversos became Christians after the pogroms of 1391. A four-generational bar would mean that in 1449 an entire generation of Christian leaders in Toledo would have no competition from conversos.

Whether motivated by cynicism or racial hatred, the introduction of exclusion laws based on something functionally equivalent to the modern concept of "race" would have a permanent and far-reaching impact in Spain. According to the historian Netanyahu, "this was the first time in Spain that any social or political organization—let alone one that represented a great city—formally adopted a racial principle and made it the cornerstone of its policy. A new ideological current was born that was to be carried along, with occasional checks, not only by the winds of social hatred, but also by the force of governmental power. Before long, and for centuries to come, Spain's attitudes towards the Marranos were to be influenced—or even determined—by the letter and spirit of the Toledan Statute."[25]

Toledo's anti-converso campaign soon spread beyond the city. On July 7, 1449, anti-converso riots broke out in Ciudad Real. The riots lasted for at least two weeks, with widespread looting and at least twenty-two conversos killed. Most of those victims were dragged through the streets and then, following the example set in Toledo, were hanged, feet upward, in the central square.[26]

Among conversos stories of the anti-Jewish terrors a generation earlier had left deep scars, and the Toledo campaign posed a significant threat. Some of the most important conversos, including the relator Fernán Díaz de Toledo, the cardinal-bishop Juan de Torquemada, and Alonso de Cartegena, bishop of Burgos, produced learned and comprehensive rebuttals of the assumptions underlying the Toledo attack. They demonstrated that the anti-converso violence carried out in Toledo was heretical because it denied the sacrament of baptism; as Torquemada pointed out, under church doctrine, baptism removed any taint of Jewishness from converts. They pointed out that the Toledo campaign violated the universal aims of the church. Punishing conversos undermined the church's ongoing campaign to convert Jews to Christianity. Why would Jews embrace the Christian religion only to suffer as conversos?

The notion that Jews as a race were "evil" undermined Christianity, a religion founded by Jews, and one in which converts had played a major role throughout history. As Cardinal Torquemada noted, "since it had been edited by persons such as Prophets, or Apostles, or Evangelists, who were all circumcised, it clearly follows from the sayings of those individuals that Holy Scripture emanated from naturally mendacious people."[27]

These and other more extensive arguments were used to exhaustively rebut the rationale behind the Toledo campaign. Ultimately, however, these writings had only a limited effect. The anti-converso campaign was not prompted by reason and canon law. It was motivated by superstition, prejudice, and class conflict. Rationality alone could not counter centuries of religious and racial bias and propaganda. When these arguments failed, conversos tried a more practical defense: they appealed to Rome. With one of the most prominent conversos, Cardinal Torquemada, in the Vatican, they had the ear of Pope Nicolas V. Their efforts were supported by the king. The rebels sent their own delegation to Rome, but—probably because of Torquemada's influence—the pope refused to accept them.

End of the Rebellion

In the end the pope signed three bulls in support of the converso position. He openly condemned the rebels as criminals: "Many of the inhabitants [of Toledo], especially among the conversos, he [Sarmiento] robbed and arrested under manipulated charges of heresy; he laid violent hands on clerics; he expelled members of the religious orders from the city; and he committed other criminal offenses, which not only work to the detriment of the faith, but also pose a danger to the state of the kingdom and bring about the destruction of its subjects."[28]

The pope excommunicated Sarmiento and his followers. Moreover, he called on Spaniards to quash the rebellion, stating, "[If] within a month after the bull is published, they be required to do so by the King, they will proceed by force against Sarmiento and his aides, seize them and keep them imprisoned until such time as due satisfaction be made to the King and all those who suffered at their hands."[29]

Finally, he openly condemned the concept of discriminating against conversos based on their Jewish descent: "Under pain of excommunication we order each and every Christian of whatever station, rank or condition, both ecclesiastic and civil, to admit each and all of those who were converted, and those who will be converted in the future, either from gentilehood or from Judaism, or from any other sect, as well as the descendants of these converts, both lay and clerical, who live as Catholics and good Christians, to all the dignities, honors, offices, notaryships, the bearing of witness and all the other things to which are usually admitted all other Christians who are older in the faith."[30]

This was only the first reversal that the rebels faced. They were now dependent on the support of Prince Enrique. The prince had no sympathy for the rebels' program. Toledo was simply a tool in his campaign against his father, propelled by his advisor Pacheco's rivalry with Álvaro de Luna. The prince held Toledo as a pawn to be used in the several conspiracies developing against the king. Juan of Navarre planned a new attack against Castile, but it was blocked by the parliament of Aragon. The prince then met with the disgruntled nobles in Coruña and agreed to plan an attack on the king's forces. The Muslim ruler of Granada began new raids and negotiated for an alliance with Juan of Navarre. The Count of Benavente eluded the king's siege and renewed his rebellion in western Castile.[31] These multiple challenges tied the hands of the king and Luna and limited their ability to deal with the Toledo rebellion and the prince's power maneuverings.

By October 1449 all these plans had fallen apart. The nobles were either having second thoughts about the wisdom of fighting the king or fighting over how to divide the spoils. Now the king was free to focus on the issue of Toledo. The prince decided to return Toledo to the king in exchange for control of the Burgos castle.[32] When the rebels learned of the prince's plan, they were divided over how to respond. Marcos García and his allies decided that they would attempt to make a separate peace with the king. Sarmiento refused, preferring to keep his alliance with the prince. When the prince learned of Marcos García's plan, he returned to Toledo. Calling the notables of the city together, he insisted that the people of the town capture Marcos García and all the rebels who had retreated to the tower of the cathedral. A mob surrounded the church. García was drawn and quartered. Pero Lope Galvez, vicar of the cathedral, who had authorized the Inquisition tribunal, was held for trial. Sarmiento attempted to escape capture by retreating to the Alcazar, the city fortress of Toledo. The prince negotiated for his surrender. He granted Sarmiento safe conduct and allowed him to keep his property but exiled him from the city. Sometime in the middle of February 1450, Sarmiento fled at night with his family. The rebellion had ended.

Unfortunately, the end of the rebellion did not bring conversos relief. The prince reestablished a government made up of Old Christian notables. The new city council demanded a royal pardon for the hundreds of people involved in the acts against conversos. Council members resisted the idea of allowing exiled conversos to return, and they continued to support the Sentencia-Estatuto ban on converso participation in public office. The prince's interest in Toledo had been nothing more than a bargaining chip with which to obtain control of the Burgos castle from his father. He let the council operate without interference.

The king initially took a stern position against the rebel leaders in Toledo. He republished the papal bulls that had condemned Sarmiento and the discriminatory anti-converso laws, along with an order demanding the annulment of all anti-converso policies. He also sought out fugitive rebels; those caught were executed. The recalcitrance of the Old Christian town council, which continued to resist returning power to their New Christian rivals and oppose any punishment for the rebellion, brought a more conciliatory approach from the king, and from Luna. Luna's goal was to gain control of the city; for that, he would need the council's support. At the king's request, the pope suspended the papal bull against the persecutors of conversos. The real negotiations, however, took place not between the king and the council of

Toledo but between the king and his son, the prince. Luna likely made significant concessions to the Old Christians of Toledo in order to win their renewed acceptance of the king's authority.

Ten days before he was to reenter the city, the king presented a letter of pardon to the townspeople of Toledo. It forgave them for all the errors they had committed during the rebellion. The letter enumerated some of these crimes but ignored the worst offenses: crimes committed against the conversos.

The prince's concession of Toledo to the king on March 30, 1451, left Luna in complete control of the city. Although the rebellion had begun based on resistance to Luna, and the town conversos were initially attacked as Luna supporters, once in charge of Toledo Luna took no action to assist his converso allies. On November 20, 1451, Pope Nicholas V nullified his previous bulls supporting conversos and condemning the rebels—probably at Luna's urging. Worse, on the very same day the pope issued a bull calling for a general Inquisition to investigate all the conversos in Castile—including high-ranking clerics—for heresy and Judaizing. This bull, if published, would have vindicated the rebel's claim that all conversos could be secret Jews and heretics. But the bull was suppressed—probably at the insistence of converso leaders.

To conversos Luna's actions in Toledo constituted an enormous betrayal. Luna seemed to be responsible for their troubles, since the initial motivation for the rebellion in Toledo was opposition to Luna. Conversos had at first only been targeted because of their association with, and loyalty to, the Constable. For thirty years converso *letratos* in Toledo had risked their positions out of loyalty to Luna. He owed them an enormous debt. During the periods of Luna's exile, converso *letratos* had kept the lines of communication between the exiled Constable and the king open, leading more than once to Luna's return to power.

For all these reasons, Luna's acceptance of Toledo's anti-converso policies was worse than a personal betrayal. The acceptance of these policies by the chief advisor to the king marked them with royal approval and helped to spread hateful policies throughout Castile. With few exceptions the converso *letratos* of Toledo would now abandon Luna and work to engineer his downfall.

The Fall of Álvaro de Luna

Luna could afford to lose the support of the conversos. He could afford to antagonize the "fifteen families"—the most powerful nobles in Castile—even if that led, in 1453, to a series of unsuccessful attempts to assassinate him. The one thing he could not afford to lose was the support of the king. When King Juan did finally abandon him, Luna would lose his power, his liberty, and his life.

There is no consensus on why, after thirty years, the king turned against his chief advisor. Several important factors contributed to the crumbling of the relationship. The first was the king's marriage to Isabel of Portugal. Luna had arranged it himself; Juan preferred a French princess, but Luna wanted to establish stronger ties with Portugal, to counter the threat from Aragon. Luna's matchmaking proved too successful. The king was smitten with his new queen. Luna resented this challenge to his special access to the king. One chronicler, Pérez de Guzmán, claimed that Luna tried to keep the king from becoming too intimate with his wife: "nor did he let him spend time with the second queen, his wife, or have intercourse with her when he wished."[33] A former servant of the relator, Fernán Díaz de Toledo, said his master once returned shocked after witnessing an argument between Luna and the queen over her arrival at court without Luna's permission. It was also claimed that Luna once pulled the royal couple out of bed after they had slept together without his permission, saying: "I married you, and I'll unmarry you."[34]

The king also complained about the domestic economies that Luna imposed on him. Luna had reasons to be frugal, foremost among them his serious mismanagement of the economy. Luna had failed to stem the flood of grants and other privileges to nobles, which had stripped the state of much of its revenue. Luna's solution—printing money—had only devalued what revenue the state had been able to keep.

Luna's material success also made him vulnerable. His enormous estate, if it reverted to the Crown, would have provided immediate relief to the king, who himself was chronically short of money. In fact, property eventually confiscated from Luna's estate amounted to two years' worth of revenue for Castile.[35] More than greed and ambition motivated Luna's constant attempts at self-enrichment. He knew that his power depended entirely on the favor (and health) of the king, and he had set out to build up his empire as insurance against loss of the king's support.

One major mistake by Luna was pivotal in bringing about his demise. One of his men discovered papers, carried by a servant to the Crown treasurer, Alonso Pérez, that demonstrated that Pérez was conspiring against Luna with a grandee, Álvaro de Estúñiga. Luna's relations with the king were already difficult, and he therefore felt he could not afford to have the treasurer remain at court as his enemy. The constable arranged to meet with Alonso Pérez in Luna's lodging in Burgos. By loosening a railing of the tower, he arranged for Pérez to be thrown over the edge, in what would be made to seem an accidental death. Luna's son-in-law bashed in Pérez's head with a mace, and the body was thrown off the tower.

Witnesses already present at the scene could attest that the death had been no accident. As one modern biographer relates, "even as it fell, the brains had bespattered an esquire who was watering his mule in the river at the foot of the tower; it was no longer a secret that the victim was dead already."[36]

One week after the murder, Luna was arrested, imprisoned in a wooden cage with his feet chained together, and taken to Valladolid. The relator provided the legal precedent for annulling royal securities previously granted to Luna. Juan II convened a commission of twelve *letrados*, many of them conversos, headed by the relator, to determine Luna's fate. They condemned him to beheading; the severed head would be placed on public display. Luna faced his execution with fortitude. His biographer Nicolas Round has described the scene:

> He prayed on the scaffold before the cross, and asked those present for their prayers. He walked to and fro about the platform, discussing with his executioner the sharpness of the knife and the purpose of that ominous hook. He received with studied coolness the news that it was for his own head. Just as coolly, he bound his own hands with a light cord, and arranged his clothes so that

they should not impede the fatal stroke. Then the executioner begged his forgiveness and passed the knife across his throat. The head was taken off and impaled; it was to remain on display for nine days.[37]

Juan II would have little opportunity to demonstrate that he was capable of independent leadership. He died less than a year later.

Before his death the king managed at least one important act: he restored the rights of conversos in Toledo. His will specifically mentioned the need to assist the conversos who had suffered from the Toledo rebellion: "Because certain Toledan citizens and residents were banished from Toledo during the time when the city was seized by Sarmiento, and because later I wanted to provide for the expelled the remedy of justice, I have restored them to their offices and possessions, and ordered that they be welcomed and received and well treated in Toledo, understanding that this would be necessary for the service of God and myself and for the discharge of my conscience."[38]

Some ascribe Juan's death to guilt over his part in Álvaro de Luna's execution. But the king had long been frail, and before he died, he had suffered from a series of illnesses. There were far more likely causes of death at the time than heartbreak.

Enrique IV and Conversos

Juan II died on July 20, 1454. His twenty-nine-year-old son, Enrique, was proclaimed king of Castile the following day. Life under the new regime would become even more difficult for the conversos. After some initial success, Enrique faced continual revolts against his rule. Without a strong central government to protect and support them, conversos were vulnerable to the same kind of scapegoating that had begun under Enrique's father, Juan II. Conflicts between Old Christians and conversos intensified, culminating in small-scale open warfare in Castilian towns between Old and New Christians.

Enrique's reign proved, if anything, more disorderly and violent than that of his father. He inherited his father's problems: a nobility whose insatiable demands drained the treasury, continually challenging the king's authority, and neighboring kingdoms with personal claims to Enrique's throne. But the primary cause for the ruin of his reign came from another direction: the treachery and personal ambition of his chief advisor, Don Juan Pacheco.

Although Pacheco rose to a similar level of power and authority as Juan II's confidant before him, Álvaro de Luna, Pacheco and Luna differed in one crucial respect: Luna never wavered in his personal loyalty to the monarch. Every action he took, no matter how misguided, could be rationalized as a means to increase his king's authority. Pacheco, in contrast, had only one goal: to increase his own—and his family's—power and wealth. To this end he betrayed everyone and everything: the nobles who supported him, whom he undermined again and again; his country, which he plunged into a senseless civil war; and Jews and conversos, who were exposed to deadly perils so that Pacheco might achieve minor political gains. As the contemporary converso chronicler Fernando de Pulgar has noted: "The Marquis of Villena [Pacheco] always tries to keep the two kings in a circle of Grandees, each friendly to the other and, putting a foot on the shoulder of both of them, pisses on all of us around."[39]

Most of all Pacheco betrayed the man who had brought him to power, King Enrique. He conspired against the king repeatedly, threatening to topple his regime. In so doing he permanently marred the king's reputation, creating the label by which he is still known: Enrique the Impotent. Much of the widespread civil disorder that Pacheco helped foment would be directed against the conversos.

The king bore some responsibility for Pacheco's success in undermining his royal power and authority in Castile. Enrique understood what was happening around him but failed to exploit many opportunities to crush his opponents. He was neither weak nor cowardly—he showed personal courage both in battle against Granada and in the civil conflicts forced on him by his domestic rivals. But Enrique was temperamentally adverse to rigor and severity. According to Pulgar he was "so humane, that only with difficulty did he have justice carried out on criminals."[40] The chaos that resulted from Enrique's clemency proved especially deadly to the conversos of his kingdom.

Pacheco is often described in histories as a converso. The rumors of Pacheco's Jewish ancestry came from a sixteenth-century book by Cardinal Francisco de Mendoza y Bobadilla. It claimed that a fourteenth-century ancestor of Pacheco's had married a descendent of Ruy Capon, a converso tax collector. This story has been discredited by some scholars.[41] If Pacheco was descended from conversos, the fact had no apparent influence on his career. Pacheco considered himself to be an Old Christian through and through.[42] He allied himself with conversos only when it benefited him to do so. When it was to his advantage to exploit anti-Jewish fanaticism and attack the converso community, he did not hesitate to do so, regardless of the costs in property and blood.

Pacheco gained recognition as the prince's *privado*, or favorite. When Pacheco was about ten years old, Luna picked him to serve the five-year-old prince. He would lead the prince into rebellion against his father, the king. As one of Pacheco's biographers has written, by the time of the battle of Olmedo, "it became clear that there were now two bases of power in Castile: on one side stood Juan II and his favorite Don Alvaro, and on the other the opposition party headed by the Prince of Asturias and the new Marquis of Villena [Pacheco]."[43]

Enrique obtained the crown of Castile in 1454 He was a nonconformist king. He disliked courtly ceremony and avoided baths and perfumes. Intelligent, he preferred, just as his father had, the entertainment provided by music and hunting over the more tedious duties of his kingship, but unlike his father, he endeavored to fulfill his royal obligations. For about ten years, Enrique was successful. The chronicler Pulgar, in his *Claros varones*, distinguishes between the first ten years of Enrique's reign, when he enjoyed "great obedience" from his nobles—and might even have conquered Aragon and Navarre—and the "adverse fortune" of his last decade.[44] The change from one decade to the next was due to Pacheco. In the first ten years, Pacheco's interests coincided with the king's. After that Pacheco entered into a series of conspiracies against the Crown that led to civil war and which would destroy Enrique's reputation.

Pacheco's break with the king began in 1462. Pacheco urged the king to use Louis XI of France as arbiter of a dispute between Enrique and King Juan II of Aragon. Enrique had been invited to head the government of Catalonia, in rebellion against Aragon. The French king quashed Enrique's ambitions to rule Catalonia in exchange for territorial concessions that were never realized. Pacheco's price for selling out his king was the marriage of his second son to the king's illegitimate daughter—a marriage that included a French title and a payoff of twelve thousand crowns a year.

Pacheco also undermined the king—and laid the foundation for civil war—upon the birth of the king's heir. Enrique's first marriage had been annulled because of the queen's infertility. Then in 1455 Enrique married the fifteen-year-old Juana, daughter of the Portuguese king. In 1462 she gave birth to the infante Juana. After the birth Enrique called a meeting of the parliament to have its members swear formal allegiance to the princess. Enrique declared that, in the absence of male heirs, Juana would inherit the throne.

Like the evil stepmother who places a curse on a fairy-tale christening, Pacheco signed a document that day claiming that his oath of loyalty to Enrique had been made under duress, out of fear of the king. He then floated rumors that Juana was illegitimate. Pacheco was responsible for the labels that would be attached to the king and to his daughter: Enrique became known as El Impotente, and Juana as La Beltraneja, because of allegations that she was the daughter of Pacheco's main rival at court, Beltrán de la Cueva. Most historians now accept Juana's legitimacy, but historians under the reign of the Catholic Monarchs supported this slander, since Queen Isabella's claim to the throne as Enrique's half sister depended on the illegitimacy of her niece Juana, who otherwise would have inherited the throne.

Pacheco soon, along with his brother and the archbishop of Toledo, organized and led a group of nobles disgruntled with the king. Together in September 1464 they published a list of complaints against the king. Their goal was to set up the king's younger half brother, Alfonso, as an eleven-year-old boy-king, under their collective control. The allegations of illegitimacy that Pacheco had made against Enrique's daughter and heir formed the basis for Alfonso's claim to the throne. The conspirators wanted not only a guarantee of succession but the effective power of the throne.

Several royal advisors urged the king to fight these demands. Instead, Enrique offered concessions to win back Pacheco's loyalty. He transferred the Order of Santiago from Beltrán to Pacheco and disinherited his daughter in favor of Pacheco's candidate, Alfonso. Pacheco and his allies were only emboldened by this move. They published a document called the *Sentencia de Medina*, listing new demands, which would result in a transfer of power from the king to the rebels. It also called for extremely repressive measures against both conversos and Jews—probably a cynical move intended to court popular favor.

At first Enrique was willing to accede to the demands of the *Sentencia*, and a committee of arbitration formed to set up new rules of governance. But the king balked at the committee's recommendations, which would effectively have removed him from power. Finally, he resisted by confiscating Pacheco's estate, demanding custody of his half brother—now also his chief rival—and planning an attack on the rebels.

On June 5, 1465, in a ceremony that would come to be known as the "farce of Ávila," the rebel league enacted a strange ritual overthrow of King Enrique, possibly motivated by Archbishop Carrillo's belief in magic and alchemy. As described by the historian H. C. Lea in his classic history of the Spanish Inquisition:

In the Deposition of Ávila, in 1465, they treated Henry IV [Enrique IV] with the bitterest contempt. His effigy, clad in mourning and adorned with the royal insignia, was placed upon a throne and four articles of accusation were read. For the first he was pronounced unworthy of the kingly station, when Alonso Carrillo, Archbishop of Toledo, removed the crown; for the second he was deprived of the administration of justice, when Álvaro de Zuñiga, Count of Plasencia, took away the sword; for the third he was deprived of the government, when Rodrigo Pimentel, Count of Benavente, struck the sceptre away; for the fourth he was sentenced to lose the throne, when Diego, López de Zuñiga tumbled the image from its seat with an indecent gibe.[45]

The "indecent gibe" thrown at the king's effigy was *a tierra, puto*, or "eat dirt, faggot." A chronicler noted that after the farce of Ávila, the witnessing crowd was ashamed at the base treatment of the king: "The people who looked on groaned and wept.... most of the people of Castile and Leon were as if astounded, marveling at what had occurred in the city of Ávila."[46]

Civil unrest marred the rest of Enrique's reign. The discontented grandees demanded more privilege and power, although the grants that they had already received had drained the Castilian treasury. Pacheco stoked their discontent, then used the resistance that he encouraged to gain personal concessions from the king, forcing the king to restore his old place of power. To Pacheco it made little difference whether he served the king, the boy-prince, or their sister, the future Queen Isabella, as long as he held the reins of power. Pacheco succeeded because he could manipulate the grandees, and because Enrique always chose negotiation and concessions over confrontation and violence. In the end the only one who benefited from civil disorder was Pacheco.

Soon Pacheco plotted to tie his family to the throne. He offered Enrique a truce in exchange for further concessions, including the marriage of Enrique's fourteen-year-old sister (and future queen of Castile) Isabella to Pacheco's brother, Pedro Giron. Enrique accepted, but Giron died before he could claim his bride. Still seeking royal connections, Pacheco now looked to Aragon. This time he obtained a match between his own daughter Beatriz and Aragon's Prince Ferdinand (future coruler of Spain, with Castile's Isabella). But again he was foiled, as Aragon's King Pedro decided instead to unite his son with Isabella.

The death of Prince Alfonso in 1468, at the age of fourteen, gave the rebels pause. The stated cause of death was plague. Alfonso had been in Pacheco's custody at the time, and some historians—both contemporary and modern—believe either that he was poisoned by Pacheco or was exposed to the plague deliberately. With the prince out of the way, Pacheco—whose treachery had alienated many of his former allies—could more easily effect a rapprochement with the king.

Enrique's settlement with the rebels made Isabella, Alfonso's sister—and the king's half sister—heir to the throne, in exchange for recognition of Enrique's sovereignty. For the duration of the year that Enrique spent negotiating his agreement with the rebels, Enrique's wife, the queen, was held hostage by the archbishop of Seville. During this period she had an affair with the archbishop's nephew and gave birth to an illegitimate child—an indiscretion that made it easier for Enrique to believe allegations of his daughter Juana's illegitimacy and to disinherit his only child.

Pacheco died a few years later, in 1474, of a throat ailment. Enrique survived him by only a few months. The conflict sown by Pacheco in the end benefited only his heirs. Pacheco failed to achieve his lifelong goal of controlling the Crown, but his titles and property were passed on to his descendants: by the beginning of the twentieth century, most of Spain's noble houses were descended from his first title, Marquis of Villena.[47] Castile paid a price for his family's success, and no one suffered more than the conversos.

Converts and Jews

Things started off well for the conversos under Enrique. He continued his father's reliance on *letratos* in the government. Fernán Díaz de Toledo stayed on as relator. Although Díaz de Toledo died a few years later, other new appointments kept conversos in the most important government positions, including treasurer, chancellor, and personal secretary to the king.

The initial threat to both conversos and Jews came from Fray Alonso de Espina. A popular preacher, like Vincent Ferrer before him, he sermonized around the country against Jews and conversos. His campaign supported a movement to expel Jews from various towns and to confiscate their property, including synagogues and cemeteries. This campaign prompted the king in reaction in 1455 to warn local authorities that Jews were under the king's protection. Anti-Jewish feelings led to a blood-libel accusation in Sepulveda in 1469 that resulted in eight executions. Anti-Jewish riots followed in which more Jews were killed, and the rest forced to flee the town.[48]

Espina, Enrique's personal confessor, actively lobbied the king to take strong measures against the Jews and conversos. He called for an Inquisition, along the lines of the movement that had eliminated the Albigensian heresy. In making this proposal to Enrique, he enlisted the support of his fellow Franciscans. Espina also tried to get support from a new popular order in Spain, the Jeronymites.

The leader of the Jeronymite order, Alonso de Oropesa, took up the idea and lobbied the king. Oropesa, however, had a different view of an Inquisition's function. He believed that an Inquisition established with royal support could reconcile the conflicts between New Christians and Old, and he obtained the king's endorsement for this plan. Archbishop Carrillo of Toledo authorized Oropesa to open an investigation in that city. It was completed in May 1462, after eight months of proceedings.

Oropesa, himself an Old Christian, concluded that the main cause of the problems in Toledo had been Old Christian jealousy of New Christians. He said in regard to the Toledo rebels, "These men are moved by the anxiety of avarice or by vainglory, or, which is certain, by their actual interests."[49] The errors of New Christians, he said, were the result either of deficiencies in instruction or misunderstandings of church doctrine and could therefore effectively be addressed by discussion and education. Very few had committed crimes or errors requiring punishment. He characterized the accusations that the conversos were by and large "apostates, feigned Christians and secret Jews" as "imputing the false under the appearance of truth."[50]

Oropesa condemned the New Christians who oppressed and falsely accused conversos. "We have to destroy these pestiferous beasts and cut off their heads, because only then will those who dwell in the prairies of the Christian faith and the woodlands of its ministries sleep in security. For only then will calm down the riots, will end the oppressions, will disappear the errors, the rugged shall be made level and the rough shall become plain."[51]

In Toledo Oropesa's work did temporarily calm the conflict, which flared up again five years later. The pope authorized the king at Enrique's request (made before Oropesa had finished his investigation) to establish an Inquisition throughout Castile. Oropesa pressed for an Inquisition to be established like the one established in Toledo, which might have avoided the repression of the later Inquisition. The king, however, took no further action. Espina continued to campaign for a "true" Inquisition, saying that if "there were made in our time a true Inquisition, countless numbers would have been delivered to the flames of those who would have been found to have really Judaized."[52]

Soon anti-converso riots would flare up throughout Castile, principally in the south. Anti-converso fervor brought on rioting in Carmona, a town northeast of Seville, in 1462. Rioters were incited and protected by the town's governor, Beltrán de Pareja. Although the rioters killed conversos and looted their homes, Beltrán, as brother of the king's favorite, Beltrán de la Cueva, was shielded from punishment. Espina defended the riots, arguing that they were caused by the peoples' impatience with converso crimes and heresy.[53]

Pacheco played an important role in the anti-converso unrest that would envelop Castile. Pacheco and the rebels adopted and exploited anti-converso passions to gain support for their attacks on the king. After the initial rebellion that Pacheco led against the king in 1465, a report put out by the committee established to arbitrate the conflict between the king and the rebels—a committee almost completely controlled by rebel sympathizers—adopted Espina's position on Jews and converts. For Jews it would have reestablished the draconian laws of Catalina, completely separating Christians and Jews. But the recommendation went even further than the earlier law, applying not only to Jews but also to Moors and increasing the penalty for violations.

The report called for an Inquisition, which, as the rebels saw it, should be established to incarcerate and punish the "many bad Christians" responsible for "great evils and harms to the Christian religion."[54] It would confiscate the property of these heretics to finance fighting against the Moors.[55] Only cynical political considerations underlay the draconian measures that the rebels proposed against Jews and converts. Nor would this be the last time that Pacheco exploited anti-converso sentiment to advance his political ambitions.

The conflict between Old and New Christians in Toledo in the riots of 1449 flared up again in 1467, becoming an armed struggle between the conversos and Old Christians. The initial cause of the fight was another tax collection dispute, but underlying it was a political conflict: The Old Christians' leader was Fernán Pérez de Ayala. His family had ruled Toledo until supplanted by Pero Sarmiento. He sought to reestablish his family's power. His rival, Alvar Gomez de Cibdad Real, a converso, was the chief magistrate of the city.

The dispute erupted into violence in the cathedral during Sunday mass. The church's treasurer and the chaplain, both involved in the tax dispute, received mortal wounds. This time the conversos were prepared for trouble. They recruited a military force of several thousand men, led by Fernando de la Torre, whose house served as an arsenal. Ayala mobilized the Old Christians for an attack: they assembled men from both the city and outlying areas and fortified the cathedral. The conversos attacked first, using artillery to break down the gates of the cathedral, and setting fire to other buildings in the vicinity. The battle lasted two days, after which the conversos returned to their homes.

The Old Christians retaliated by setting fire to converso homes. The wind cooperated, spreading the fires to create a conflagration that destroyed houses along eight streets, encompassing the most heavily populated converso neighborhoods. Fighting continued, with the conversos now trying to save their homes, at the same time warding off New Christian attacks. One converso leader, a lawyer named Alfonso Franco, was captured while attempting a counterattack. The fire lasted two more days, destroying sixteen hundred converso homes. Looters made off with whatever the fire spared. Over 150 conversos were killed. The survivors took shelter with sympathetic nobles, churchmen, and other Old Christians.[56]

Pero López de Ayala now had effective control of Toledo, and he began to take revenge on the conversos. Fernando de la Torre, caught in the Church of Santa Leocadia when he was trying to flee the city, was hanged, feet up, from the beams of the church's bell tower. His brother Alvaro de la Torre, the *regidor*, was caught a day earlier and similarly executed. Both corpses were carried to the city's central square of Zodocover, accompanied by a large crowd and a town crier proclaiming: "This is the justice which the community of Toledo ordered to be done to these traitors, captains of the heretical conversos, because they were against the Church. It ordered to have them hanged with feet up and head down. He who thus acts, thus pays." They hung there, feet up and head down, for four days, as Old Christian passersby mutilated the corpses. They were finally turned into shapeless bulbs of flesh, emitting an unbearable stench. The city then ordered the Jewish community to remove them from the gallows and bury them. They were interred near the Jewish cemetery.[57]

Pacheco, the archbishop of Toledo, and Prince Alfonso all pleaded for clemency for the captured lawyer, Alfonso Franco. He was executed. The other conversos obtained leave to take their possessions and flee the city. The Toledans then restored the Sentencia-Estatuto, barring conversos from city offices. A delegation of Toledans went to Prince Alfonso asking for approval of the anti-converso laws, as well as pardons for any acts they had committed during the riots. The prince rejected the delegation's request: "Let them do what they want. It is enough that matters are in such bad shape that they can pass the evil acts under dissimulation, but it would be dishonorable and shameful for me to confirm abominable and abhorred deeds."[58]

Toledan Old Christian representatives later approached King Enrique. In order to reestablish his sovereignty over the city, he issued the requested pardon and recognized their rights to all confiscated converso offices and properties. This earned him welcome into the city, where he signed a form banning conversos from office and granting Pero López de Ayala control of the city. Three years later, however, with Prince Alfonso dead and Enrique firmly in control of the state, he would reverse his stance, ordering that conversos be returned to office.

Six years after these riots in Toledo, anti-converso rioting fanned out across southern Castile. The violence began in Córdoba. There conversos had forged a close relationship with the leading nobleman, Alonso de Aguilar. They had also aroused the jealousy of the bishop of Córdoba, described by one chronicler as "more inclined toward avarice than toward religion, and it was said that, forgetting his own lewdness and infamous corruption, he devoted himself to engineer harmful enmities."[59]

Reportedly, Pacheco got involved, too, seeing an opportunity to create discord and gain more allies in Córdoba. The anti-converso forces supported by Pacheco formed a confraternity called the "Brotherhood of Charity" that banned conversos from membership. Another chronicler called them "a conspiracy in the city, under the color of devotion."[60] The Brotherhood arranged weekly religious processions through converso neighborhoods, looking for opportunities to provoke trouble.

They found their opening on March 16, 1473. During Lent a procession carried an effigy of the Virgin through a converso neighborhood. A young girl from a converso household reportedly threw a liquid on the procession. Alonso Rodriguez, a blacksmith known for his hatred of conversos, claimed that the girl had thrown urine on the sacred image. He yelled out: "Let us go and avenge the offense to the faith from these reprobated enemies of the faith and of charity."[61]

A crowd had begun setting fire to converso houses when a gentleman tried to stop them. When the blacksmith Rodriguez and his followers attacked the man, other Old Christians came to the protester's aid. A fight broke out, with both Old and New Christians opposing the blacksmith's mob. Rodriguez fled, seeking refuge with his supporters in the Church of San Francisco. Hearing of the incident, Alfonso de Aguilar rode out to the church and demanded to speak with the blacksmith. Rodriquez only insulted him. Incensed, Aguilar struck him with a lance. The blacksmith was carried home with a mortal wound. His supporters rallied once again, erupting in riot against the converso community. They vowed to avenge his death.

Don Alfonso de Aguilar tried to stop the looting. Overwhelmed by the mob, he was forced to retreat. Rural workers and peasants from outside Córdoba joined the rioters in the city. Conversos resisted for two days without assistance from Aguilar, but their defenses finally collapsed, and a massacre ensued. According to a contemporary account: "There was not a cruelty in the world that was not exhibited on those occasions. Maidens and matrons were not only violated ... [but] made to suffer a horrible death."[62] The fact that the mob focused on the commercial district of Córdoba suggests that their main motivation was greed, not religious fervor. The cathedral chapter later referred to the riots as "the robbery of the conversos which was carried out in the city."[63] Aguilar spent the three days of rioting sheltered in his fortress, protecting only those conversos who were able to join him. After the riots Aguilar supported the city council's decision to exile all New Christians, as well as to institute a ban on converts holding office in Córdoba.

Anti-converso riots soon spread to the southern towns of Montor, Adamuz, Bujalance, La Ramble, and Santaella. In a few towns, such as Jerez, Baeza, and Écija, conversos were saved by the interventions of nobles. In Calatrava peasants found guilty of killing conversos were hanged by Pacheco's nephew, Rodrigo Giron.

Noble protection could not always save the conversos. In Jaén the Old Christian noble Don Miguel Lucas de Iranzo, a former favorite of King Enrique, was assassinated by anti-converso forces after he made it clear that he would protect the converso community He was shot with a crossbow while praying in church, and his body was then mutilated with swords and lances. Once Don Miguel was dead, a mob massacred the conversos and pillaged their homes. Refugees from Córdoba fled first to Palma del Rio and then to Seville. At that time Seville was in the grip of a famine. Complaints that conversos should not be welcomed—given the town's scarce food stores—prompted the leading noble, the Duke of Medina Sedona, to send the refugees back to Palma. There they were attacked and robbed of their possessions. Sixty conversos were killed.

Seville remained tense. Conversos mobilized a small army to defend against an attack. Anti-converso agitators began accusing conversos of heretical acts. According to the chronicler Alonso de Palencia, the real motive of the agitators was greed: "Surely there were some conversos at the time who were attached to such superstitious practices; but the intention of the accusers was manifest; they wanted the sack and the shedding of blood, following the example of what happened in Cordoba."[64]

A fight between a young converso and an Old Christian provided the pretext for mob violence. A crowd started looting the quarter where all the apothecaries were located. The conversos, supported by nobles and other Old Christians, managed to quell the riots. The precautions taken by the conversos in their defense proved successful, and Seville remained peaceful thereafter.

The chronicler Palencia claimed that it was Pacheco who promoted the riots of Andalusia, hoping that the general unrest would give him an opportunity to gain control of the southern cities. There is little evidence of what action—if any—Pacheco took there. His role in the unrest in Segovia, however, is clear. King Enrique had entrusted Andrés Cabrera, a converso, with control of Segovia's fortress, which still held the king's treasury. Cabrera had been a rebel but now was aligned with the Princess Isabella. Pacheco asked the king to transfer control of the fortress to him, but the king delayed in answering. Pacheco then conspired with several local nobles, including Diego de Tapia, to set off anti-converso riots as a smoke screen, thereby allowing them to capture the fortress. The plot, however, was leaked to the papal legate, who informed the king. The king passed the information on to Cabrera, giving him several days' notice to prepare a defense of the fortress, with help from both Old and New Christians. The attackers were defeated, and Diego de Tapia killed.

Soon after this incident, both Pacheco and King Enrique died. Conflicts in Castile now were focused on succession. Throughout the civil war politicians had exploited the anti-converso propaganda of Espina and other friars, using long-standing anti-Jewish prejudice to obtain narrow political gain. While the unrest they had spread throughout southern Spain momentarily halted with the end of the civil war, the prejudice that this propaganda and civil unrest had ignited would soon provide popular support for the establishment of what would come to be known as the Spanish Inquisition.

18

Anti- and Pro-Converso Writings

Anti-Converso: The Tale of the Two Tents

The final act of mercy that Juan II granted to Álvaro de Luna was to obtain as his last confessor the Franciscan friar Alonso de Espina, the best known preacher of his day. Espina had another distinction: he was to become the leading anti-Jewish, anti-converso speaker and propagandist. His writings, his claim that conversos were secret Jews and heretics, and his call to establish an Inquisition to investigate conversos would play a significant part in the establishment of the Spanish Inquisition.

Espina belonged to the Observant branch of the Franciscan order, and he would eventually become the leader of the Spanish branch. The Observants were the most militantly anti-Jewish branch of the order. One Observant, Giovanni da Capistrano, ordered forty-one Jews to be burned at the stake in Breslau in 1454 over accusations that they had desecrated the host. Another, Bernardino da Feltre, advocated a blood-libel prosecution that resulted in fourteen executions.[1] Espina became confessor to Juan II's son, Enrique IV, who succeeded his father as king of Castile. He actively campaigned for an Inquisition to be formed to investigate Jewish practices among the conversos, openly citing as a model the illegal Inquisition formed in Toledo.

Espina's best known work was the *Fortalitium Fidei*, or *Fortress of Faith*, completed in the 1460s. Ostensibly a defense of Catholicism, which Espina considered under attack by Jews, heretics, Saracens, and demons, it contained the largest collection of anti-Jewish lore and libel ever assembled. The book proved extremely popular, appearing in multiple editions, mostly outside Spain. It was particularly popular in Germany and may have played a significant role in the development of anti-Semitism there.[2] The arguments in Espina's book and his personal advocacy would be marshaled as justification for the Spanish Inquisition and would provide it with much additional popular support two decades later.

The book contains examples of all the traditional forms of anti-Jewish libel. There are stories of blood libel—the ritual murders of Christians by Jews, desecration of hosts, and poisoning of wells. Jewish physicians kill their Christian patients: "for every Christian they cure, they kill fifty others."[3] Jews caused the Black Plague. Espina is absolutely credulous when it comes to these stories. He tells all without skepticism, even though the blood-libel stories had already been condemned as false by four popes.[4] The stories related in his book sound patently absurd to modern ears, and yet he states that many were supported by his personal observations or had been related to him by trustworthy eyewitnesses.

There was at least one time during his life, however, when the veracity of Espina's claims was challenged. In 1463 Espina headed a delegation of Observants in an attempt to convince King Enrique IV to authorize an Inquisition. One of the delegates, Fernando de la Plaza, claimed in a sermon on behalf of Espina that he had proof of Jewish practices by the conversos—a collection of one hundred foreskins from converso children circumcised by their parents. As a contemporary chronicler has noted:

> Informed of the matter, the King ordered the members of the Franciscan delegation to come to him, and facing them, he told them that what they related about the circumcised new Christians was a grave insult to the Catholic Faith, and that he was in duty bound to have it punished. He then ordered them to have the foreskins brought to him and also let him know the names of the culprits, as he wished to be fully acquainted with everything pertaining to this matter. In response, Fray Fernando told the King that he did not have the foreskins in his possession, but that the matter was related to him by persons of authority. The King then asked him: Who were those persons? But Fernando refused to mention their names; so that it was all found to be a lie.[5]

Espina attributed Jewish perfidy to an inherited condition functionally equivalent to the modern concept of race. There are, according to him, at least two reasons for Jewish evil. The responsibility borne by the Jews, collectively, for the death of Christ caused Jewish blood to be forever cursed. Worse, they are literally demonic. Espina claimed of Jews that they are literally "sons of the Devil" and as such they are a danger not only to their neighbors and to those who deal with them but to humankind as a whole.[6] He considered the ancestors of the Jewish race to have been half beast (snakes and asses) and half demon.[7]

Because Espina claimed an inherited basis for Jewish evil, he considered conversos to be as untrustworthy as the Jews. Overtly Espina advocated that all Jews be exiled; for conversos he favored the establishment of an Inquisition that would find and burn conversos responsible for the heresies he believed had been uncovered by the rebels in Toledo.

But *Fortalitium Fidei* goes further than this, implying that the solution to the converso problem is what we would now consider genocide. Although Espina did not openly advocate the mass killing of Jews and conversos, his book is filled with stories of Jewish and converso heresies resolved by the massacre of entire Jewish or convert communities. For example, in one story a Jew convinces a Christian executioner to sell him the heart of a recently executed man for use in a black magic ritual. The executioner's wife, discovering this deal, convinces her husband to substitute a pig's heart for the criminal's. A few days later a huge crowd of pigs appears in the field, and the animals tear each other apart: had a Christian heart been used, the victims would have been Christians instead. When the king of France learns of this, he orders all the Jews in the region killed.[8]

In another story a nobleman is told to pay a border duty by Jewish tax gatherers. He refuses to pay, arguing with the Jews and hitting one in the head. The Jew returns the blow. The nobleman draws his sword but, surrounded by armed Jews, is unable to retaliate. On his journey home, the nobleman wonders how he came to merit such a disgrace and remembers that when the French king had ordered the expulsion of the Jews, he had defended them and allowed them to remain on his lands. He returns home and puts all the Jews in his domain to death by the sword.[9]

At least one story, the "Tale of the Two Tents," applies directly to the conversos. The story is set in England in a time contemporary to Espina.

This strains credulity, because the Jews of England had been expelled in 1290. The England of the "Tale" appears to be cursed and suffering from disease, famine, and war. The king turns to the saintly men of the country, who are told by God through prayers that this curse is due to crimes committed by the Jews. The king responds by requiring all the Jews to convert. The evils continue. Then the king learns that the Jews have only pretended to convert and have used this ruse to take control of all the offices in the kingdom, so that the Christians now are in thrall to the Jews. Realizing the trick that the Jews have played, the king calls all the conversos to the shore. He sets up two tents. One contains a cross, the other the Torah. He tells them:

> I have made you all become Christians, and you have accepted my orders voluntarily; but after your conversion the evils in my kingdom have multiplied, and perhaps the cause of this was that you came to Christianity against your will. It is therefore my wish that you be left free. Behold, in that pavilion near the sea, there is the Torah of the Jews, in the second the cross of Christ. Choose for yourself the lot you wish to have, and rush to it immediately. [Rejoicing in the freedom granted them by the King] the Jews ran at once, with their wives and children, to the pavilion of the Torah, and when they emerged from it on the other side they were slaughtered one after another and thrown into the sea. Thus was the said kingdom purged, and the plague ceased forthwith; nor has any Jew lived in that kingdom ever since. Let the Spaniards take note and see whether a similar plague is not flourishing among them![10]

This is almost an explicit a call for mass violence against the conversos. As Netanyahu points out: "The lesson was evident. There is a way of ridding Spain of its Jews—a way both simple and direct. Kill them all—man, woman and child. This is the shrill genocidal cry that rises from Espina's work again and again. Kill them for violating a Host, for killing a Christian child, even for standing up against a Christian nobleman who offends them; kill them for converting disingenuously to Christianity; kill them when they live under the name of Jews, as well as when the live under the name of Christians."[11] Espina, heir to Ferrand Martínez's pogrom, faced a dilemma. Martínez had adopted the slogan, "Convert or be killed." But if conversion does not work, if Jews are inherently too evil to adapt to Christianity, then only one part of that slogan is left: kill. And this message was soon to spread as anti-converso pogroms broke out throughout southern Castile.

Pro-Converso: "That Old Faggot Jew"

By the reign of Enrique IV in the mid-fifteenth century, most conversos had been Christian for two generations or more. No converso of this generation had the political power or religious stature of men like the relator Fernán Díaz de Toledo, Cardinal Torquemada, or Alonso de Cartagena. The instinct of Jews and early conversos to side with the king for protection had led the first generation to side almost unanimously with Juan II and with Álvaro de Luna—until Luna sold them out. Now conversos could be found on all sides of the civil war: some stuck by King Enrique, some sided with Prince Alfonso, while others supported Pacheco—even after he had demonstrated that he could be just as treasonous to conversos as he had been to the king.

The new political loyalties of the conversos reflected their assimilation to and adoption of Old Christian manners. But while conversos rejected Judaism (whether by free will or compulsion), they were still distrusted and discriminated against by Old Christians. This blocked full assimilation. Circumstances required conversos to develop their own perspective and customs. The converso soon became an important force in Spanish art and culture.

The converso perspective first broke into Spanish culture through humor. The court jester, or *truhán*, became prominent in the fifteenth century. These jesters were almost always conversos. Converso dominance in this profession may have been due, in part, to a Jewish cultural acceptance of humor. It also reflected the conversos' marginal status—it was easy for Old Christians to make fun of these former Jews, and the conversos, in turn, as the butt of the joke, could look more skeptically and satirically than Old Christians at Castilian society.

A school of poetry developed during this period, with the poets called the *cancioneros*, or songsters. While these poets wrote in a wide variety of styles, much of their poetry was burlesque—jester poetry written to entertain and to gain the patronage of the royal court and grandees. Many of these poets—if not the majority of them—were conversos. Among the *cancioneros*, Anton de Montoro stood out in his open admission to his Jewish heritage. He dramatized the plight of the converso and protested the killings of conversos and the discrimination they suffered in Castile.

Born a Jew around 1404 in or near Córdoba, Montoro probably converted around 1414. His Jewish name was Saul, and his mother remained Jewish. He became known as the Ropero, or used-clothes peddler. Trade in general had a low status in Castilian society, and dealing in used clothes was one of the lower-status trades. A tailor could service the aristocracy, and anyone with money would have his clothes made to order. A seller of used or ready-made clothes, however, only serviced those too poor to buy fashionable wear.

Montoro became known as a poet late in life. His first known poems date from the 1440s, when he obtained the patronage of the dominant aristocrat of Córdoba. He became one of the most successful poets of his day, engaging in public feuds and correspondence with other well-known poets and leaving behind a substantial estate. Montoro may have stressed his low class and Jewish background partly as a pose. Like jesters the comic *cancioneros* poked fun at themselves. Juan Baena, for example, a prominent converso poet, made light of his physical ugliness and short stature.[12] In lieu of a physical defect, Montoro's low-class occupation and Jewish background allowed for self-deprecating humor. Montoro often satirized his Jewish descent. In a poem to his wife, he noted that they were well matched as conversos; he had won her hand because she was considered unworthy of any reputable Christian, while with a fellow converso her Jewish background would "pervert a single house only":

You and I
and to have but little worth,
we had better both pervert

a single house only, and not two.
For [wishing] to enjoy a good husband
would be a waste of time for you,
and an offense to good reason;
So I, old, dirty, and meek,
will caress a pretty woman.[13]

Montoro could be bawdy even by our standards. One of his poems is called "Montoro a una mujer que todo era tetas y culo"—"Montoro to the Woman Who Is All Tits and Ass."[14] In "Montoro to the Woman Who Called Him Jew," his response to what was meant as an insult is to call the insulter a sodomite, implying that the mouth that sent out that insult was used to perform oral sex.[15]

In several of his poems, without entirely abandoning his satiric voice, Montoro bitterly protested against the mistreatment of the conversos described in the previous chapter. After the attacks on the conversos of Carmona in 1462, he addressed King Enrique IV: "What death can you impose on me / That I have not already suffered?"[16]

The massacre in Montoro's hometown of Córdoba elicited a lengthy and complicated poem to Alonso de Aguilar, the aristocrat who, after befriending the conversos, deserted them during the attack, then allowed them to be exiled and barred from public office. "Montoro to Don Alonso de Aguilar on the Destruction of the Conversos of Córdoba" begins as a fulsome panegyric to Aguilar, possibly reflecting Montoro's need to go on living under Aguilar's protection in Córdoba. Only after eight verses of excessive praise does Montoro turn to the massacre, noting that after this disaster, "it would serve the conversos better to be Jews than Christians."[17]

By verse 19, he is again praising the grandee, while abjectly begging that mercy be shown to conversos in a despairing tone: "We want to give you tributes, be your slaves and serve you, we are impoverished, cuckolded, faggots, deceived, open to any humiliation only to survive." In the next verse Montoro describes himself as "wretched, the first to wear the livery of the blacksmith" (the man who started the anti-converso riots), implying that he would have quickly surrendered to the rioters.

He pleads for the grandee's mercy, while he remains "starving, naked, impoverished, cuckolded, and ailing."[18]

His most explicit depiction of the plight of the conversos comes in a poem he dedicated to Queen Isabella. The poem opens by describing Montoro's embrace of a Christian lifestyle, including eating non-kosher food:

O sad, bitter clothes-peddler [ropero]
who does not feel your sorrow!
Here you are, seventy years of age,
and have always said [to the Virgin]:
"you remained immaculate,"
and have never sworn [directly] by the Creator.
I recite the credo, I worship
pots full of greasy pork,
I eat bacon half-cooked,
listen to Mass, cross myself
while touching holy waters—
and never could I kill
these traces of the confeso [converso].
With my knees bent
and in great devotion
in days set for holiness
I pray, rosary in hand,
reciting the beads of the Passion,
adoring the God-and-Man
as my highest Lord,
Yet for all the Christian things I do
I'm still called that old faggot Jew.[19]

The epithet at the end of the verse, puto judío, is a generic insult, not an imputation of homosexuality; it was, moreover, the worst insult in the language. As one modern academic, Barbara Weissberger, in the book Queer Iberia, explains: "Behind the sodomite, bearer of pestilence, is the outline of the converso. They are joined in the worst popular insult that could be hurled: 'faggot Jew!'"[20] "The English translation of 'puto judío' cannot fully convey the pejorative sense of this masculinization of 'puta,' which figures the Jewish male subject both as a whore and as the passive partner in the homosexual act."[21] The poem ends with a chilling prediction of the soon-to-be-established auto-da-fé, in which thousands of conversos would be burned at the stake. Montoro asks Queen Isabella that if she must burn conversos, to do so at Christmastime, when the warmth of the fire will be better appreciated.

Montoro himself managed to evade the Inquisition: he died soon after writing the poem, probably before the Inquisition had come into force. He showed his lack of respect for the church by leaving it only a nominal sum in his will. His wife was not as fortunate: she was burned as a heretic sometime before April 1487.[22]

The poems of Anton de Montoro represent both a creative dead end and a harbinger of more important art. By 1480 and the imposition of the Spanish Inquisition and "purity of blood" laws, conversos could no longer like Montoro proudly proclaim their Jewish roots. Such an attitude would have resulted in death by fire for heresy. The nineteenth-century Spanish historian Amador de los Ríos has said that Montoro "seemed to be boasting of his sambenito," the punishment that would be inflicted on conversos by the Inquisition.[23]

Instead, converso writers would turn to secrecy and indirection. It is no coincidence that the two most important works by conversos, *La Celestina* and *Lazarillo de Tormes* (both classics of world literature), were both first published anonymously. But Montoro also pioneered some of the same attitudes and devices that would mark works of later converso artists. Irony, irreverence, and the use of low-class characters to attack the pretensions of the higher classes would soon inspire a much more important genre. Picaresque literature came out of the *cancionero* tradition.[24] The picaresque novel, in its turn, was to become part of the foundation of modern literature.

PART 4

The Spanish Inquisition

19

The Catholic Monarchy

Insecure Beginnings

Ferdinand and Isabella received their title—"the Catholic Monarchs"—from Pope Alexander VI, aka Rodrigo Borgia. Their reign would become the bedrock of the Spanish state: they ended a century of civil strife, united the separate Spanish kingdoms, completed the reconquest of Moorish territory, and oversaw the earliest discoveries and conquests that eventually would make Spain into one of the largest empires in human history.

The monarchs' fame in Spanish history is mirrored by their infamous roles in the history of the Jews and conversos. If there is a spectrum in Spanish history from the tolerance of the *convivencia* to the intolerance of the *reconquista*, the Catholic Monarchs rank at the far end of the reconquest side; they demolished what was left of *convivencia* and completed the reconquest by conquering Granada and eliminating the Jewish presence in Spain. After ordering the expulsion of Jews from Castile and Aragon, they engineered the banishment of Jews from Portugal and Navarre, banning Jewish worship in the whole Iberian Peninsula. For the conversos they established and oversaw the development of the Spanish Inquisition, which for centuries would become a byword for political repression.

While in retrospect the joint monarchy seems to be a monument to both Spanish glory and religious intolerance, when viewed from the other end of history, there was nothing inevitable about their rise to power or their acts of intolerance. Both monarchs began their reign embracing tolerance. They allied themselves with Jews and conversos, who assisted their rise to power and held important positions in the royal court. Even at the height of the Inquisition, the monarchs had close ties to conversos who played important and powerful roles in the courts of both Castile and Aragon. The monarchs had similarly close ties to the Jews, and Jews played an important role at their court up to the eve of expulsion.

There is no evidence that either monarch came to power intending to repress conversos and expel the Jews. These actions developed incrementally. The Inquisition, founded to deal with the tension between the Old and the New Christians in Seville, grew rapidly in scope and mission because the friars entrusted to operate it turned it into a crusade managed with fanatic aggression. The Inquisition, in turned, spent years lobbying for the expulsion of the Jews.

Similarly, there was nothing inevitable about the monarchs' successful reign. It is easy to forget how much the monarchs struggled to achieve power, and how fragile was their early hold on the Crown. Neither had been born to succession. The marriage of Ferdinand and Isabella was not inevitable nor was even for a long time considered likely. After their marriage the royal couple faced the same internal and external enemies who had shattered the rule of their predecessors.

It is important to remember this background, when considering what happened to the conversos and Jews. The Spanish Inquisition, founded in 1481, was not the act of a confident, mature monarchy set to impose uniformity on their kingdom. It was the act of two young, relatively untested monarchs, who only five years before had to battle to establish Isabella's dubious claim to the throne of Castile. They struggled all their lives to achieve power over unstable kingdoms, one of which—Castile—suffered armed conflicts between Old and New Christians. When they established the Inquisition, they were not autocrats exerting arbitrary power, but rather monarchs desperate to establish their authority and stabilize a kingdom—Castile—that had suffered through two generations of civil unrest.

Isabella's Rise to the Throne

Of the two Isabella faced the greatest struggle to reach the throne. Her father, Juan II, died when she was only three. She was raised away from her half brother King Enrique's court, in the town of Arévalo. Her mother, consumed with depression after the death of her husband, left responsibility for her two children, Isabella and her younger brother, Alfonso, in the hands of their Portuguese maternal grandmother, Isabel de Barcelos.

For most of her childhood, Isabella was not considered a serious candidate for the throne. She stood in line behind the king; his daughter, Juana; and Isabella's younger brother, Alfonso. She was instead a marriageable commodity, to be traded at the whim of—and to the advantage of—the Crown. When she was six, she was engaged to her cousin (and future husband), the five-year-old Ferdinand, not yet heir to the throne of Aragon. Three years later an attempt was made to promise her to Ferdinand's older brother, Charles of Viana. When she turned thirteen, she was engaged to the thirty-two-year-old widowed king of Portugal, Afonso.

The treacherous Don Pacheco manipulated Isabella to further his own family ambitions. He arranged for her to marry his brother, Pedro Giron, who had a mistress and out-of-wedlock children. According to her chroniclers, Isabella and her lifelong companion Beatriz de Bobadilla dreaded the marriage and prayed continuously for the death of Giron. Isabella's famous religious devotion may stem from the granting of this prayer: Giron died on his way to claim Isabella as his bride. Pacheco also tried, unsuccessfully, to marry Ferdinand to one of his own daughters. Isabella's brother, Alfonso, died in 1468. With Juana labeled a bastard, Isabella was now a serious contender to the throne and thus a much more valuable commodity on the royal marriage market. King Louis XI of France made her a marriage offer of his brother and heir, Charles, Duke of Berry and Guienne. King Edward IV negotiated on behalf of one of his brothers, possibly the Duke of Gloucester, later crowned as Richard III.

Isabella, however, now had the political support of certain conspirators against Enrique, particularly the admiral of Castile, Alfonso Enriquez (Ferdinand's maternal grandfather) and the powerful Archbishop Carrillo of Toledo, one of the sponsors of the farce of Ávila. No longer the helpless ward of her older brother, she had the power and determination to choose her own consort.

Ferdinand: A Childhood in Civil Disorder

Ferdinand grew up in as much turmoil as Isabella, but his problems were political, not familial. His father, Juan II of Aragon, had already exhausted his rancor on his first son, Charles of Viana. Juan had married Blanche of Navarre, and it was in Navarre that Charles was raised. When Blanche died, Juan refused to yield Navarre to his son.

In 1447, at the age of forty-nine, he married Juana, the daughter of the hereditary admiral of Castile and much Juan's junior. In 1458, at the age of sixty, Juan succeeded his brother to the throne of Aragon. Enamored of this new family, he reserved rights of succession for his and Juana's young son, Ferdinand. Still seeking support for his claims on Navarre, Juan's older son, Charles, negotiated again with Enrique IV, now seeking an alliance through a promise of marriage to the future Queen Isabella. This rapprochement with Enrique again drew Juan's wrath. The king had Charles of Viana arrested in December 1460.[1]

The arrest set off a violent reaction in Catalonia. The Catalans resented Juan's ambitions in Castile, because Catalan commercial interests wanted him instead to focus on promoting their trade in the Mediterranean and rivalry with Genoa. The Catalans used the arrest to justify protest against royal abuses of power. In 1461 a Catalan revolt, supported by a rebellion in Navarre, forced Juan to capitulate. The accord that Juan signed freed Charles, formally recognized Catalan liberties, and barred Juan from entering Catalonia without the permission of the Catalan parliament.

Charles died soon afterward, probably of tuberculosis. With Juan effectively barred from Catalonia, the nine-year-old Ferdinand became king of Aragon. His mother, Juana, became the real ruler. The strong-willed and impatient queen quickly entered Barcelona and tried to arrange for her husband Juan's readmission to Catalonia. The queen soon antagonized the Catalan leaders. Rumors spread that she had poisoned Charles. Charles was transformed into a martyred saint and symbol of Catalan rights: Even before his funeral, while lying in state, rumors grew that Charles could work miracles, curing the paralyzed, blind, and dumb. The civil war of 1462–72 promoted a cult of Charles as the symbol of

Catalan revolutionary unity.[2] The war for the independence of Catalonia lasted ten years. Queen Juana campaigned on behalf of her husband until her death from cancer in February 1468. Ferdinand's apprenticeship with his single-minded mother prepared him for his future union with another woman of similar mettle, Queen Isabella.[3]

Juan fought on, despite his own infirmities. He was blinded by cataracts from 1466 to 1468, when a Jewish physician, demonstrating Jewish superiority in medicine, restored his sight. Ferdinand kept a Jewish personal physician up until the time of the expulsion of the Jews, in 1492.

After the death of Isabella's youngest brother, Juan II intensified his campaign to unite her with his own son. As a likely heir to King Enrique, Isabella had now become Juan's potential gateway to achieving his lifetime goal of political power in Castile. Juan made plans to pass on the crown of Sicily to his son, to enhance the marriage prospects. It was Isabella who chose Ferdinand. In January 1449, Isabella told her confederates that she would marry only Ferdinand, that "it has to be he and absolutely no other."[4] This put her at odds with her brother, King Enrique, who wanted her to marry the Portuguese king or, alternatively, the French Duke of Guyenne. Either choice would have removed Isabella from Castile and thus from competition for the crown. She committed herself to marriage with Ferdinand. Early in 1469 she formally consented to the marriage before witnesses, in exchange for a promised gift of forty thousand gold florins.

With Enrique opposing the marriage, and allies of Enrique controlling the territory between Aragon and the bride-to-be, Ferdinand had to ride to the wedding incognito. He disguised his party as merchants and servants and rode to Valladolid. There the cousins met for the first time. Isabella's supporter, Cárdenas, pointed Ferdinand out to her with an excited *ese es, ese es*—"that's him, that's him"—words Cárdenas later emblazoned on his coat of arms.[5] The future monarchs spoke together for two hours. The marriage negotiations preserved Isabella's rights over Castile. Ferdinand would be named royal consort but succession would go to their children, and Castile and Aragon would retain separate identities and rights.

The Royal Couple's Struggle to the Throne

The public ceremony took place on October 19, 1469. The couple consummated the union that evening, and witnesses waiting outside the bedchamber were called in soon afterward to retrieve the bloody bedsheet, which was shown to the crowd as musicians played triumphant songs with trumpet, flutes, and drums. Witnesses examined the room to satisfy themselves that the royal marriage had really been consummated.[6] Sexual union had become a public concern during the reign of Enrique "the impotent."

A daughter was born to the couple a year later. The longed-for son and heir did not arrive until 1478. His death at the age of nineteen meant that the crown would eventually go to their daughter, Juana, who came to be known as Juana la Loca, "the Mad."

The monarchs had very different but complimentary personalities. Isabella was known for her piety and her regular devotion to church attendance and confession. Yet her state duties always took precedence over her faith. While the monarchs devoted substantial time and resources to campaigning for church reform, their main concern was always the subordination of the church to royal control. Isabella's piety was, in part, a product of her obsession with maintaining the propriety and pomp of her person and office. Her attention to the dignity of her station would keep her from becoming the butt of public ridicule like her brother Enrique, "the Impotent." However, it also led to accusations of rigidity and reluctance to compromise.

Ferdinand's personality provided a counterbalance to Isabella's. As J. N. Hillgarth has described him: "[He was in] some ways closer to his mother, Juana Enriquez, than to his formidable father, Juan II of Aragon, as more sentimental than intellectual, fonder of studying history than Latin, of music than astronomy, sensual in his liking for women, gold and jewels, with which he loved to adorn not only his person but the trappings of his horses."[7] "Fernando's greater suavity tempered Isabel's rigor, and, in general, his views prevailed."[8] Ferdinand had a much wider range of political interests than his wife. While she focused on Castilian affairs, he dealt with Castile, Aragon, Catalonia, and his holdings in Italy. Eventually, he would become known as a pragmatic strategist, skilled in dissimulation; Machiavelli later cited Ferdinand as a model leader in *The Prince*. Both monarchs had one thing in common: they were raised in violent and dangerous times. Neither would hesitate to sacrifice lives—including lives of conversos and Jews—in order to further their own interests or those of the state.

Isabella tried to effect a reconciliation with her half brother Enrique, while at the same time building up domestic alliances. The unpopularity of Don Pacheco, who was stirring up trouble throughout Spain, helped her garner support.[9] In 1473 her aristocratic allies arranged for her to meet with her half brother while Ferdinand was away. The meeting turned into a post-Christmas family reunion. It went so well that Enrique extended an invitation to Ferdinand, who arrived on New Year's Day.

Tensions soon rose again, but there was little time for open conflict to develop. Pacheco died on the fourth of October. Enrique followed after his minister, expiring on the eleventh of the same month, at the age of forty-nine. Isabella's career would intersect with many sudden and mysterious deaths. Some have suspected foul play, though not on the part of the queen. Her brother, for example, may have been killed by Pacheco. As for the murders of Pacheco, his brother, and the king, Ferdinand's father Juan II is a possible suspect.[10]

Although succession was disputed between Isabella and her twelve-year-old niece, Isabella did not hesitate to claim the throne for herself. She arranged for a coronation the day after Enrique's death, while Ferdinand was away. Enrique's body, unwashed and untended, was quickly sent to Guadalupe for burial in the same miserable clothes in which he had died.[11] It was not long before the usual enemies, foreign and domestic, would resist royal authority as they had in the course of the last two reigns. But with the two kingdoms unified by the marriage of Isabella and Ferdinand, Aragon no longer posed a threat to Castile.

The conspirators against Isabella, which included Archbishop Carrillo of Toledo and Pacheco's son the Marquis of Villena, found a foreign patron in King Afonso V of Portugal. He agreed to marry Juana, his niece, and to invade Castile. Then he allied himself with King Louis XI of France. The young monarchs were now surrounded by external enemies, while within Castile most of the powerful aristocrats in Andalusia also opposed them. Alfonso invaded Castile in May 1475. He reached Plasencia on the thirtieth of May, where he was formally betrothed to Juana and proclaimed king of Castile. But a rebellion in the lands of the Marquis of Villena tied the rebels down. Nor was Archbishop Carrillo able to secure the city of Toledo for King Alfonso. This left the Portuguese army without significant Castilian support. Alfonso made attempts to advance as far as Burgos but eventually settled near the Portuguese border. The final battle took place on March 1, 1476, in the town of Toro, which lies just east of Zamora, between León and Salamanca.

Although Ferdinand won the battle of Toro, he did so without capturing either the king or the prince of Portugal, so that most troops remained in play, and the victory was not decisive. The real victory was obtained, not on the battlefield, but through politics. By the time of the battle of Toro, most of Portugal's allies were already negotiating with Isabella and Ferdinand. Portuguese forces had withdrawn from Spain by June. Castile would now be free from war or invasion.

Jews and Conversos

The monarchs owed their victory in significant part to converso and Jewish support. The converso keeper of the royal treasury in Segovia, Andrés de Cabrera, had been an early supporter of the queen. He helped to reconcile Isabella with her half brother, King Enrique. He also married the queen's favorite lady-in-waiting, Beatriz de Bobadilla, and would remain a member of her inner circle his entire life.

Cabrera was joined by the most prominent Jew in Isabella's court: Abraham Seneor. Seneor had worked in the royal treasury under Diego Arias. He became an early supporter of Isabella and brought Cabrera into her party.[12] Isabella rewarded Seneor with prominent positions, most profitably as treasurer for the newly created militia, the Santa Hermandad. Seneor brought his son-in-law Meir Melamed with him to court and, later, Isaac Abravanel, one of the most talented Jews in Spanish history. Both Seneor and Abravanel played key roles in the fiscal administration of Isabella's court. Though he was not a rabbi,

Seneor would also become the head of the Jewish community, with the informal title of chief rabbi.

Isabella honored the memory of her late father, Juan II, and emulated the practice of his administration by appointing *letrados* to prominent positions in the court. Many of these were jurists from Spanish schools like the University of Salamanca, and many, if not most, were conversos. The University of Salamanca recognized the favor shown to it by the monarchs by placing a portrait of Ferdinand and Isabella on its facade, with the Greek inscription: "The Monarchs for the University; the University for the Monarchs."[13]

Conversos also played important roles in the court of Aragon. Some families, like the Caballerias, once wealthy as Jews, became powerful aristocrats as conversos. Aragon-Catalonia escaped most of the political tension that poisoned New and Old Christian relations in Castile, making the converso rise to political prominence there easier and less contentious.

As purity of blood became a Spanish obsession, both monarchs would be tagged with rumors that they had Jewish ancestors. Fernán Díaz de Toledo, Juan II's leading converso official, claimed that Ferdinand's mother was of Jewish descent.[14] Another Jew who left Seville at the time of the expulsion also cited rumors that Ferdinand had been the grandson of a Jewish woman named Paloma.[15] A sixteenth-century Jewish chronicler, Elijah Capsali of Candia, elaborated on this rumor. According to Capsali, Paloma was a married Jewish woman who had an affair with Fadrique Enriquez, the admiral of Castile. Their son was raised by the admiral as his own and took over the admiralty. His fourth daughter, Juana, married Ferdinand's father.

Rumors also traced Jewish descent on part of the monarchs through two royal mistresses: Pedro the Cruel's mistress, María de Padilla; and Doña Leonor de Guzmán, mistress to Alfonso IX.[16] María de Padilla's daughter Costanza married John of Gaunt, and their daughter Catherine of Lancaster was Juan II's mother and Isabella's grandmother. Doña Leonor was the mother of Enrique II, and matriarch to the Trastamara dynasty, from which both monarchs were descended. Both royal mistresses came from aristocratic backgrounds before the age of conversions, when it was rare to find aristocrats of Jewish descent, and there is little evidence to show that they were descended from Jews. María de Padilla may have been a victim of the anti-Jewish propaganda campaign of Enrique II, which labeled her lover, Pedro the Cruel, a "secret Jew." Doña Leonor was hailed as a savior of the Jewish community because of her opposition to an anti-Jewish minister, Gonzalo Martínez de Oviedo. Rumors of her Jewish descent may have stemmed from this, although her son Enrique aggressively exploited anti-Jewish sentiment.

Practically, whether either or both of the monarchs were of Jewish descent is irrelevant. If either was aware of Jewish ancestors, neither acknowledged the fact, nor did either one show any affinity with the converso community. The monarchs would end the Jewish presence in Spain, and those New Christians who would survive by converting, would nevertheless find their freedoms stifled by the smoking bonfires of the Spanish Inquisition, stoked by the bodies of hundreds or thousands of converso victims.

20

Origins of the Inquisition

As described elsewhere in this book, Ferdinand and Isabella could be among the most open and tolerant of Spanish monarchs and had close associations with both conversos and Jews. So why did Ferdinand and Isabella request permission from Rome in 1478 to establish an Inquisition, a request that initiated the most repressive state-sponsored policies against conversos and Jews in Spanish history?

There are a number of possible motives, but no single one seems to sufficiently explain such a significant shift in royal policy. The actions were probably the result of several factors, but short-term political considerations may have been the primary motivation. Once initiated the Inquisition provided its own engine for growth, using terror to spread itself throughout Spain and to prepare the way for the expulsion of the Jews.

Several of the following factors played some part in the monarchs' decision to establish the Inquisition.

Religious Concerns

Both the mass conversions of 1391 and the Spanish Inquisition were due in large part to the campaigns of clerics in Seville. In the case of the Inquisition, the responsible cleric was the contemporary Dominican friar Alonso de Ojeda. He took over the anti-converso campaign of Alonso de Espina, becoming known as "Frey Vincente el Segundo," after Saint Vincent Ferrer.[1] His campaign might have had only a local impact had the queen not taken up court in Seville from July 1477 through October 1478. This gave him direct access to the queen, who at that time had also become a tertiary, or lay, sister of the Dominican order.[2] Soon after the queen left Seville, Ojeda claimed to have evidence of a secret meeting in the city of conversos practicing as Jews. This led the monarchs to commission a report on the situation—sponsored by the archbishop and by a Dominican friar in Segovia, Tomás de Torquemada—which supported the allegation of widespread Judaizing in Castile. The letter issued by the monarchs on December 27, 1480, authorizing the establishment of the Inquisition in Seville seemed to endorse Ojeda's view of the conversos. It observed that there "have been and are some bad Christians, apostates, heretics and confesos" who have "turned and converted, and do turn and convert, to the sect and superstition and perfidy of the Jews."[3]

There are reasons to question the depth of the monarchs' concern over religious deviation on the part of conversos. Ferdinand is not normally viewed as a devout monarch obsessed by religious orthodoxy. Niccolò Machiavelli's book *The Prince* cites Ferdinand as a model for what would be known as a "Machiavellian"—a politician cynical of ideals and pragmatic in morality. Machiavelli praised Ferdinand's ability to use religion as a pretext for achieving secular political ends: "Always using religion as a plea, so as to undertake greater schemes, he devoted himself with a pious cruelty to driving out and clearing his kingdom of the Moors; nor could there be a more admirable example, nor one more rare. Under this same cloak he assailed Africa, he came down on Italy, he has finally attacked France; and thus his achievements and designs have always been great, and have kept the minds of his people in suspense and admiration and occupied with the issue of them."[4]

The queen was known for her public piety, and she could have been swayed by the arguments of Ojeda and others. A well-known story, still repeated in popular histories, ascribes her support of the Inquisition to her religious piety, claiming that she established the Inquisition as a way of fulfilling a vow she had made at confession to Fray Torquemada before becoming queen. This story does not come from a credible source. As the historian H. C. Lea has described: "It is said that her confessor, Torquemada, at an earlier period, had induced her to take a vow that, when she should reach the throne, she would devote her life to the extirpation of heresy and the supremacy of the Catholic faith, but this may safely be dismissed as a legend of later date."[5]

There is another reason why this story of Torquemada's influence over Isabella is unlikely. While Torquemada probably acted as one of her confessors, her chief confessor and spiritual advisor at the time was Hernando de Talavera. Talavera, head of the Jeronimite order and probably a converso himself, was noted for his spiritual purity and devotion; contemporaries described him as "Christlike in appearance, way of life, and attitude."[6] While Talavera supported the death penalty for obdurate heretics and did not object to the idea of some kind of Inquisition, he believed that salvation lay in education and persuasion, not repression. He probably envisioned an Inquisition more like the one administered by his patron and predecessor in the order, Oropesa, whose Inquisition in Toledo did more to absolve than to punish the converso community.

Talavera would later have the opportunity to put his ideals into practice. After the conquest of Granada in 1493, he was named first archbishop, charged with bringing Islamic citizens into Christianity. He sought to encourage conversions by preaching and showing respect for local culture, using charitable persuasion and the use of Arabic during religious services.[7] He worked incessantly and tirelessly at preaching and caring for his new parishioners. As J. N. Hillgarth notes:

> He preached so continually and simply that his cathedral church was fuller at matins, said at night, than other cathedrals at High Mass. The Laity confessed and received communion there not only at Easter, as was normal, but on all major feasts. Talavera's humility, when treated discourteously by laymen or clerics, was carried to a point which seemed unbelievable in an age when prelates were great lords. To the German visitor Munzer he seemed "a new St. Jerome, for his continual studies, his constant labours and rigorous fasts had so debilitated his body that his bones were visible." Unlike Cisneros, Talavera refused to use ecclesiastical position to advance his family, nor did he profit financially, as was customary, from the regular visitations of his diocese ... spending much of his revenues every year on the poor.[8]

Although Talavera was popular in Granada, he was criticized by many for the slowness of his methods in getting Muslims to assimilate and convert to Christianity. In 1499 Ferdinand ordered Archbishop Francisco Jiménez de Cisneros to step in and institute more repressive measures. This led to violent confrontations between the Moors and the Christians, which in turn provoked further repressive measures against Muslims.

At the age of eighty, Talavera was accused of heresy by one of the most corrupt and abusive inquisitors general, Diego Rodriguez Lucero, who was trying to extend the Inquisition's authority by accusing Old Christians of heresy. Specifically, Talavera was accused of maintaining a synagogue, and he was arrested along with his entire household, including his sister, nieces, and servants. Confessions from the household were obtained by torture. Papal intervention obtained his release in April 1507, but he died the following month. He had been so devoted to his mission that he had neglected his own estate. His household had to resort to the charity of the bishop of Málaga.[9]

There is another reason to doubt the importance of religious concerns as a motivation for establishing the Inquisition. If the Judaic practices of conversos had posed a major threat to the Spanish church and state, one would expect there to have been a major effort to counter Jewish reversions in the period following the initial conversions. The first generation of converts, raised as Jews, would have felt the greatest temptation to turn back to their old religion. Yet neither the church nor the state expressed any concern over the religious practices of that first generation. It was only in 1449, fifty-eight years after the first wave of conversions, that the rebels in Toledo made a political issue of converso beliefs. Contemporaries of the rebels recognized that they were acting on political and economic, not religious, motives.

Finally, outside Seville and its environs, there did not appear to be significant political concern in Castile over the religious views of the converso. As the historian H. C. Lea notes: "In the fourteenth century there were many complaints about the Jews and petitions for restrictive laws, but these diminish in the fifteenth century and the later Cortes, from 1450 on, are almost free from them."[10] In short, while it is possible that religious concerns may have factored into the decision of either or both of the monarchs to establish the Inquisition, there are substantial grounds for considering other possible motives for royal support of the Inquisition's founding.

Money

The monarchs began their reign with treasuries depleted by decades of civil wars and unrest. While the queen made some efforts to reform the *mercedes* system that had diverted potential royal revenue into grants to nobles, she also made new grants to cement allegiances to her regime, and these grants continued to drain the royal treasury. The new military commitment to the conquest of Granada also placed an enormously expensive burden on the royal purse.

The Inquisition presented Ferdinand and Isabella with a short-term fix for their financial woes. Confiscation of property was a traditional punishment for heretical behavior. It derived from the Roman punishment for treason and had been applied to heretics—those deemed traitors to God—since at least the twelfth century. The property of heretics normally fell to the church. In 1477 the monarchs manipulated the Inquisition in the Aragon-controlled kingdom of Sicily to provide for a grant to the king of one-third of all confiscations. This demonstrated that even before the formation of the Inquisition in Spain, the monarchs recognized that profit was to be had from an Inquisition and that they considered inquisitional procedure to be under royal control.[11]

When the monarchs negotiated the right to establish an Inquisition in Castile with Pope Sixtus, they ensured that the Crown, not the church, would control the Inquisition, and that the right to confiscate property would be under the control of the Crown. The Crown made receipt of this income one of its first priorities in setting up the Inquisition. As H. C. Lea has noted: "When the first inquisitors were sent to Seville, in 1480, they were accompanied by a receiver of confiscations—a royal official whose appointment shows what were the expectations entertained."[12]

The Inquisition did in fact generate huge revenues, providing the monarchs with a major source of funds for their war against Granada, among other projects. The amount raised is difficult to calculate, particularly since the currency of the time cannot be converted to its equivalent in modern currency, but it probably involved millions, whether measured in *maravedis* or ducats.[13]

For two reasons the Inquisition was a less valuable fund-raising tool than it appeared to be. First, although it raised an enormous amount of money over the short term, confiscating the property of the most productive class in Spain had a devastating economic impact—both on the economy as a whole and, over the long term, on the royal purse because it eliminated an important source of tax revenue.

Ferdinand and Isabella were aware from the beginning of the negative consequences of confiscating productive assets. Pulgar, the queen's royal secretary, advised the monarchs of the economic impact of the Inquisition in Seville, namely, that as the number of conversos declined, commerce in Seville was beginning to suffer. According to Pulgar the queen belittled the threat that this would lead to the diminution of her rents and, esteeming very highly the cleansing of her lands, said that her interest was to rid her lands of that sin of heresy, for she knew it was to the service of God and herself. And the supplications that were made to her in this affair did not make her change her mind about this decision.[14]

The town council of Barcelona later complained to Ferdinand about the economic havoc wrought by the Inquisition. The king acknowledged the problem but insisted that religious concerns had made the Inquisition necessary, stating: "Before we agreed that this inquiry should be held in any of the cities of our realm, we weighed the matter well and foresaw all the losses and also the effects upon our royal rights and revenues. Since, however, our purpose and our zeal prompt us to set the service of our Lord God above our own service, we wish this Inquisition to proceed, come what may, in preference to all other considerations."[15]

As one modern Spanish historian has observed:

> We will have to state that Ferdinand and Isabella were totally intransigent when they decided to sacrifice the country's economy to its spiritual well-being. There can be no doubt whatever on this score, for in the face of the reasonable arguments made to them by

the city governments of Seville, Toledo, Barcelona, Valencia, and Saragossa, in the face of the serious dislocation which the establishment of the Inquisition and the consequent flight of the conversos meant for these cities, the king and queen always replied that in the first place, they were taking into account the religious benefit of the country, that they had the economic factor well in mind, and that in consequence they were sacrificing it to the spiritual policy which had been decreed.[16]

The monarchs' awareness of the long-term danger to the economy of confiscating productive assets did not necessarily preclude economic motivations for establishing the Inquisition. The monarchs' economic policy did not go much beyond filling the royal treasury, and this confiscatory policy would not be the only example of the Crown pursuing short-term gain at the expense of the long-term economic health of the kingdoms. Another example of their short-sighted economic policy is their relationship to the *mesta*, the sheep-raising cooperative that garnered enormous funds for the royal treasury. To promote wool production for export to the looms of England and Bruges, the monarchs enforced open-grazing practices that caused substantial damage to agricultural development. Farming losses led to food shortages and eventually required the importation of grain to a country that should have been self-sufficient. As the prominent twentieth-century Spanish historian Jaime Vicens Vives notes:

> No historian, no matter how great an apologist he has been for the Catholic Monarchs, has been able to defend this decision. Ballesteros Gaibrois states in a work on Queen Isabella, "The result was permanently harmful for the Spanish economy." And, trying to find some excuse, he adds, "This was one of the subjects which the great policy-makers of the time simply did not have within their mental range." This conclusion seems unfounded to us, for the problem of famine in Castile was one that Ferdinand and Isabella lived with daily, and it was intimately related to the dilemma which they found already in existence and solved in favor of livestock.[17]

A second problem with the Inquisition as a source of funds was that it was an enormously inefficient way to raise money. The Inquisition itself required a large bureaucracy, entirely supported through the confiscation of assets. Even though the Inquisition brought in an enormous profit, this money had to pay for the expenses of the courts; the salaries of the inquisitors, the notaries, jailers, and others; and the costs of feeding prisoners. By 1501 the pope was obliged to earmark several church sources of income in order to maintain the Inquisition.[18]

Although money may have factored into the royalty's decision to establish the Inquisition, the damage that Inquisition confiscation caused to the economy and the enormous expenses of the Inquisition itself indicate that profit was not the major, or even a principal, motive for starting the Inquisition in Spain.

Politics

Throughout Castilian history most attacks against Jews or conversos, while fueled by religious and class antagonism, were driven and shaped by political aims and ambitions—the ambitions of Enrique II in the civil war against Pedro the Cruel, of Sarmiento in his leadership of the Toledo rebellion, and of Don Pacheco in his machinations against Enrique IV. The one great exception to this pattern was the outbreak of riots of 1391, and even those riots followed and grew out of the politically motivated anti-Jewish campaign of Enrique II.

The origin of the Spanish Inquisition, too, may have been politically conditioned. At the end of the war of succession in which Isabella had to fight against her niece Juana's claim to the throne, the greatest challenge facing the monarchs lay in southern Castile. Much of the opposition to Isabella's claim came from the south, and it was controlled by powerful nobles. This is where Pacheco's nephew and his son, the Marques of Villena, held power. Enrique de Guzmán, who held the titles of Viceroy and Duke of Medina Sidonia, largely controlled Seville and resented not being granted the title and monies of Master of Santiago. His archrival, Rodrigo Ponce de León, the Marques of Cadiz, was married to a Pacheco.

These grandees had long operated almost independently in Seville, where the kings had consistently been too weak or preoccupied with fighting revolts to exercise control. The Guzmán and Ponce de León families had openly battled for control of Seville. They siphoned off much of the tax revenue from the rich southern ports and evaded other taxes through smuggling. Isabella stayed in Seville from July 1477 until October 1478. She worked to bring under her control Enrique de Guzmán, the strongest and wealthiest of Andalusia's great barons, as well as the other nobles, and to reimpose effective royal authority over Seville.[19]

In the context of the problem of establishing royal control over a difficult region, the monarchs may have viewed an Inquisition as a useful tool to bolster royal power in the city. It was Seville where the preaching of Ojeda had brought the issue of the conversos to public attention. By showing through the establishment of an Inquisition that they were taking action on these concerns, the Crown gained popular support that they could use over the nobles. In Seville conversos held important positions in the local government and provided administrative and political support to local aristocrats. Establishing the Inquisition promised not only to bring these powerful conversos under royal control but also to undermine the support they gave to local grandees.

There may have been another concern. Many of the converso refugees who fled Córdoba for Seville eventually settled in Gibraltar, under the sponsorship of the Duke of Medina Sidonia. The duke subsequently had second thoughts and ordered all conversos expelled from his territory. The return of these conversos to Córdoba may have caused the monarchs and others to fear further unrest between Old and New Christians, which an Inquisition could forestall.[20]

All these considerations reflect contingencies, not long-term plans or strategies. Yet there is no evidence that the Inquisition was initially seen as anything more than a local contingency—a way of meeting the need to impose royal authority in the region, and to appease the critics of conversos in southern Castile. The idea that the Inquisition arose as an expediency to address local concerns has been supported by the historian Henry Kamen: "Was there a long-term strategy, or was the tribunal intended to be purely local and temporary? Neither the Crown nor the early supporters of the Inquisition looked, around 1480, much further than the frontiers of Andalusia. The immediate purpose was to ensure religious orthodoxy there. For the first five years of its existence the tribunal in Castile limited its activity only to the south, particularly to the sees of Seville and Córdoba. It was the area where the social conflicts of the preceding century had concentrated. There was, as yet, no thought of a nation-wide Inquisition."[21]

21

The Inquisition

The principal cause of the Spanish Inquisition was the Spanish Inquisition. I do not mean to imply that the Inquisition founded itself. But once founded, it operated in such a way as to become a machine that fueled its own momentum.

Critics of the conversos had long looked for evidence to bolster their claims that conversos were secret Jews and, as such, constituted a serious threat to the church. As described in an earlier chapter, the Friar Espina had even once tried to make this case with King Enrique IV by citing an imaginary bag of five hundred foreskins. The Inquisition used terror, torture, imprisonment, and death by fire and looked upon harmless rituals as heretical acts. These extreme measures produced the very evidence that critics of conversos had been searching for: confessions, induced by fear. It was not necessary to rely on imaginary bags of foreskins when anti-conversos could point to hundreds or thousands of confessions to heretical behavior.

Did the monarchs intend for the Inquisition to be such an aggressive institution? The king's directive authorizing the establishment of the Inquisition in Seville seems to call for aggressive action. The letter of appointment to the inquisitors urged them to proceed against the "infidels" with all the means and methods provided by the laws, carrying out their duties "until the achievement of the proper end." It warned them that failure to fully carry out their duties would result in a loss of "natural" citizenship and dismissal.[1] Yet the letter lacks specific directions and may have been designed only to ensure that all conversos were thoroughly investigated. There is no evidence that either of the monarchs intended for the inquisitors to operate using the extreme methods they adopted from the beginning.

There was no precedent of which the monarchs would likely have been aware that would have led them to expect such an aggressive Inquisition. Ferdinand was familiar with the papal-authorized Inquisition that still existed in Aragon and Sicily, having operated for centuries. This institution was largely quiescent, investigating only a few cases each year. The king and queen would also have remembered the Inquisition led by Oropesa in Toledo in 1461, which largely absolved the conversos from the charge of heresy. Some conversos may even have supported the founding of the Inquisition in Seville, on the expectation that it would provide them with absolution from the charges brought by Ojeda and other critics.

The Dominican inquisitors had a longer tradition to draw on, however. They took as their model the bloody thirteenth-century Inquisition that their order had led against the Cathars. The Cathars, however, had drawn their members from Catholics and thus had represented a direct threat to the church. Conversos did not pose a threat to the same degree, since Jewish rituals held no appeal to Old Christians.

Given the overwhelming "evidence" of widespread heresy uncovered by the inquisitors in Seville, the monarchs had only two options. The first was to repudiate the Inquisition's findings. This, however, would require an admission of error on the part of the Crown. Moreover, the inquisitors were respected Dominican friars without ulterior motives, although they did have their own preconceptions and prejudices. They were seen as credible sources, and their findings, while criticized by some—mainly conversos—were generally accepted and almost certainly believed by the monarchs.

Their other option—probably inevitable given the evidence provided by hundreds of confessions from conversos in Seville—was to embrace the methods and findings of the Inquisition. There was no logical distinction to be made between conversos in Seville and conversos in other southern towns or, for that matter, in the rest of Spain. If, as appeared from the confessions extracted by the Inquisition, a substantial portion of conversos in Seville were heretics, then it stood to reason that heresy was widespread throughout Spain or at least wherever there were substantial converso communities.

This logic, based on the operation of the Inquisition in Seville, meant that the Inquisition would have to serve as more than a temporary solution for a local political problem. The evidence gathered through the Inquisition by the Dominicans showed that the Inquisition was a necessary institution, addressing a problem endemic throughout the Spanish kingdoms. The Inquisition justified its expansion—first throughout Castile, then to Aragon—by continuing to use the same extreme methods to elicit evidence of heresy. The Inquisition would become the basis for the Crown's decision to expel the Jews in 1492. It converted itself into one of the longest lasting institutions in the history of Europe.

The Legend of the *Fermosa Fembra*

On September 17, 1480, the sovereigns commissioned two Dominicans to begin the Inquisition in Seville. Juan de San Martín had been prior of the Dominican house of San Pablo in Burgos and vicar of the reformed congregation of the order in Castile. Miguel de Morillo had been elected the previous year as Dominican provincial of Aragon. Their assessor was Dr. Juan Ruiz de Medina, a secular cleric and member of the Castilian royal privy council.[2]

Many histories of this period tell this story of the converso resistance to the Inquisition in Seville. One converso leader, Diego de Susan, assembled a meeting of the most prominent conversos of Seville and its surrounding towns. Susan exhorted the crowd, which included high-ranking ecclesiastics and government officials, to form an army and collect weapons. If a single converso was arrested by the Inquisition, Susan said, he would call out the army to kill the inquisitors. One later account reported that the men asked, "Are we not the most propertied members of this city, and well loved by the people? Let us collect men together." And thus between them they allotted the raising of arms, men, money, and other necessities. "And if they come to take us," they resolved, "we, together with armed men and the people will rise up and slay them and so be revenged on our enemies."[3] The plot was foiled by Susan's daughter, Susanna de Susan, a famous beauty known as the *fermosa fembra*, the "lovely woman." Susanna loved a man from an Old Christian family. Concerned that he would be injured in the uprising, she warned him of the plot, and he betrayed her father to the Inquisition.

The inquisitors arrested Pedro Fernandez Venedera, majordomo of the cathedral, and discovered enough weapons in his house to arm one hundred men. The most powerful conversos, all involved in the plot, were quickly incarcerated. On February 6, 1481, six men and women were publicly burned to death in the Inquisition's first auto-de-fé. Another burning soon followed, an execution of three of the richest and most powerful men in Seville, including Diego de Susan. As the historian Cecil Roth describes the execution: "He went to the stake calm and unperturbed as usual. The halter round his neck was trailing uncomfortably in the mud, and he had to solicit the help of one of the crowd of bystanders. 'Be so good as to lift up the end of my African scarf,' he requested, urbanely."[4]

The death of her father and confiscation of his property left Susanna de Susan reduced to a life of poverty and shame. Rainaldo Romero, bishop of Tiberias, offered her entrance into a convent on behalf of the church. She soon left the nunnery and drifted from lover to lover, ending her life in the arms of a grocer, bereft of her riches and beauty. As Cecil Roth recounts, her dying instructions were

> that her skull should be placed as a warning over the door of the house which had been the scene of her disorderly life, in what was subsequently known as the *Calle de la Muerte* ("Street of Death"). Here it remained for centuries, and it was said that in the middle of the night strange cries of grief and remorse were sometimes heard to issue from the fleshless, grinning jaws. In the course of structural alterations in the middle of the last [nineteenth] century, the house was swept away. But . . . romantic Sevillans still imagine that in the Barrio de Santa Cruz, haunted as it is by the shade of Pedro the Cruel seeking for amorous adventure, the voice of the loveliest of Andalusian women may still sometimes be heard uttering shrieks of anguish for her share in the Great Betrayal.[5]

Traces of the legend of "La Susona" remain in modern Seville. In the Barrio de Santa Cruz there is a street called Calle de Susona, still nicknamed Calle de la Muerte. While her skull is gone, if it ever hung there, two *azulejo* tiles mark her memory. One is a picture of a skull. The other bears the caption:

En estos lugares, antigua calle de la muerte,
pusose la cabeza de la hermosa Suona ben Suzón,
quien por amor a su padre traicionó y, por ello,
atormentada dipúsolo en testamento.

[Here, in the ancient street of death
was placed the skull of the beautiful Suona Ben Suzon,
who for love betrayed her father,
and tormented, placed her skull here in testament of that betrayal.]

Scholars have recently challenged the veracity of this story, arguing that it was concocted in part to justify the brutality of the Inquisition in Seville, by making the inquisitors the potential victims of a conspiracy. This shift is reflected in the works of British historian Henry Kamen, who in his histories of 1975 and 1985 tells the story without qualification. But by the time his book *The Spanish Inquisition: A Historical Revision* was published in 1997, he had decided that "the whole story about the plot and betrayal was in reality a myth: Susan had died before 1479, the plot is undocumented, and there was no daughter Susanna."[6]

Burned at the Stake

While the existence of a converso resistance is in doubt, it is clear that the Inquisition started in Seville with great severity. The tribunal quickly adopted extreme measures against conversos. On February 6, 1481, the first auto-da-fé was performed. Fray Alonso de Hojeda, who had done more than anyone to lobby for the establishment of the Inquisition, triumphantly preached the sermon as six of Seville's most prominent conversos were publicly burned alive. Three more converso leaders were burned in a ceremony a few days later.

The practice of burning heretics originated with the Inquisition against the Cathars in 1017. It was not unknown in Spain: Alfonso the

Wise adopted burning as punishment for Christians who converted to Judaism or Islam. It had, however, been used rarely, if ever, as a punishment. The Dominican friars, bringing back a practice they had adopted through their leadership in the crusade against the Cathars, were now establishing a new standard of severity in Spain.

The frequency with which inquisitors now resorted to the stake required the construction of a new public site for burnings. As H. C. Lea describes:

> As though to show that the work thus begun was to be an enduring one, a *quemadero*, *brasero*, or burning-place was constructed in the Campo de Tablada, so massively that its foundations can still be traced. On four pillars at the corners were erected statues of the prophets in plaster-of-Paris, apparently to indicate that, although technically the burning was the work of secular justice, it was performed at the command of religion.... The cost of the four statues was defrayed by a gentleman named Mesa, whose zeal won for him the position of familiar of the Holy Office and receiver of confiscations. He was, however, discovered to be a Judaizer and was himself burnt on the *quemadero* which he had adorned.... According to a contemporary, by the fourth of November they had burnt two hundred and ninety-eight persons and had condemned seventy-nine to perpetual prison.[7]

The story of Mesa and his burning, found in Francisco Javier García Rodrigo's 1877 history of the Inquisition, is probably as fictitious as the myth that D. Guillotin was the first to have been decapitated by his own device.[8]

Quemaderos would soon be constructed throughout Spain. By 1488, about seven hundred conversos had been committed to the flames in Seville, either alive or in effigy.[9] While the Inquisition in the seventeenth century and later may have been defamed through exaggerated reports of violence and brutality, the severity of the Inquisition in its earliest stage is rarely disputed.[10]

The ambition of the inquisitors soon required more resources. The number of prisoners required them to shift their headquarters from the convent of San Pablo to the Castle of Triana, the stronghold of Seville, of immense size and with appropriately gloomy dungeons.[11] Application was made to Pope Sixtus IV for more appointments. He commissioned seven more inquisitors, all Dominicans, including the man whose name would become most closely linked to the Spanish Inquisition, Tomás de Torquemada.

Converso Reaction

The coming of the Inquisition set off a panic among the conversos. So many fled that guards were placed at the city gates, and more people were detained than the city had space to confine. According to the chronicler Hernando de Pulgar, thousands of families fled, and "depopulated a large part of the country."[12] Some conversos fled to other parts of Spain, Portugal, northern Africa, or Rome. Others sought shelter with local aristocrats. To counter this flight, the two leading inquisitors issued a proclamation ordering nobles to search their lands, seize all who had fled there, and turn them and all their property over to the Inquisition. According to Lea: "In vigorous language they were told that any failure in obeying these orders would bring upon them excommunication removable only by the inquisitors or their superiors, with forfeiture of rank and possessions and the release of their vassals from allegiance and from all payments due."[13]

The tone of this proclamation was extraordinary. Low-level clerics threatened grandees like the Marquis of Cádiz, who until recently had run their lands as fiefdoms effectively independent of any royal or other authority. This tone reflected the clerics' confidence that they had the full backing of the monarchs, whose motivation for supporting the Inquisition included a desire to curb the independence of these aristocrats. The threats were at least partially effective. The Marquis of Cádiz, for example, sent back thousands of refugees.[14]

Some conversos sought relief from the Inquisition through appeals to the church. The church gave lip service to the possibility of appeal from

Inquisition orders. Complaints by the conversos and others prompted the pope to write to the monarchs, forwarding complaints of Inquisition excesses in Seville. His criticism rested on the argument that the Inquisition should be a general inquiry into heresy, not exclusively focused on alleged Judaizers. When Isabella applied to Sixtus in 1482 to preclude church review of Inquisition judgments, the pope conferred authority on the archbishop of Seville to hear appeals. All these actions were likely prompted by lobbying from conversos, and probably profited church officials, but gave the conversos little real relief. Ultimately, the pope never exercised oversight over or inspection of Inquisition activities.

The papal penitentiary sold confessional letters, which authorized confessors to absolve all sins and provided—in theory—church absolution from the crimes prosecuted by the Inquisition. At one point the Duke of Medina Sidonia called in church officials and tried to use such a letter to shield his estate manager from the Inquisition.[15] The church continued to profit from these letters, but they gave the conversos little protection. According to Lea, "they were disregarded and many fugitives who had procured them found on their return that they had been burnt in effigy during their absence and that the document on which they had relied was of no avail."[16]

The Inquisition placed an agent in Rome in 1484 to complain about these letters. Shortly thereafter King Ferdinand issued a decree ordering death and confiscation to anyone who used such letters without first obtaining royal authorization. In 1485 the monarchs issued a further order claiming that the letters were obtained without papal knowledge and therefore that they were to be disregarded until papal intention could be ascertained.[17]

Only one obstacle could not be evaded by the inquisitors: their own mortality. Soon after the Inquisition began, the plague, which had decimated Spain in the previous century and subsequently flared up from time to time, broke out again in Seville. Fray Alonso de Hojeda, the architect of the Seville Inquisition, succumbed to the disease shortly after preaching at the first auto-da-fé. With the disease raging as the Inquisition continued to light its human bonfires and to fill the prisons with thousands of conversos, Seville must have been a kind of hell. As Lea concludes: "God and man seemed to be uniting for the destruction of the unhappy Conversos."[18]

Plague forced the inquisitors to relocate temporarily to the town of Aracena, but it did not stop the trials and punishments. Conversos petitioned Diego de Merlo for permission to flee the epidemic. Passes were issued, but only to conversos who left their property behind. Those who did not return could be tried in absentia, their property subject to confiscation by the church and the Crown.

The Inquisition in Seville provided the enemies of the conversos for the first time with substantial evidence of converso heresy. Based on this evidence, new tribunals were soon established in Córdoba, Jaén, Ciudad Real, and possibly Segovia. The success in Seville, however, was only mixed; the relatively ad hoc activities of the first tribunals allowed many conversos to escape Inquisition review. But the Inquisition learned from its mistakes. Soon, under the leadership of Tomás de Torquemada, the Inquisition would become a significantly more efficient bureaucracy of repression.

Tomás de Torquemada

In popular memory Torquemada epitomizes the worst excesses of the Spanish Inquisition. The name has become one of the most infamous in history, a symbol for fanatical and cruel violence, both personal and institutional.[19] This is the figure Mel Brooks burlesqued in *History of the World*, who sings the praises of the Inquisition as he tortures Jews. The popular novelist and historian Rafael Sabatini once noted that the surname itself seems to inherently invoke horror: "It almost seems a fictitious name, a *nom de guerre*, a grim invention, compounded of the Latin 'torque' ('twist') and the Spanish '*quemada*' ('burnt') to fit the man who was to hold the office of the Grand Inquisitor."[20]

In reality Torquemada probably had no direct involvement in torture and, except for a few significant exceptions, had no jurisdiction over the Jews. Even his name has an innocent derivation: it came from his native town's Roman name, Torre Cremata (Burned Tower).[21] Rather than characterizing Torquemada as a medieval torturer, it would be more accurate to link him to a more modern stereotype: the true believer or party functionary.

It is easiest to define what he was not. He was no innovator. His aggressive and rigid prosecution of perceived heresy among conversos and Jews followed an agenda laid out by his predecessors, especially his fellow Dominicans, Alonso de Espina and Alonso de Hojeda. Torquemada was not an intellectual. He left behind few writings, most of them official documents. He was not a demagogue. He made few public appearances and was not known for his oratory.

He was principally a bureaucrat. He built an institution, the Inquisition, almost from scratch, oversaw regulations to make it operate uniformly under central control, fought turf battles with the Vatican to maintain and expand the institution's authority, and kept it funded and growing, extending its reach across all of Spain in less than a decade.

Born in 1420 Torquemada probably found his vocation with help from his uncle Juan. Both began their careers in the Dominican priory of San Pablo in Valladolid. Tomás followed the "Observant" reform movement, which stressed spiritual devotion over intellectual approaches to religion. He became prior of the Dominican house of Santa Cruz in Segovia in 1455. He rose to national prominence, acting as confessor to Cardinal Pedro González de Mendoza, archbishop of Seville and later Toledo. He also became chaplain and confessor to one or both of the monarchs.

While his uncle published tracts urging tolerant treatment of conversos, Torquemada adopted a different position. In 1478 he wrote a memorandum to the monarchs titled "The Things the Kings Must Remedy." In it he warned against the Jews' baneful influence on conversos and urged the readoption of measures from the Laws of Catalina, such as physical separation of the communities and use of identification badges for the Jews.[22] This paper, and his general advocacy of measures to counter heresy among conversos, led to his appointment by Pope Sixtus as an inquisitor in February 1482.

There has been common speculation that Torquemada was a converso. Some historians have even seen Tomás de Torquemada's shame at his converso origins as the motivating force behind his persecution of conversos.[23] For example, the popular historian and journalist James Reston writes: "His grandmother had been a Jew, and this dirty little secret seemed to drive his passion against Jews and Christians of Jewish heritage into a determined and permanent rage."[24]

There is some evidence that Torquemada may have had Jewish roots. Historians generally accept that his uncle, Juan, was of Jewish descent. The contemporary chronicler and converso Fernando de Pulgar claimed that Juan's grandparents were "of the lineage of Jews who were converted to [the] holy Catholic faith."[25] The sympathy shown by the elder Torquemada with the plight of the conversos corroborates this evidence of his converso origin.

There are numerous examples in Spanish history of apostates persecuting Jews to prove devotion to their new faith and bury the shame of their converso heritage. This motivation, however, does not fit with Tomás's background. His uncle, if a converso, was not a rabbi; he was, instead, a cardinal, the "Defender of Faith" for the Vatican, and one of the most respected Spanish clerics of the fifteenth century. Even as a devout Catholic, Tomás should have been proud, not ashamed, of his heritage. Moreover, there is no need to seek out hidden motives to explain Torquemada's zeal. His dedication matched that of his fellow Dominicans, as well as that of other contemporaries. He marched in the footsteps of Saint Vincent Ferrer and numerous others who had no taint of Jewish blood to overcome.

Torquemada himself provided the best evidence that he was not of Jewish origin. He founded a convent of Saint Thomas Aquinas in Ávila. In 1496 he applied to Pope Alexander VI and received permission to bar anyone of Jewish descent from admission to the convent. Though so-called purity of blood laws would, starting in the sixteenth century, make such restrictions common, at this time it was still unusual to regulate membership based on Jewish descent. The monarchs generally opposed such rules, preferring instead to use the Inquisition as the sole basis for regulating converso behavior.

Groucho Marx famously told the Friars Club that he didn't want to join any club that would have people like him as a member. That makes a good joke, but for Torquemada to take this position in real life would have required either deep hypocrisy or pathological self-hatred. It is more likely that he was not of Jewish origin. Even if his uncle was of Jewish descent, Torquemada may not have been. His uncle could have been descended from Jews through his mother's side, and he and Torquemada's father could have had different mothers.[26] In those times of high childbirth mortality and high mortality in general, serial marriages were common. The wife of Bath, in a famous fictional example, had five husbands. There is an example closer to hand. Both of the Catholic Monarchs were children of second wives.

Soon after his commission as an inquisitor on February 11, 1482, Torquemada took control of the growing Inquisition. On October 17, 1480, he received a papal brief appointing him inquisitor of Aragon, Catalonia, and Valencia. He had probably already been formally recognized as inquisitor general for Castile. One of Torquemada's first acts was to oversee the writing of extensive rules regulating the function of the Inquisition. On October 29, 1484, he authorized the issuance of twenty-eight articles, or "instructions." Influenced by the fourteenth-century *Directory for Inquisitors* of the Catalan Dominican Nicolau Eymerich, the instructions governed every aspect of the Inquisition, from the opening "edict of grace" to provisions for punishments.

Around the same time, a central governing body, the "Council of the Supreme and General Inquisition," or La Suprema, was established to ensure that uniform procedures were followed by the various tribunals. Another eleven articles were issued in January 1485 that began to address the corruption that had tainted the Inquisition from its earliest days. A further set of instructions in 1488 returned to the problem of corruption. It also established direct oversight of the local tribunals by the Suprema; now the Suprema would retain official advisors (*consultores del Santo Oficio*) to review the sentences handed down by local tribunals.[27] The Suprema oversight ceded greater control over the general functioning of the Inquisition to Torquemada.

The detailed, uniform instructions written under Torquemada's supervision began the process of converting the Inquisition's mission of examining religious fidelity into an institution that functioned more like a secular court of law (although one lacking many procedural safeguards for defendants' rights) than a religious tribunal. One inquisitor noted that in 1545 it had become "more useful to choose inquisitors who [were] lawyers rather than theologians."[28]

There was a fundamental contradiction in Torquemada's character. As one modern historian notes, he was "a curious mixture of austerity and magnificence."[29] He was famed for his asceticism, as the historian H. C. Lea has noted: "We are told, indeed that he refused the archbishopric of Seville, that he wore the humble Dominican habit, that he never tasted flesh nor wore linen in his garments or used it on his bed, and that he refused to give a marriage-portion to his indigent sister, whom he would only assist to enter the order of *beatas* of St. Dominic."[30]

At the same time, he accepted as least some of the trappings of a powerful noble. He lived in palaces. He maintained a personal retinue of 250 armed men and 50 horsemen. He accumulated a large personal fortune, which he spent on building the monastery of Saint Thomas Aquinas in Ávila and other church structures, as well as on improvements to his native town of Torquemada. He also lived in personal fear that his enemies would exact vengeance. He kept at his dining table what he believed was a unicorn horn, said to be a universal remedy for poisoning.

One thing remained consistent: Torquemada's belief that most conversos were heretics who required purging, and that Jews undermined converso faith and should be expelled from Spain. His rigid adherence to this belief is demonstrated by his actions in one case involving his oversight. An inquisition tribunal in Medina found and punished a number of conversos for heresy but referred some acquittals to Torquemada for review. He decided to send an official to the tribunal so that these cases could be retried. After the prisoners were tortured, a few more were found guilty, but the rest were again acquitted. This incensed Torquemada, who declared that he would burn them all. He had them arrested again and sent to Valladolid, to be tried outside their district, where they were likely all convicted.[31]

Torquemada was over sixty when he began his career with the Inquisition, and his age would cut his tenure short. On June 23, 1494, when Torquemada was seventy-four, the pope appointed a committee of four bishops to assist him in his work. Four years later he died. He left his own epitaph, inscribed on the walls of the monastery of Saint Thomas at Ávila, where he is buried: "Pestem Fugat Haereticam," "he drove away the pestilence of heresy."

Although Torquemada's leadership of the Inquisition lasted only a little over ten years, his rigid determination and organizational talent succeeded in establishing the Inquisition throughout the Spanish kingdoms, and he probably bore primary responsibility for convincing the monarchs to expel the Jews from Spain. He laid the foundations that established the Inquisition as one of the strongest and most long-lived institutions in Spanish history, as noted by the American historian H. C. Lea:

> Full of pitiless zeal, he developed the nascent institution with unwearied assiduity. Rigid and unbending, he would listen to no compromise of what he deemed to be his duty, and in his sphere he personified the union of the spiritual and temporal swords which was the ideal of all true churchmen. Under his guidance the Inquisition rapidly took shape and extended its organization throughout Spain and was untiring and remorseless in the pursuit and punishment of the apostates.... He at least deserves the credit of stimulating and rendering it efficient in its work by organizing it and by directing it with dauntless courage against the suspect however high-placed, until the shadow of the Holy Office covered the land and no one was so hardy as not to tremble at its name.[32]

22

Arrest, Trial, and Punishment

Edict of Grace

The Inquisition opened in each town with an offering of amnesty, but within narrow limits and at a very high price.

The rules governing the Edict of Grace, derived from the earlier Inquisition, are to be found in the First Instructions of Torquemada. Article I of the instructions calls on inquisitors first to "summon by proclamation all the people and convoke the clergy" to assemble on a Sunday or holiday, where they would hear a sermon of the faith. At the end of the sermon, all the faithful were to come forward and take an oath of allegiance to the Holy Inquisition. Article III called for the reading at the end of the sermon of an Edict of Grace, which granted a term (initially thirty days) within which conversos could come forward and freely confess their guilt. The article provided that such a confession would be punished by fines or other suitable sanctions, but that the confessor would not be subject to death, imprisonment, or confiscation of property.

The Edict of Grace proved extremely effective for the Inquisition. As Henry Kamen observes: "Hundreds of conversos, well aware that they had at some time been lax in observing the rules of their faith, came forward to admit their offences and be reconciled. In Seville the prisons were filled to overflowing with conversos waiting to be interrogated as a result of their voluntary confessions. In Mallorca 300 persons formed a procession during the first ceremony of contrition in 1488. The tribunal at Toledo initiated its career by reconciling an astonishing total of 2,400 repentant conversos during the year 1486."[1]

The Inquisition made public the identities of those who confessed. The secret nature of these proceedings meant that no one could know what the conversos had confessed to or who the confessing heretics may have named as fellow sinners. Fear that family and neighbors were informing on them spurred many conversos to take advantage of the period of grace and confess to heresy on their own part while informing on others.

The fines imposed on conversos who confessed formed an important source of funding that allowed the Inquisition to establish itself in new cities and towns. Moreover, the confessions became an invaluable font of evidence for later Inquisition arrests and trials as Israeli academic Haim Beinart describes in his study of the Inquisition in the city of Ciudad Real:

> The confessions and statements made during the Period of Grace produced a mass of valuable information on the Conversos of Ciudad Real and other places, on the connection between the local Conversos and the Jews who came to Ciudad Real, as well as on the Conversos who went to Jewish centres and observed mitzvoth there. Each penitent was examined to ascertain whether his confession and deposition were complete; as is known, he was required to reveal all he knew about even the closest members of his family. The number of instances in which wives accused their husbands of forcing them to observe mitzvoth, of sons who informed on their parents and relatives who had taught them Jewish precepts, and like cases, were far from rare.[2]

While the Edict of Grace proved profitable for the Inquisition, it was considerably less advantageous for conversos. The catch to the offer of clemency was that in order to be effective, a confession had to be complete. As stated in Article III of the instructions, conversos were assured of clemency only if their confession involved "a sincere penitence, divulging all that is known to them or that they remember, not only of their own sins but also of the sins of others."[3]

Even after a converso had confessed and received clemency—along with a fine or other penalty—that converso could still be accused of heresy based on evidence of unconfessed crimes. For example, in Talavera Andrés González, the parish priest, made an early confession before the tribunal. Based on further evidence, he was arrested, at which point he made an even "fuller" confession. He was still brought to trial, and although the witness testimony confirmed nothing more than the very acts to which he had confessed, he was burned to death as a heretic in 1486.[4]

H. C. Lea has pointed out the tremendous advantage enjoyed by the Inquisition in this offer of grace: "The multitudes who came forward contributed large sums in their 'alms'; they gave the tribunals wide knowledge of suspects and a means of subsequently convicting them on the score of their imperfect confessions—for their confessions could not fail to be technically imperfect. Moreover, the necessity of denouncing all accomplices furnished an invaluable mass of testimony for further prosecutions."[5]

Investigation

Throughout the "period of grace," inquisitors employed teams of notaries to record confessions and accusations. They compiled the evidence into numerous books, including volumes labeled, for example, "Book of Testimonies" and "Book of Confessions."[6] These would become sources for further investigations and, following the normal rules of evidence, were included in the official record of cases going to trial.

The inquisitors believed that they faced an organized conspiracy against the church, and they fought it by first attacking the leaders of the converso community, as the historian Haim Beinart established in his research on the Inquisition in the city Ciudad Real: "The sequence in which the trials were held reveals that those tried in their own presence were also tried according to a fixed order: first came the prominent Converso figures of Ciudad Real, whose cases, to which wide publicity was given, were to serve as a lesson to the entire Converso public."[7]

The Inquisition protected the identity of informants, which meant that anyone with a grudge against a converso could inform without fear of repercussions. The earlier Inquisition, under the instructions of the thirteenth-century pope Boniface VIII, had introduced the practice of giving inquisitors discretion to conceal witness identities on the basis that heretics were dangerous offenders who could seek revenge against their accusers. While this remained, nominally, a "discretionary practice" in the Inquisition Instructions of 1484, it soon became standard practice.[8] Eventually, using the same rationalization—that heretics posed a special threat—inquisitors would bring secrecy into every aspect of Inquisition practice.

Citing the threat posed by heretics, the Inquisition increased the pool of potential informants by suspending almost all the restrictions on witnesses under the accepted rules of evidence that would have applied in standard criminal proceedings. In normal criminal cases, the age of majority was twenty-five, and minors were not admitted as witnesses. This restriction did not limit the Inquisition. As H. C. Lea has noted: "In the Spanish Inquisition, the rule was observed that, where heresy was concerned, all witnesses were admissible, no matter how infamous.... It would appear that even the insane were regarded as competent.... All other exceptions known to the secular law—minority, heresy, perjury, infamy, complicity, conviction for crime—were disregarded, although they might affect [the witness's] credibility."[9]

Conversos would betray even family members out of fear that the relative could first betray them.[10] It was not uncommon for wives to accuse their husbands of Jewish practices or for children to inform on parents and other relatives.[11] Secrecy allowed neighbors and servants to punish slights and resentments with betrayal to the inquisitors, without fear of reprisals. Henry Kamen has described the problem of false or malicious accusations:

> Petty denunciations were the rule rather than the exception. The Inquisition became a useful weapon for paying off old scores. "In Castile fifteen hundred people have been burnt through false witness," a villager asserted in the 1480s. ... The records of the Inquisition are full of instances where neighbours denounced neighbours, friends denounced friends, and members of the same family denounced each other.... Many of these cases would have arisen through sheer malice or hatred. Vengeful witnesses had everything on their side: their hearsay evidence was usually unveri-

fiable, their identity was always kept secret; and the costs of prosecution were borne not by them but by the tribunal.[12]

These betrayals led to numerous arrests and imprisonment, presenting the Inquisition with logistical problems. Lengthy imprisonment was uncommon in Spain. The sudden influx of large numbers of prisoners under the Inquisition led to the requisitioning of castles throughout Spain, most of which had valuable dungeon space. The Inquisition took over the royal castle of the Aljafería in Saragossa, the royal palace in Barcelona, the archepiscopal palace in Valencia, the castle of Triana in Seville, the Alcázar in Córdoba, and other similar castles and palaces. Dungeons were used where available, or prison cells were constructed.[13]

Arrest could mean ruin for the converso and his or her family. Upon arrest all of the person's possessions were confiscated and inventoried by the Inquisition and held pending final disposition of the case. If the prisoner was exonerated, the property would be returned, minus trial and jail costs. No provision was made for dependents, who could be driven into destitution by the loss of the converso's business and property.

Torture

Outside Spain the Inquisition would become linked in the popular imagination with the image of the sadistic torturer. Centuries later this image would even invade the horror stories of Edgar Allen Poe. In "The Pit and the Pendulum," the inquisitors offer their prisoners a choice of death by falling into the eponymous pit or being cut by the razor-sharp pendulum, as the narrator, a prisoner, describes:

> And now, as I still continued to step cautiously onward, there came thronging upon my recollection a thousand vague rumours of the horrors of Toledo. Of the dungeons there had been strange things narrated—fables I had always deemed them—but yet strange, and too ghastly to repeat, save in a whisper. Was I left to perish of starvation in this subterranean world of darkness; or what fate perhaps even more fearful awaited me? That the result would be

death, and a death of more than customary bitterness, I knew too well the character of my judges to doubt.

The Inquisition did employ torture, but its use of torture was consistent with contemporary standards in Europe; torture had been adopted as a legitimate method to obtain confessions by the earlier Inquisition. By the time of the Spanish Inquisition, torture was in common use in criminal cases in Castile, though it was not yet legal in Aragon, and inquisitors made use of Castilian methods and experienced criminal torturers. In the early Inquisition, torture was used less often than it was in the criminal system. The huge number of confessions and informants coming out of the period of grace normally made torture unnecessary. It became more common, however, in subsequent centuries.

Inquisitors used two primary justifications for torture. The first was in instances where some evidence of heresy existed, but the evidence was considered insufficient to convict. The second was in instances where heresy had been established, but there was suspicion that the converso might still be able to reveal other practices of heresy. In the latter example, even a converso condemned to death for heresy could be tortured to compel testimony against others.

In this period there were two primary forms of torture. The *garrucha* involved a pulley from which a victim was suspended by the wrists, with hands behind the back, and lifted. Sometimes weights were added to the feet.

In the other method, the *potro*, a type of waterboarding (the Inquisition considered waterboarding a form of torture), the victim was tied lying down on a trellis with the head in a depression lower than the feet. The head was bound with an iron band, while tight cords tied the victim's arms and legs to the trellis. The *toca*, a linen strip, was stuffed into the mouth. A jar holding about a quart of water dripped onto the *toca*, slowly saturating it, and thereby giving the victim the impression of drowning. The victim would flail about, but the movements of the limbs only made the restraints, sometimes tightened by tourniquets twisted into the cords, dig into the victim's flesh. The intensity of the torture session could be measured by the amount of water consumed.

A lengthy session would require six or eight jars. The victim, male or female, wore no or minimal clothing during the torture session. Nudity induced shame, but the primary reason for nudity was that clothes interfered with the torture restraints.

The inquisitors avoided direct questioning, instead commanding the victim to confess and to tell the "whole truth." Because the victim tended not to know the specific nature of the charges, the vague command to confess increased the victim's anxiety, and with it the chances of breaking down and implicating the largest number of people. The avoidance of direct questioning bolstered the credibility of the confession. However, it did have one drawback for the inquisitors: When trying to establish imagined conspiracies (as in the blood-libel trial involving the "holy child of La Guardia"), it became nearly impossible to put together cohesive testimony from the confessions of multiple witnesses forced to guess at their own crimes.

The Inquisition did allow for some due process protections. In order for a confession obtained under torture to be usable in a prosecution, it had to be ratified by the confessor twenty-four hours after the torture was inflicted. However, because the victim was under threat of further torture in the case of a retraction, renewed pleas of innocence were rare.

Trial

Conversos who managed to resist enticements or compulsions to confess but who remained under suspicion were moved on to the next stage: the trial. The Inquisition trial, of course, lacked much of what we would now expect in the way of protections for the accused. Like the normal criminal system of that day, judges/inquisitors also acted as investigators, prosecutors, and triers of fact. They carried into the trial a deep distrust of conversos, which created a presumption of guilt very difficult to overcome.

The inquisitors also viewed their role as including something more—something fundamentally different—from the role of a judge. Namely, they were charged with stamping out heresy, a threat to the church and to the welfare of the souls of the accused being tried in the court. They viewed the court as something like a confessional. As H. C. Lea has noted: "The guilt of the accused was assumed, and he was treated as a sinner who was expected to seek salvation by unburdening his conscience and contritely accepting whatever penance might in mercy be imposed on him."[14]

Inquisitors did grant one important right to the defendant: the right to be represented by counsel if the accused could afford a lawyer. This was customary in Spain. The royal court even maintained two public defenders, or *abogados de los pobres*.[15] The right to a lawyer was acknowledged in Article XVI of the First Instructions of Torquemada, though with certain limitations: "If the accused should demand the services of an advocate, he shall be supplied. The advocate must make formal oath that he will faithfully assist the accused, but that if at any stage of the pleadings he shall realize that justice is not on his side, he shall at once cease to assist the delinquent and shall inform the inquisitors of the circumstance."[16]

The principal role of the advocate, according to the inquisitors, was to coax a confession from the accused. Some lawyers, however, rigorously defended their clients, to the extent of challenging some of the basic premises of the Inquisition trials, such as the use of hearsay evidence. Some lawyers also challenged—with little success—the use of evidence relating to acts prior to confessions in church, on the theological basis that the confession would have absolved the converso of all prior sins. Acting as a defense advocate in these trials involved some risk; in at least one case, an advocate was convicted by the Inquisition for defending a man condemned to the auto-da-fé.[17]

Enforced secrecy posed the main obstacle to an effective defense. The accused was allowed to see only a heavily censored indictment, ostensibly to protect the identities of all witnesses. As a result the defendant often did not know the exact nature of the crimes of which he or she was accused.

The most effective defense was to impeach the credibility of the witnesses by showing them to be of bad character or to have had an ulterior motive for smearing the accused. Such statements to impugn and discredit witnesses were called *tachas*. But *tachas* were often made blindly, since the accused was often in the position of having to guess the names of the witnesses. The secrecy of the charges also inhibited the use of alibi defenses, since the accused did not know the dates and actions that required alibis. Thus, the best defense was to discredit any and all potential accusers and charges.

In one extreme case, an unpopular man from the town of Vayona had been accused of heresy by 35 witnesses. In his defense he impeached the character of no fewer than 152 villagers, including his wife and daughter, and sought to demonstrate why they would have had cause to hate him and inform against him. He succeeded in escaping with a moderate penance. As. Lea wryly observes: "Life must have been scarce worth living in Vayona when he was let loose."[18]

Inquisition rules placed other restrictions on an effective defense, making it almost impossible to have a fair trial. The Inquisition put few if any limits on who could serve as a witness, but witnesses brought by the defense could be excluded at the discretion of the inquisitor. Relatives were routinely disqualified on the grounds that their testimony was biased on behalf of the defendant, yet their testimony could be used by the prosecution.[19] Inquisition secrecy presented another dilemma: the witness called by the accused to confirm an alibi or serve as a character reference might turn out to be the very same witness who had informed on him or her to the Inquisition in the first place.

Many trials involved the missing or deceased. Those who fled the Inquisition were subject to prosecution. Failure to appear in court would result in condemnation, though defendants had some right to subsequently appear and clear their names. The dead could be defended by their heirs. Trial and condemnation of a dead heretic involved more than theoretical punishment: the estate of the deceased was subject to confiscation. This meant that heirs could be ruined, even when no suspicion of heresy existed on their part. Moreover, some institutions refused to hire or admit into their ranks the descendants of heretics. The Inquisition's participation in this destruction of the lives of innocent people constitutes one of its greatest injustices.

Punishment

The Inquisition exercised enormous discretion in meting out punishment. With heresy considered a capital offense, inquisitors could sentence the guilty with a range of penalties from a simple reprimand to death at the stake.

Even the lightest penalty normally included confiscation of property, along with various civil disabilities. These could include sumptuary penalties that barred the penitent from wearing gold or silver, coral, pearls, or other precious stones or garments of silk or other finery; riding on horseback; or bearing arms. More onerous were bans on performing public duties, including holding public office, working as a physician or a notary, or as tax collectors, grocers, apothecaries, or brokers.[20] The confiscation of property and the ban on common professions impoverished many penitents.

Shaming the heretic was a primary goal of the Inquisition, for which a key tool was the *sanbenito*, or penitential garment. The garment, inherited from the older Inquisition, was a yellow robe marked with one or two diagonal crosses, to be worn with a tall, pointed dunce cap. The penitent would wear the garment in public for a period ranging from a few months to life. Those condemned to the stake wore a black garment marked with flames or sometimes figures of demons dragging the condemned into hell.

The *sanbenito* became a perpetual mark of shame for entire families as the custom developed of displaying the garments prominently in local churches as perpetual reminders of the family's heresy. With the adoption of racial exclusion through purity-of-blood practices, this reminder of a family's converso roots would serve to permanently punish generations of people accused of heresy. Many changed their names to erase this blot on their reputations. In Toledo, for example, the surnames initially adopted by conversos disappeared and were replaced by new surnames.[21]

Even before the Spanish Inquisition, perpetual prison had been a penalty laid down in canon law for heretics otherwise subject to capital punishment but who had sought timely reconciliation from the church.

This penalty posed problems for the Inquisition, because long-term imprisonment was uncommon in Spain for criminal offenders, and there was little available space to accommodate the masses convicted by the new tribunals.

At first the Inquisition dealt with the shortage of space by impounding castles and fortresses. Later the Instructions of 1488 allowed inquisitors to instead use house arrest or confinement in institutions such as monasteries and hospitals. The difficulty and expense of keeping people in prison for life ultimately led to such sentences as "perpetual prison for one year," which allowed the Inquisition to balance legal strictures with practical limitations.[22]

King Ferdinand came up with yet another solution to the prison dilemma: the substitution of galley service for imprisonment, which had the advantage of saving on the prisoner housing costs while at the same time providing slave labor for the Spanish navy. This practice would become relatively common after the mid-sixteenth century, particularly for the Moors. Other than death at the stake, it was the most dreaded punishment inflicted by the Inquisition.[23]

Flogging, a common form of penance—often self-inflicted—became a frequent punishment of the Inquisition too, with the heretic condemned to be whipped through the streets. The convict condemned to flogging would appear in the auto-da-fé with a knotted rope halter around his or her neck. The number of knots reflected the severity of the punishment withstood; one hundred lashes was the minimum, but two hundred lashes was not uncommon.

Death at the stake was the ultimate penalty, one that had originated during the Albigensian Inquisition—the first such execution was recorded in 1017. Scripture provided justification for this extreme punishment: "If a man abide not in me, he is cast forth as a branch, and is withered; and men gather them, and cast them into the fire, and they are burned" (John 15:6, King James version).

As with torture the Inquisition maintained the fiction that the civil authorities, and not the church, were responsible for capital punishment. The Inquisition determined guilt and turned the convicted over to the state for appropriate punishment, adding a plea for mercy and urging the state not to spill blood. Yet the Inquisition knew that the penalty required for the offense of heresy was death. If the civil authorities responded with a request that the evidence be reexamined to determine whether the sentences were just, the church made it clear that the state could not question the verdict but was required to carry out the sentence of death at the stake.[24]

Four legal justifications existed for death at the stake: pertinacity, *negativo*, *diminuto*, and relapse.[25] Pertinacity applied to those of the accused who resisted the judges and defended their actions as correct. *Negativos* were persons who denied their guilt despite "sufficient evidence" of heresy. *Diminutos* made confessions to the Inquisition, but their confessions were considered insufficient. And relapses were people who had confessed and been reconciled with the church but had committed subsequent acts of heresy.

Confession could forestall punishment, but the confession had to precede the sentencing, or it would be considered coerced and insincere. Devout Christians risked a death sentence by defending their innocence before the Inquisition and holding out for acquittal. Even those accused who thought they had provided a full confession and who sought reconciliation during the trial could be condemned as *diminutos* for not having confessed all their suspected sins. A person could also be condemned on the same grounds if that person confessed to all of his or her errors but did not name persons who were considered accomplices, including close family and friends.

The sentencing phase culminated in a public ceremony: the auto-da-fé. In the mid-sixteenth century the inquisitor general Fernando de Valdés converted the public burning into an elaborate public ceremony that would dramatize the power of the Inquisition. The "auto" would be held on public holidays, preceded by the great procession of the Green Cross, followed by an evening of prayer. Royalty attended with local nobility and officials, and nearby windows were requisitioned to provide views for the privileged.

The auto of the fifteenth-century Inquisition was much simpler. It was an efficient exhibition of the convicted and public announcement of their punishments. Those tried in absentia were represented in effigy, while the dead, if convicted, were disinterred from consecrated ground to join the living and the effigies at the stake.

There is a contemporary account of the first Inquisition to be held in Toledo in February 1486:

> All the reconciled went in procession, to the number of 750 persons, including both men and women. They went in procession from the church of St. Peter Martyr in the following way. The men were all together in a group, bareheaded and unshod, and since it was extremely cold they were told to wear soles under their feet which were otherwise bare; in their hands were unlit candles. The women were together in a group, their heads uncovered and their faces bare, unshod like the men and with candles. Among all these were many prominent men in high office. With the bitter cold and the dishonour and disgrace they suffered from the great number of spectators (since a great many people from outlying districts had come to see them), they went along howling loudly and weeping and tearing out their hair, no doubt more for the dishonour they were suffering than for any offence they had committed against God. Thus they went in tribulation through the streets along which the Corpus Christi procession goes, until they came to the cathedral. At the door of the church were two chaplains who made the sign of the cross on each one's forehead, saying, "Receive the sign of the cross, which you denied and lost through being deceived." Then they went into the church until they arrived at a scaffolding erected by the new gate, and on it were the father inquisitors. Nearby was another scaffolding on which stood an altar at which they said mass and delivered a sermon. After this a notary stood up and began to call each one by name, saying, "Is X here?" The penitent raised his candle and said, "Yes." There in public they read all the things in which he had judaized. The same was done for the women. When this was over they were publicly allotted penance and ordered to go in procession for six Fridays, disciplining their body with scourges of hemp cord, barebacked, unshod and bareheaded; and they were to fast for those six Fridays. It was also

ordered that all the days of their life they were to hold no public office such as *alcalde, alguacil, regidor* or *jurado*, or be public scriveners or messengers, and that those who held these offices were to lose them. And that they were not to become moneychangers, shopkeepers, or grocers or hold any official post whatever. And they were not to wear silk or scarlet or coloured cloths or gold or silver or pearls or coral or any jewels. Nor could they stand as witnesses. And they were ordered that if they relapsed, that is if they fell into the same error again, and resorted to any of the forementioned things, they would be condemned to the fire. And when all this was over they went away at two o'clock in the afternoon.[26]

Although now associated with death at the stake, the auto-da-fé did not include executions. For the executions stakes were set up in *quemaderos* or *braseros*, in fields outside the city, where crowds gathered to watch the public executions. Victims who confessed after the sentencing were granted the mercy of garroting, or strangulation, before burning. The unrepentant, or, in some cases, those who had failed to provide sufficient bribes to corrupt executioners, went to the flames alive.

There are no accurate figures for how many were executed, but over three-quarters of the total number of executions are thought to have occurred within the first fifty years after the Inquisition's founding.[27] The total number of those killed during this period probably amounted to anywhere between one and several thousand.[28]

The smoke from the burning bodies, effigies, and condemned books could be seen as far as fifty to sixty kilometers away, sending the message of Inquisition power into the countryside.[29] One Rodrigo Alonso, returning to the town of Guadalupe in response to an inquisitor's summons, was witnessed standing still in the town watching the smoke. When told that his brother Diego was one of those burned alive, he fled in fear. Three years later he returned to face the Inquisition, which, after his case was transferred to Toledo, condemned him to death. He was executed in 1491.[30]

The fires were meant to reduce the bodies to ashes, which would then be scattered over fields or thrown into running waters, "so that the memory of the impious might vanish from the earth," and so that remains could not be preserved as relics by fellow heretics.[31] However, bonfires did not always produce the energy required to reduce bone to ash. The charred bones of Inquisition victims can likely still be found buried in the earth beneath fields throughout Spain.

23

··

Inquisition Expansion

Assassination of an Inquisitor

On the evening of September 15, 1485, Pedro Arbués, a leader of the Inquisition in Aragon, knelt in prayer on the floor of the cathedral in Saragossa as the canons chanted the service of matins. Dressed more for battle than worship, he wore a coat of mail and a steel helmet and bore a lance that he rested against a pillar.

Arbués had a good reason for taking precautions. The Inquisition had aroused both political and popular resistance in Aragon. At the beginning of the year, King Ferdinand had written to the governor of Aragon, warning him of rumors of a conspiracy against the Inquisition; an attempt had been made on Arbués's house in the spring. But Arbués's precautions proved inadequate. As he prayed, eight or ten paid assassins entered the church by the chapter door. One sneaked up behind the praying figure and, with a backhand stroke, slashed Arbués's neck above his mailed coat. Another pierced him through the arm, and a third stabbed him yet again, before all the attackers fled the church. The mortally wounded man was carried to a nearby house, where he survived another twenty-four hours.

The death of Pedro Arbués marked the most "successful" act of violent resistance by conversos against the Inquisition. That success was heavily qualified, however, because the murder would have disastrous consequences for conversos. It would spell the end of popular resistance to the Inquisition by providing the Inquisition with a pretext to crush the converso establishment in Aragon.

Opposing the Inquisition

Soon after the Inquisition was established in Castile, King Ferdinand planned to extend it to Aragon. There was, however, a legal impediment:

the papal authorization to establish an Inquisition under the control of the monarchs extended only to Castile. There was also a legal loophole: a long-established and largely moribund Inquisition in Aragon left over from the Inquisition established to deal with the Cathars. Dominicans controlled this institution. At the King's request, they authorized him to appoint new personnel for a revived Inquisition in Valencia.

This new move quickly faced widespread opposition. Both Old and New Christians resisted attempts to extend the Castilian Inquisition into Aragon. Nationalism drove some of this resistance. The union of the monarchs had not united the kingdoms themselves, which continued to have separate governments and institutions. Aragon's subjects saw the movement to impose the Castilian Inquisition, staffed largely by Castilian personnel, as a breach of their *fueros*, or rights.

Nor did Aragon share Castile's popular resentment and distrust of conversos. Exploitation of conversos as scapegoats during decades of civil strife in Castile had made conversos into ready targets for the Inquisition. Aragon had suffered similar levels of civil unrest, but conversos had been irrelevant to those political struggles, which were driven by a Catalan desire for independence, as well as a separate peasant revolt.

Conversos became part of Aragon's political establishment. Powerful converso families held some of the highest positions in the kingdom. Converso success in Aragon suggests that had Castile enjoyed stronger leadership, Castilian conversos may have been allowed to assimilate there without interference from the Inquisition.

Inquisition opponents managed to get papal support, as Pope Sixtus IV issued what H. C. Lea has called "the most extraordinary bull in the history of the Inquisition—extraordinary because, for the first time, heresy was declared to be, like any other crime, entitled to a fair trial and simple justice."[1] The bull stated that "in Aragon, Valencia, Mallorca and Catalonia the Inquisition has for some time been moved not by zeal for the faith and the salvation of souls, but by lust for wealth, and that many true and faithful Christians, on the testimony of enemies, rivals' slaves and other lower and even less proper persons, have without any legitimate proof been thrust into secular prisons, tortured and condemned as relapsed heretics, deprived of their goods and property and handed over to the secular arm to be executed, to the peril of souls, setting a pernicious example, and causing disgust to many."[2]

Papal support, as always, proved unreliable. King Ferdinand responded to the bull with indignation and strongly defended the Inquisition:

> Things have been told to me, Holy Father, which, if true would seem to merit the greatest astonishment. It is said that Your Holiness has granted the conversos a general pardon for all the errors and offences they have committed.... To these rumors, however, we have given no credence because they seem to be things which would in no way have been conceded by Your Holiness, who have a duty to the Inquisition. But if by chance concessions have been made through the persistent and cunning persuasion of the said conversos, I intend never to let them take effect. Take care therefore not to let the matter go further, and to revoke any concessions and entrust us with the care of this question.[3]

The pope yielded to the king (there may have been material inducements offered to the Vatican, both to obtain and then to override the bull). The pope agreed to let the king appoint Torquemada inquisitor general of Aragon. The Inquisition now became the only institution that operated throughout all the kingdoms of the united Crown.

Open resistance broke out in one of the Inquisition's first targets, the town of Teruel. Town leaders refused to allow Inquisition officials admission to the walled city and forced them to withdraw to a nearby town. The outraged inquisitors excommunicated the town magistrates and issued an interdiction on the town. The magistrates then obtained absolution from two priests in Villaquemada. Both priests paid for their intervention; King Ferdinand secretly ordered his illegitimate son, the archbishop of Saragossa, to seize them and have them imprisoned.

The town of Teruel next tried to negotiate with the king. He commanded the town to submit unconditionally. The Inquisition issued a decree confiscating all town offices, and the Crown stopped payment of all salaries to Teruel. When the deputation of Aragon tried to intercede with the king, Ferdinand responded that the people of Teruel were guilty of madness and outrage. The king then ordered the officials of Aragon to raise an armed force under Inquisition control to seize all town inhabitants and their property and place them under Inquisition judgment. When the officials did not respond quickly enough, he called on Castilian officials near the border to respond with armed forces. The town surrendered to the king's orders. The whole town of Teruel was subject to banishment, and all property placed at the mercy of the inquisitors.

Barcelona also resisted the entry of the Inquisition, but its residents had a legal basis for their objection. The position of "inquisitor" already existed in Barcelona, as outlined in a 1461 grant by the pope; thus there was no room, legally, for a new, royally appointed inquisitor. Once again the king had to lobby the Vatican, and as always the Vatican eventually sided with the king, but in this case the city gained years of delay. The king requested that the city agree to Torquemada's control of the Inquisition in 1484; it was not until 1486 that the pope would agree to remove all previous inquisitors and name Torquemada "special inquisitor" for Barcelona.

Barcelona's resistance was partly motivated by the city's concern over the economic impact of the Inquisition. Nearby France welcomed conversos, who were essential to the economic health of Barcelona. City councilors complained to the king in 1485 of the "losses and disorder caused in this land by the Inquisition that Your Highness wishes to introduce ... The few remaining merchants have ceased to trade.... Foreign realms are growing rich and glorious through the depopulation of this country." The following year they added that the city would be "totally depopulated and ruined if the Inquisition were introduced."[4]

The Inquisition, once introduced, produced few victims in Barcelona. In its first two years, only ten people met their fate in the flames of the auto-da-fé. The two-year delay in receiving papal approval for Torquemada's appointment gave most potential victims an opportunity to flee, including the regent of the city council, Antoni de Bardaxi.[5]

Attack on the Conversos

The assassination of Pedro Arbués effectively ended Aragon's resistance to the Inquisition. Immediately afterward the Inquisition began to promote Arbués as a holy martyr. It was said that, grievously wounded, he spent the twenty-four hours before his death making pious statements. Lea describes the stories that attended his death:

> Miracles at once attested his sanctity. On the night of the murder the holy bell of Villela tolled without human hands, breaking the bull's pizzle with which the clapper was secured. His blood, which stained the flagstones of the cathedral, after drying for two weeks, suddenly liquefied, so that crowds came to dip in it cloths and scapulars and had to be forcibly driven off when he was buried on the spot where he fell: when the conspirators were interrogated by the inquisitors, their mouths became black and their tongues were parched so that they were unable to speak until water was given to them. It was popularly believed that when, in their flight, they reached the boundaries of the kingdom, they became divinely benumbed until seized by their captors.[6]

The king promoted Arbués's veneration. He sponsored a sacred commemoration in Arbués's honor, had a tomb built for him, and a statue erected with a relief depicting the assassination. In 1490 the municipality of Saragossa paid for two solid-silver lamps in the cathedral to provide an eternal flame in his memory.[7] Spaniards assigned him a feast day. The Vatican was less impressed by his credentials—he was not canonized until 1867.[8]

The Inquisition took the position that the murder was planned by a widespread conspiracy of important conversos. The investigation of this conspiracy became the pretext for arresting, imprisoning, or torturing the most powerful conversos in Aragon. Many conversos quickly fled the kingdom. Some may have been motivated by guilt, others by fear of Inquisition abuses. There was an immediate incitement to panic: once news of Arbués's stabbing spread, crowds filled the streets before dawn shouting: "Burn the conversos who have slain the inquisitor."[9] The king, the Inquisition, and the *diputados* took immediate steps to catch the fugitives. They offered a reward for the fugitives' return. Foreign lands were requested to assist in the criminals' repatriation, and a proclamation was issued threatening excommunication of all persons who assisted the conspiracy.

The monarchs approached the Vatican and obtained papal letters ordering everyone to return the fugitives to the Inquisition, under pain of excommunication. This was one of the first attempts at international extradition. When some converso fugitives took refuge in Tudela, in the neighboring kingdom of Navarre, the king demanded their return, threatening war if his demand was not met. Only Ferdinand's embroilment in a local conflict in the westernmost province of Galicia, putting down a rebellion, prevented him from marching into the small kingdom. The authorities of Tudela submitted to the jurisdiction of the Inquisition.

Many of the most important converso families—some of the most powerful in the kingdom—were accused by the Inquisition of guilt in the murder of Arbués. This included the Santángel family: Luis de Santángel, knighted by Juan II for his military service was beheaded and burned, while his cousin Luis, the king's financial secretary, whose loan would finance Columbus's voyage, was penanced in 1491. More than fifteen members of that family were punished by the Inquisition.

Lea describes the fate of another prominent converso group, the Sanchez family:

> There was in Aragon no Converso house more powerful than the descendants of Alazar Usuf and his brothers who took the name of Sanchez and furnished many officials of rank such as treasurer, bayle, dispensero mayor, etc. Of these, between 1486 and 1503, there were burnt, in person or in effigy, Juan de Pedro Sanchez, Micer Alonso Sanchez, Angelina Sanchez, Brianda Sanchez, Mossen Anton Sanchez, Micer Juan Sanchez, and, among the Tamirit, with whom they were allied by marriage, Leonor de Tamarit and her sister Olalia, Valentina de Tamarit and Beatriz de Tamirit. Of the same family there were penanced Aldonza Sanchez, Anton Sanchez, Juan de Juan Sanchez, Luis de Juan Sanchez, Juan Sanchez the jurist, Martin Sanchez, Maria Sanchez and Pedro Sanchez.[10]

The fury of the inquisitors led to unusually harsh punishments for those directly implicated in the murder of Arbués. Vidau Durango had his hands cut off and nailed to the door of the Diputación; he was then dragged to the marketplace, beheaded, and quartered. The fragments were suspended in the streets. Juan de Esperandeu was dragged to the cathedral door, where his hands were cut off; then he, too, was dragged to the marketplace, beheaded, and quartered. Luis de Santángel was beheaded in the marketplace, his head put on a pole, and his body burned.[11]

Some killed themselves rather than face the Inquisition's wrath. Francisco de Santa Fe, counselor to the governor of Aragon and grandson of the apostate who led the attack on the Jewish community in the disputation of Tortosa, jumped from a tower; his remains were burned, encased in a box, and thrown into the Tagus River. Juan de la Badia broke a lamp in his cell and swallowed the fragments. The next day his corpse was drawn and quartered, and the hands were chopped off.

A few converso suspects in the Arbués murder were so valuable to the king that they escaped punishment. Gabriel Sanchez, the king's treasurer, and Alfonso de la Cavallería, the vice chancellor, both fell under suspicion, and the Inquisition had evidence of either conspiracy or heresy against them both. In Cavallería's case, the investigation lasted nearly twenty years and filled almost five hundred folios. While the evidence was largely hearsay or circumstantial, conversos had been regularly condemned to death on similar or lesser evidence, and both men had relatives who had been either sanctioned or killed. Yet Cavallería was never punished. As the historian Henry Kamen has noted: "The King protected them firmly, and ordered the Inquisition to exempt them from its jurisdiction."[12]

How many of the accused and punished were really guilty? A substantial body of evidence compiled by the Inquisition supports the conspirators' guilt, but that evidence, as was always the case with the Inquisition, was obtained using coercion and torture. It is hardly believable that such a large group of prominent and respected officials could have known of the murder conspiracy without one of them informing against the plotters in advance of the assassination.

Even less credible is the speculation by the historian Benzion Netanyahu: "The question 'who killed Arbués?' can be given only one answer: the Inquisition itself."[13] Netanyahu based his conclusion that the conversos were innocent and the Inquisition martyred Arbués on the Inquisition's successful exploitation of the murder to shatter the converso opposition to its authority, and the disastrous effect of the murder on the converso community. The aftermath was indeed disastrous, but at least a few conversos almost certainly were responsible for the act that would lead to their destruction.

The Holy Child of La Guardia

In early June 1490, Benito García, an itinerant converso laborer and wool washer in his sixties, made a fatal decision. He checked into an inn at Astorga, one of the northern Spanish towns that prospered as way stations on the popular pilgrimage route to the legendary burial site of Saint James in Santiago de Compostela. While García was at the inn, one or more men ransacked his baggage and claimed to have found a consecrated wafer. Apparently no one questioned these men's motives. The Inquisition had turned Castile into a nation of informers, with all conversos fair game.

The provisor of Astorga, Pedro de Villada, also a local agent of the Inquisition, took charge of García. García later told a fellow prisoner that under Villada's hospitality he received two hundred lashes, waterboarding, and torture by thumbscrews. Under torture García confessed to possession of the wafer. He also admitted to consorting with a group of Jews who encouraged him to embrace his old religion. The Inquisition normally had no jurisdiction over Jews. Inquisitors, however, could claim jurisdiction if the Jews attempted to proselytize Christians. Based on this legal precedent, on July 1, 1489, they arrested a group of Jews, all, like García, simple laborers, for attempting to bring back to Judaism the converso Benito García.

One, a young Jewish shoemaker named Yuce Franco, took ill in prison. He asked for a fellow Jew to visit him in his cell to provide him some comfort. Instead, a monk who claimed to know Hebrew was brought in and dressed as a Jew, in order to operate as a prison informant. The monk later alleged that Yuce had asked him to tell Abraham Seneor, head of the Jewish community, that Yuce and his fellow Jews had been imprisoned because of an accusation that a boy had been killed during Holy Week in place of "that man" (meaning Jesus).[14] This admission became the basis of the blood-libel accusation known as the story of the holy child of La Guardia.

Blood-libel accusations—stories of Jews who killed Christian children in magical rituals—were common in Europe and had been condemned by the pope. The inquisitors did not need much imagination to concoct a version of this crime and a story about the magical abuse of consecrated wafers: Alonso de Espina's well-known anti-Jewish tract, the *Fortalitium Fidei*, or *Fortress of Faith*, provided blueprints for both accusations.

Once the Inquisition began to investigate a ritual killing by Jews, Torquemada took notice and control of the inquiry. Because the accused Jews were imprisoned in Segovia, jurisdiction over the matter rested with the court in Toledo. Torquemada wrote to have all the prisoners whom he named brought to Ávila, where he was constructing a monastery, for trial. Torquemada, tied up with other matters at the royal court, added that he could not take personal charge of the trial and would delegate responsibility.

Torquemada had a compelling incentive for taking a personal interest in the case. From its inception the Inquisition had argued that Jews constituted a fifth column that undermined converso faith. According to this logic, the Jews had to be forcibly separated from conversos, preferably by expulsion. A case involving a Jewish conspiracy against Christians would provide strong support for the Inquisition's anti-Jewish campaign.

By October 27 Yuce Franco had elaborated on his initial admission. He now said that he had been told that Alonso Franco and his brother once crucified a boy in the same manner in which the Jews had killed Jesus Christ. Histories of this trial have tended to center on the testimony of Yuce, in part because only his trial record was preserved; other records have been lost or destroyed.

A Lengthy Trial

The trial began in Ávila on December 17. Defendants were accused of the ritual murder of a Christian child on Holy Friday and of stealing a consecrated host, with the intention of using it to stage a magical ceremony on Passover—also involving the heart of the murdered Christian child—in order to infect all Christians with rabies. With this magic, the accusation went, the Jews would destroy all Christians and take over Castile.[15] Yuce Franco, when he heard the charges, responded that it was "the greatest lie in the world."[16]

Yuce was imprisoned in a cell next to the converso Benito García. The Inquisition allowed him to speak with García, that he might gather information against him and share it with the Inquisition. Benito's admissions mainly conveyed his bitter feelings toward Christianity for having him jailed and tortured. He asked for a knife so that he could circumcise himself and is supposed to have said that if he were freed, he would go to Israel. Ironically, although he had been arrested for stealing a host for use in a magical ritual, he belittled the wafer, saying that Christians mixed some flour with water and called it God.[17]

Questioned in April 1491, Yuce now admitted to involvement in a magical ceremony but still denied knowledge of the blood-libel accusation. He said that a Jewish physician had requested that Benito García bring him a host for use in a magical ceremony, and that he himself had only been used as a messenger. After constant interrogation, possibly including torture, by the ninth of June Yuce admitted to having heard that the magical ceremony also used the heart of a Christian child.

By July 19 Yuce began to give inquisitors the full story that they had been demanding. He claimed he had not admitted it sooner because he had sworn an oath to keep it secret until he had been imprisoned for a full year. Approximately three years earlier, he said, the conspirators had met in a cave. There they handed the heart and host to the physician, who retreated to the back of the cave to perform a magical ceremony. Later, on the nineteenth, Yuce described the killing of the child. Those present at the ritual, mimicking the passion of Christ, he said, had abused and crucified the child.

The interrogation continued into the fall, with the inquisitors solic-iting fresh details and attempting to smooth out the contradictory con-fessions made by different defendants. On October 11 the inquisitors took the unprecedented step of bringing the defendants together in pairs and having them confess in front of each other. This arrange-ment violated even the low legal standards of the Inquisition. It dem-onstrates that by this point the purpose of the trial was not, if it had ever had been, to determine the guilt or innocence of the defendants but rather to prepare a version of a ritual murder that was consistent and credible by the standards of the time.

Had the Inquisition merely been concerned with the guilt or inno-cence of particular defendants, there would have been no need for so many months of interrogation—the Inquisition had long since gath-ered more than enough evidence from confessions to convict the defen-dants. The Inquisition could also have followed other evidentiary paths that seem obvious today. It could, for example, have traced the identity of the presumed victim—there is no historical evidence that any child had been reported missing, or that the Inquisition looked for a possible victim. They might have looked for a body. The inquisitors asked about the location of the murder and burial, and the defendants repeatedly confessed to details of the murder, but there is no record that anyone searched for or discovered a body.

To the Inquisition these details were less important than obtaining a full and plausible story. That is because the real defendants were not the few Jews before the tribunal but the collective Jews of Spain. Just as the assassination of Arbués had become an excuse for the Inquisition to try the most prominent conversos of Aragon, the blood-libel accu-sation, by demonstrating the iniquity of the Jewish defendants, was an excuse for the condemnation of every Spanish Jew.

Another month of interrogations and confessions followed. The defendants were finally executed on November 14, 1491. It is said that Yuce Franco embraced Christianity before his execution. If he did so, his motivation was almost certainly a desire to receive the relative mercy of the garrote rather than death by fire.

The Blood-Libel Cult

This blood-libel accusation may be the longest lasting anti-Jewish blood libel in history. It was not until 1544 that a popular account was published, the *Memoria muy veradero de la passion y martirio, que el glorioso martir, innocent nino llamado Cristobal, padescio . . . en esta villa de la guardia* (Very true account of the passion and martyrdom of the glorious martyr, the innocent child called Cristobal, that was suffered in this town of La Guardia), by Licenidado Vegas, the apostolic notary of the town of La Guardia. This account describes the tortures that the child suffered in imitation of the passion of Christ, saying that the child received 6,200 lashes but complained only of the last one thousand, since they were more than Christ had received.[18]

Other versions, all glorifying the child as a sainted martyr, followed. Spain's greatest playwright, Lope de Vega, produced his version, *El Nino Inocente de la Guardia*, around 1610. His play opens with Queen Isabella receiving a vision from the founder of the Dominicans telling her, in a dream, to found the Inquisition and expel the Jews. The dream is followed by a lament from converso/Jews. Any sympathy for the Jews ends as Lope de Vega portrays them first as buffoons, then as villains who kidnap a young child. The child has a chance to escape but embraces martyrdom and receives his torments happily, watched over by an angel who promises him redemption.[19] The child became known as "Little Christobalico," the patron saint of La Guardia, and his shrine was visited by several kings (though the child was never formally recognized as a saint by the Vatican). The shrine is still maintained; in the Church of La Guardia, parishioners still gather before it to sing the hymn named for it (videos of the hymn and images of the child can be readily found on the Internet).

Spanish historians long accepted the truth of the Inquisition's account of this trial. Even in the latter part of the twentieth century, Spanish historian Julio Caro Baroja provided a weak defense of the trial, stating that the killing was plausible, because people in the Middle Ages still believed in the dark arts, and some really did commit acts of black magic.[20]

This last defense has a logical flaw to it which demonstrates the fundamental absurdity of the blood-libel charges. There were, indeed, Jews who believed in magic, particularly given the popularity in that period of Kabbalah, Jewish mystical tradition. But Jews believed in *Jewish* magic—for them, magical power derived from Jewish sources. Such sources included hidden messages in the Torah, or the Tetragrammaton, the secret name of God. In order to believe that a consecrated host had magical efficacy, Jews would have had to believe in transubstantiation, the mystical presence of Christ in the Eucharist. This belief would require the Jews *also* to believe in the divinity of Christ, making them, effectively, Christians. Yet Benito García, in his conversation with Yuce Franco, belittled the sacred nature of the host. The same error in logic exists in the charge that Jews staged a magical imitation of the passion: Jews who did not believe in Christ's divinity would not have found any magical power in the ritual. If the Jews had believed in Christ's divinity, they of course would not be Jews. But the Inquisition saw no contradiction in their charges, because the Inquisition had little knowledge or interest in Judaism and viewed the Jews as little more than bad Christians. To the inquisitors Jews were basically Christians in league with the devil.

A modern academic has pointed out that this blood-libel trial was fundamentally a witchcraft trial, adding that such trials were relatively uncommon in Spain (outside the Basque country) because in Spain widespread accusations of secret Jewish practice took up the space in the popular imagination otherwise occupied by witches: "The converted Jew substituted for the witch as a pariah, reflecting through antithesis and projection society's most ingrained fears and repressed longings."[21]

The story of the Holy Child of La Guardia, still told today, had an immediate impact. Although there is no direct documentation of how this trial may have been used, most historians speculate that Torquemada used it as evidence to convince the monarchs that the Jews posed a danger to the country and should therefore be expelled.

Expulsion was only a few months away.

PART 5

The Last Iberian Jews

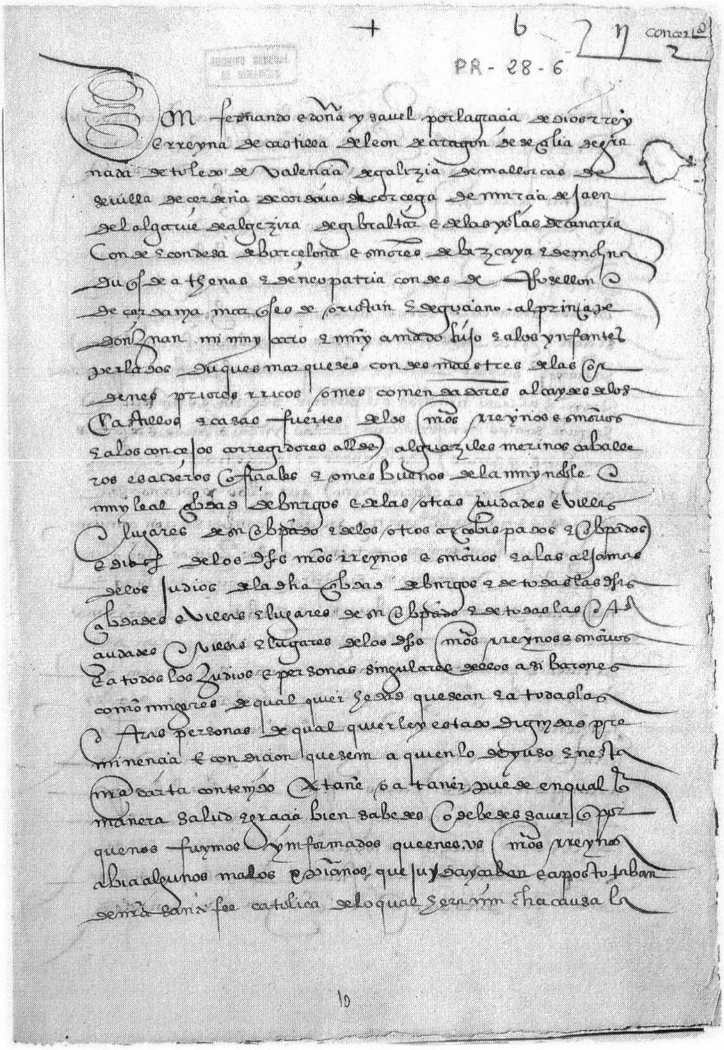

Fig. 3. Decree of Expulsion of the Jews, Granada, March 31, 1492.
Manuscript on paper; uncertified copy. Courtesy of Simancas
(Valladolid), Archivo General de Simancas (PR 28-6).

24

Spain and Expulsion

After Conversion: The Jews, 1391–1492

From the perspective of the Jews, the Catholic Monarchs were like the little girl with a little curl from Longfellow's nursery rhyme: when they were good they were very, very good, and when they were bad, they were horrid.

At the start of Ferdinand and Isabella's reign, life for the Jews was mostly very good. Jews prospered in two ways: they revived their trades in crafts and other businesses in small towns and villages across Spain; and they achieved a greater prominence in the royal court that they had in over a century. At the beginning of the fifteenth century after the mass conversions, many of Spain's larger cities remained without Jewish communities. Jews instead received shelter and prospered in smaller towns like Morvedre in the province of Valencia, in Aragon, or in Trujillo, in the western province of Estremadura. It has been estimated that by 1474 the Jewish population of Castile was about 30,000 families, with another 6,000 families in Aragon, about 150,000 people in a total Spanish population of about 6 million.[1]

While Valencia and some other cities prohibited Jews from reestablishing permanent settlements within the city limits, Jews could carry on trade with these cities on an itinerant basis, sometimes working with conversos to whom they still had family ties. A royal letter of 1461 describes the Jew's itinerant trade:

> The greater part of the Jews of the said aljama [Morvedre] are merchants, silkweavers, shoemakers, and artisans ... accustomed, in almost any week and for the greater part of the time, to travel outside the said town through the valleys and villages near it and

through other places, whether of Christians or of Muslims, and to stop in them to sell their handicrafts and their goods—for example, silverware, silk, and other items—and to farm some taxes, and this [they do] pacifically and tranquilly, and without molestation, vexation, and contradiction of any kind, just as the place and as the law provides for.[2]

The monarchs initially accepted their traditional roles as protectors of the Jewish community. Queen Isabel issued several decrees to prevent oppression of the Jews. On July 7, 1484, she sent this directive to the town of Trujillo: "I order each and every one of you that from now on no gentleman or squires or other persons or any people from this city or outside of it compel or oblige these aforementioned Jews ... to clean his stables or wash his water jars ... or threaten them or send ruffians, strumpets or people to their houses against their wishes." Only two years before the expulsion decree, she wrote to the Bilbao council: "According to canon law and according to the laws of our kingdoms, the Jews are tolerated and accommodated, and We hereby order that they be tolerated and permitted to live in our Kingdoms as Our subjects and vassals."[3] The queen's actions prompted a Polish traveler, Nicolas de Popielovo, who visited Spain in 1484, to remark on the queen's tolerance: "Their subjects in Catalonia and Aragon speak of it publicly and I heard it said by many in Spain that the Queen is the protector of the Jews and herself the daughter of a Jewess."[4]

Jewish intellectual and cultural activities also flourished under the monarchs. The Jewish astronomer Abraham Zacuto won an appointment to a chair in astronomy and astrology at the University of Salamanca, the oldest and most respected university in Spain and normally closed to Jews. His astronomical studies contributed to the voyages of discovery of Columbus and Vasco da Gama, among others. He personally consulted with Columbus and advised the monarchs on the advantages of the voyage.

In 1497 Zacuto created the first mariner's astrolabe. Astrolabes that allowed for measurements of latitude by sighting the pole star at night had long been in use. Such astrolabes, however, became ineffective near or below the equator and could not be used at night. Zacuto's astrolabe allowed for measurements to be made using the position of the sun. The device he designed was the first one small and sturdy enough to be used abroad ships. He personally handed one to Vasco da Gama, who used it on his first voyage to India.[5] After the expulsion Zacuto would become court astronomer to the king of Portugal. The twentieth-century Portuguese monarch Manoel II said of him: "Truly the great astrologer ... gave grand, enormous service to Portugal, his knowledge. Zacuto's science served not only the Portuguese, but also Spain, beginning with Columbus, who possessed a copy of *Almanach Perpetuum*."[6] Zacuto managed to evade the 1497 Portuguese mass conversions of Jews. He and his son escaped to North Africa, where they reached Tunis in 1504 after twice being imprisoned by pirates. He died in 1515 in Jerusalem, where he had taught in a rabbinical seminary.[7]

As for religious study, one contemporary Jew claimed that at the time of the expulsion the country had "never been so full of academies and students."[8] Most remarkable was the new Jewish influence at the royal court. The Jewish role in court was almost entirely due to the influence of the financier Abraham Seneor. The queen had not forgotten his early support, which may have included help in financing her wedding. In 1475 she tried to reward him with a lifetime annuity of 150,000 *maravedis*. When it was determined that it was illegal to assign such revenues to a Jew, she tried to pass the money to Seneor through a Christian agent. A law banning such assignments led to other paths of preferment. In 1488 she made him treasurer-general of the Hermanidad, an innovation of the monarchs that was to become a kind of national police.[9] One modern historian has described the importance of Seneor's role at court, which he compares to that of a modern secretary of the treasury: "If the text-book description 'minister of finance' is both fanciful and anachronistic, it is true that his documented activities go far beyond those of previous Jews in the service of the crown: the extension of his activities which encompassed even [the frontier towns of] Llerena and Jerez, the strategic importance of timely payments and provisions to frontier castles at a time of war and of course his office as treasurer of the Santa Hermandad are difficult to understand within the context of the putative 'decline' of the Jewish 'courtiers.'"[10]

Although noted for neither his religious knowledge nor his piety, Seneor was named chief rabbi of Spain. One contemporary Jew praised Seneor as the protector of the Jewish community: "And blessed be our God, who in His great mercy and loving kindness did not and will not remove the scepter from Judah. He is our exilarch, in whose hand is the seal from the king over the aljamas, to banish or to fine."[11] Seneor promoted the career of his son-in-law, Meir Melamed, who attained important tax collection positions. Melamed also joined Seneor in assisting the Hermanidad as the agency's chief tax collector.

Isaac Abravanel

The most talented Jew to work at the court came to it late, after exile from Portugal in 1483. Isaac Abravanel, a brilliant financier, was also the last great Jewish religious commentator and historian to work in Spain. Though born in Portugal, where he lived until the age of forty-six, Abravanel had deep roots in Castile. His family claimed descent from the house of King David and residence in Spain from before the time of the Romans. His grandfather, Samuel, had served as Enrique III's chief financial administrator. Abravanel's grandfather was also responsible for the family's exile and shame. Samuel converted to Christianity around the time of the 1391 riots. It is unclear whether the conversion was voluntary or compelled. He took on the name Juan Sanchez de Sevilla but soon fled with his family to Portugal, where he could return to his ancestral faith.

Abravanel later wrote that he was "brought up from childhood in wealth and honor."[12] Abravanel's father, Judah, served as treasurer to the Portuguese king's son, Fernando, who died in an ill-fated expedition to Tangiers. Fernando's will specified repayment of a large debt to "the Jew Arbarbanel."[13] Abravanel's education included Hebrew, Latin, Portuguese, and Castilian. The breadth of his learning, apparent in his early writings, in part reflected the Renaissance breakthroughs that were beginning to be felt in Iberia. In his earliest known book, *Forms of the Elements*, an exercise on classical philosophy and possibly the only work of Abravanel not related to religion, he showed a deep familiarity with classical and Muslim works, including Aristotle, Alexander of Aphrodisias, Themistius, al-Ghazali, Avicenna, ibn Tufayl, and Averroës.[14] As one recent biographer has written, "Among Iberian scholars, . . . few if any rivaled Abarbanel for broad immersion in Latin literature."[15]

Abravanel followed this work with *Crown of the Elders*, a monograph explaining a passage in the biblical book of Exodus. He then became occupied with business affairs, as he began to step in for his aging father. He also started to assume a leadership role in the Jewish community. When 250 Jews were enslaved after Portugal captured the North African city of Arzilla in 1471, Abravanel led a group of twelve prominent Jews in raising the money to negotiate for their freedom.

Abravanel became closely associated with the Duke of Bragança, the most powerful aristocrat in Portugal. Abravanel would later be described by the government of Portugal as "extremely rich and land-wealthy" and the Duke of Bragança's "most great servant and friend."[16] His wealth can be seen in an enormous loan of 12 million *reales* given to the Portuguese Crown after the war with Castile; Abravanel personally raised over a tenth of the total amount.[17] The association with the duke would both enrich Abravanel and lead to his exile from Portugal. In 1481, after King Afonso succumbed to the plague, his son João II took power and began to try to take back for the Crown the wealth and power previously ceded to powerful aristocrats. João complained openly about the grants that had been given to these nobles: "All my father left me are the highways of Portugal."[18]

On May 29, 1483, the Duke of Bragança was arrested while in conference with the king. The next day Abravanel was summoned to appear at the palace. Abravanel started toward Lisbon, but when he learned of the duke's arrest, he turned and fled to Castile, leaving his wealth and family behind. The Duke of Bragança was beheaded, and then King João ordered the houses that belonged to Abravanel in Lisbon destroyed, in case he had hidden any documents or valuables there. The houses were rebuilt and given to the son of Abravanel's former business partner; even Abravanel's library and seats in the synagogue were given away. Abravanel wrote to King João protesting his innocence—for the rest of his life he would claim he had never been involved in any conspiracy against the king. João granted Abravanel's family permission to leave the country unharmed, but Abravanel was sentenced to death in absentia and thus never again able to return to Portugal.

Late in life, looking back to his time in Portugal, Abravanel complained that his responsibilities at court had kept him from study and writing: "For all the days that I was in the courts and palaces of kings occupied in their service I had no time to study and looked at no book but squandered my days in vanity and years in futile pursuit so that wealth and honor would be mine."[19]

Abravanel's enforced exile in Castile now afforded him time to work and write. In only five months he produced commentaries on the early books of the biblical prophets, Joshua, Judges, and both books of Samuel, four volumes comprising about four hundred thousand words.[20] These works were marked by Abravanel's erudition and the breadth of their sources. Instead of limiting himself to Jewish authorities, his commentaries included citations from the classical Romans Seneca and Cicero and Christian writers including Thomas Aquinas, Augustine, Jerome, and Nicholas de Lyra, and even the convert Paul of Burgos.[21]

Opportunity soon shifted Abravanel's focus back to finance and the court. In the spring of 1484, he arranged an audience with the Spanish monarchs. His son-in-law joined Abravanel from Portugal, and with his wealth, together with what Abravanel had salvaged from his Portuguese holdings, he now had the resources to return to large-scale tax farming. The huge expenses of the war to take Granada, the last outpost of Muslim Spain, made his resources and financial expertise essential to the state.

Abravanel took over the tax farming operations of Cardinal Mendoza, whose power and wealth had earned him the nickname "the third King of Spain."[22] He also became paymaster to the cardinal's nephew, the Duke of Infantado. By 1491 he had become the queen's personal financial representative, and he would later claim that during this time most Spanish Jews considered him their unofficial leader.[23] When in 1491 the Crown renewed its contracts with Jewish tax farmers for four more years, Abravanel must have felt relatively secure in his position of authority, after having lost nearly everything he owned fewer than ten years earlier.

The Expulsion Decree

The year 1492 was Spain's *annus mirabilis*, the year that, more than any other, shaped the country's destiny and changed the fate of the world. On January 2, one year after Granada had capitulated, ceding the last piece of Muslim soil to Spain, the victorious monarchs marched into the city; on August 3, Columbus set sail for the western seas; and on March 31, the king signed the Edict of Expulsion, ordering all Jews to leave Spain.

Scholars differ in their assessments of the monarchs' reasons for ordering expulsion, but the source of the idea is clear. Almost from its inception, the Inquisition had argued that Jewish communities undermined converso faith by encouraging a return to Judaism. Using this argument inquisitors obtained authorization for the expulsion of Jews from Andalusia in 1483 and in 1486 from portions of Aragon, though it remains unclear how extensively either of these orders was enforced. Shortly before the signing of the Edict of Expulsion, Torquemada had signed a decree ordering Jews to leave the bishopric of Gerona, a decree that closely prefigured, in its language and arguments, the far broader edict that soon followed.

The king acknowledged the influence of the Inquisition on his decision in a letter to the Count of Aranda on the day the edict was signed: "The Holy Office of the Inquisition, seeing how some Christians are endangered by contact and communication with the Jews, has provided that the Jews be expelled from all our realms and territories, and has persuaded us to give our support and agreement to this, which we now do, because of our debts and obligations to the said Holy Office; and we do so despite the great harm to ourselves, seeking and preferring the salvation of souls above our own profit and that of individuals."[24]

In the decree the king adopts a common Inquisition complaint—that communication between Jews and conversos encouraged the conversos to revert to heretical Jewish practices, claiming that the Jews proselytized to the conversos, instructing them in their ceremonies and observances of the Law, holding gatherings where they read unto them and teach them what they ought to believe and observe according to their Law, trying to circumcise them and their children, giving them books from which to read their prayers, and declaring the fasts that they ought to fast, and joining with them to read and teach them the histories of their Law; notifying them of Passover before it comes, advising them what they should observe and do for it, giving them and taking unto them the unleavened bread and the [ritually] slaughtered meats with their ceremonies, instructing them on the things they should stay away from, thus in the foods as in the other matters, for observance of their Law, and persuading them as much as they can there is no other law nor truth besides it.[25]

The king stated that he had first attempted to prevent Jews from undermining converso faith by separating them from Christians and expelling the Jews from Andalusia, but that did not solve the problem of Jewish "contagion." Therefore, he resorted to full expulsion, with all Jews required to leave Spain by the end of July or face capital punishment; the state would retain all remaining Jewish property.

Approximately one month elapsed between the signing and the publication of the decree. The king probably spent the intervening time in consultation with Jewish leaders. Abravanel later claimed that he had met with King Ferdinand three times and had offered to pay enormous sums if the king would withdraw the order. He further claimed he had met with the queen, too, who told him: "Do you believe that this comes upon you from us?" adding, "The Lord hath put this in the heart of the king."[26] However, in another account Abravanel portrayed the queen as worthy of blame for the king's decision: "All this time, it was the queen who stood behind him and hardened his resolve to carry out the decree."[27]

In one popular and probably apocryphal story, Torquemada interrupted negotiations—just after the Jews had offered to pay King Ferdinand to reconsider his decision—in order to shame the monarchs into not brokering a deal that would have allowed the Jews to stay in Spain.

According to the sixteenth-century inquisitor Luis de Paramo, Torquemada arrived at the palace, a crucifix hidden in his cloak, and spoke to the king "with great and holy frankness," saying, "I know about the king's business. See here the crucifix of our Savior, whom the wretched Judas sold for thirty pieces of silver to his enemies and betrayed to his persecutors. If you applaud this action, sell him for a higher price. I, for my part, resign from all power. I will not take any blame, you will be responsible to God for this business deal."[28]

One can only speculate about the motives behind the monarchs' decision to expel the Jews, in addition to those given in the edict. Wealth does not appear to have been a motive: in his letter to the Count of Aranda, King Ferdinand acknowledged the economic harm that expulsion would cause. While he did take some steps to ensure that Jewish wealth would remain in Spain, he also made an enormous effort to convert the Jews, even though it meant that those who did convert were allowed to remain in Spain and keep their property, which otherwise would have enriched the Crown.

Nor does personal hatred of Jews on the part of either the king or the queen seem to have been a factor, given the prominence of both Jews and conversos at court, where the monarchs maintained close personal relations with both groups. It is tempting to link the conquest of Granada to the edict of expulsion and a scheme for accomplishing religious purity, but Muslims were initially allowed to remain in Granada after the *reconquista* and to continue practicing Islam.

Some historians blame the expulsion on class conflict, since the emerging urban middle classes viewed both conversos and Jews as competitors. The Catholic Monarchs, however, fresh from their popular successes in Granada, were firmly in power and had no need to exploit anti-Jewish sentiment to curry favor with urban populations.

It may simply be that the reasons stated by King Ferdinand in his decree and adapted from the Inquisition were the real motives. It is not that the king or queen had succumbed to pressure from the Inquisition: the monarchs controlled the Inquisition. But they had spent an entire decade incorporating the institution and its methods into their own policies and probably found the Inquisition's arguments—which may have included exploiting the La Guardia trial and its accusation of blood libel—persuasive.

The decision also has to be placed in the context of the times. I previously suggested that the real issue relating to *convivencia* is not why Spain sometimes seemed intolerant but rather why it was ever tolerant at all—it was tolerance, not intolerance, that was outside the norm. The Edict of Expulsion brought Spain's policy toward the Jews into conformity with much of the rest of Europe; both England and France had already expelled their Jews. There was no recognition anywhere in the world at that time of modern principles of religious freedom and tolerance. Even Italian humanists like Machiavelli, Guicciardini, and Pico della Mirandola considered the decree as an act of good governance.[29]

The Spanish Jews themselves viewed the expulsion as part of a wider movement to eliminate Jews from much of Europe. As Abravanel wrote while living in exile from Spain:

> At the beginning [the movement to expel the Jews] was in France, which was not all-inclusive, only from certain towns. But the first total expulsion from a kingdom was from the island that is called "end of the earth" which is Inglaterra [England]....And after this in 5,066 [1306] was the first total expulsion from France during the reign of Philip, son of Philip, son of Louis....And from thence there followed in our time the expulsions from Savoy and Provence and Milan and Ashkenaz and this last one itself, the expulsion of Jerusalem that was in Spain, and Sardinia and Sicily.[30]

The recognition that the Spanish decree was part of a wider anti-Jewish campaign was later echoed by Abraham Zacuto: "And we, for our sins, have seen ... the expulsion from Spain, Sicily, and Sardinia in 1492, and in the year 1497 after the expulsion from Portugal. For from France they came to Spain. But we [in Portugal] had the enemies on one side and the sea on the other."[31] The sixteenth-century writer Samuel Usque, reflecting on the suffering that Jews had endured after being forced out of so many homes in different kingdoms, lamented:

"Europe, which swallowed me with its noxious mouth, now vomits me out.... Now Europe, O Europe, my hell on earth!"[32]

Some Spanish Christians criticized the expulsion. For example, the contemporary inquisitor and official chronicler of Aragon, Jerónimo de Zurita, wrote: "Many were of the opinion that the king was making a mistake to throw out of his realms people who were so industrious and hard-working, and so outstanding in his realms both in number and esteem as well as in dedication to making money. They also said that more hope could be entertained of their conversion by leaving them in the country, than by throwing them out, referring mainly to those who eventually went to live among the infidel."[33]

It may be that the monarchs' principal motivation was not in fact expulsion but conversion. Although King Ferdinand did not mention conversion in the decree, by law Jews who converted could remain in Spain and keep their property. Jews who left could choose to return to Spain, convert, and have their property returned to them. Enormous resources were expended in an effort to convert as many Jews as possible before they left.

The powerful court Jews were a particularly important target for conversion, because the monarchs hoped to keep their talents and capital in the country, as well as to provide an example for other Jews. The most prominent Jew to convert was Abraham Seneor. He and his son-in-law converted in a ceremony held at the monastery of Guadalupe, in which both monarchs acted as godparents. Seneor changed his name to Fernán Núñez Coronel, and as a reward he was named governor of Segovia, a member of the royal council, and treasurer to Prince Don Juan, heir to the throne. Soon after Seneor's conversion, another prominent Jew, Abraham de Córdoba, was baptized, with Cardinal Mendoza and the papal nuncio acting as godfathers.[34]

The sixteenth-century Jewish chronicler Elijah Capsali claimed that Seneor may have been extorted into converting: "I have heard it rumored that Queen Isabella had sworn that if Don Abram Seneor did not convert, she would wipe out all the communities, and that Don Abram did what he did in order to save the Jews, but not from his own heart."[35] A more likely reason for the conversion was age: Seneor was in his eighties, too old to make the difficult journey and try to establish a life in a new country. Many Jews viewed him as a traitor, calling him, in Hebrew, "Abraham Sone Or," or hater of light.[36]

Isaac Abravanel's son Judah later reported an attempt by the monarchs to force the family to convert by planning to kidnap and baptize Judah's son. As a Christian the child would have been forced to remain in Spain, providing an incentive for the rest of the family to convert. But to protect the child, the child's wet nurse smuggled the baby out of the country into Portugal, while the rest of the family planned for their own departure into exile.[37]

Convivencia can best be understood as a marriage of convenience, in which Jews received a secure home in exchange for services valuable to the Crown. The expulsion decree, in part, represented the monarchs' recognition that after the completion of the reconquest and the conversion of much of the Jewish population, the presence of the remaining Jews in Spain was no longer convenient, nor were they needed.

While it is tempting to blame Spain's eventual economic and political decline on the loss of the talent and capital provided by the Jews, the Inquisition's campaign against the conversos in the 1480s, which confiscated the assets of the most productive class in Spain, proved far more damaging to the economy than did the expulsion of 1492.[38] The expulsion did have some economic impact, causing significant damage to small communities dependent on their Jewish settlements. For the kingdom as a whole, however, a large percentage of the former Jewish community remained in Spain as "New Christians" and had supplanted the Jews' economic roles and importance in Spain. Rather than leading to decline, the loss of the Jews preceded the period of Spanish history now called the golden age, or *siglo de oro*.

Exodus

The first problem that the Jews faced was money. They had only two months to liquidate all their assets. The monarchs had prohibited them from taking gold, silver, or other precious metals with them.

Andrés Bernáldez (1450–1513), a curate from the town of Palacios, wrote a history of the reign of Ferdinand and Isabella that is now one of the primary sources of that period. He was a supporter of the Inquisition, and some of his attitudes toward the Jews would now be considered anti-Semitic. Even he, however, was moved by the difficulties that the Jews faced in their expulsion from their homes:

> In the ... time of the Edict, they sold and misspent whatever they could of their estates. The young and old prepared themselves for the journey, demonstrating great courage and hope of having a prosperous exit and divine happenings. And in everything, they had miserable misfortunes. Indeed, the Christians took their many estates, rich houses, and landed properties for a small amount of money, and they would go about begging to sell them, but they could not find anyone to buy them. They exchanged a house for an ass, and a vineyard for a small piece of cloth or linen, because they could not take out either gold or silver.[39]

To add to the burden, the king required that every Jewish community pay all communal taxes in advance of leaving. All debts owed to Jews not paid by their departure escheated to the Crown. The need to quickly close out affairs included family concerns. According to Bernáldez: "They married all the young men and women who were twelve years of older, one with the other, so that all the young girls from this age on up would be under the protection and company of a husband."[40]

The Dominicans and others exploited the crisis to push for conversions. For example, in Teruel thè rabbi was detained in his house while Franciscans went through the town proselytizing. Even Teruel's municipal councilors, fearful of the economic consequences of the expulsion, went door-to-door preaching conversion.[41] These efforts at conversion continued even as the Jews set out to leave Spain. Bernáldez, with remarkable sympathy, described their journey out:

> And foregoing the glory of all this, and confiding in the vain hopes of their blindness, they took to the difficulties of the road, and left the lands of their births—the small and the large, the old and the young, on foot and riding on donkeys and other beasts of burden,

and on carts; and they continued their journeys, each one unto the ports of destination. And they went by the roads and fields with great difficulties and misfortunes, some falling, others rising up, others dying, others being born, others becoming sick, that there was not a Christian who did not feel their pain.

Always, wherever they went, they were invited to be baptized, and some in their misery converted and stayed, but very few did so. And the rabbis were encouraging them, and made the women and young men sing, and made them play timbrels and frame drums in order to make the people happy. And thus they left Castile and arrived at ports, where some boarded ship and others went on to Portugal.[42]

There are no reliable figures for how many Jews left, compared to how many converted. The best estimate by a contemporary comes from Bernáldez:

At the time, Rabbi Mayr wrote to the chief rabbi Don Abraham Seneor, his father-in-law, that he knew for certain that the king and queen were expelling 35,000 vassals, that is, 35,000 Jewish families. And among the ten or twelve rabbis who returned from their exile and whom I baptized, there was one, very sharp-witted, who testified to me that there were in Castile over 30,000 Jewish households, and that there were 6,000 in Aragon, by which he meant also Catalonia and Valencia. So that there were over 170,000 souls at the time that the king and queen issued the decree.[43]

Yitzhak Baer has put the number of exiles at between 100,000 and 120,000.[44] Somewhat more recently, Henry Kamen has estimated that as many as half of all Jews converted (many upon returning from unsuccessful attempts to emigrate), while about 40,000 Jews were expelled.[45] One recent account notes that estimates by historians of the numbers of Jews leaving Spain range from 40,000 to over a million, and that by 1500 Spain's population was 7 to 9 million, including about a quarter of a million conversos.[46]

There were few options for escape. England and France were closed to Jews. Jewish leaders negotiated an agreement with Portugal's King João II allowing Jews a temporary stay for a hefty fee. The small independent kingdom of Navarre also proved open to the Jews. Both of these countries would become traps. The remaining destinations for escape lay across the sea, but a sea voyage was fraught with dangers. Jews found themselves exploited by greedy sea captains or pirates. Some were abandoned, others sold into slavery. Outbreaks of plague were still common, and some of the vessels became plague ships.

The Journey to Fez

Most of North Africa was closed to Jews, but the kingdom of Fez, in Morocco, allowed for Jewish settlement. Bernáldez describes how the Jews were mistreated on their way to Fez: "En route, they were robbed in diverse manners, and they took their young girls and women, and the valuables of the estate, and they assaulted the women in plain vision of their parents and husbands, doing a thousand outrages and misfortunes unto them."[47] In Fez the Jews' presence was tolerated by the king, but the community of exiles suffered the consequences of famine, drought, and a fire that ravaged the shelters that the Jews had built themselves.

Several eyewitness accounts have survived of the dangers faced in the difficult journey to Fez, as well as the terrible privations suffered there. For example, the Kabbalistic scholar Judah ben Jacob Hayyat, who left by boat from Lisbon to North Africa in 1493 with 250 Jews, wrote that after embarking they could not find a port to receive them. They sailed for four months, with few provisions. They were then waylaid by a Basque crew that took them captive, looted their property, and took them to Málaga. There they were imprisoned in the ship, while priests came aboard at the order of the bishop, to proselytize to them. After seeing that the Jews refused to convert, the bishop ordered them to be deprived of food and water until they converted. This continued for five days while city notables and priests made many visits to the ship. Close to one hundred souls apostatized in one day, but ben Jacob Hayyat's wife died from the deprivations, as did nearly fifty others, including women and children. Ben Jacob Hayyat himself lay near death. At that point the bishop relented and allowed the ship to sail on to Fez.

In Morocco ben Jacob Hayyat was imprisoned on false charges of apostasy against Islam, ransomed by the Jewish community, and only then was allowed to proceed to Fez. When he arrived, he only discovered more privations:

> Famine prevailed in this city, until we were reduced to eating the grass in the fields. Every day I ground grain with my two hands at the homes of the Moslems, in return for a small slice of bread, thinner than thin, not fit even for dogs to eat. And during the nights my stomach sagged to the ground and my swollen belly was my bolster. Because of the intense autumn cold, because we had no covering against the cold, and also because we had no houses in which to spend the night, we used to dig holes in the rubbish heaps in the city and burrow unto them.[48]

Judah ben Jacob Hayyat eventually sought refuge in Italy.

Abraham ben Solomon left Spain for Fez at the age of ten and was an eyewitness to the fire that raged through the Jewish encampment outside the city:

> After they had been living in Fez for about eight months, a fire erupted in the Jewish section in the month of Tammuz and a number of people there burned to death, as if fire had descended from heaven. I was about eleven at the time, and was saved from the fire....
>
> Immediately after the great fire which I mentioned, there was a great drought, and more than 20,000 Jews in Fez and the surrounding area died. And when they saw this terrible thing, there were those who returned to the land of Edom [i.e., of the Christians]. For they said: "We will all die here." Others fled to the tents of the Ishmaelites. Some died of hunger in the markets and streets, and the daughters of Israel were unclothed.[49]

The suffering that Jews encountered in Fez compelled many to return to their former homes in Spain, even though this meant abandoning their religion and converting to Christianity. Bernáldez saw Jews returning from Fez and claimed to have baptized over one hundred of them himself. He described the privations they related to him and the difficulties they suffered in their journey back to Spain:

> All those Jews who had passed through the Kingdom of Fez, and who returned here, came naked, barefoot and full of fleas, dying of hunger and having undergone evil calamities, that it was a pain to see them. And on the roads by which they came from Fez to Mazalquivir, and from there to Arcila, the Moors came out and stripped them nude to their bare skins. They threw themselves upon the women with force and murdered the men, and they would open them up in the middle, searching for gold in their abdomen, because they knew that they had swallowed it. And they would pull them aside off the road, make them open their mouths so that they give them the gold, and thrust their hands below for the same purpose.[50]

Abravanel and Italy

Another route of escape lay in Italy, and Abravanel chose to flee there. He set sail from Valencia and arrived in Naples on August 14, in one of nine caravels. He was welcomed by King Ferrante and received a place at court. Others experienced more hardships on their way to Italy. One Genoese historian described the pitiful condition of the boats that arrived from Spain: "One might have taken them for specters, so emaciated were they, so cadaverous in their aspect, and with eyes so sunken; they differed in nothing from the dead, except in the power of motion, which indeed they scarcely retained."[51]

Naples provided Abravanel with only a short-term refuge. King Ferrante died on January 25, 1494, after which a French invasion unleashed a war of succession. Abravanel fled Naples less than a year later, on January 21, 1495. Unrest would require him to continue to wander through

Italy, including a seven-year stay in Monopoli. There, unable to pursue business or court activity, he concentrated on writing and study.

His son settled in Salonika, which was under Ottoman control. The Ottomans welcomed Jewish settlement, and Salonika and other Ottoman lands would house important Sephardic communities. However, the difficulty of reaching these lands from Spain meant that most of the Sephardic settlers in the Ottoman lands came much later, after first attempting to settle in Portugal and other more accessible refuges.

Rather than joining his son and adjusting to life in a Muslim land, Abravanel clung to life in Christendom. He finally settled in Venice, where he helped with trade negotiations with his native Portugal. Abravanel's writing during his years of exile in Venice exemplified a traditional Jewish response to disaster: to hope fervently for the coming of the Messiah. In traditional Judaism the Messiah is conceived of as a human figure, like Moses, whose coming will usher in the kingdom of God on earth. Jews believed that the coming of the Messiah would be accompanied by miracles, including the resurrection of the dead. Jewish messianism would have provided consolation and given meaning to the suffering that followed the expulsion of 1492.

Abravanel turned to prophecies of the Messiah in several of his post-exile books, and these prophecies became an obsession with him. He proved, through three separate and complicated calculations based on the biblical book of Daniel, that the Messiah would come around the year 1503, though his presence might not become manifest until the 1530s or 1570s.[52] After predicting the date of the Messiah's coming, Abravanel went on to describe how a Jewish kingdom would be established, a scenario that included the destruction of Christendom, which he saw as just retribution for the privations that Christendom had inflicted on Spanish Jews. According to Abravanel the destruction would begin in a war between Christian and Muslim forces over control of Israel, a war that Abravanel predicted would be the bloodiest battle in history, with destruction magnified by heaven-sent torrents of fire, sulfur, and brimstone, all of it directed mainly against the Christians.

The Christian defeat there would bring the war between Christianity and Islam to Europe, culminating in an assault on Rome. Abravanel associated Rome, as the capital of Catholicism, with the biblical predictions of the doom that would be suffered by Edom. Rome would be utterly destroyed, and then the Messiah would appear in Rome and announce a new order for humankind.[53] All nations would miraculously yield to him. Jews all over the world, including all of those who had died over the many generations of exile from Israel, would now reappear in Israel. The Messiah would rule the earth, establishing God's kingdom and justice in this world, and nature would be restored to its original condition, as it was in Eden.[54]

Abravanel, of course, never saw the fulfillment of his vision of the coming of the Messiah and retribution for injustices inflicted on the Jews. He was vindicated, however, in other ways. He died in Venice, where he was honored by both Jews and Christians. His son Judah became an important Renaissance thinker, known as the Leone Ebreo, or "Hebrew lion." His *Dialoghi d'amore*, authored around 1502 (but not published until 1535), became one of the most influential Renaissance Neoplatonic works of all time.[55]

In 1992, 130 Abravanels (only some of whom were known descendants) gathered in New York City to pay tribute to Don Isaac Abravanel on the quincentennial of his exile from Spain.[56] They listened to a taped greeting from Don Isaac's most prominent direct descendant of that time, Maurice Abravanel, one of the best known conductors in twentieth-century United States. He eventually assumed the leadership of the Utah State Symphony Orchestra, turning it from an obscure ensemble into a world-renowned orchestra with recording contracts on several labels and over one hundred recordings, and he was a pioneer in the worldwide revival of Gustav Mahler's reputation. Because of him the Abravanel name is honored in Salt Lake City only a few blocks from the Mormon Temple complex, as the name of the city's main performing arts complex: Abravanel Hall.

25

The Last Jews of Iberia

Portugal: The Jews Prior to Spanish Expulsion

Portugal's physical and cultural proximity to Spain made it a tempting refuge from Spanish repression for Jews and conversos. It served as a refuge after the mass conversions of 1391, when some converts (including Abravanel's grandfather) had sought shelter there, where they could revert to their old religion. King João I of Portugal publicly recognized the hardships suffered by the Jews in Spain: "Know that the Jews of the *comuna* of Lisbon have informed us that the Jews in the realms of Castile and Aragon have suffered many thefts and evils and some of them have been converted against their will . . . in the hope of escaping death until such a time when they might reach safety."[1] King João promulgated a law that placed evidentiary burdens on prosecutors of persons accused of reverting to Judaism in Portugal. The law also echoed the provisions from the papal bull of Boniface IX condemning the forced conversions of Jews.

Jews who fled Spain at the turn of the fifteenth century, either as Jews or as converts, do not appear to have been prosecuted in Portugal. The same cannot be said for the next wave of immigrants: Spanish conversos who came to Portugal fleeing persecution by the Inquisition. Anti-converso fervor stirred up in Spain by the Inquisition spread to Portugal. The unpopularity of the conversos increased due to outbreaks of plague, common at the time, which sometimes coincided with the arrival of converso immigrants.

In 1484 the municipal council of Lisbon ordered the immediate expulsion of all Spanish conversos, using an outbreak of the plague as a pretext. In Porto anti-converso sentiment culminated in an expulsion order enacted in 1485 and renewed two years later. In 1488 the king issued a decree prohibiting any Castilian converso from entering Portugal and took steps to encourage emigration of conversos already residing in the kingdom. By 1493, one year after the Spanish expulsion decree had gone into effect, the king ordered that any Castilian converso discovered entering Portugal be put to death.[2]

After Expulsion: King João

After the expulsion decree was issued, the Spanish Jews negotiated with Portugal to allow for access to Portuguese territory, as either a refuge or a transit stop to other lands. The deal they made provided a windfall for Portugal but relatively few benefits for Jews. Portugal granted only about six hundred families a right to permanent resettlement. The others, perhaps as many as one hundred thousand Jews, only received an allowance to stay for eight months, along with assurances that arrangements would be made for their transit out of Portugal.[3]

Even this temporary shelter required Jews to pay a burdensome tariff. According to one of the refugees, the prominent astronomer Abraham Zacuto:

> Most of those in Castile entered Portugal because they were unable to take passage by sea, and had to leave by the assigned date. This required them to pay a tithe of all they owned. Furthermore, each person had to pay a ducat per person and a third of a ducat for permission to pass through the country. Then they had to pay a quarter of all they brought with them, and some of them almost a third. Even one who had no money whatsoever had to pay ten ducats, and if not he was imprisoned.[4]

The chronicler Elijah Capsali described the efforts of the Portuguese to ensure that the Jews paid the full entrance fee: "King João, even before the sons of Israel had entered Portugal, sent zealous agents, angels of destruction, to decimate them and deprive them of their ornaments. As they were emptying their bags, the messengers of the Gentiles appeared before them, insulting them; they searched their tents in search of loot and to take away their gold and silver."[5] Portugal imposed on refugees arriving from Spain both an entrance fee and a tax on all property brought into the country. These imposts contributed millions of *reais* to the royal treasury.[6]

Many of the exiles were placed in refugee camps close to the border. Royal documents refer to various encampments, each with four thousand to five thousand Jews, near different towns along the border. Refugees in these encampments suffered from disease, especially plague. Several towns took measures to block the entry of Jews for fear of plague. Even the Jewish community in the town of Loulé tried to keep the foreign Jews out, due to plague fears.[7]

King João II did not wait long before retaliating against Jews who overstayed or failed to pay the required tax. In his most shocking action, he enslaved Jewish children, had them converted to Christianity, and then shipped them to a new experimental colony in São Tomé, an uninhabited island near the equator, about 120 miles off the African coast. By the mid-fifteenth century, the Portuguese had already established profitable sugar plantations on the island of Madeira, and the king hoped to emulate this success in São Tomé, using Jews, criminals, and African slaves from northern Angola as laborers. Several later Jewish commentators bewailed the mistreatment of these children, whose suffering on the island reportedly included being eaten by crocodiles. As recorded by Samuel Usque in the mid-sixteenth century: "They were thrown ashore and mercilessly left there. Almost all were swallowed up by the huge lizards on the island, and the remainder, who escaped these reptiles, wasted away from hunger and abandonment. Only a few were miraculously spared that dreadful misfortune.[8]

There are no firsthand reports of the conditions that the children faced on the island or of how many survived. However, the fears of contemporary Jews that all the children died appear excessive. The colony eventually succeeded and was prospering by the sixteenth century, although this prosperity would not survive competition with more-efficient sugar producers in the following century. Given the young age of the Jewish settlers, the lack of any Jewish resources or contacts, and the likelihood that they eventually mixed with the other settlers, it is improbable that any Jewish faith or practices survived. However, the descendants of the original colonists continued to be called New Christians as late as the seventeenth century. In 1529 one plantation owner complained that the Jews held all the best land.[9]

When Pedro da Cunha Lobo was appointed bishop of the island of São Tomé in 1621, he arrived with ambitions to eliminate imagined Jewish practices on the island. One modern historian records his paranoid reactions after arrival: "Then on the night of October 26, 1621, he was awakened by the sounds of a noisy celebration. Looking out his window, he saw marching past the cathedral a procession of Jews carrying a 'golden calf'! Rushing out to confront the 'Jews,' he was beaten and abused by them. Shocked and disgusted, he took the next ship back to Portugal."[10]

In addition to enslaving the children sent to São Tomé, João II also enslaved adult Jews. Capsali claimed that fifteen thousand were enslaved, and that two-thirds of those were ransomed by the Jewish community. The Spanish chronicler Bernáldez set the figure at only one thousand.[11]

King Manoel and the General Conversion

Some relief came to the Jews with João's death in 1495, at the age of forty. The new king, João's cousin and brother-in-law, Manoel, immediately adopted a more favorable position toward the Jews. On the day of his succession, Manoel issued letters urging the town councils of Porto and Évora to take steps to protect the Jews against anti-Jewish riots that might break out in reaction to the death of his predecessor.[12] In one of his first acts as monarch, he freed the Jews in Portugal who had been enslaved by King João II. Manoel wanted to expand Portuguese holdings in North Africa and to further Portuguese explorations and settlements toward India; today he is best remembered as the patron of the explorer Vasco da Gama. Jewish capital and expertise would help further his political ambitions. His ambitions, however, proved fatal to Portugal's Jews. Manoel hoped to marry Princess Isabel, the eldest daughter of Ferdinand and Isabella, and widow to João II's son. Among other advantages the marriage would make a union between the two countries possible, if unlikely (the heir apparent to the Spanish throne, Prince Juan, did not die until October 1497).

Princess Isabel initially refused to remarry, despite her parents' interest in pursuing the alliance with Portugal. But her reluctance was overcome, and a marriage contract was signed in November 1496. Although no mention of the Jews is made in the contract, it is generally agreed that the marriage conditions included the expulsion of the Jews from Portugal. This stipulation reflected more than the personal fanaticism of the bride-to-be. Her parents had just gone through enormous efforts to rid Spain of its Jews and would not have wanted to see the same Jews reappear on the border with their daughter's new kingdom.

A written Portuguese edict of expulsion was signed one month after the marriage contract, in December 1496. Unlike the Spanish edict, which had given a lengthy justification for the expulsion based on the Inquisition's argument that the Jews undermined converso faith, the Portuguese edict is supported by a perfunctory recital of Jewish perfidy: "We are convinced that the Jews, obstinate in their hatred of the Holy Catholic Faith of Our Lord Jesus Christ who redeemed us by his death, have committed and continue to commit against him great wrongs and blasphemed in these Our realms. As sons of wickedness, they do not do this only amongst themselves but, with their hardened hearts, they also plunge Our kingdoms into a greater condemnation and induce many Christians to leave the one true path that is the Holy Catholic Faith."[13]

The decree then ordered the expulsion of both Jews and Muslims from Portugal. No justification was provided for the Muslim expulsion. Jews would be required to leave by the end of October 1497. They were promised provisions—including ships—to aid in their departure. King Manoel made some early efforts to comply with his promise to assist the Jews in leaving the country. In January 1497 one town's municipal council noted that the king had ordered the forced requisition of ships to ferry the Jews out of Portugal.[14] But it soon became apparent that the king wanted to keep the Jews in Portugal as converts (even though the expulsion decree was premised on Jewish wickedness). Thus he issued several decrees to port cities ordering that no Jew could leave without royal license.[15] He also limited the number of ports that could be used by the Jews. The king was probably motivated by fears that the Jewish expulsion would have dire economic consequences for Portugal. In the next century, Rabbi Gedalya ibn Yahna would write that the king "feared that the kingdom would remain like an empty fishing net, for the Jews were extremely numerous and they possessed most of the kingdom's wealth."[16]

Early in 1497 the king ordered the seizure of all communal property, including all synagogues and schools, as well as objects of worship, such as Torah crowns and ornaments. He then ordered all religious books confiscated, making Jewish religious worship nearly impossible. The books were locked away. Some may eventually have been burned; others were sold. One chest of books was sold in 1505 to the Jews in Chochin, India.[17] In the spring of the same year, the king decided on a new, more drastic measure to compel conversion. In late March—Passover for the Jews, Easter for the Christians—he sent soldiers throughout the country to seize all the Jewish children. These children were to be taken away and raised as Christians. Only Jews who agreed to conversion could retrieve their children.

The brutal separation of children from their parents shocked even Christians. The chronicler Jerónimo Osório, bishop of Silves (who was born in 1506 and thus did not personally witness the act), wrote:

> Dom Manuel, who was troubled in his soul that so many millions of men would suffer eternal punishment, devised a plan which would at least save their children. The plan was unjust; it was unfair, even though it was born out of laudable purposes. He ordered that every child of a Jew who was not beyond the age of fourteen years be taken away from the parents so that, removed from their sight, they be indoctrinated in the Christian religion. But the king did not accomplish this without great spiritual affliction. It was such a piteous thing to see the children being wrested from the breasts of their mothers, and the parents being dragged, struck, and whipped as they clutched their little children in their arms. A cry was raised and the air trembled with the laments and the weeping of the women. There were some among them who, turbid with indignation, drowned their children in the wells; some of them fell into such madness that they killed themselves.[18]

Fernando Coutinho, the bishop of Lamego, at the time a member of the royal council, witnessed Jews "dragged by the hair to the baptismal fonts; how a father, his head covered as a sign of his intense grief and with a broken heart, went to the baptismal font accompanied by his son, protesting and calling upon God as their witness that they wished to die according to the Law of Moses."[19] As a further act of coercion, the king evoked an old law stipulating that any convert who was an only child had a right, once baptized, to immediately receive two-thirds of his parents' estate. The king used this law as grounds for seizing Jewish property.[20]

The king used carrots as well as sticks to encourage conversion. On May 30, 1497, he issued a decree promising that those who converted would be free from any inquiry into their beliefs for twenty years. Any denunciation based on heresy would be admissible in court only if it reflected acts committed within twenty days of the denunciation. Any crimes committed by Jews before conversion would be pardoned. Many of the Jews in Portugal had seen the Spanish Inquisition persecute conversos; King Manoel promised to shield them from a similar fate.

As the day of expulsion from Portugal drew near, the king restricted embarkation to the port of Lisbon. Jews were crowded into the Estaus palace on the Rossio Square. Contemporary accounts estimated that between ten and twenty thousand Jews were housed on the palace grounds, awaiting transport out of Portugal. Because space was limited in the palace, Jews may have camped out in the stable yards.[21] The king then ordered that the Jews be taken into nearby churches and converted by force. As one Jewish eyewitness recounted: "When the time had passed, and the Jews did not want to change their faith of their own free will, they were taken by force in all the king's provinces, and were beaten with sticks and straps, and carried to the churches. There they sprinkled water on them, and gave them Christian names, men and women alike."[22] According to Jewish chroniclers, some of the Jews attempted suicide rather than be converted. Some of those who resisted were allowed to leave for North Africa. One rabbi left an account of being abused, tortured, and imprisoned in Lisbon; he eventually made his way to Egypt, one of a party of twenty-seven rabbis and other hold-outs allowed to leave Lisbon in the spring of 1498.[23]

After Conversion

The conversions effected by King Manoel in Portugal were so extensive that they came to be called the "general conversion." The king kept his pledge to shield the converts from prosecution and investigations into heresy. He did, however, also take some steps to keep them within their new faith. On April 20, 1499, he published a decree forbidding the New Christians from leaving the country without a special royal license.[24] Other laws were aimed at encouraging settlement of New Christians outside the old Jewish quarters and intermarriage of New and Old Christians.[25]

Although the king made some attempts to encourage the conversos to assimilate into the Christian culture, they remained a separate and cohesive community, and tensions soon developed between the New and the Old Christians. The New Christians suffered occasional attacks of persecution from the Old Christians. In 1503, after a poor harvest, anti–New Christian riots broke out in Lisbon and Évora. The worst of these incidents took place in 1506, a year when plague had broken out in Portugal, and the royal court had fled Lisbon. The city suffered, too, from famine and drought. Daily processions prayed for "water and mercy."[26]

A chapel in the Convento de São Domingos contained a crucifix that some claimed could be seen on occasion to shine brightly, a miracle that attracted huge crowds. On Sunday, April 19, a riot broke out after a New Christian was supposedly heard to remark scornfully that no miracle had occurred in the convent. The alleged blasphemer was beaten, taken out to the plaza, and dismembered. When his brother arrived, he, too, was killed, and both bodies were burned.[27] The Dominicans egged the mob on, encouraging the crowd to attack the New Christians. While one friar preached a sermon against the Jews, two others held up a crucifix to the crowd shouting: "Heresy, heresy . . . ! Destroy this abominable people."[28]

The anti-converso riots set off by this event lasted for days. One witness, a German whose vessel was docked in Lisbon, left an anonymous account of the riots, including this description of the following days' events: "On Monday, I saw things that I would certainly not have believed had they been reported or written, or unless I had witnessed them myself. Women with child were flung from the windows and caught on spears by those standing underneath, their offspring being hurled away. The peasantry followed the example of the townspeople. Many women and girls were ravished in the fanatical pursuit. The number of New Christians slain is estimated at between 2,000 and 4,000 souls."[29]

The mob targeted one of the king's financial advisors and tax farmers, João Rodrigues Mascarenhas. They attacked his home on Sunday, and after he had escaped, on the following day he was recognized before he could make his way outside the city. He was beaten to death by the mob, and his corpse repeatedly stabbed. The crowd brought the body back to his house, which they looted and tore apart.

Today there is a small, round monument in Lisbon's main square, the Rossio, to the victims of the massacre. It is inscribed: "Tribute from the City of Lisbon to the victims of the Jewish Massacre of 1506. In memory of the thousands of Jewish victims of fanatic religious intolerance, murdered in the massacre that began on the 19th of April, 1506 in this place." It is interesting that the monument describes the events of April 1506 as a massacre of Jews, since all the victims were technically Christians. But since the "general conversion" decreed by King Manoel had taken place fewer than ten years earlier, "Jewish" is probably a more accurate description of the victims.

The massacre did provide one important benefit to the New Christians. They immediately lobbied the king to rescind the prohibition on travel outside Lisbon. After almost a year of negotiation, the king issued a decree on March 1, 1507, lifting limits on travel and promising that New Christian would be treated as the equals of Old Christians in every respect.[30] In practice, though, the Crown continued to restrict converso emigration, but large numbers of conversos managed to leave Portugal for places of refuge in both the Old and the New World.

The establishment in Portugal of a repressive inquisition in the late sixteenth century at the request of King João III provided a further impetus for converso flight from Portugal. There is substantial literature on this diaspora—generally speaking, the Iberian Jews who left Spain and Portugal after the expulsions of 1492 and 1497 are better documented in popular literature than are the Jewish communities of Iberia before the expulsions.

In Spain conversos had lived for several generations as "New Christians" and were purged of Jewish practices by the repressive machinery of the Spanish Inquisition. The Portuguese New Christians, in contrast, were relatively free from church or state religious coercion and therefore remained relatively unprocessed by the Christian faith. Many quickly reverted to Judaism after emigrating, and other emigrants brought with them a mix of faiths and customs or alienation from religion. The persistence of Jewish culture or faith among the Portuguese converso who left for other European countries led these countries to associate Portuguese with Judaism. As the historian Cecil Roth has noted (echoing the lament of the seventeenth-century Portuguese Jesuit Padre António Vieira): "throughout Europe ... the terms 'Portuguese' and 'Jew' were regarded as almost synonymous."[31]

Navarre

Like Portugal Navarre's geographical proximity to Spain and religious tolerance made it a tempting refuge for Spanish Jews. But it also had major drawbacks: Navarre was politically unstable, land-locked, and surrounded by countries that denied entrance to Jews. In the end it became a trap from which few Jews could escape.

Jews living in the kingdom of Navarre had suffered some bouts of repression. The Shepherd's Crusade of 1320, invading from France, targeted Jews. Local anti-Jewish riots had broken out in 1328, resulting in the killing of hundreds of Jews, mainly in the town of Estella.[32] Jews in Navarre, however, had escaped the mass riots of 1391, which had led to forced conversions throughout Spain. By the end of the fifteenth century, Navarre was host to about 3,550 Jews in a kingdom of about 100,000 people.[33] Most Jews lived in the south near the Aragonese or Castilian borders, in towns like Tudela, Estella, and Olite, as well as in the capital, Pamplona. Few Jews lived in the rural Basque regions north of Pamplona.

Although Jews in Navarre had not been subject to mass conversions in 1391, a significant number of conversos from the neighboring kingdoms of Castile and Aragon did eventually settle in the kingdom. In the town of Tudela, by the late 1400s conversos had taken up several high level positions in the city government, as well as in local churches.[34]

The growth of Navarre's converso population attracted the attention of the Spanish Inquisition. In the aftermath of the Arbués assassination in Aragon, the Spanish Crown demanded the return to Aragon of conversos who had fled to Navarre. When Ferdinand wrote to officials in Tudela demanding that they accede to Inquisition authority, city officials reacted by blocking Inquisition access to the city. In one case an Inquisition official who took a group of conversos from Tudela into custody was chased down by thirty horsemen from the city who freed the prisoners.[35] In response in April 1487, the Spanish monarchs obtained a letter from Pope Innocent VII barring any ruler from admitting refugees fleeing the Spanish Inquisition and ordering that such refugees be returned to Spanish custody. The standoff was resolved on February 21, 1488, when the city of Tudela agreed to submit to the Inquisition in exchange for the actions taken against them by Spain being lifted.[36]

After Ferdinand and Isabella decreed the expulsion of Jews from Spain in 1492, Navarre's Queen Catherine and King Consort Jean allowed Jews free access to their kingdom. Several cities protested against the admission of Jews into the kingdom, possibly fearing economic consequences, retaliation from the Spanish, or increased scrutiny of Navarre's conversos by the Inquisition. Navarre's monarchs, however, maintained their policy of granting refuge to the fleeing Jews. The historian Benjamin Gampel has estimated that approximately 1,800 Jews fled to Navarre from Spain, while earlier historians had put the figure at 12,000.[37]

For some Jews Navarre was a way station to a more permanent refuge. Navarre's proximity to Spain meant that Jews expelled from Spain were still able to close out their abandoned estates through agents, without having to accept the fire-sale prices imposed by the tight expulsion deadline. Because Navarre was landlocked, on March 9, 1493, Ferdinand granted Jews in Navarre safe passage through Aragon in order to reach the southern ports, to sail from Iberia.[38] Other Jews remained in Navarre, settling in cities like Tudela that already had Jewish centers. Tax collectors maintained records distinguishing "native Jews" from the "newcomers," so that—at least for tax purposes—Navarre now had Old Christians, New Christians, Old Jews, and New Jews.[39]

While the Jews found safe refuge in Navarre, the country's history of political instability and military weakness made it an insecure home. Two rulers died in quick succession. Their heir, Catherine, married the French aristocrat Jean d'Albert, but the couple remained more focused on their holdings in southern France than on the small state of Navarre.[40] Rival factions—the Beaumonts, who supported Castile, and the Agamontes, allied with France—plunged the country into periodic civil strife. Only several years in advance of the Spanish expulsion, the Treaty of Valencia, signed on March 21, 1488, had made the kingdom an official protectorate of the Spanish monarchs. Possibly inspired by their Spanish neighbor, factions in Navarre began to promote anti-Jewish measures. At the request of the Cortes, the kingdom barred Jews from appearing in public on Sundays until noon and on feast days.[41] The Cortes continued to complain about Jewish lending and other practices—a complaint that the monarchs acknowledged in 1496.[42]

For Navarre's Jews the end came in 1498, when King Jean and Queen Catherine ordered all Jews to convert or to leave the kingdom. No copy of an expulsion decree survives, but the motive for the decree was probably to appease the Spanish monarchs and to ease political pressure on Navarre from the more powerful neighboring kingdom.[43] Any relief from Spanish interference in Navarre's affairs was short-lived: in 1512 Ferdinand conquered Navarre and absorbed it into Spain.

The alternative given to Navarre's Jews in 1498—to convert or to leave—was a false choice. Ferdinand no longer allowed Jews to transit his kingdom; the only lawful way into Spain was through conversion. France similarly barred Jews from admission. For all but a few Jews, there was no exit from Navarre. As one contemporary Jewish chronicler noted: "The road was closed upon them and they turned from God, the

Lord of Israel."[44] Another contemporary, Francisco Aleson, reported: "Not many left since almost all converted to our Holy Faith."[45] A few Jews managed the treacherous escape from Navarre. Shemtov ben Shmuel Gamil left an account of his harrowing journey to Morocco, which did not come to light until 1928. Gamil left first for a town in Valencia, where he had left children and a business before the expulsion of 1492. He found his children gone and his business plundered.

The Inquisition had eyes throughout Spain, with informants everywhere. Gamil was imprisoned and then released after three weeks, presumably by posing as a Muslim. Gamil then contacted his children and attempted to leave from Tortosa. He changed his plans in order to evade capture and headed for Almería. There he was again arrested and again released by posing as a Muslim with the assistance of an Islamic contact. Now he and his family went to Granada and paid a large sum of money to join a group of Muslims traveling to Fez. Again, he was discovered and imprisoned, and the family spent months in prison in several locations. Gamil managed once again to obtain release and finally escaped to Morocco.[46]

Based on the reasonable assumption that Navarre's monarchs acted to appease the Spanish monarchs, Ferdinand and Isabella can be considered the main architects behind the complete eradication of overt Jewish worship on the Iberian peninsula. As the historian Benjamin Gampel notes: "Thus ended the almost six-hundred-year-long existence of the Jewish community of Navarre and, with it, the distinguished history of the Jews in the Iberian Peninsula."[47]

PART 6

After Expulsion

26

Purity of Blood

In the nineteenth century Thomas Carlyle proposed the "great man" theory of history, arguing that history was shaped by heroic men with great ideals. The story of the Jews of Spain seems to have been shaped instead by a "little man" theory of history. Individual decisions and actions impelled many of the major events in their history. But these decisions were made not by men with great ideals but rather by men driven by narrow, parochial ambitions, who did not expect, imagine, or care about the far-reaching consequences of their actions. Examples include the cynical anti-Jewish campaign of Enrique II, the religious fanaticism of Ferrand Martínez, the papal ambitions of Benedict the antipope, and the marriage ambitions of King Manoel of Portugal.

This is not to dismiss the importance of underlying social and economic factors. Such factors as the church-sponsored campaign against the Jews provided the kindling for these actions, without which these individual decisions may never have caught fire. But the underlying social factors did not compel the conversion or the expulsion of the Jews. Had different decisions and actions been taken—for example, had the archbishop of Seville survived to restrain Ferrand Martínez from his anti-Jewish campaign—the Jews may have been able to cling to life in Spain for centuries more, just as they held on to their religion and customs in towns and villages throughout the rest of Europe.

Pero Sarmiento and Marcos García's invention of racial exclusion laws was one such narrowly motivated action with far-reaching unexpected consequences. The Toledo revolt of 1449 started as an improvised means to punish allies of Álvaro de Luna and grab some quick loot. What began as a local political dispute, however, led to an invention of historic importance—namely, what the noted expert on anti-

Semitism Leon Poliakov has deemed "the first example in history of legalized racism."[1] The exclusion bars initiated in Toledo marked the beginning of modern anti-Semitism: for the first time, people were formally discriminated against based on a racial—rather than a religious—definition of Judaism.

Toledo's experiment in racial exclusion stained Spanish history and character for centuries to come. Though never imposed on a national level, discriminatory restrictions based on *limpieza de sangre*, or "purity of blood"—sometimes referred to simply as *limpieza*—were adopted locally by city and provincial governments, as well as by institutions including schools, parishes, and church and military orders. The new racial distinctions became an integral part of the Spanish concept of honor and national pride. "Purity of blood"—*limpieza*—laws would provide a template for the racist attitudes and racial slavery that accompanied Spain's conquest of the New World.

Almost immediately after the Toledo rebels of 1449 imposed restrictions based on Jewish descent, other communities proposed similar discriminatory rules. Soon schools and religious orders followed, barring admission from persons of Jewish descent. Conversos actively opposed these measures. They lobbied the kings and popes for relief. They produced a large literature in their defense, some written by Old Christian allies acting disinterestedly since they were not of Jewish descent. These arguments from the conversos and their allies demonstrated that *limpieza* violated Christian doctrine because it rejected the sacrament of baptism, contradicted the claim of Christianity to be a universal church open to all, and slandered all sanctified Christians of Jewish descent, including Christ, Mary, and most of the apostles.

Supporters of *limpieza* did not deign to respond to most of these arguments and provided little in the way of written argumentation to bolster their claims. The early supporters of *limpieza* largely relied on old anti-Jewish popular prejudice for support, and this prejudice continued to drive the spread of restrictions based on purity of blood.[2]

Rather than respond directly to the arguments of conversos, the purity-of-blood movement relied on two main justifications. The first was the evidence obtained by the Inquisition: starting with the Jeronymites, institutions used the Inquisition's discoveries (or alleged discoveries) of heresy to argue that this generation of conversos could not be placed in positions of trust. While this argument carried some logic as a pretext for *limpieza* at the time, these restrictions would continue in Spain long after any significant evidence remained of Jewish practices among conversos.

The second justification cited by supporters of *limpieza* was the accusation of deicide. The Jewish role in the killing of Christ was seen as a kind of original sin, inherited by succeeding generations of Jews.[3] Because the act superseded the rite of baptism, even baptism could not purge the conversos of the taint of this crime.[4] The belief that all people of Jewish descent were permanently stained by a curse made purity-of-blood restrictions an early version of modern racism, an inheritable religious curse mirroring the modern belief in inherited biological characteristics.

The fifteenth-century friar Espina, one of the principal writers to push for discriminatory restrictions on conversos, cited the thirteenth-century writer Thomas of Cantimpré as the basis for his claim that Jews, including conversos, suffered from this curse, which was also the basis for the Jewish guilt in blood-libel crimes. Thomas of Cantimpré claimed that Jews habitually kill Christians because of the curse brought on the Jews when they shouted: "His blood be upon us and our children." According to Thomas the guilt of the deicide passed to these Jews' descendants and afflicted their blood with disease. When this cursed blood courses through their veins, they suffer torment, unless they admit their share in killing Christ. Thomas claimed that the Jews believe they could be cured of this agony by the use of Christian blood; "and thus they kill at least one Christian annually, and they cast lots among themselves to determine which province should supply the victims."[5]

By the end of the fifteenth century, the idea that Jews suffered a curse from their part in deicide had passed into Spanish popular literature. The popular Catalan novel of knighthood *Tirant lo Blanc*, written sometime in the mid-fifteenth century (the author, Joanot Martorell, died in 1468) was published in 1490. It is regarded as a classic of Catalan literature—one of the few books of knighthood rescued, for its merit, from the famous auto-da-fé of books in *Don Quixote*. Still in print in both English and Spanish, it was filmed in Spain in 2006.

In the latter part of the book, King Escariano, accompanied by the knight Tirant, summons a Jew and offers to assist him in marrying the daughter of a rich Jewish merchant. The Jew responds that he would "sooner die than commit such a misdeed" and proceeds to explain how some Jews are cursed by the sin of deicide:

> "May the great God of Liberty," replied the Jew, "shield my heart from such baseness, and when I explain why this marriage cannot take place, you will certainly excuse me. Ever since Jesus Christ was crucified, all Jews have been of three lineages, the first of which consists of those who called for His death. Their restlessness reveals them, as they are forever fidgeting and their souls know no peace, nor have they much sense of shame. The second lineage is those who took part in His crucifixion. . . . You can recognize them by the fact that, unable to meet your gaze, they look down or to one side and can barely turn their eyes Heavenward. The Jew who wants to be my father-in-law is of this type. The third lineage . . . opposed Christ's execution and, moved by compassion, took refuge in Solomon's temple lest they see that Holy Man so cruelly abused. These kind and generous Jews . . . treat their neighbors with love and can look in all directions. Being of this type, I do not wish to taint my blood with perpetual grief, since by children's lineage would be eternally corrupted. I fear such Jews more than death and feel ashamed to speak with them."[6]

In 1674 the Franciscan Francisco de Torrejoncillo, in his widely known book *Centinela contra judios, puesta en la torre de la Iglesia de Dios*, developed what may be the most elaborate description of this curse, a version so fantastic that to modern ears it is comical. Torrejoncillo claimed that Jews inherited a hatred of Christ, and that one-eighth Jewish blood was sufficient to be infected. Some Jews had a tail at the end of their spine painful to sit on, an indication that their ancestors had sat on the tribunal that condemned Christ. According to Torrejoncillo each of the twelve tribes played a different role in the passion of Christ and, as a result, suffered different curses. Those descended from Ruben seized Christ on Gethsemane and as a result are unable to cultivate the soil. Those of the tribe of Asher, who slapped Jesus in the face, now have their right arm nearly one palm shorter than their left. Those of the tribe of Simeon, who nailed Jesus to the cross, suffer from bleeding wounds on their hands and feet on the twenty-fifth day of each month. According to Torrejoncillo, the crimes and punishments of the remaining tribes, though too gross to repeat, had been verified in Turkey by Antonio Carrasa, a great Hebrew rabbi who had converted to Catholicism.[7]

Limpieza laws initially spoke in terms of a stain that passed through race or lineage. The link between impurity and blood began to appear infrequently in the fifteenth century. There is a reference to unclean blood in Alonso de Oropesa's mid-fifteenth-century defense of the conversos: "Those who come to Christ should not be excluded because of an improper class of blood."[8] A satire written about the same time referred to Marrano physicians who killed Old Christian patients and married their widows in order "to dirty and stain their pure blood."[9]

The phrase "purity of blood" did not come into common use, however, until the sixteenth century. According to the standard medical belief at the time, derived from the classical physician Galen, blood was not just a fluid; rather, it was one of four principal humors in the body. It had particular importance because it also circulated the other humors. Blood therefore played an essential role in establishing a person's character, which explains why the English language still uses adjectives that originated in terms relating to blood and other humors to describe traits of character like sanguine, phlegmatic, choleric, and melancholy.[10] One mid-seventeenth-century writer, Diego de Castejón y Fonseca, in his book *Primacia de la Santa Iglesia de Toledo*, directly linked racial blood purity to classical medicine, saying that the poisonous inclinations caused by Jewish descent came from the humors.[11]

"Impure blood" was understood literally, not as a metaphor. This contributed to the belief in seventeenth-century Spain that Jewish males menstruated. Menstruation was thought to involve the body trying to purge impure blood, since woman's menstrual blood was commonly believed to have contained excess humors.[12] As a result it was believed that female saints did not menstruate; since their holy bodies contained only pure blood, they had nothing to purge.

A belief in menstruation among men arose partly in response to confusion over bleeding from hemorrhoids. Hemorrhoids, too, were the sign of a curse: according to a physician Dr. Quiñones, "among other bodily and spiritual curses which they suffer, inside and outside the body, for having persecuted the true Messiah, Christ our redeemer, to the point of placing him on a Cross, is that every month many of them suffer a flowing of blood from their posterior, as a perpetual sign of infamy and shame."[13] A Dr. Huarta, the personal physician to King Felipe IV, advocated applying *limpieza* rules to the medical profession and suggested that looking for male menstruation or hemorrhoids could be used as a test for the presence of impure blood.[14]

Once word spread of the discriminatory practices of the Toledan rioters, public demand quickly led to widespread attempts to impose these restrictions throughout Castile. Several localities followed Toledo's example. Córdoba both banned conversos from office and exiled most conversos from the city. Guipúzcoa, a Basque province bordering France, took the most extreme step, prohibiting conversos from living or marrying there (although Guipúzcoa never had a significant Jewish or converso community).

Schools were quick to adopt "purity of blood" standards. They were responsible for moral education and by excluding conversos, could claim that they were acting to shield students from exposure to persons of impure blood. The Colegio de Santa Cruz de Valladolid adopted *limpieza* rules in 1488. A school in Sigüenza passed a "statutum contra Hebaeos" in 1497. By 1522 conversos were barred from the Universities of Salamanca, Valladolid, and Toledo. The University of Seville, although it had been founded by a converso, in 1537 adopted a statute of *limpieza* after someone had carefully blotted out of the original charter the clause making the university open to all.[15] The Colegio Viejo de San Bartolomé de Salamanca falsely claimed to have begun the practice in 1414, which would have made it the first to institute a ban on converts and the purest school in Castile. Records show that *limpieza* was not established there until 1498.

The first order to impose *limpieza* was the Jeronymites. The pro-converso views of Alonso de Oropesa, the leader of the order, attracted numerous converso recruits. After the imposition of the Inquisition, the large number of conversos in the order attracted allegations of Judaizing among the order's monks and a violent purge followed, including several public burnings of conversos adjudged as heretics. Based on these alleged discoveries of heresy, one prior, Gonzalo de Toro, began a campaign to impose *limpieza* on the order. He faced strong opposition within the order, but Toro prevailed in 1486. He then appealed secretly to Pope Innocent VIII to issue a bull affirming the validity of the decree. The pope deferred the issue to his successor, Alexander VI (the Catalan Borgia, father to Lucrecia), who affirmed the decree in 1495, barring descendants of conversos to the fourth generation from the order, except by special consent of the General and the Private Chapter.[16]

Tomás de Torquemada, the leader of the Spanish Inquisition, established the convent of Saint Thomas Aquinas in Ávila. In 1496 he applied to Pope Alexander VI and received a decree forbidding the reception of anyone descended, directly or indirectly, from Jews. Julius II, who became pope in 1503, soon therefore issued a bull denouncing *limpieza* and banning its use in religious and secular orders. The pope was probably supported by King Ferdinand, who wanted the authority over conversos to be vested only in the Inquisition, which acted under royal authority and control. After Ferdinand's death, however, orders once again started to adopt *limpieza de sangre* bans on converso membership. By the early sixteenth century, cathedral chapters began to bar conversos from office in their churches. The church of Seville, in 1515, was the first to do so. In 1532 Pope Clement VII extended this law to nephews of conversos, and a decade later it was further extended to great-nephews.

The chapter at Córdoba followed suit, citing the religious crimes, dissensions, ambitions, and arrogance that these Judeo-Christians had brought to the church and the city of Córdoba.[17] Córdoba went even further and established a formal procedure for testing candidates. On his knees, right hand placed over an image of the crucifix in the missal, each candidate would swear that he was not descended from Jews or Moors. He would then recite the last names of his parents and grand-parents and the place of their birth. There followed an investigation into the veracity of the claims, and if necessary an official investigator would be chosen to interrogate witnesses. After all evidence was collected, a majority vote would allow the candidate to be sworn in, with an oath that included faithfulness to the purity-of-blood law.[18]

The monarchs did not take a fully consistent position toward these efforts. Fernando and Isabel opposed Jerónimo's purity law. But when the Colegio of San Bartolomé had trouble ejecting a converso, the queen responded that if he would not leave through the door, then they should throw him out the window.[19] The most important conflict over an attempt to impose *limpieza* discriminatory restrictions came in the mid-sixteenth century, when the archbishop of Toledo, Juan Martínez Silíceo, emerged as the strongest proponent yet of *limpieza* restrictions. He dedicated himself to winning approval for *limpieza* from both king and pope.

Silíceo, born Juan Martínez Pedernales, came from a family of peasant descent. He went to Paris as a mendicant and managed to obtain six years of study at the University of Paris, followed by three years there as a teacher. After he was recruited to teach at Salamanca, he became tutor to Prince Felipe (who, as Felipe/Philip II, raised the Spanish Armada against England). Ten years as the prince's tutor won him the appointment in 1546 as archbishop of Toledo. Silíceo, with reason, called this post the most important one in the world after Rome. Toledo was the largest archbishopric in Spain, and Spain was the leader of the Counter-Reformation, the Catholic nation leading the church's campaign against the rise of the Protestantism. The previous archbishop had attempted to impose *limpieza* in 1539—with no success. Silíceo would dedicate himself to overcoming his predecessor's failure. *Limpieza* often involved class conflicts. Many of the conversos were prosperous, with ties to the aristocracy, and the lower classes were often the most fanatic supporters of purity-of-blood laws.

Silíceo inherited the prejudices of his origins. He had also long been associated with the Colegio de San Bartolomé, which was proud of its tradition of racial purity (though it was less strict than the Colegio Mayor de Cuenca, which barred not only those with "stains" of Jewish or Moorish blood but also anyone even falsely rumored to have such stains). The pretext for Silíceo's campaign arose when he heard that a candidate for a canon benefice had a father who, after being accused by the Inquisition, had fled Spain and reverted to Judaism. Silíceo protested that such a candidate would transform the most important church in Spain into a synagogue. He then recommended imposing purity-of-blood restrictions in his archdiocese. All candidates for office would be called upon to swear unyielding allegiance to the principle of purity of blood and bear the cost of proving the truth of their "pure blood" claims.

The dean of the cathedral, Diego de Castilla, a high-born converso, objected that the church of Toledo could better protect its honor by admitting only people of nobility (which would have barred the archbishop) or only those who could pass rigorous university exams. People of low birth, he said—not Judeo-Christians—threatened to stain the honor of the church of Toledo.[20]

Silíceo hurriedly convened a chapter meeting to push through a vote on *limpieza*. His proposal won by a vote of twenty-four to ten. But protesters complained that the proposal should have been presented before all cathedral dignitaries, and they threatened to appeal to the pope. While conversos led the opposition—Silíceo pointed out that nine out of ten of the votes against *limpieza* came from conversos—they were joined by some prominent Old Christians, who called for the immediate annulment of the statutes. These groups appealed collectively to both the Crown and the pope. Prince Felipe ordered the archbishop to suspend the provisions of the purity statute. Silíceo then appealed to Felipe's father the emperor (Felipe's father, King Carlos of Spain, also ruled the Holy Roman Empire as Charles V). Carlos told his representative to consult with Rome, while submitting the issue to the royal council.

The New Christians had already appealed to Rome and obtained assurances of the pope's opposition to these restrictions. The archbishop's representative, however, convinced the pope on Silíceo's behalf to refer the issue to three cardinals, who declared it "saintly and just."[21] Based on that recommendation, Pope Paul III signed a secret brief approving the decree. Papal statute in hand, Silíceo agreed to submit the decree to the royal council, which backed the prince against Silíceo. Silíceo then appealed yet again to the emperor, claiming a fair judgment from the royal council was impossible, since some members, as conversos, would be personally affected by enforced *limpieza*. Silíceo now prepared several papers for the emperor in defense of *limpieza*, citing the huge number of *limpieza* laws already approved in Spain, beginning with the first, adopted in Toledo in 1449.

Like the fifteenth-century book *Fortress of Faith*, Silíceo's papers provide an extensive record of anti-Semitic ideas current at the time. He recapitulates all the treasonous acts allegedly committed by Jews, including the betrayal of Spain to the Moors. He also enumerates the crimes of conversos, blaming all outbreaks of civil disorder, including the Toledo revolt of 1449, on them. He even claims that the followers of Martin Luther were descended from Jews. Silíceo called for the imposition of *limpieza* as an extension of the *reconquista de España*. Instead of an exterior Islamic enemy, Old Christians now had to liberate Spain from the dominion of the New Christians, who had not only succeeded in controlling the property and lives of the Old Christians but now had reign over their souls.

Silíceo would not end with banning conversos from positions in the church. He would ban them from working as judges, lawyers, and scribes; he would also ban them from medicine, fearing that they only brought about the deaths of Old Christians.[22] He also condemned miscegenation. He called for a ban on marriages between Old and New Christians. He said that people should breed with pure blood just as with horses one should seek out seed of good caste for a pure-blooded mare.

In a remarkable statement, he claimed that correspondence had been discovered between the Jews of Constantinople and Spain at the time of the expulsion. The modern scholar and expert on anti-Semitism Léon Poliakov has called this "one of the most widespread anti-Semitic forgeries of the sixteenth century."[23] According to this correspondence, the Spanish Jews, facing the forced choice between conversion and expulsion, conspired to only pretend to convert. Then, under the guise of New Christians, they could work to expel Old Christians from their churches, thus avenging their own expulsion from the synagogues. As paraphrased by Netanyahu, the letter called on the conversos "to train their sons as merchants and financiers so that they may strip the Christians of their wealth; they should equip them with the skills of government officials so that they may subjugate the Christians and oppress them; they should educate them in the disciplines of the priesthood so that, as priests, they may destroy the Christian temples; and they should teach them the arts of medicine and surgery so that they may freely kill Christian patients."[24]

The nineteenth-century Spanish historian Alfonso de Castro calls this a forgery written by Silíceo.[25] The claims made in the letter echo similar claims made by Friar Espina in his fifteenth century *Fortress of Faith*. But Espina's paranoid fantasy was written at a time when the conversos held important positions in the royal court and in the church. As the historian Netanyahu notes: "By the time Silíceo began his campaign, no converso served as bishop, archbishop, or cardinal; nor, with rare exceptions, could conversos be found in high posts of the royal administration, such as those of royal councilors; major judges, governors, or corregidores. The absence of common educational prerequisites (such as graduation from a major college), coupled with the pressure of the racialist movement, had led the kings to abstain from appointing or even nominating conversos for such high posts."[26]

Silíceo even found an argument to deal with the fact that Christ and his disciples were Jews. By his reasoning Christ chose to come among the Jews because he recognized their perversity. He wanted to cure those most in need. As for the apostles, despite all the benefits they received from Christ, they denied him at the moment of his passion.[27]

Prince Felipe continued to oppose the decree, but Silíceo put it into effect anyway. He began examining applicants for purity of blood. In 1555 Pope Paul IV approved the decree. When Felipe took the throne soon afterward, he yielded to pressure from Silíceo and his supporters and approved it. While this approval did not end the debate, the acceptance of this principle by the highest civil and religious authorities meant that no obstacles blocked the full promulgation of such restrictions for any purpose.

The most prominent clergy to resist Silíceo's campaign of *limpieza* was Ignacio de Loyola, founder of the Jesuit order. Born Inigo Loyola in the Basque mountain village of Azpetia, he was the youngest of thirteen children of a minor aristocrat. Loyola's mother died when he was still an infant, and the child was brought up by his wet nurse. From her Loyola learned to speak only Euskerra—Basque—a non-Indo-European language. He first spoke Spanish as an adult and would never achieve full proficiency.[28]

Loyola began his career as a page for the chief treasurer of Castilla, Juan Velázquez de Cuellar. From Castilla he was transferred to the Navarrese court of the Duke of Najera, where he and his brother became embroiled in a military dispute. While defending the town of Pamplona against a French assault, Loyola was struck by a cannonball that shattered his right leg. During his long convalescence, Loyola steeped himself in works of religious devotion and in this way found his vocation. His new ambition, however, would require formal education he had not needed as an aspiring courtier and knight. He therefore resumed his studies, first in Spain and later at the University of Paris.

In France Loyola befriended Spanish conversos, who may have been seeking educational opportunities denied them in Spain owing to *limpieza* restrictions. These conversos became some of his closest colleagues and founding members of the new Society of Jesus. These first Jesuit conversos included Juan Polanco, Loyola's personal secretary; Francisco de Toledo, the first Jesuit cardinal; and Diego Lainez, who succeeded Loyola as the superior general of the Jesuits. Loyola's acceptance of his converso colleagues is reflected in a claim later made by one Jesuit that he once heard Loyola say it would have been a great favor from God to be descended from the Jews and thus to be of the same blood as Christ.[29]

The prominence of conversos among the Jesuits in the early days of the order made it popular among the New Christians. It also made confrontation with Archbishop Silíceo, the most powerful prelate in Spain, inevitable. Silíceo first expressed his displeasure with the Jesuits when they established a school at Alcalá without first obtaining his permission. As a punitive measure, the archbishop banned members of the order from acting as priests without first being personally examined by him, on pain of excommunication and payment of a large fine.

It soon became apparent that Silíceo's real concern was the order's openness to conversos, and that the Jesuits could win his favor only by adopting *limpieza* restrictions. Loyola refused to comply. At one point the pope intervened, sending a cardinal who obtained an agreement that the archbishop would rescind his edict if the Jesuits would adopt the same rules on purity of blood as the other orders in the diocese. Loyola again refused.

Loyola's resistance to imposing *limpieza* in his own order did not lead him otherwise to oppose the archbishop or to denounce *limpieza* in general. In 1552 he wrote to the archbishop expressing his respect and loyalty and promising to do nothing that might bring him disgrace. Loyola's resistance to *limpieza*, however, continued to elicit the displeasure of Silíceo. Loyola resolved this problem in part by sending New Christian disciples to Rome, where their converso background would be less controversial.[30]

The Jesuits' initial openness to conversos significantly impeded their success in Spain. Although Ignatius and most of his first companions were Spaniards, the early growth of the Jesuits was much slower in Spain than in Portugal and Italy, largely due to the opposition of leading churchmen such as Silíceo.[31] Old Christians refused to join the Jesuits because they were reputed all to be "Jews." If a noble from an Old Christian family did join the order, it was said his family would cry at the disgrace. When another converso, Juan de Polanco, who had been the order's acting leader, stood to take on the leadership of the Jesuits after the death of Lainez, some members of the order sympathetic to *limpieza* had the king of Portugal and Cardinal Infante ask the pope not to permit another converso to head the order. While the pope could not deny the nomination on the basis of Jewish descent, he could and did object to yet another Spaniard heading the order. In 1573 a Belgian took up the position instead.[32]

The obstacles that the Jesuits faced in Spain eventually forced a compromise. By the late fifteenth century, the Jesuits in Spain had problems recruiting due to rumors by their enemies characterizing the society as a party of Jews. This led to a vote by the order in 1593 to yield to the critics of the order and adopt *limpieza* in Spain. Continued resistance to *limpieza* restrictions within the order—mainly the campaign of Father Pedro de Ribadeneira, who may have been a converso—resulted fifteen years later in a compromise allowing conversos who had been Christians for five generations to enter the society.[33] This allowed the Jesuits to appease the supporters of *limpieza* without compromising Loyola's principles, since almost all conversos by this time had been Christians for five generations or more.[34]

By the end of the sixteenth century, purity laws had become so strict that some involved *limpieza de sangre de tiempo immemorial*, or "purity of blood from time immemorial," demanding, according to the modern scholar Alfred Sicroff, a purity of blood so absolute that the stain of only one drop of impure blood, even if it came from the distant past, was sufficient to disqualify any descendent of that lineage. It became common to disqualify people using rumors and anonymous poison-pen letters. As Sicroff notes: "The combination of these two practices (requiring an absolute purity of blood, and allowing almost any type of testimony as evidence) constituted, even for old Christians, an impossible standard of evidence.... No one could be certain of their purity of blood, because from night to morning an enemy could appear to despoil ones reputation with false rumors. It therefore soon became known in Spain that more important than being a pure Christian was being able to prove being one, even if this involved the need to buy false testimony to secure this purity."[35]

Contributing to the growth of *limpieza* discriminatory laws and frequently accepted as evidence of Jewish descent was a library of genealogical books claiming—often based on little more than personal vendettas—that prominent families were descended from conversos. Ironically, the first of these books was written by a converso, the relator Fernán Díaz de Toledo, who had set out to defend the conversos by showing how respectable they had become.

Later books appeared in order to malign numerous families, including some of the most prominent in Spain. The Green Book of Aragón was prepared by a sixteenth-century assessor of the Saragossa Inquisition, and as Henry Kamen notes: "The document...became a source of major scandal, for copies were passed from hand to hand, added to and distorted, until the government decided it could not tolerate the slander. In 1623, all available copies of the *libros verdes* were ordered to be burnt."[36]

Even more insidious was another book, circulated underground: As Kamen recounts: "In 1560 Cardinal Francisco Mendoza y Bobadilla, presented to Philip II a memorandum, later to be known as *Tizon de la Nobleza de Espana* (Blot on the Nobility of Spain), in which he claimed to prove that virtually the whole of the nobility was of Jewish descent. He was motivated to malign prominent families after two members of his family were denied admission into a military order. The proofs he offered were widely credited, and the *Tizon* was reprinted many times down to the nineteenth century, almost always as a tract against the power and influence of the nobility."[37] These books spawned imitations, generally known as *libros verdes* or *del becerro*. Much of the information in these books was born of rancor and has since been relegated to the category of "idle hearsay."[38]

The excesses of *limpieza* received frequent criticism and, by the seventeenth century, were eliciting calls for reform. Proposed reforms included putting an end to investigations after a family had been examined for "purity of blood" three times and restricting evidence of conversions to the past century. Despite royal support these attempts at reform had limited success. Resistance to reform was due only in part to bigotry; greed also played a role. The institutions that required proof of purity of blood also required applicants to pay for the investigations themselves. These fees could be extortionate and, in an age of corruption, provided significant opportunities for filling coffers by graft and bribery.

Limpieza outlived the Inquisition. It was not until 1835 that the minister of the interior abolished the application of *limpieza* in schools under his jurisdiction. The Cortes abolished *limpieza* in the corps of military cadets in 1860. Another law of 1865 abolished *limpieza* as a condition for marriage and for state careers.[39] Sicroff has observed that by the mid-sixteenth century, the "purity of blood" principle had become "a type of religious and Spanish national dogma."[40] Some modern historians, however, while acknowledging the widespread popularity of *limpieza* restrictions, have argued that the actual effect of *limpieza* was more limited than the popularity of such measures would suggest. It was largely confined (within Spain) to Castile. In regard to the church, it applied to only about a sixth of the sees in Spain.[41]

Limpieza restrictions could be evaded. One scholar, Linda Martz, has shown that in Toledo, where almost all important institutions had imposed *limpieza*, prominent families of converso descent were able buy their way into important positions and pass as Old Christians.[42] In Toledo, for example, converso families like the Franco, Villareal, Herrera, and Ramirez continued to occupy posts freely throughout the period.[43]

Many offices were sold by the Crown, which in its desperate need for funding had a strong economic incentive to sell to people who claimed to be "Old Christians" but whose pedigree could not stand up to close scrutiny. While the major universities were all subject to *limpieza*, conversos could be found among both students and professors. *Limpieza* also proved no obstacle to the most powerful Spanish politician of the seventeenth century, a favorite of Felipe IV, the Count-Duke of Olivares, who was descended from Jews on his mother's side.

While, as these scholars show, it was possible to evade purity-of-blood restrictions, such evasions could come with a high price. For example, in 1585 a prominent Toledan who paid numerous witnesses to support his claim to "pure blood" was found to be of converso descent on both sides of his family. The authorities imposed large fines on the false claimant and all his witnesses.[44]

The legal constraints that purity-of-blood laws imposed on conversos and their descendants, even if they could sometimes be skirted, significantly reduced status mobility for the affected population.[45] Moreover, evasion of the law required money, power, or prominence—poorer conversos had little choice but to comply.

The cultural impact of *limpieza* may have been greater than the specific laws that it created. Honor played an enormous role in Spanish society, and by the fifteenth century honor included purity of blood: "In Spain," wrote a Franciscan in 1586, "there is not so much infamy in being a blasphemer, robber, vagabond, adultery, sacrilegious person or in being infected with any vice as in having descended from the line of the Jews, even if one's ancestors had been converted for two or three hundred years to the holy Catholic faith."[46] The seventeenth-century writer Juan Escobar de Corro, in his treatise on the purity of the nobility, equated the word "purity" with "honor" and considered death preferable to infamy.[47]

Ironically, the enormous efforts to purge Spain of Jews and Moors through *limpieza* and the Inquisition gave it the false reputation abroad of being a country heavily populated by Jews and Moors. Marrano, a word that had come to be used in Spain as a derogatory description of conversos, now was used against all Spaniards. The Spanish were aware of this dilemma. "I do not know," wrote Diego de Hermosilla, "why this misfortune has struck Spanish nobility, so highly qualified and held in such wretched esteem, because of the ignominious name of Marranos which the other nations persist in applying to the Spaniards."[48] According to the Dominican Agustín Salucio, Spain was considered a land of Marranos, "whose inhabitants must be either vile or mad to dishonor themselves so."[49]

As *limpieza* was incorporated into the Spanish sense of honor, anti-Semitism became a central feature of Spanish culture. According to Kamen: "As the western region with the longest experience of Jewish culture, Iberia breathed anti-Semitism through every pore. It was a common, vulgar response to almost any communal or personal friction."[50]

The anti-Jewish vituperation common among the *cancionero* poets of the fifteenth century as part of a comic exchange of insults became a frequent motif in Spanish literature. As noted by Gustavo D. Perednik, the Israeli-Argentine author of *Judeofobia*:

> The main authors of the golden Age of Spanish literature . . . gave uninhibited vent to their Judeophobic inclinations. Tirso de Molina, Lope de Vega, Calderon de la Barca, and Alonso Castillo Solórzano attacked alleged Judaizers, who seldom defended themselves in the hope that their accusers would relent. . . . Quevedo wrote . . . the *Execration against the Jews' Stubborn Blasphemy* in which he addressed King Philip IV with the explicit request that

"all of them should perish, with their possessions. Their god is slag, their silver is stench, their wealth is a pest. By birth our Lord Jesus Christ taught us to escape from the Jews' gold.... The Jews do with us what Satan did with Christ." Quevedo ends with the wish for "the total expulsion and desolation of the Jews, always evil and every day worse, ungrateful to their God, and traitors to their king," without bothering to notice that there were no Jews left in Spain to expel.[51]

Even the respected modern Basque ethnographer and historian Julio Caro Baroja, whose *Jews in Contemporary and Modern Spain*, published in the 1960s, is a frequently cited history of the Spanish Jews and conversos, tossed a gratuitous anti-Semitic remark into his history when describing the typical Jewish quarter: "There is no harmony between its exterior appearance and what it contains; the outward appearance is miserable, vile. Something similar happens with the Jew: his exterior is frequently repugnant. What goes on in his interior? Only those inside his narrow circuit know."[52] It is inconceivable that such a phrase would appear in a respected history of the Jews written by a modern historian from any other European country.

27

....

Jewish Blood, Black Blood

For historians of racism, *limpieza* is an anomaly. It is generally assumed that the modern concept of race originated in the seventeenth and eighteenth centuries, a by-product of the scientific discovery of the inheritance of biological traits. Yet in the fifteenth and sixteenth centuries, the Spanish concept of purity of blood was already operating much like modern racism, supporting a system of discrimination based on supposedly inherited characteristics. Although the Spanish believed that inheritance followed from a religious curse, rather than from genetics, in other respects the conceptual underpinnings of *limpieza* resembled a modern system of racial discrimination.

The impact of Spain's experiment in racism was to reach far beyond Europe. Contemporaneous Iberian initiatives—the establishment of African race slavery, the discovery of the New World, and the development of plantation agriculture—would bring *limpieza* onto the stage of world history as a direct progenitor of modern racism. When large-scale Spanish and Portuguese plantations using African slaves were established in the Americas, *limpieza*, or discrimination based on "blood" or descent, proved to be an ideal off-the-shelf tool to maintain class structures and barriers, with *limpieza* transformed into a racial classification system called the *systema de castas*, based on purity of blood.

Although the large-scale plantation slavery that began to be established in the seventeenth century was new in scale, slavery as in institution had long roots in Iberia. Slavery had existed in Europe throughout the Middle Ages. The word "slave" comes from the Latin *sclavus*, meaning a person of Slavic descent. For centuries first the Vikings and later Italian merchants had grown wealthy in slave trade with captives from Eastern Europe. As early as the tenth century, Prague operated as an important slave market, from which purchased slaves were transported to the West by way of southern Germany. In Gaul the city of Verdun was renowned for its slave mart and as a site where castrations were performed—the Moors used Eastern European slaves as eunuchs, using castration to maintain control over the slave.[1]

During the period of Muslim rule in Spain, Slavs were bought on the Eastern European slave market and brought to Spain to serve as administrators. They were often trusted with important positions because their only hope of advancement was loyalty to their masters. By the time of Abd al-Rahman's death, it is reported, there were some 3,750 Slavs in Córdoba. Bought usually as children, often castrated, brought up as Muslims, and with an Arabic education, these Slavs had no roots in al-Andalus itself. They were attached to their ruler as slaves or as clients (*mawali*). Their masters could rely on their loyalty since they had no other source of support, even if their loyalty rested largely on their own sense of their self-interest.[2]

At the time of the destruction of the caliphate, about fifteen thousand Slavs were living in Muslim Spain, and some took control of the smaller party states.[3] Trade in Slavs soon declined. By the late Middle Ages slavery had largely been supplanted in western Europe by feudal vassalage. By the fifteenth century opposition from the tsar and blockage of trade routes caused by Ottoman expansion dried up the flow of slaves from the Black Sea countries.[4]

Islamic kingdoms in Iberia also traded in slaves from Africa. These African slaves then made their way into Christian Spain through capture or purchase. Portuguese explorations in Africa allowed Portugal to challenge Islamic control of the African slave trade. Beginning with slave raids in the 1440s, the Portuguese eventually broke the Islamic monopoly by trading directly with the Africans. By 1448 the Portuguese had established a permanent trading post off the coast of Mauritania. The first slave fort, on the coast of Ghana, dates from 1482.[5] The Spanish obtained their own direct source for slaves through their conquest of the Canary Islands.

At first these slaves were brought principally to Portugal and Castile. In Portugal they were put to work draining marshes and clearing land in the south. In the period before 1492, Portugal took between 80,000 and 150,000 slaves from Africa, all destined to work in Europe, principally as domestic helpers.[6] So many slaves were imported to Castile that by the mid-1500s observers claimed that Seville resembled "a giant chessboard with an equal number of black and white chessmen."[7] Slaves were so common that in 1466 when the Bohemian knight Leo of Rozmital asked for two black slaves after being granted the choice of any present he wished by the king of Portugal, the king's brother broke out laughing at the waste of this boon on such a valueless asset.[8]

The discovery of the New World and the development there of large-scale plantation agriculture considerably expanded the market for African slaves. The plantation system started when the Portuguese adapted Muslim sugarcane cultivation successfully on the island of Madeira in the mid-fifteenth century, an experiment they soon repeated with Jewish and African slave labor in the deserted island of São Tomé. The expansion of the plantation into the New World and the impracticality of American Indian slave labor due to disease, contributed to a tremendous increase in the importation of African slaves to the New World. The Spanish Crown licensed slave export to the New World in 1518, calling for the delivery of 4,000 slaves.[9] Between 1500 and 1580 approximately 74,000 Africans were enslaved and shipped to the New World; this number increased exponentially to approximately 714,000 shipped between 1580 and 1640.[10]

Along with slavery Spain exported another institution: *limpieza de sangre*. The Crown barred Jews and Moors from entry into the American possessions and in order to enforce this ban in 1552 decreed that potential emigrants to the New World must furnish proof from their home towns of their *limpieza de sangre*, demonstrating the absence of Jewish or Moorish blood.[11] The ban proved largely ineffective, as conversos fled in large numbers to the New World, partly to escape *limpieza* restrictions in lands where, even though the same restrictions applied, there was less state and church control.

Soon *limpieza* took on a much larger role: as a standard to establish class and other restrictions based on blood purity among the combined offspring of Europeans, indigenous Americans, and Africans. The influence of *limpieza* restrictions on the development of racist practices in the New World is often underappreciated as scholars tend to associate the concept of race with the Enlightenment discovery of biologically inherited characteristics. Some modern historians, however, have acknowledged the important role that Spanish purity-of-blood restrictions played in the development of racial discrimination in the Americas.

The scholar María Elena Martínez, for example, in a much-cited article about purity-of-blood restrictions in Mexico, has noted how *limpieza* was adapted from Spain as a basis for applying race restrictions in the New World: "Used mainly against converted Jews and Muslims ... on the Iberian Peninsula, this concept began to be deployed against colonial categories at the end of the sixteenth century, a process that is reflected in *probanzas de limpieza de sangre* (purity certifications) made by certain colonial institutions, among them the Inquisition and the Franciscan Order."[12]

David Brion Davis, the prominent American authority on the history of black slavery, describes the problems that conversos faced in Spain in his history of American slavery, *Inhuman Bondage*, in order to demonstrate how *limpieza* became a basis for racist practices in the New World: "In one of history's bitter ironies, it was the Spanish and Portuguese treatment of Jews, ... that provided the final seedbed for Christian Negrophobic racism, including the desire to make use of black labor while protecting the 'purity' of white blood.... In other words, there is much evidence that the Christians' growing fears and anxiety over the mass conversion and intermixture of Jews in late medieval Spain gave rise to a more general concern over 'purity of blood'—*limpieza de sangre* in Spanish—and thus to an early conception of biological race."[13]

The Oxford University historian of Spain J. H. Elliott has also cited the importance of *limpieza* in Spanish America as a tool for ensuring white dominance over other races: "In effect, *limpieza de sangre* became a mechanism in Spanish America for the maintenance of control by a dominant elite. The accusation of mixed blood, which carried with it the stigma of illegitimacy—compounded by the stigma of slavery where there was also African blood—could be used to justify a segregationist policy that excluded the castas from public offices, from membership of municipal corporations and religious orders, from entry into colleges and universities and from joining many confraternities and guilds."[14]

The nineteenth-century German explorer Alexander von Humboldt noted the parallel between the *limpieza* restrictions in Spain and the racial discrimination he found in the Spanish colonies in the New World: "In Spain it is a kind of title of nobility not to descend from Jews or Moors. In America, the skin, more or less white, is what dictates the class that an individual occupies in society. A white, even if he rides barefoot on horseback, considers himself a member of the nobility of the country."[15]

Another contemporary observer, Fray Prudencio de Sandoval, in a text of 1604, analogized the impure natures of black and Jewish blood, in order to justify the imposition of *limpieza* to both: "Who can deny that in the descendants of Jews there persists and endures the evil inclination of their ancient ingratitude and lack of understanding, just as in the Negroes [there persists] the inseparability of their blackness. For if the latter should unite themselves a thousand times with white women, the children are born with the dark color of the father. Similarly, it is not enough for the Jew to be three parts aristocrat or Old Christian, for one family line (that is, one Jewish ancestor) alone defiles and corrupts him."[16]

Davis cites this quote from Fray Sandoval as evidence of how the Spanish were expanding their concerns over Jewish blood to cover the African blood they carried to the New World through the importation of African slaves: "They began to transfer to the newly imported blacks the kind of racial concerns originally ignited by the Jews who had converted and then intermixed with Christians."[17]

The Spanish deployed *limpieza de sangre* throughout Spanish America, including present-day Mexico and Venezuela, and the Portuguese adopted it in Brazil.[18] The ubiquity of *limpieza* in Mexico can be seen in the hundreds of *limpieza de sangre* certificates preserved in the Mexican Inquisition files.[19] When Louisiana became part of the Spanish Empire in the 1760s, *limpieza de sangre* was imposed as a way to apply restrictions to different racial mixtures.[20] One modern historian, writing about the significance of *limpieza* restrictions in what is now New Mexico, wrote: "Purity of blood, therefore, had become equated with conquest;

it was the defining symbol of Spanish Catholic identity, and would remain so for the better part of three centuries in the New World. . . . In America, as in Spain, blood remained the axis around which social identities were formed."[21]

The concepts of *limpieza* and *casta* even spread to India. The Portuguese applied these concepts to deal with the social divisions in Hindu culture. Adopted by the British, it became the basis for the use of the word "caste" in India.[22] *Limpieza* became the basis for a society structured on race distinctions called castes. J. H. Elliott describes how the caste system developed in the seventeenth century: "What became known as a society of *castas* was in process of formation—casta being a word originally used in Spain to denominate a human, or animal, group, of known and distinctive parentage. The *mestizos* born of the unions of Spanish men and Indian women were the first of these castas, but they were soon joined by others, like *mulatos*, born of the union of creoles with blacks, or *zambos*, the children of unions between Indians and blacks."[23]

For each new "combination" of races, the caste system produced a new descriptive category, some closer than others to the Spanish ideal of pure blood. One's place in society was determined according to this racial hierarchy. The Swedish ethnologist Magnus Morner in a study of race in the history of Latin America cites the following examples of combinations generated by the caste system: "Spaniard plus Indian equals mestizo; Spaniard plus mestizo equals cuarteron de mestizo; Spaniard and cuarterona equals quinteron; Spaniard and quinterona equals Spaniard, or requinteron de mestizo; Spaniard and Negress equals mulatto; Spaniard and mulatto equals quarteron de mulatto; Spaniard and cuarterona de mulato equals quinteron; Spaniard and quinterona equals reqinteron; Spaniard and reqinterona equals white; Mestizo and Indian equals cholo; Mulatto and Indian woman equals chino; Spaniard and china equals cuarteron de chino; Negro and Indian equals sambo de Indio; and Negro and mulatto woman equals zambo."[24]

Although *limpieza* applied to both "Indians" and "Negros," and while "Indians" also suffered discrimination in colonial Spanish society, the main target of discrimination was black blood.[25] The primary reason that *limpieza* was seized on as a tool for discriminating against Africans was its practical value both to justify race slavery and to enforce the race distinctions that a race slave system require. But while the system may have developed principally out of economic motivations, several rationalizations were expounded to justify discrimination. Some of these rationalizations ran parallel to—or developed out of—long-standing Spanish attitudes toward the Iberian Jews.

Like the Jews Africans were said to carry an inherited biblical curse—not the deicide of which Jews were accursed but the "curse of Ham." In Genesis, Ham sees his father, Noah, drunk and naked. He relates what he has seen to his two brothers, who cover their father: "When Noah woke up and learned what his youngest son had done to him, he said, 'Cursed be Canaan / the lowest of slaves / Shall he be to his brothers.' And he said, 'Blessed be the Lord / the God of Shem; / Let Canaan be a slave to them. / May God enlarge Japheth, / And let him dwell in the tents of Shem; / and let Canaan be a slave to them.'"[26]

The association of the curse of Ham with Africans began with Rabbi Hiyya in the third century CE and was taken up by Muslim writers.[27] These writers associated sub-Saharan Africans with the son of Ham. The Hamitic curse provided a justification for the increasing use as slaves of sub-Saharan Africans.[28]

These Jewish and Muslim myths were passed on to Christians in Iberia. As one modern historian observes: "Over time, Iberian Christians became acquainted with the Muslim system of black slavery and adopted the same sets of symbols and myths, with additional arguments. Not only were blacks not Christians, but they were the Muslims' servants, the heathen's heathen, doubly cursed by their status as nonbelievers and by their servile conditions."[29]

The curse of Ham never had the emotional resonance of the story of Jewish deicide. Alleged Jewish guilt for the death of Jesus directly inspired anti-Jewish passion. In contrast the curse of Ham provided a rationalization, not a motivation, for enslaving Africans. Like the conversos Africans were considered "new Christians." Their loyalty to the Christian faith was suspect because their conversion was thought to have been forced, and this suspicion justified further repression, including relatively frequent trials for blasphemy, often for remarks made while being beaten.[30]

The identification of Africans as New Christians was intensified by their continued identification with the Moors. Africans were subject to the same *limpieza* rules that the Spanish applied to Muslims, based on the belief that all Africans adhered to Islam, even though few African slaves had been Muslims at the time of capture. Finally, Africans were denigrated by a circular logic: they lived a degraded life as slaves, and therefore they must be a degraded people. The use of Africans as slaves led to the general association of Africans with traits of servility and inferiority.[31]

Limpieza rules excluded persons with black blood from numerous occupations and privileges: Blacks, mulattoes, and *zambos* (mixed black and Indian) were barred from civil and religious offices and various fields of commercial endeavor.[32] *Limpieza* controlled entrance into the priesthood. Those of impure blood were barred from ordination into the priesthood. As one modern historian has noted: "For half of the sixteenth century, the ordination of any person of 'impure blood' was absolutely prohibited. A growing need for priests who spoke both Spanish and the assorted Indian tongues, however, led the royal government in 1558, to authorized *mestizos* of legitimate birth to receive training as clerics."[33]

This liberalization measure only assisted people of "Indian" descent, not mulattoes. It was not until 1707 that persons of African descent would be allowed to take up Holy Orders, because of a shortage of priests in Santo Domingo. The ban on blacks in the priesthood meant that Friar Martin de Porres, a Peruvian of African descent, who died in 1639, could not be a priest, although his devotion to his faith received wide respect during his lifetime, and he was eventually recognized as a saint and canonized in 1962.

Limpieza was also applied in schools. Many schools barred students with impure blood. Royal decrees barred entry to universities of people having any African blood, and specific prohibitions barred their admission to the universities at Lima, Mexico City, and Havana.[34]

From Spanish America *limpieza* influenced the development of racial attitudes in the British colonies. By the time slavery was introduced in Virginia, the Spanish had over a century of experience with the administration of slavery and race relations. England had no significant tradition of slave ownership outside the colonies and was not involved in large-scale slave trade until the Treaty of Utrecht in 1713.[35] The American colonies looked to their southern neighbors for a model that would help them develop this peculiar institution. As the historian Alden Vaughn has noted: "Because the Latin American model of lifetime, inheritable servitude was apparent to everyone—Spanish and Portuguese colonists held a quarter of a million black slaves by 1617—Virginians had no need to invent a new status."[36]

One of the first attempts at a legal definition of race was a Virginia law of 1662 that adopted the doctrine of *partus sequitur ventrem*, meaning that the slave status of a child would be determined by the status of the mother. This doctrine came from Roman law and was contrary to English common law, under which status was inherited from the father. *Partus sequitur ventrem* came to Virginia via the Siete Partitas of Alfonso the Wise, in common use in the Spanish colonies.[37]

The colonies, therefore, looked to Spain, rather than England, in their search for a legal precedent that would address certain "problems" faced by slave owners. Specifically, these "problems" involved potential threats to the property and status of white male landowners posed by the claims of mixed-race children, offspring of landowners and black slaves. The legal solution was to be found in the Spanish tradition— inherited from the Romans—of status-by-matrilineal-descent, which deprived mixed-race children, as slaves, of any right to legal claims. The focus of this shift in inheritance law seemed to be on class, rather than race. It was also common for white serving girls to marry black men. According to records from one county in the 1660s, one-fourth of all children born to white servant girls in several counties were mulattoes. Five out of ten free black men on the eastern shore were married to white women.[38] The status of servants, however, did not threaten the propertied classes.

All the vocabulary and formulas that the colonies adopted to define and deal with race had their roots in the Spanish colonies. The term "Negro" itself was incorporated into English from the Spanish in the mid-sixteenth century and "mulatto" a half century later. Previously "black" or "blackamoor" had been used to refer to people of African descent, but the Spanish terms would become the standard.[39]

The word "mulatto" comes from the Spanish word *mulo* meaning "mule," which of course is a cross between a donkey and a horse. It may also have come from the Arabic word *muwallad*, used to refer to people of mixed ancestry. Other race words taken from Latin America include "quadroon" (or quarter black, from the Spanish *cuarterón*) and "octoroon." "Sambo," which in the Spanish commonly referred to a mix of "black" and "Indian," became a derogatory race term for blacks in English.

Even the word "race" itself, in the sense from which the word "racism" is derived, probably came into English from Spanish, where it came to be used to refer to people of Jewish descent. While some controversy remains about the word's origin, it probably first appeared in fourteenth-century France in the context of animal husbandry.[40] The *cancionero* poets in Spain were using the term to refer to people of Jewish descent by the early fifteenth century.[41]

The instigators of the Toledan revolt, in 1449, adopted the word *raza*, or "race," to refer to people of Jewish descent, and by the sixteenth century it had come into common use to refer to people descended from Jews and Moors. The English adopted this term much later and probably following the Spanish example, as the social anthropologist Audrey Smedley explains in her book *Race in America*: "In fact, 'race' did not appear in the English language as a technical term with reference to human groups until the seventeenth century. . . . During the fifteenth and sixteenth centuries, Spanish hegemony in Europe was extensive, and the country's contacts with the English increased significantly. It is quite likely that the English adopted the term 'race' from the Spanish, applying it also to New World indigenes. At that time, the Spanish pronunciation *reazza* could have been easily transformed into the English 'race' in a manner consistent with other known linguistic transformations."[42]

A final concept that likely came out of Spanish and *limpieza* was purity of blood. The *Oxford English Dictionary* attributes the phrase "blue blood" to the Spanish concept of *limpieza*: "that which flows in the veins of old and aristocratic families, a transl. of the Spanish *sangre azul* attributed to some of the oldest and proudest families of Castile, who claimed never to have been contaminated by Moorish, Jewish, or other foreign admixture; the expression probably originated in the blueness of the veins of people of fair complexion as compared with those of dark skin." While the Spanish commonly used the word "blood" in the racial context in connection with racial purity by the sixteenth century, the English examples of this period cited in the OED pertain to family relationships or royal or aristocratic descent. It was not until the eighteenth century that the English colonies commonly used "blood" in a racial context.[43]

Both Spain and the United States arrived at the most extreme standard for racial purity: the "one drop" rule. They came to this independently— the "one drop" rule did not come into common use in the United States until after the Civil War, when it was used to implement Jim Crow racial segregation. Yet the rule derived from the same root concept: *limpieza*. It was a logical extension of the idea, conceived in fifteenth-century Spain, that one's blood would be stained by admixture with an impure race.

The book *Memoirs of a Huguenot Family*, the account of an American settler in Virginia printed in 1757, contains a condemnation of miscegenation that incorporates purity-of-blood concerns. The author writes of whites who mixed with blacks, complaining of "this abominable practice which has polluted the blood of many among [them]," adding, "We ... should not have smutted our blood."[44]

Thomas Jefferson expressed similar concerns about miscegenation (without regard to his personal practices). He advocated removal of blacks from the United States, due in part to concerns over maintaining blood purity. He stated that Negro "amalgamation with the other color produces a degradation to which no lover of his country, no lover of excellence in the human character can innocently consent."[45] Resettlement of blacks would mean that they would "be removed beyond the reach of mixture" so that they could not stain "the blood of [their] master."[46]

It was now the eighteenth century. The concept of purity of blood had embedded itself in the consciousness of the new American nation.

28

....

Conversos and the Beginnings
of the Modern Novel

Conversos faced an unusual dilemma. Torn from their old Jewish traditions, they were persecuted by the inquisitors, the official guardians of their new religion; at the same time, they faced the discriminatory measures imposed by *limpieza de sangre* restrictions. Most conversos, despite these burdens, sincerely embraced the Catholic faith, and conversos rank among some of the greatest Spanish religious figures, including Saint Teresa of Ávila. Others, however, turned away from religion, becoming premature secularists in what was still a religious age.

A few of these conversos transmitted this secular viewpoint into their art. They produced, in the sixteenth century, a series of books shaped by the converso experience that seem from our perspective strikingly modern. Estranged from religion by the persecution of the Inquisition, the conversos wrote books with a wholly secular perspective, books that treat established religion with skepticism or even blasphemy. The protagonists of these books were society outcasts—prostitutes, villains, thieves, and scoundrels, reflecting the low status conferred on conversos by purity-of-blood discrimination. Finally, these books had no moral center: the characters committed or suffered from sins and crimes without consequences, with no religious or secular authority to provide clear justice or punishment for transgressions. The lack of moral center reflects the conversos' unfair persecution from the institutions that should have provided justice as the arbiters of morality, the church and the state.

These converso works would play a central role in the development of the greatest modern secular art form: the novel. Converso books include *Lazarillo de Tormes*, which many consider to be the first modern novel. Conversos also created a new literary genre, the picaresque novel, novels with a *pícaro*, or rogue, as protagonist. Cervantes may have been a converso, and even if he was not, he showed sympathy to the converso condition. These and other books by conversos were enormously popular and influential throughout Europe and became one of the cornerstones of the modern novel. The influence of these books, shaped by the converso experience, infused the converso vision into modern thought and culture.

La Celestina

The first of these books was *La Celestina*, by the converso attorney Fernando de Rojas. One of the great classics of Spanish literature, *La Celestina* first appeared in an anonymous edition of 1499, under the lengthy title: "The Comedy of Calisto and Melibea with its arguments newly added which contains, in addition to its agreeable and sweet style, many philosophical maxims and warnings very necessary to young men who are shown the deceits practiced by servants and go-betweens."[1] Its popularity led to a new edition in which the author playfully concealed his name in an acrostic, the first letters of which read, "The Bachelor [reflecting his education, not marital status] Fernando de Rojas finished the Comedia of Calisto and Melibea, and he was born in the Pueblo de Montalbán." The book eventually appeared in an expanded version, with the authorship acknowledged, as the "Tragicomedy of Calisto and Melibea." It has come to be known by the name of its most prominent character, Celestina. In a prologue to a later edition, Rojas claimed that while studying law in Salamanca he came across a rough draft of the first act and, impressed by its literary quality, took advantage of a two-week vacation to complete the book. Some now discount this story as a deliberate attempt to trivialize the book in order to divert attention from the radical and possibly blasphemous views scattered throughout the text.

The story that Rojas tells about expanding on a found fragment does, however, explain the unusual structure of the book. The first act opens with the relatively conventional subject of unrequited love. Calisto, an aristocrat, catches a glimpse of the young maiden Melibea when he enters her household, enclosed by a wall, in search of his lost falcon. He accosts her. When she rejects him, he becomes obsessed with her beauty and seeks help from his servants in wooing her.

At this point the book takes a strange and radical turn. The story shifts to focus on characters who would normally be considered subsidiary: the servants and their lower-class peers, including a number of prostitutes. Most of *La Celestina* describes the various plots conceived by the servants to profit from their master's obsession. Farces from Plautus to Beaumarchais have used servants to drive the plot, but *La Celestina* is not a farce: all the main characters die.

The focus on lower-class or criminal characters would become a mark of converso literature. It reflects converso criticism of a society that awards status based on descent rather than on individual achievement. In the Spain of the time, the minimum title of respect someone could aspire to was based on descent—the title of hidalgo, derived from the words *hijo de algo*, or "son of someone." That someone, to confer status, could not be a converso. The purity-of-blood laws put conversos in the lowest rank in society.

The converso use of low-class characters, like the *pícaro*, provided converso writers with a platform to criticize established society. As the Israeli scholar Yirmiyahu Yovel has noted: "Picaros were anti-hidalgos; they paraded their lowly origins as opposed to the Spanish cult of noble stock and 'pure blood'; in their inverted, ironic way they challenged the Spanish obsession with nobility or *hidalguia*."[2]

Celestina takes an even stranger turn upon the introduction of what will become the principal character, after whom the play is generally known: La Celestina, the "celestial woman." The servants introduce her to Calisto as a go-between who can help him to seduce Melibea. The "celestial" appellation is ironic: Celestina is an old woman, a procuress, and former prostitute whose character would become the archetype for a witch in Spanish literature.[3]

Celestina's intelligence and vitality take over the play, just as her fingers reach into every corner of town. One character describes her professions: "She had six trades, to wit: Laundress, perfumer, a master hand at making cosmetics and replacing damaged maidenheads, procuress, and something of a witch. Her first trade was a cover for the rest."[4] As a laundress and seamstress she has access to every house, where she befriends—and corrupts—the servant girls. "She was a great friend of students, purveyors, and priest's servants," whom she uses as customers, acting as a procuress to sell sexual favors from her servant clients.[5] Her inventory of chemicals and medicinal herbs that she sells as spells and beauty ointments fills over a page and accurately reflects the kinds of materials that the Inquisition would have documented as a witch's inventory.[6] She even services monasteries and nunneries and goes into detail regarding the clergy whom she claims she has provided with prostitutes.[7]

As a witch Celestina commits one act of black magic in the book, invoking Pluto to create a love charm, although the book does not clarify whether she has actual magical powers. Her real power is psychological. She can persuade any character to follow his or her passion, whether it be ambition, greed, or lust, and in the case of each major character, the passion she arouses leads to destruction.

There is a mystery at the heart of *La Celestina*. Why does Calisto risk his life and reputation by plotting in secret to woo Melibea, instead of openly approaching her parents to ask for her hand? Shakespeare opens *Romeo and Juliet*—a play often compared to *La Celestina* (though written almost a century later)—with an explanation of the feud that divided the lovers' families. Rojas gives no explanation of what separates Calisto from Melibea. Moreover, while Romeo and Juliet plot secretly to marry, Calisto apparently harbors no plan for Melibea beyond sexual satisfaction.

Some believe that the lovers are divided by ethnicity, by the divide between Old and New Christians. This is an interesting explanation that would turn the work into a tragedy driven by ethnic hatred. However, there is little in the play to support this hypothesis, and proponents of this view are divided over which character would represent the converso.[8] A more credible explanation for Calisto's covert approach to love is that Calisto's aim is seduction, not marriage. This interpretation makes him an early version of the most famous seducer in literature, Don Juan, who first appeared in the 1630 play *El burlador de Sevilla* (The Trickster of Seville), by yet another converso author, Tirso de Molina.

From a moral standpoint, the Calisto-as-Don-Juan theory also makes the book much darker. There is no moral center to *La Celestina*: the characters are motivated only by passions that destroy them in the end. When Melibea's father, the only blameless character in the play, delivers a long, final speech lamenting his daughter's death, he turns to Greek and Roman rather than church authorities for an explanation of his fate, and his tone is stoical; he makes no attempt to find redemption in Christianity.

Throughout the book one finds antireligious or blasphemous references that seem to reflect Rojas's own disillusionment with the church. While his characters frequently invoke the name of God, Jesus is named only five times—always as an expletive—and Mary's name appears three times, twice only in an exclamation.[9] One Spanish scholar, Ciriaco Morón Arroyo, has claimed that "the quantity of sacrilegious allusions in Celestina is so great that the whole text could be read as parody of the most sacred dogmas of Catholicism."[10] These allusions, however, are scattered throughout the book in such a way that they seem to reflect the views of characters rather than of the author. As a result *La Celestina* long escaped condemnation by the Inquisition or the church. It was not until 1640 that the Tridentine Index ordered the expurgation of about fifty lines. *La Celestina* was banned in 1790.[11]

Rojas had reason to resent the church. He wrote during the most violent period of the Spanish Inquisition, and there is evidence that his father was condemned by the Inquisition when Rojas was twelve.[12] Fear of the Inquisition may explain why he chose to publish anonymously, and why the author of a popular and highly influential book, a classic of world literature, never published again, although he lived for another forty years.

La Celestina became enormously popular. More than thirty editions were printed in Spain in the sixteenth century, and despite the book's strange morality, its popularity led to its use as a schoolbook.[13] Six years after the first Spanish edition appeared, an Italian translation was published in Rome. The Hebrew edition appeared a few years later. By the mid-seventeenth century *La Celestina* had been translated at least once into Latin, four times into German and English each, five times into Flemish, nineteen into Italian, and twenty-four times into French.[14]

It also inspired numerous imitations, including Spanish books titled *The Second Celestina*, *The Third Celestina*, and *The Daughter of Celestina*.

Lozana, the Lusty Andalusian

One book—now recognized in Spain as a classic—inspired by *La Celestina* is *The Portrait of Lozana, the Andalusian* by Francisco Delicado. Published in 1530, it is a frank and bawdy account of a prostitute in Rome, written by a syphilitic Spanish converso priest who worked in Rome. Delicado expresses his debt to Rojas in his dedication, as well as on the title page, where he describes his book as "containing a great deal more than *La Celestina*."[15] He wrote it in a similar, play-like format, in dialogue but probably not meant for public performance.

The book is not of the same literary quality as *La Celestina*. It lacks a plot, consisting instead of short sketches that describe the life of Lozana and her fellow prostitutes and her schemes to make money. Delicado claims that there are 125 characters in the book, and as a result, few besides Lozana are sharply drawn. On the other hand, it is an experimental book that includes a dose of what might now even be considered postmodernism, where Delicado appears as a character in the book and Lozana offers to bear his child.

But what Delicado lacked in poetry, he made up for in reportage, providing an intimate and sympathetic account of prostitution in Rome. Parts of the book read like transcripts of conversations among prostitutes. He lays out his intent to act as a documentarian in his dedication: "I shall report only what I saw and heard ... should anyone be amazed that I spent my time writing about such things, I shall only reply that 'words feel no shame at what they record.'"[16]

The heroine's birth name is Aldonza. She has earned her nickname, Lozana (Lusty), by her early proclivity to sex. *Lozana* was condemned during the nineteenth and much of the twentieth centuries for being pornographic. It utilizes many words not allowed to be used in Spanish literature until the post-Franco period and depicts several explicit sexual scenes, in particular the scene in which Lozana first meets her servant (and lover) Rampín, and they copulate six times. *Lozana* was the first of several sexually explicit books about prostitutes written in that period in Italy. Paula Findlen claims that modern pornography emerged from these books, which may have been inspired by the ancient Roman author Lucian's *Dialogues of the Courtesans*. This genre in that period would include works by authors such as Pietro Aretino, Lorenzo Venier, and Niccolo Franco.[17]

These books about prostitutes reflected the ubiquity of prostitution in a Rome that was populated predominantly by men, with a few local women but many male clergy, soldiers, or traveling traders. *Lozana* provides a long list of the prostitutes' national origins, which includes entries for most of the provinces in Spain, documenting the large number of Spanish prostitutes working in Rome. A census taken in Rome in 1490 found a total of 6,800 concubines among the city's total population of 50,000.[18] While Delicado's syphilis may reflect his intimacy with prostitutes, he had other sources of knowledge, too: Delicado had served in the church of Sancte Maria in Posterule de Urbe on a street frequented by prostitutes.[19]

Delicado, writing outside the jurisdiction of the Spanish Inquisition, is at liberty to talk frankly about converso life in Italy. Upon her arrival in Rome, Lozana takes up with a community of converso women, all of whom have left Spain following the institution of the Inquisition. Before they can trust Lozana one of the women says they will have to test her: "I'd just like to find out whether or not she is a new Jewish convert so we can talk freely."[20] The women decide to ask her how to make empanadas; only when Lozana reveals that she cooks them the converso way do they admit her to their group.

Lozana decides to rent a house in the Jewish quarter, where each group of Jewish immigrants—according to her converso lover and pimp Rampin—attends its own separate synagogue. Rampin criticizes the Italian Jews for acting like gentiles and being ignorant of Jewish law but praises the Spanish Jews for their learning. Later, when someone coerces Rampin to eat ham, he violently regurgitates the meat all over the dining table—he cannot tolerate this nonkosher meat. Lozana takes the ill Rampin home to recover, noting that his father had suffered from intermittent fevers for seven years after once eating ham.[21]

Lozana documents the scourge of syphilis—the HIV of its time—which first appeared in Europe at the end of the fifteenth century, and which may have been brought back from the New World. Lozana herself suffers from syphilis, which has eaten away at her nasal cartilage (some characters joke that she will never wear glasses because she has no nose to hold them up). In a city of prostitutes and johns, the disease affected almost everyone, and characters frequently complain in the story of genital pain, the "French disease," and loss of hair. Delicado had written a pamphlet promoting the use of a particular New World wood to cure syphilis, and he promotes this work on occasion in *Lozana*.

Unlike *La Celestina*, *Lozana* had little impact on contemporary literature. It probably received limited distribution, and its absence from the church's indexes of forbidden books testifies to its relative obscurity.[22] When *Lozana* was rediscovered in the mid-nineteenth century in the Imperial Library of Vienna by the scholar Pascual de Gayangos, prominent Spanish intellectuals condemned it as pornographic. Today *Lozana* is an accepted classic of Spanish literature.

In *Lozana* Delicado provides a good example of the secular converso attitudes that would work their way into the foundations of the modern novel. The converso style includes an embrace of realism, criticism of corruption, and a focus on outcasts and the lower classes. As in *La Celestina* there is no moral center to the book. The prostitutes are not censured for their trade, nor are they punished by the author. Syphilis is depicted as a physical affliction, not a moral punishment. As in *La Celestina*, while the name of God appears frequently in the book, Mary is never mentioned, and the name Jesus rarely appears in the book.[23]

Lozana, like Celestina, is an enterprising opportunist who explores all possible avenues for advancement; alongside her prostitution, she sells beauty treatments and homemade remedies to fellow prostitutes, and she practices minor witchcraft, telling fortunes and removing the evil eye. She prospers enough to retire to the island of Lipari, without being punished for what the church would view as her many sins.

While *Lozana* had limited distribution and influence, in 1554 another book appeared that would have a revolutionary impact on literature within and beyond Spain: *The Life of Lazarillo de Tormes and His Fortunes and Adversities*. Some consider *Lazarillo* to be the first modern novel. Manuel Duran has compared the author of *Lazarillo* to Columbus, discovering, not a New World, but a new picaresque literary landscape, realistic and centered on middle- or lower-class characters.[24]

Lazarillo became the model for a new literary genre—the picaresque—a genre focusing on the adventures of a *pícaro*, or rogue. Picaresque books would come to dominate Spanish literature, and the genre would prosper throughout Europe—there are classic examples of picaresque books based on this Spanish model in English, French, and German literature.

Lazarillo was revolutionary, too, in its elevation of an ordinary figure from the lowest ranks of society to the status of the protagonist. It was the first book not dealing with a saint or a historical figure that used in the title the terms "The Life of" to highlight the importance of the title character; after *Lazarillo* the phrase became common in the titles of novels featuring the life of an "ordinary" main character.[25]

Lazarillo, though published anonymously, is commonly held to be the work of a converso. There are several reasons for this view. The book was published in Antwerp, indicating that the author, like many other conversos (including Delicado), had chosen to live on the fringes of what was then the Spanish Empire, far from the Inquisition. Moreover, the book takes a relentlessly critical view of the church.

A novella in length, *Lazarillo* is the concise and darkly comic story of a young man whose adversities far outweigh his fortunes. Lazarillo's troubles begin as a child, when his father, a miller, is caught pilfering and is sent to the wars, where he dies. His widow takes up with a black slave and has a child by him. When the slave, caught stealing to support the mother, is separated from her, she sends her child away from home to a series of miserable apprenticeships.

Lazarillo begins at the bottom of the career ladder: lower than even a beggar, he is the unpaid servant of a blind beggar. This first master is both hot-tempered and stingy, and Lazarillo learns he must steal to eat: hunger remains his principal motivation throughout the novel. The education provided by the blind man is literally a school of hard knocks—it begins when the master instructs Lazarillo to put his ear to a stone shaped like a bull, in order to hear a loud noise inside. When Lazarillo obeys, the blind man slams Lazarillo's head into the stone, admonishing him that the servant of a blind man needs much sharper wits.

Only when the beggar beats Lazarillo for stealing a sausage does the boy find a new master—this time a parish priest—who proves to be even stingier than the first. The second master keeps his bread locked up like treasure in a chest and feeds Lazarillo onion sandwiches and leftover scraps.

Stealing from the bread chest gets Lazarillo expelled from service. His third master, a minor nobleman, proves kindly, but his only asset is his pride in his station. He spends his days strutting about town and displaying his rank, when in fact he is so impoverished (though he never admits it) that Lazarillo has to beg to support them both. This character illustrates the converso frustration with the Spanish system of granting status based on descent. The hidalgo has nothing in his life except his rank obtained though his descent—a parasite, he is unable to survive without the beggary of his servant.

Lazarillo ends the story at what he considers to be the height of his good fortune, in his new position as town crier. He is supported by an archpriest, who arranges for Lazarillo to marry the archpriest's mistress, to hide the archpriest's adultery. Lazarillo rationalizes his agreement to earn a living as a cuckold by concluding that his wife is as good (i.e., as bad) as any woman in Toledo. The ending foreshadows trouble ahead: Lazarillo's story is a confession, indicating that he may be under investigation for the crime of assisting in adultery.

Lazarillo is filled with descriptions of church-related corruption. In one short, enigmatic chapter, Lazarillo works for a friar in the Order of Mercy. The friar spends his whole day in "worldly affairs and visiting people," gadding about so much that Lazarillo wears out his first pair of shoes, given to him by the friar, in a week. He leaves the friar's service for reasons he would "rather not mention," implying that the friar has committed what Lazarillo would consider unspeakable acts. Lazarillo then works for a "pardoner," a seller of counterfeit papal indulgences, who engages in several con games to sell his worthless merchandise. The adulterous archpriest is only the last in a line of unpleasant or corrupt clerics. *Lazarillo*, like *La Celestina* and *Lozana*, lacks any clear moral center. The protagonist adapts as best he can to survive in a corrupt world. There is no description of Christian redemption or forgiveness—nothing to indicate that the imperfect figures who represent the church are aberrations, rather than archetypical members of an empty institution.

In 1559 *Lazarillo* became one of the first books to be banned by the Spanish Inquisition because of its criticism of the church. The book would eventually be released in an expurgated edition, called *Lazarillo Punished*, printed in 1573.

The Pícaro

Possibly due to the Inquisition's ban, it took fifty years from the date of first publication for the seed of *Lazarillo* to germinate. In 1599 the converso Mateo Alemán published the book that put the *pícaro* into the picaresque, *Guzmán de Alfarache*, popularly known as *El Pícaro*, or "the rogue." *Guzmán* became an international best seller. It went through thirty editions in six years, outselling the later *Don Quixote* and, like *Quixote*, inspiring a spurious sequel.[26]

Guzmán is, stylistically, the antithesis of *Lazarillo*. Whereas the older book is short and concise, *Guzmán* is enormous—about 250,000 words, over a thousand pages long. At least half of the book consists of digressions from the main plot, mainly in the form of sermons and excoriating diatribes that furnish examples of corruption in contemporary society. When Guzmán is cheated by an innkeeper, the author describes at length cheating and theft by innkeepers. Guzmán's apprenticeship to a butcher gives the author opportunity to document the crimes of thieving butchers. And when Guzmán is unjustly imprisoned after accusing a judge's son of robbery, an essay on legal corruption ensues. The novel proceeds in this way, citing corruption at every level of society. Only the church escapes direct criticism.

The main character—Guzmán, the rogue—alternates between being a victim and a victimizer. If he develops at all in the novel, it is mainly in his growing sophistication and expertise at swindling and theft. Only at the very end does he repent: sentenced to be a galley slave, Guzmán informs on a mutiny and is made the galley equivalent of prison trustee, whereupon he resolves, for the moment, to lead an honorable life.

The unending attacks on corruption would seem to make *Guzmán de Alfarache* a moral book. However, no countervailing moral institution appears in the book as an antidote for the corruption. While the book avoids direct criticism of the church, and the protagonist often goes to mass, neither religious doctrine nor redemption is expressly sought or invoked. The constantly recurring lectures on corruption have the ironic effect of justifying Guzmán's own immoral habits; in a society so fundamentally corrupt, his thievery is necessary to his survival.

The success of this novel sparked numerous imitations. One scholar estimates that between 1599 and 1688 some twenty-five to thirty picaresque novels appeared in Spanish. Many, but not all, were written by conversos. Of these books the most stylistically refined is *El Buscón*, or "the swindler," by Francisco de Quevado. Not only was Quevado an Old Christian; he may also have been the most rabidly anti-Semitic writer of the Spanish golden age.[27] Yet even Quevado acknowledged that the picaresque world comes out of the converso experience: the father of his protagonist is a converso thief, the mother, a converso witch-prostitute.

The popularity of these books about rogues may be due in part to the fact that they appeared in an age of rogues. Spain had just sent an army of *pícaros* into the Western Hemisphere, where they dismantled the Aztec, Incan, and other civilizations in their quests for easy riches. The Spanish Empire was built on the thefts of the *pícaro*.

Cervantes

The greatest novel of this period, also one of the greatest and best-known novels in history, Miguel de Cervantes's *Don Quixote* was published between 1605 and 1615. Ever since Américo Castro suggested the idea, speculation has circulated that Cervantes was also of converso descent. There is circumstantial evidence to support this idea. As Castro pointed out, if Cervantes had been a converso, many of the difficulties he faced in advancing his career might be more easily explained.[28] The Cervantes family was among the families listed as conversos in Fernán Díaz de Toledo's *Instrucción*. Members of the Cervantes family traditionally took up trades commonly associated with conversos, such as work in the cloth business or as barber-surgeons. While Miguel de Cervantes was able to obtain proof of his "purity of blood," fraudulent certificates were easy to obtain. Absent direct evidence of Cervantes's background, however, it cannot be determined with certainty whether he was a converso.

It is clear that Cervantes learned from his converso predecessors. He was familiar with both *La Celestina* and *Guzmán*, and he called *Lazarillo* "divine."[29] While *Quixote* has a range and depth of imagination beyond any of the picaresque novels, its realistic and secular setting and prominent use of characters from ordinary—not noble—backgrounds carries on the converso, picaresque tradition.

Cervantes also shows no sympathy for the purity-of-blood laws and other racial legislation of the time. The now-famous book-burning scene at the beginning of the *Quixote* is generally seen as a satire of the Inquisition's auto-da-fé. The only character in *Quixote* who repeatedly brags about his blood purity is Sancho Panza, the peasant. Sancho's belief that his pure blood elevates his status in society illustrates what Cervantes's contemporary, the monk Agustín Salucio, protested against— that purity-of-blood laws elevated peasants over people superior to them in rank and education: "It is a difficult thing to think that a farrier's son or the son of someone with an even lower occupation should regard himself as being more honorable and of a better caste than a very noble gentleman, even if the latter were the grandson of a grandee, but happened to have a drop of non-Christian blood. . . . All that is necessary to be an Old Christian is to be a man of low rank, and not to know who one's ancestors are, even if they were Jewish."[30]

The middle-class Quixote never mentions his blood and shows all the signs of being a converso character. Even his title, "Knight of La Mancha," implies a joke on Quixote's background: La Mancha, the region where Quixote lives, also translates to mean "the stain." *Mancha* was a common code word at the time, used to indicate impurity of blood. Quixote also shares with many conversos an outlook that is secular, not religious; while religion plays an important role in some knighthood romances, such as the stories of Parsifal and the Grail knights, Quixote is loyal only to the secular ideals of chivalry and courtly love.

When Quixote does discuss lineage, he describes status rankings in which race or ethnicity have no role. In part 2, chapter 6 he states that all families in the world can be reduced to four kinds: those that rose from humble beginnings; those that began with a high rank and have maintained it; those that went from high rank to oblivion; and the vast majority of common, plebeian people. When someone impugns the background of his beloved (and imaginary) Dulcinea, Quixote defends her honor by praising her virtue, not her descent.

The novel also criticizes the racial policies of King Felipe III, who ordered the expulsion of all Moorish converts to Christianity from Spain between 1609 and 1614. Cervantes describes the dilemma of a devoutly Christian Moorish woman, daughter of Christians of Moorish descent, unfairly forced into exile and separated from her Christian lover because of this decree.

Cervantes's most direct attack on the purity-of-blood rules came in a short farce called *El Retablo de Las Marvillas*, "The Wondrous Pageant," published in a collection of farces called *Entremeses*, meant to be performed during the interludes of full-length plays. *El Retablo* is a variation on the plot later found in *The Emperor's New Clothes*—both works were probably based on similar folktales. In the play con men tell the provincial governor that they propose to put on a miraculous play, but that the play can only be seen by people of legitimate descent, with no Jewish blood: "*Ninguno puede ver . . . que tenga alguna raza de confeso,*" "no one can see . . . who has any converso blood."[31] The con men, after receiving their pay in advance, describe the marvels being portrayed on the stage, but nothing is produced, and the audience keeps silent rather than admit to having Jewish blood.

Cervantes through one character describes the basic equality of human beings, regardless of race: "That flock of mice running there is descended in direct line from the ones Noah had in his ark; some are white, some are streaked, some speckled and some blue; but they're all mice."[32]

The Converso Legacy

The secular novels of Spain soon were published and widely read in other countries. *Lazarillo*'s popularity increased after the publication of *Guzmán*: the popularity of *Guzmán* led to nine editions of *Lazarillo* in four years.[33] Translated into English in 1586, it appeared in many English-language editions.[34]

Guzmán, translated into English in 1622 by James Mabbe with an introduction by Ben Jonson, had appeared in four editions in English by 1656.[35] It inspired both a spurious sequel in Spanish and an English imitation, *James Hind, the English Gusman*. Even the relatively minor *Pícara Justina* by Ubeda (another converso), was published in English in 1707 as *The Spanish Libertines* and translated into French by Alain-René Lesage. In France the Spanish picaresque books were imitated in a novel by Lesage, *Gil Blas*, completed in 1735. *Gil Blas*, in turn, became an important influence on the development of the English novel.

Most scholars locate the origins of the modern novel in eighteenth-century England. But these eighteenth-century English books by authors like Defoe, Fielding, Smollett, and Sterne used the sixteenth- and seventeenth-century Spanish books as a model. *Don Quixote*, in particular, had an enormous influence on eighteenth-century English literature. Henry Fielding, author of *Tom Jones*, called his novel *Joseph Andrews* an "Imitation of the Manner of Cervantes, Author of *Don Quixote*." He also wrote a play in 1734 called *Don Quixote in England*. Daniel Defoe, too, cites the influence of the Quixote in his book *Memoirs of Captain Carleton*, and Defoe's *Moll Flanders* is a type of picaresque novel. Charlotte Lennox's *The Female Quixote*, of 1752, would later inspire Jane Austin's *Northanger Abbey*.

Tobias Smollett, one of the most important English novelists of the century, was particularly influenced by the picaresque genre, as well as by *Don Quixote*. He translated *Gil Blas* (its author, Legase, had translated Spanish picaresque books into French) as well as *Don Quixote* into English and wrote *Sir Launcelot Greaves* as an explicit imitation of

Quixote.[36] Laurence Sterne's *Tristram Shandy* also cites *Quixote* several times and coins the adjective "Cervantick."[37] Even Sir Walter Scott paid tribute to Cervantes in the introduction to his novel Waverley, while his novel *Rob Roy* bore the influence of the Spanish picaresque.[38]

The revolutionary converso embrace of secular realism did not limit itself to fiction. The great Spanish painter Velázquez is generally believed to have been a converso, and images of *picaros* staring brazenly out at the viewer appear in many of his paintings, most dramatically in *The Feast of Bacchus*, also known as *The Drunkards*. Spinoza, who was born into a family of conversos (his father was born a Christian in Portugal), brought this inherited converso skeptical realism to philosophy: he tried to construct a philosophical system outside the framework of traditional religion, for which he was excommunicated from the Jewish community of Amsterdam.[39] But the Spanish converso experiments in fiction, which became one of the cornerstones of the modern novel, proved to be the conversos' most important contribution to the creation of the modern mind.

29

Coming to America

The year 1492 proved to be a pivotal one in Jewish history. The expulsion brought a major phase of Jewish civilization to an end. At the same time, the Columbus expedition would provide new shelters and unprecedented opportunities for the Jews. Most Sephardic Jews settled in North Africa, the Levant, and the Near East. They flourished, both materially and culturally, and their story—which is beyond the scope of this book—is well related in books like Jane Gerber's *The Jews of Spain*; Howard Sachar's *Farewell, España*; and Paloma Díaz-Mas's *Sephardim*.

What is less well known is that from the beginning, conversos and Sephardic Jews played an important part in the European settlement of the New World. Conversos sailed with Columbus, who noted in his journal that he assigned one converso, Luis de Torsent, to an exploration party because the sailor understood both Hebrew and Aramaic, in case the party might encounter Indians descended from the Ten Lost Tribes (Jews enslaved by Assyria in about 720 BC whose fate is unknown).[1]

The legend that Native Americans descended from the Lost Tribes would persist for a long time. One explorer, the converso Antonio de Montezinos, claimed that he found a tribe of Indians near present-day Medellín, Colombia, who told him that they were descended from the lost tribe of Reuben. This account was disseminated throughout Europe by a book known in English as *The Hope of Israel*, the work of a rabbi from Amsterdam named Menasseh ben Israel; it appeared in English in 1650 after being published in Ladino and Dutch. The idea that the Americas were populated by descendants of Israel was also incorporated into the most successful indigenous American religious text, the Book of Mormon.

From Holland to Brazil

The Dutch were the primary sponsors of Jewish settlements in the New World, at least in the seventeenth century. By that time Amsterdam had become an important Jewish refuge, particularly for the Portuguese Sephardim. Holland had been incorporated into the Spanish Empire through the marriage of Ferdinand and Isabella's daughter Juana (also known as Juana la Loca, or Juana the Mad) to the Habsburg monarch Phillip the Handsome. During the Reformation the newly Calvinist Dutch resisted the rule of Spain's staunchly Catholic Phillip II.

Dutch resistance forced Phillip to grant autonomy to the Dutch states in a 1573 agreement known as the Pacification of Ghent. Because of the religious repression they had suffered under the Spanish Hapsburgs, the Dutch proceeded to forbid religious persecution in the Union of Utrecht, which united the Dutch provinces. The Dutch never granted full equality to the Jews, so legal discrimination and occasional attempts at repression of the Jews continued. Nonetheless, the Dutch granted the Jews a level of freedom and religious tolerance beyond anything in any other state in Europe at the time. Because Dutch Protestants had suffered from repression of their religion by the Catholic Spanish, popular resentment in Holland tended to focus on Catholics rather than Jews.[2]

Jewish immigration to Holland began early in the seventeenth Century. Many of the first Jews to arrive were Portuguese conversos who returned to Judaism after settlement in Holland. By 1620 there were approximately one thousand Jews in Amsterdam.[3] By 1672 this population had increased to 7,500, or about 3.75 percent of the city's population.[4] The congregations united in 1638 to form one that would worship in the temple known as the Portuguese Synagogue, or "Esnoga." Their synagogue, built in 1675 and still in use today, would be the largest in Europe and was the model for London's Bevis Marks and the Touro in Rhode Island.[5]

Jews were valued by the Dutch in part because of their trade contacts, which contributed to Holland's mercantile economy. The Spanish Diaspora meant that Jews had contacts with fellow Sephardic Jews and conversos all over the world, including commercial ties to the Ottoman

Empire, a trade relationship not accessible to Christians. The Dutch Jew's most significant commercial ties were with the conversos in Brazil. Portugal's successful experiments with plantation sugarcane cultivation on the island territories of Madeira and São Tomé met with even greater success in Brazil. From the very beginning, conversos played a major role in the development of this commodity. According to the historian Arnold Witnitzer, a significant percentage of the population of Pernambuco, in northern Brazil, consisted of conversos.[6] This reflected the large number of Portuguese conversos who came to the New World seeking trade opportunities and relative freedom from the Inquisition.

In the first half of the seventeenth century, the governor of Panama, Francisco de Valverde y Mercado, complained about these Portuguese conversos to Spain's King Phillip III: "Today the traders of the Indies are the Portuguese because they have the contracts for supplying slaves and the dispatch of the fleets and squadrons on the good journey, of which all trade depends and of their nation there have been many Jewish merchants around here who live within their Law and they, upon getting rich, go to other kingdoms before they fall into the hands of the Inquisition."[7] Registration records show that in Caracas in 1606, forty-one out of forty-six resident foreigners were Portuguese, and in 1630 in Cartagena, Colombia, 154 of 184 registered foreigners were Portuguese.[8]

Not all the conversos in Brazil came voluntarily. For several hundred of them, Brazil was a place of exile, imposed as punishment by the Inquisition for a sentence of guilty to the charge of "Judaizing."[9] The conversos in Brazil soon played a major role in the development of the sugar trade. One converso, Duarte Coelho, the son of an astronomer-navigator, became the first person to cultivate sugar in Brazil. Appointed *donatario* of the province of Pernambuco, he established several large sugar plantations and brought in workers from Portugal—many of them fellow conversos—to construct sugar mills.[10] By the 1630s conversos had developed fifty-nine sugar mills, of which they were both owners and operators.[11]

The Brazilian conversos often maintained family ties with their fellow conversos in Amsterdam, many of whom had previously resided in Brazil and worked on the sugar plantations. One of the founding members of the Portuguese Jewish community in Amsterdam, Jacob Lopes da Costa, owed his fortune to a stint in Brazil as a tax farmer and sugar-mill owner. Another Sephardic resident of Amsterdam, Duarte Saraiva, belonged to a prosperous Pernambuco family.[12]

Due to the Sephardic Jewish ties to conversos in Brazil, Holland had become the principal conduit of sugar into Europe. In a document of 1622, the Jewish community of Amsterdam described the importance of its role in the sugar trade: "More than 10, 12, and even 15 ships were built in this country each year. Those ships brought here by way of Portugal 40, 50 thousands of cases of sugar each year.... It caused the number of sugar refineries in Amsterdam to increase from three to twenty-five in 50 years. Some of the refineries processed 1,500 cases of sugar each year."[13]

The profits from the sugar trade prompted an initiative to conquer the Brazilian sugar territories, an effort promoted and led by the privately held West India Company (WIC), a company somewhat akin to a modern corporation in what may be the first example of corporate imperialism. To support the invasion, the WIC estimated that a successful conquest would yield a profit of fifty kilograms of gold, most of which would come from sugar profits. Another factor cited by the WIC in support of invasion was the claim that most Portuguese were really Jews who would support a Dutch incursion, particularly if the Dutch proclaimed religious freedom.[14]

An initial attempt to conquer Bahia, the first Portuguese settlement in Brazil (and the capital of the colony), succeeded in holding Bahia for one year, at the end of which the Dutch were driven out. A second expedition, in 1629, succeeded in conquering Pernambuco, the epicenter of Brazilian sugar production, including the capital of Pernambuco state, Recife. The WIC had little Jewish capital: Jews had invested only 36,100 guilders of the initial capitalization of over 7 million.[15] But from the beginning, Jews played a major role in the Dutch conquest of Pernambuco. The Dutch Jews and conversos, fluent in both Portuguese and Dutch, could act as intermediaries between the invaders and the resident Portuguese planters. The struggle to control Pernambuco destroyed much of the sugar infrastructure, and the Jews had both the knowledge and the capital to rebuild.

The Dutch invasion force consisted of thirty-six ships and over seven thousand soldiers. A Jew named Antônio Dias Paparrobalos, who had worked as a merchant in Pernambuco, became the invaders' principal guide. The mercenary soldiers also included some documented Jews— Moses Navarro, Antonio Manoel, David Testa, and Samuel Cohen— who were, effectively, the first Jewish soldiers in America. Navarro would become wealthy as a sugar-mill owner and tax farmer.[16] Other Jews came with the Dutch as settlers. The arrival of the tolerant Dutch prompted many of the local conversos to revert openly to Judaism. Manoel Calado, a contemporary Brazilian chronicler, complained that many conversos had in fact been "secret Jews" who, after the arrival of the Dutch, had themselves "circumcised in public and openly declared themselves as Jews ... greatly scandalizing the Christians."[17]

The successful Dutch invasion also encouraged many Jews to immigrate to Brazil. In 1638 two ships alone delivered 200 Jews from Holland.[18] By 1639, ten years after the initial invasion, so many Jews had come over from Amsterdam that the three Sephardic congregations there were consolidated into just one.[19] By 1641 there were approximately 1,450 Jews in Dutch Brazil; between one-third and one-half of the entire European population in Dutch Brazil was Jewish.[20]

Jews prospered in a number of ways. They owned many of the sugar mills, though still fewer than half, and they worked as sugar brokers and exporters, as well as creditors to the Portuguese planters and millers.[21] Jews controlled most of the tax farming—and taxes were a major source of Dutch revenue from Brazil. The local slave brokerage was also dominated by Jews, although the importation of slaves from Africa was monopolized by the WIC.[22]

In 1641 the Jews of Recife, who had formed a congregation called Kahal Kadosh Tsur Israel, or Holy Congregation of the Rock of Israel, built a temple in town on the street Rua do Bode, which was also known as the Rua dos Judeus, or Street of the Jews. This was the first synagogue to be constructed in the New World. The site now serves as the location of a Jewish museum, exhibiting archeological remains from the original synagogue (little from the Dutch colonial period remains in modern Recife). Jews soon built a second synagogue, Kahal Kadosh Magen Abraham (the Shield of Abraham), in nearby Mauritia. Other congregations gathered less formally in nearby regions, including Olinda.[23]

During the 1640s Recife's novelty as a Brazilian "City of Jews" led to enough firsts to fill a Guinness Book of Jewish World Records. Isaac Aboab de Fonseca became the first ordained rabbi in the New World, and he served as the spiritual leader of Recife's Jewish community from 1642 to 1654.[24] Born in 1605 Fonseca had been raised Catholic. After his family emigrated to Amsterdam via France, he converted to Judaism and took up religious studies. Fonseca returned to Amsterdam after the Dutch loss of the Brazilian colony.

The first Jewish physician and pharmacist in the New World was Abraham de Mercado. An early settler in Brazil, he subsequently left first for Amsterdam, then London, where he obtained permission from Oliver Cromwell to settle in Barbados.[25] Michael Cardoso, the first Jewish lawyer in the New World, received permission to practice from Dutch authorities. When the Recife Council of Justice barred him from practice due to his religion, authorities in Amsterdam—upon request from the Dutch Jews—ordered the court in 1646 to admit him to the bar.[26]

The political movement that would lead to the end of the Dutch settlement in Brazil, ironically, initially received both Dutch and Sephardic support. Portugal had come under Spanish rule in 1580. In 1640 Portugal declared its renewed independence, and the Duke of Bragança crowned himself King João IV. Holland supported Portuguese independence, with the main aim of weakening its Spanish rival and enemy. In 1641 Portugal and Holland signed a ten-year truce, which included Brazilian territories.[27]

Despite the truce, King João IV began to discuss the possibility of a revolt against Dutch rule in Brazil with Portuguese rebels. The insurrection first broke out in the province of Maranhão in February 1644 and quickly spread to other Dutch holdings. When a Dutch ship with three Jewish merchants on board dropped anchor in August 1645 at a part of the Brazilian coast that, unbeknown to them, had been captured by Portuguese rebels, two of the Jews—because they were conversos born as Christians—were arrested and executed as apostates.[28]

In the course of the insurrection, the rebels captured other Jews, too, some of whom were executed, while others were turned over to the Inquisition. One of the captured Jews, Isaac de Castro de Tartas, was shipped to Lisbon and, at the orders of the Inquisition, burned alive in an auto-da-fé. Rebel mistreatment of Jews infuriated the Amsterdam Jewish community, who changed their traditional title of "the Portuguese nation" to *"gemeene Joodsche natie,"* or "general Jewish nation."[29]

By September 1645 rebels had captured most of the Dutch territories. In only three months practically everything had been conquered or devastated. The sugar infrastructure, the basis for the Dutch colony's economy, was completely destroyed.[30] Recife came under siege. Jewish volunteers, including a forty-man naval contingent, helped to defend the besieged town.[31] As one of the German employees of the WIC in Brazil noted, "the Jews, more than anyone else, were in a desperate situation and therefore, preferred to die sword in hand than face their fate under the Portuguese yoke: the flames."[32]

The Amsterdam Jews showed their support of the Jews in Brazil by helping to finance a privateering campaign that captured approximately 220 Portuguese vessels, effectively imposing a blockade on Río de Janeiro.[33] The Portuguese, in turn, enlisted local converso capital to purchase vessels large enough to resist the privateering raids. The Dutch attempted several times to break the rebel forces, but their land efforts were defeated by poor Dutch strategic decisions and the rebels' superior knowledge of the terrain. This led to a standoff, with the pro-Portugal rebels controlling the land, and the Dutch in control of the seas.

By summer of 1646 the siege had been dragging on for nearly a year, and the inhabitations of Recife were beginning to lack supplies. Soldiers for the Dutch went from door to door requisitioning stocks for public warehouses. Bread was rationed to one pound per person each week. Slaves, in particular, suffered; there were reports of slaves digging up horse cadavers for food. Cats and dogs were used for food. The mercenary soldiers of the WIC, left without pay, were bought off with a loan from the local Jews. The population planned for a desperate assault, to be led by the remaining soldiers followed by the entire population of the town. But on June 23, 1646, two WIC relief vessels arrived, with news that a further relief expedition was to follow.[34]

In their effort to control Pernambuco, the Dutch suffered the traditional disadvantage faced by colonial or foreign intervention forces, from the American Revolution to the war in Vietnam: the native population, in this case born planters, was willing to make sacrifices for its homeland beyond anything that the Dutch, motivated mainly by profit, could endure. In 1651, after two military defeats in Guararapes, the Dutch suffered defeats to their navy in the first Anglo-Dutch War. The Dutch began negotiations with Portugal over surrender of the Brazilian colony. While some Jews attempted to leave Brazil during the Dutch-Portuguese conflict, most were stuck in Recife. The destruction of the sugar trade during the siege reduced the number of trade-related vessels, so hardly any were available for transport out. The collapse of the sugar economy also left the Jews unable to pay for travel, and they could not leave until they repaid their debts to the WIC.

The capitulation agreement was signed in January 1654 in Taborda, Brazil. The Dutch negotiated protection guarantees for Jews in Brazil, and the agreement also allowed all Dutch subjects retention of their property, as well as future treatment equal to treatment of Portuguese subjects. As residents of Recife awaited ships for departure, however, the Portuguese general Francisco Barreto de Menezes exempted " the Jews who had been Christians" from his earlier promise of general amnesty for the city's residents, subordinating the law of Recife to the authority of "the Holy Inquisition, wherein [he could not] interfere."[35] Because many of the city's Jews had been born Christian, and because even those who had been born Jews and never baptized could have difficulty proving that they had not been born Christians, most Jews opted for emigration.

Settlements in the Atlantic Colonies

Of the Jews who left Brazil following the attempted Dutch invasion, the majority returned to Holland. However, the prosperity and freedom that they had experienced in Brazil tempted many to return to the Americas and inspired other Jews to follow. The Dutch continued to sponsor Jewish settlements. Of these the two most important were located in the Dutch colonies of Suriname and Curaçao.

Jews first settled in Suriname in the 1650s, when it was a British colony. When the Dutch took over the colony at the end of the second Anglo-Dutch war in 1667, a group of Jews established an agricultural community in an area the Dutch called Jodensavanne, or Jewish Savannah. While the colony was small—only about 105 men, and fewer women—its isolation made it practically autonomous, probably the only politically independent, Jewish-led society in the world.[36] Located in the Surinamese jungle, it eventually consisted of a few dozen Jewish-run sugar plantations.

Much of the labor was supplied by African slaves, and the mixing of Jews and blacks, combined with the relative scarcity of Jewish women, produced, over time, a significant community of black Jews. At the end of the eighteenth century, black Jews had their own synagogue in Suriname's capital city of Paramaribo, as well as their own society, founded in 1759, called Darkhei Yesharim (The Ways of the Righteous).[37]

In 1685 the Jews of Jodensavanne built a large synagogue, Brach veShalom. The brick ruins of the temple still remain, but the community itself suffered on account of the poor soil and found it difficult to compete with communities in more fertile regions. By the time the original settlement was destroyed by fire in 1832, most of the Jodensavanne Jews had left for the Suriname capital of Paramaribo and other locations. As early as 1817, about one-third of the white population of Paramaribo was Jewish.[38]

The most important and longest-lasting Jewish-Dutch settlement was established on the island of Curaçao. The island had poor potential as an agricultural center due to its poor soil and the chronic lack of rainfall. Instead, it flourished as a center for contraband to and from the colonies of Spain and Portugal. The Spanish banned direct trade with Holland, but settlers on Curaçao were able to evade Spanish patrols by using small vessels and by docking in small coves along the Venezuelan coast. They brought over merchandise from Europe, including textiles and manufactured goods, as well as spices from East India. To Europe they brought American silver, dyewoods, and tobacco, but the most important export crop was cacao.[39] Many, if not most, of the sloops and schooners that serviced this trade were owned by Jews. This trend is reflected in many of the vessels' names, including the Masal-tob, the Abraham en Isaac, the Bathseba, and the Bekeerde Jood (Converted Jew).[40]

By 1789 there were over a thousand Jews in Curaçao, or about one-third of the white population. The Curaçao synagogue, Mikveh Israel, constructed in 1732, was the largest in the Western Hemisphere, and is still in use. The Jewish cemetery, consecrated in 1659, is one of the oldest European cemeteries in the New World.

Jewish prosperity in the Dutch colonies encouraged immigration, creating significant Jewish communities in other Atlantic colonies. Jews prospered in French colonies such as Martinique until 1685, when they were expelled by Louis XIV. The British, aware of the significant contribution that Jews made to the Dutch colonies, actively encouraged Jewish immigration. When the British invaded French Cayenne with orders to burn the town and destroy it, Captain Sir John Harman, who led the invasion, had orders to take on board the town's Jews. This directive led to resentment among the British officers who were "aggrieved that any of the French should be left behind, being Christian, and the Jews numbering fifty to sixty should be carried off." When the orders were questioned, the official response was "It is necessary for the Jews to be transported for the several reasons fit to be given to his Majesty."[41]

By 1689 fifty-four Sephardic families lived on Jew Street in the British colony of Barbados, including the family of Abraham de Mercado, the first Jewish physician in the New World.[42] By the mid-1700s approximately four hundred Jews lived in Barbados and nine hundred in British Jamaica.[43]

New Amsterdam

One settlement, relatively small and unimportant, has particular value for Jews of the United States. In February 1654 a small group of refugees from Recife was stranded by bad weather in Jamaica, then still a

Spanish possession. The Spanish imprisoned the refugees from Recife, but the Dutch consuls in Cádiz and San Sebastián, at the urging of the Jewish community in Amsterdam, requested their release. In September 1654 twenty-three Jews sailed out of Cabo São Antonio, Cuba, on the French bark Sainte Catherine, headed for the Dutch colony of New Amsterdam.[44]

These were not the first Jews to arrive in New Amsterdam—an Ashkenazi Jew, Jacob Barsimson, had arrived from Europe shortly before the group disembarked—but they were the first to arrive as a community. Altogether they owed more than 1,500 guilders to the crew in payment for the voyage and found their furniture and other property confiscated to pay the debt, leaving them destitute.[45] They subsisted at first on handouts from Barsimson and from the local Dutch Reformed Church, whose dominie noted that the "Jews have come weeping and bemoaning their misery."[46]

Almost immediately they faced the opposition of the colony's governor, Peter Stuyvesant. Stuyvesant, the son of a Calvinist minister, was a career official with the WIC. His right leg had been shattered during a 1644 expedition to wrest control of St. Martin from the Spanish. One biographer has called him "God-fearing, honest, hard-working, abstemious."[47] As governor of Curaçao, he wrote that he considered the Jews "a crafty and generally treacherous people in whom not much confidence must be placed."[48]

Only three weeks after the Jews' arrival, Stuyvesant wrote to the WIC that "for the benefit of this weak and newly developing place," he had "require[d] them in a friendly way to depart." He called them a "deceitful race" and "hateful enemies and blasphemers of the name of Christ" who should not be allowed "further to infect and trouble this new colony."[49] The Amsterdam Jews came to the support of the refugees from Recife, citing their loyalty to Holland and the value they provided to the company as productive members of the WIC venture in Brazil. They argued that the Jews in New Amsterdam, which so sorely needed new settlers, should be allowed to enjoy the same rights as the Jews in Holland.[50]

In spite of the support that Stuyvesant received from the church for his anti-Jewish policy, he was obliged to comply with the WIC's orders that the Jews be allowed to remain. But Stuyvesant succeeded in placing strict limitations on the Jews' activities. The New Amsterdam council ordered the Jews to pay a fee for exemption from service in the militia and refused the requests of two Jews to volunteer for militia service (they had hoped to avoid the fee). It prohibited the Jews from trading outside the city and denied them the right to own real estate. Council members also denied them the right to a synagogue or, as Stuyvesant phrased it, "the free and public exercise of their abominable religion."[51]

Faced with these obstacles, most Jews left the colony. By 1664 only four Jews were known to be living in the New Amsterdam.[52] This represented the core of what would be a permanent Jewish presence in the colony. Asser Levy became a butcher, one of only six licensed butchers in the city, and the only one allowed an exemption, out of regard for kosher practice, from slaughtering hogs. He hired a housemaid, and when he died in 1682, he left a sizable estate, including an inventory of 440 people who owed him money.[53] Another, later arrival, also a refugee from Recife, Joseph Bueno, purchased a site in the New Bowery, where in 1683 he buried his father, Benjamín Bueno de Mesquita. Mesquita's gravestone, inscribed in Spanish, is the oldest decipherable Jewish tombstone in New York and the second oldest Jewish tombstone on the island on Manhattan.[54]

When the British took over the colony, they adopted a policy of religious tolerance. By 1730 enough Jews—about 225 Jews in a city with a total population of 8,000—had arrived to build a synagogue, the first temple built in British North America. The Jewish community in Curaçao donated 272 ounces of silver toward its construction.[55] The congregation that built the temple, Shearith Israel (Remnant of Israel), was formed in or around 1706; this Sephardic congregation is the oldest in the United States.

In 2003, in honor of the 350th anniversary of the American Jewish Community, the U.S. Congress passed a resolution to commemorate the 1654 arrival at New Amsterdam of the Jews from Recife. Considering the relative failure of the original settlement, the significance of this particular date can be questioned (one recent scholarly article criticized what it called "mythologizing 1654"). It is clear, however, that the Sephardic experience in general—there would be more Sephardic settlements—formed the foundation for the creation of the first American Jewish communities, a creation that would transform both Jewish and world history.[56]

Conclusion

Assimilation and Its Discontents

While *convivencia* never provided the Jews with the same level of acceptance into society as modern assimilation, it did give them many opportunities for integration in the larger, non-Jewish society—and this absorption of Jews into a larger Christian and Muslim culture created friction and pressures that affected both the individuals and society as a whole.

Until the forced conversions of 1391, *convivencia* probably had a limited impact on most Jews. They lived in separate communities and most probably had only business dealings with the Muslim and Christian populations. The Jews who more actively participated in Christian and Muslim society, either at court or as physicians or in other occupations, had to balance their Jewish identity with their status in a non-Jewish society. Some obtained wealth and/or power and seemed to have had no problem succeeding in a non-Jewish culture while maintaining a strong Jewish identity—examples include Hasdai ibn Shaprut, physician and courtier to the caliph; Samuel ibn Nagrela, vizier in Granada; and Samuel Halevi of Toledo, in the Christian period.

But material success was only part of what assimilation could offer the Jews. Exposure to foreign cultures, particularly to the accomplishments of a culturally surging Islamic empire (and the Greek and Roman classical literature that this empire rediscovered and preserved), provided them with enormous cultural stimulation. Many, most prominently Maimonides, incorporated classical and Islamic philosophical ideas into a Jewish structure. Others explored new developments in mathematics, astronomy, and other sciences. The Arabic poetic tradition stimulated an enormous body of secular poetry in Hebrew. Jews also mastered and became dominant in a new profession—medicine—based on classical principles.

Religion and Philosophy

While many Jews were able to incorporate new ideas and cultures into their religious traditions, some found another way to deal with a life that bridged two different religious worlds: they gave up their religious practice. While the "secular Jew" is considered a modern phenomenon, there are indications that as early as the Muslim period some Spanish Jews were attracted to and adopted a secular outlook. This trend most likely began in the Muslim period with the embrace of classical philosophy.

Philosophy did not necessarily require abandoning Judaism. It was possible, as Maimonides demonstrated, to reconcile philosophy with faith. That said, there were others who saw philosophy as a threat to their Jewish faith. Judah Halevi, for example, in his twelfth-century *Book of the Kuzari*, devoted a significant section to demonstrating the superiority of Jewish faith over rational philosophy. In the thirteenth century, the "anti-Maimonides" movement attempted to ban the study of philosophy, believing it undermined Jewish faith. After the mass conversions of 1391, Solomon Alami, in his *Iggeret Musar* (*Epistle of Ethical Admonition*), claimed that the attraction to philosophy was one of the reasons Jews opted for conversion over martyrdom:

> Then there were those scholars who attempted to interpret the scriptures in the Greek manner and clothe it in Greek dress. They believed that Plato and Aristotle had brought us more light than Moses our master.... Now, if a man should not be able to "live by his faith," why should he suffer death for it and endure the joke and the shame of dispersion among the nations? It serves no good purpose to quote Scriptures as support for philosophical opinions: the way of reason and the way of faith are too far apart and will never meet.... Those who read a few columns in a book of Greek philosophy will soon tear to shreds the scroll of the Torah.[1]

Writing in the same period as Alami, Joshua ha-Lorki (before he became the apostate Geronimo de Santa Fe), in his letter to the new convert Pablo de Burgos, cited philosophy and reason as factors that might have led Pablo away from his Jewish faith.

The conversos faced a more radical form of assimilation—forced conversion—and some went even further in embracing a wholly secular point of view. This secular perspective fostered a body of literature like *La Celestina*, which would become a foundation for the modern novel.

A threat to faith can also stir religious creativity. The popularity and growth of Jewish mystical literature may have been partly a reaction to the frictions caused by increased exposure to a Christian world. The Kabbalah, which was seen as an esoteric, powerful belief system representing an ancient tradition, was particularly effective in strengthening a Jewish sense of identity for many.

Converts in the Christian World

Assimilation did not have an impact just on the Jews. It was also perceived as a threat to Spanish society as a whole, because it was forced to accept within it a foreign religion and culture. (We see this reaction to assimilation today in the controversies in the United States and abroad surrounding immigration policies.) After the mass conversions, the conversos were particularly vulnerable to being viewed as a threat by the Old Christian society. Many lived in separate neighborhoods and continued to socialize and marry within their own group. (One can see this tendency in the book *Lozana*: Lozana is not accepted into the community of converso prostitutes in Rome until she shows that she practices converso customs.) Centuries of anti-Jewish propaganda, revived and expanded in fifteenth-century Spain through works like Alonso de Espina's *Fortress of Faith*, served as a basis for stigmatizing the New Christians.

The Toledo revolt of 1449 became the pivotal event in creating the perception that the assimilation of New Christians posed a threat to Old Christian society. It did this by introducing two innovations: an inquisition that operated without any pretense of objectivity, bent on proving that the conversos were secret Jews; and the racial exclusion provisions that eventually became known as *limpieza de sangre*, or purity-of-blood restrictions. While the leader of this revolt may have promoted these concepts as a pretext to loot and weaken the converso community, the rapid popularity and spread of *limpieza* and the proliferation of anti-converso riots show how ready Old Christian society was to feel threatened by the conversos.

In the end Spanish monarchs chose to respond to assimilation with repression. The Spanish Inquisition dealt with the perceived threat with mass arrests, torture, large-scale imprisonment and galley enslavement, and death at the stake. Assimilation finally brought to Europe the first modern bureaucracy of repression, an institutional model that would be imitated many times over, right up to today.

Spanish Jews after Spain

While Spain closed itself off for protection from the perceived threats from assimilation, the Jews who survived the expulsion carried with them to new lands a rich culture that benefited from exposure to other traditions. The rationalism Maimonides brought to Judaism, for example, was carried forward by Joseph ben Ephraim Karo, who was four years old at the time of the expulsion, and who eventually settled in Israel. Karo's codification of Jewish law in his classic work, the *Shulchan Aruch*, built on and superseded Maimonides as a source for religious rulings. Sephardic Jews also continued to explore the mystical world of Kabbalah; the hilltop town of Safed in Israel became an important center for Kabbalah studies, particularly through the teachings of Isaac Luria (1534–72).

Amsterdam would in the seventeenth century offer to Sephardic Jews an important shelter and greater opportunities to engage in a larger world. It was here that Baruch Spinoza, whose parents were conversos, developed what many consider to be the first modern system of philosophy. The Dutch also brought Jews to the New World, where they played an important role in the establishing the Atlantic trading system.

The Ottoman Empire, both in the Middle East and in Europe, like the Greek city of Salonika, also became an important shelter for Sephardic Jews, where they adapted to these new cultures while preserving their old traditions, such as their own language, Ladino, a variation of old Castilian. The contemporary Sephardic folksinger Flora Jagoda, who wrote a well-known Hanukkah song, "Ocho Kandelikas," once said that when she grew up in Bosnia she knew who was Jewish because they spoke Spanish (Ladino).

Today 20 percent of modern Jews are descendants from the Spanish expulsion. Ironically, the expulsion decree, designed to put an end to Spanish Jewry, instead spread a vital and flourishing Sephardic culture throughout the world.

Notes

1. A Marriage of Convenience

1. Américo Castro, *Structure of Spanish History*, 467.
2. Menocal, *Ornament of the World*.
3. Kamen, *Disinherited*, 50.
4. Rohr, *Spanish Right and the Jews*, 66.
5. Marías, *Understanding Spain*, 135.
6. N. Roth, *Jews, Visigoths and Muslims*, 1.
7. Fletcher, "Early Middle Ages," 84.
8. Cited in Peréz, *History of a Tragedy*, 107.

2. The Visigoth Persecution of the Jews

1. Gerber, *Jews of Spain*, 39.
2. Parkes, *Conflict of the Church*, 347.
3. Bachrach, *Early Medieval Jewish Policy*.
4. N. Roth, *Jews, Visigoths and Muslims*, 37.
5. Gerber, *Jews of Spain*, 15.
6. Gonzalez-Salerno, "Catholic Anti-Judaism in Visigothic Spain," 128.
7. Parkes, *Conflict of the Church*, 348.
8. Ashtor, *Jews of Moslem Spain*, 1:13.

3. Muslim Rule

1. Holmes, *Terrorism and Democratic Stability Revisited*, 248.
2. Murphy, *God's Jury*, 71.
3. Makki, "Political History of Al-andalus," 5–7.
4. Makki, "Political History of Al-andalus," 9–10.
5. Lowney, *Vanished World*, 38.
6. Makki, "Political History of Al-andalus," 11.

7. Fletcher, *Moorish Spain*, 44.
8. Fierro, *Abd al-Rahman III*, 84.
9. Fletcher, *Moorish Spain*, 53.
10. Fierro, *Abd al-Rahman III*, 51.
11. Fierro, *Abd al-Rahman III*, 55.
12. Fierro, *Abd al-Rahman III*, 112.
13. Fierro, *Abd al-Rahman III*, 112.
14. Fletcher, *Moorish Spain*, 66.
15. Menocal, *Ornament of the World*, 32.
16. Fierro *Abd al-Rahman III*, 1.
17. Fletcher, *Moorish Spain*, 70–71.
18. Crompton, *Homosexuality and Civilization*, 167.
19. Fletcher, *Moorish Spain*, 73.
20. Fletcher, *Moorish Spain*, 76.
21. Wasserstein, *Rise and Fall*, 52.

4. Jews of Muslim Spain

1. Hillenbrand, "Medieval Cordoba as a Cultural Centre," 1:124.
2. Gampel, "'Letter to a Wayward Teacher,'" 390.
3. Bat Ye'or, *Dhimmi*, 44–46.
4. M. Cohen, *Under Crescent and Cross*, 99.
5. Hillenbrand, "Medieval Cordoba as a Cultural Centre," 1:120–21.
6. Lowney, *Vanished World*, 75.
7. Siraisi, *Medieval & Early Renaissance Medicine*, 72.
8. Seed, "Origin of Modern Navigation," 75.
9. Sirat, *History of Jewish Philosophy*, 5.
10. Siraisi, *Medieval & Early Renaissance Medicine*, 101–9.

11. Nuland, *Maimonides*, 12.

12. Nuland, *Maimonides*, 16.

13. Ashtor, *Jews of Moslem Spain*, 1:282–83.

14. Benjamin of Tudela, *Itinerary of Benjamin of Tudela*, 9–10.

15. Benjamin of Tudela, *Itinerary of Benjamin of Tudela*, 38–40.

16. Benjamin of Tudela, *Itinerary of Benjamin of Tudela*, 62.

17. Brann, *Power in the Portrayal*, 74.

18. Cited in Brann, *Power in the Portrayal*, 56–58.

19. Benjamin of Tudela, *Itinerary of Benjamin of Tudela*, 52–53.

20. Benjamin, *World of Benjamin of Tudela*, 20.

5. Judah Halevi and *The Kuzari*

1. Cole, *Dream of the Poem*, 5.

2. Fierro, *Abd al-Rahman III*, 71.

3. Ashtor, *Jews of Moslem Spain*, 1:153, 184–93.

4. Ashtor, *Jews of Moslem Spain*, 1:218–24.

5. Ashtor, *Jews of Moslem Spain*, 1:221, 230.

6. Ashtor, *Jews of Mòslem Spain*, 1:199–200.

7. Gerber, *Jews of Spain*, 50.

8. Scheindlin, *Song of the Distant Dove*, 16.

9. Regarding panegyrics, see Scheindlin, *Wine, Women and Death*, 6.

10. Halevi, *Selected Poems of Judah Halevi*, 118.

11. Scheindlin, *Song of the Distant Dove*, 53.

12. Halevi, *Selected Poems of Judah Halevi*, 1.

13. Halevi, *Kuzari*, 36.

14. Halevi, *Kuzari*, 40.

15. Halevi, *Kuzari*, 99.

16. Brann, *Compunctious Poet*, 90.

17. Halevi, *Selected Poems*, 40–41.

18. Brann, *Power in the Portrayal*, 101.

19. Brann, *Power in the Portrayal*, 128.

20. Halevi, *Selected Poems*, 21.

21. Halevi, *Selected Poems*, 249.

22. Sachar, *Farewell España*, 17.

6. A Golden Age of Poetry

1. Scheindlin, *Gazelle*, 6–7.

2. Menocal, *Ornament of the World*, 125.

3. Carmi, *Penguin Book of Hebrew Verse*, 298.

4. Abu-Haidar, "Review of Abraham Ibn Ezra y su Tiempo," 550.

5. N. Roth, "'Deal Gently with the Young Man.'"

6. Pagis, *Hebrew Poetry of the Middle Ages*, 47.

7. N. Roth, "'Deal Gently with the Young Man,'" 23.

8. Pagis, *Hebrew Poetry of the Middle Ages*, 65.

9. Pagis, *Hebrew Poetry of the Middle Ages*, 13.

10. N. Roth, "'Deal Gently with the Young Man,'" 23.

11. Cole, *Dream of the Poem*, 85.

12. Scheindlin, *Gazelle*, 13.

13. Scheindlin, *Gazelle*, 39, 77.

14. Scheindlin, *Gazelle*, 23.

15. Scheindlin, *Gazelle*, 37.

16. Cole, *Dream of the Poem*, 79.

17. Ashtor, *Jews of Moslem Spain*, 1:32.

18. Brann, *Compunctious Poet*, 75–76.

19. Scheindlin, *Wine, Women and Death*, 173.

20. Solomon ibn Gabirol, *Selected Religious Poems*, 7.

21. Sachar, *Farewell España*, 13.

22. Baer, *History of the Jews*, 1:61.

23. Baer, *History of the Jews*, 1:63.

24. Baer, *History of the Jews*, 1:61–62.

25. Ben Ezra, *Selected Poems*, 101.

26. Cole, *Dream of the Poem*, 185–86.

27. Cole, *Dream of the Poem*, 181.

28. Cole, *Dream of the Poem*, 173.

29. Glick, "Science in Medieval Spain," 94–97.

30. Glick, "Science in Medieval Spain," 90.

7. The End of the Caliphate

1. Glick, "Science in Medieval Spain," 83–98.
2. Glick, "Science in Medieval Spain," 57.
3. Glick, "Science in Medieval Spain," 58.
4. Brann, *Power in the Portrayal*, 129.
5. Wasserstein, *Rise and Fall*, 97.
6. Brann, *Power in the Portrayal*, 16.
7. Ashtor, *Jews of Moslem Spain*, 2:112.
8. Brann, *Power in the Portrayal*, 25.
9. Sachar, *Farewell España*, 7.
10. Brann, *Compunctious Poet*, 34.
11. Cole, *Dream of the Poem*, 38.
12. Brann, *Power in the Portrayal*, 131.
13. Fletcher, *Moorish Spain*, 96.
14. Cole, *Dream of the Poem*, 45.
15. Cole, *Dream of the Poem*, 38.
16. Cole, *Dream of the Poem*, 61.
17. Cole, *Dream of the Poem*, 65.
18. N. Roth, "'Deal Gently with the Young Man,'" 96–97.
19. Sachar, *Farewell España*, 9.
20. Lewis, *Islam in History*, 170.
21. M. Cohen, *Under Crescent and Cross*, 165.
22. Fletcher, *Moorish Spain*, 108.
23. Weinberger, *Twilight of a Golden Age*, 96.

8. Maimonides

1. Gerber, *Jews of Spain*, xv.
2. Kraemer, *Maimonides*, 42.
3. Kraemer, *Maimonides*, 24.
4. Kraemer, *Maimonides*, 44.
5. Kraemer, *Maimonides*, 60.
6. Kraemer, *Maimonides*, 199.
7. Nuland, *Maimonides*, 45.
8. Kraemer, *Maimonides*, 124.
9. Kraemer, *Maimonides*, 106.
10. Kraemer, *Maimonides*, 107.
11. Kraemer, *Maimonides*, 115.
12. Nuland, *Maimonides*, 92.
13. Kraemer, *Maimonides*, 163.
14. Kraemer, *Maimonides*, 328.
15. Kraemer, *Maimonides*, 222–23.
16. Kraemer, *Maimonides*, 303–4.
17. Kraemer, *Maimonides*, 301.
18. Kraemer, *Maimonides*, 441.
19. Nuland, *Maimonides*, 183.
20. Kraemer, *Maimonides*, 381.
21. Kraemer, *Maimonides*, 443.
22. Kraemer, *Maimonides*, 374.
23. Maimonides, *Guide for the Perplexed*, 4.
24. Kraemer, *Maimonides*, 374.
25. Kraemer, *Maimonides*, 399.
26. Maimonides, *Guide for the Perplexed*, 638–39.
27. Maimonides, *Guide for the Perplexed*, 454–55.
28. Gerber, *Jews of Spain*, 88.

9. Christian Rule

1. Sirat, *History of Jewish Philosophy*, 141.
2. Ray, *Sephardic Frontier*, 12.
3. Ray, *Sephardic Frontier*, 12.
4. Baer, *History of the Jews*, 182.
5. Ray, *Sephardic Frontier*, 12.
6. Stanley Payne, *History of Spain and Portugal*, 1:67.
7. Quoted in Payne, *History of Spain and Portugal*, 1:135.
8. Klein, *Jews, Christian Society, & Royal Power*, 58.
9. Payne, *History of Spain and Portugal*, 1:67.
10. Payne, *History of Spain and Portugal*, 1:99–100.
11. Ray, *Sephardic Frontier*, 32.
12. Sachar, *Farewell España*, 10.
13. Sachar, *Farewell España*, 43.
14. Sachar, *Farewell España*, 30.
15. Lowney, *Vanished World*, 220.
16. Sachar, *Farewell España*, 33.
17. Siraisi, *Medieval & Early Renaissance Medicine*, 31.
18. Baer, *History of the Jews*, 1:122.
19. Scholem, *Major Trends in Jewish Mysticism*, 80.

20. Gampel, "'Letter to a Wayward Teacher,'" 406.

21. Scholem, *Origins of the Kabbalah*, 377.

22. Klein, *Jews, Christian Society & Royal Power*, 118.

10. Jews in Castile and Aragon

1. Fletcher, *Moorish Spain*, 8.

2. Mariana, *Historia general de España*, 13:20.

3. O'Callaghan, "Paths to Ruin," 43.

4. N. Roth, "Jewish Collaborators," 63.

5. Neuman, *Jews in Spain*, 2:104.

6. Baer, *History of the Jews*, 1:116.

7. Boonstra, Jansen, and Kniesmeyer, *Antisemitism*, 32.

8. O'Callaghan, "Paths to Ruin," 43.

9. Martínez, "Black Blood of New Spain," 388.

10. Martínez, "Black Blood of New Spain," 243.

11. Baer, *History of the Jews*, 1:129–30.

12. Baer, *History of the Jews*, 1:308.

13. Klein, *Jews, Christian Society, & Royal Power*, 145.

14. Baer, *History of the Jews*, 1:149.

15. Baer, *History of the Jews*, 1:148.

16. Assis, *Golden Age of Aragonese Jewry*, 52.

17. Baer, *History of the Jews*, 1:160.

18. Burns, *Worlds of Alfonso the Learned*, 7.

19. Burns, *Worlds of Alfonso the Learned*, 10.

20. Assis, *Golden Age of Aragonese Jewry*, 139.

21. Assis, *Golden Age of Aragonese Jewry*, 13.

22. Baer, *History of the Jews*, 1:175.

23. Baer, *History of the Jews*, 1:175.

11. *Book of Splendor* and Kabbalah Mysticism

1. Scholem, *Major Trends in Jewish Mysticism*, 174.

2. Scholem, *Major Trends in Jewish Mysticism*, 190.

3. See, for example, Scholem, "The Sefirotic Doctrines of a Pseudepi-graphic Epistle," in his *Origins of the Kabbalah*, 355.

4. Lachter, "Jews as Masters of Secrets," 295.

5. Scholem, *Origins of the Kabbalah*, 197.

6. Green, "Zohar."

7. Moses de León, *Zohar*, 94.

8. Scholem, *Origins of the Kabbalah*, 211.

9. Scholem, *Major Trends in Jewish Mysticism*, 230.

10. Scholem, *Major Trends in Jewish Mysticism*, 230.

11. Koren, "Christian Means to a Conversa End," 45.

12. Idel, *Kabbalah*.

13. Green, "Zohar," 35.

14. Scholem, *Major Trends in Jewish Mysticism*, 179–80.

15. Scholem, *Major Trends in Jewish Mysticism*, 162.

16. Moses de León, *Zohar*, vii–viii.

12. Toward 1391

1. Pagels, *Origin of Satan*, 10.

2. Pagels, *Origin of Satan*, 88.

3. Carroll, *Constantine's Sword*, 271.

4. Carroll, *Constantine's Sword*, 271.

5. Augustine, *City of God*, 18:34.177.

6. Carroll, *Constantine's Sword*, 218–19.

7. Boswell, *Christianity, Social Tolerance, and Homosexuality*, 272.

8. Carroll, *Constantine's Sword*, 278.

9. Boswell, *Christianity, Social Tolerance, and Homosexuality*, 272.

10. Carroll, *Constantine's Sword*, 282.

11. Schroeder, *Disciplinary Decrees*, 236–96.

12. Carroll, *Constantine's Sword*, 282.

13. Lowney, *Vanished World*, 200.

14. Baer, *History of the Jews*, 1:181.

15. Ashley, *Dominicans*, 12.

16. J. Cohen, *Friars and the Jews*, 42–43.

17. Morris, *Papal Monarchy*, 472.

18. Morris, *Papal Monarchy*, 474.

19. Baer, *History of the Jews*, 2:14.

20. J. Cohen, *Friars and the Jews*, 239–40.

21. J. Cohen, *Friars and the Jews*, 69.

22. J. Cohen, *Friars and the Jews*, 69.

23. J. Cohen, *Friars and the Jews*, 63.

24. J. Cohen, *Friars and the Jews*, 66.

25. J. Cohen, *Friars and the Jews*, 67.

26. Chazan, *Barcelona and Beyond*, 52.

27. Baer, *History of the Jews*, 1:102.

28. Chazan, *Barcelona and Beyond*, 42.

29. Chazan, *Barcelona and Beyond*, 75–76.

30. Chazan, *Barcelona and Beyond*, 139.

31. Nachmanides, "The Disputation at Barcelona," in *Writings and Discourses*, 2:82.

32. Nachmanides, *Writings and Discourses*, 2:662, 668.

33. Chazan, *Barcelona and Beyond*, 126.

34. Chazan, *Barcelona and Beyond*, 128.

35. Nachmanides, "Prayer at the Ruins of Jerusalem," in *Writings and Discourses*, 2:12–713.

36. J. Cohen, *Friars and the Jews*, 146.

37. J. Cohen, *Friars and the Jews*, 245.

38. J. Cohen, *Friars and the Jews*, 24.

39. Nirenberg, *Communities of Violence*, 229.

13. Seeds of Destruction

1. Hillgarth, *Spanish Kingdoms*, 1:76.

2. Baer, *History of the Jews*, 1:356.

3. Estow, *Pedro the Cruel of Castile*, 183.

4. Estow, *Pedro the Cruel of Castile*, 194.

5. Baer, *History of the Jews*, 1:363.

6. Estow, *Pedro the Cruel of Castile*, 81.

7. Estow, *Pedro the Cruel of Castile*, 202.

8. Baer, *History of the Jews*, 1:364.

9. Netanyahu, *Origins of the Inquisition*, 102.

10. Baron, *Social and Religious History*, 11:44.

11. Estow, *Pedro the Cruel of Castile*, 259.

12. Baer, *History of the Jews*, 1:368.

13. Estow, *Pedro the Cruel of Castile*, 155–56.

14. The Conversion of the Jews

1. Amador de los Rios, *Estudios historicos*, 69, my translation.

2. Netanyahu, *Origins of the Inquisition*, 131.

3. Netanyahu, *Origins of the Inquisition*, 132.

4. Lea, *History of the Inquisition*, 1:104.

5. Netanyahu, *Origins of the Inquisition*, 133.

6. Netanyahu, *Origins of the Inquisition*, 134.

7. Netanyahu, *Origins of the Inquisition*, 134.

8. Hillgarth, *Spanish Kingdoms*, 1:385.

9. F. Danvila, quoted in Netanyahu, *Origins of the Inquisition*, 155.

10. Netanyahu, *Origins of the Inquisition*, 144.

11. Ortiz de Zuniga, quoted in Netanyahu, *Origins of the Inquisition*, 149.

12. Baer, *History of the Jews*, 2:98.

13. Baer, *History of the Jews*, 2:101.

14. Gutwirth, "Towards Expulsion," 54.

15. Baer, *History of the Jews*, 2:101.

16. Baer, *History of the Jews*, 2:104.

17. Netanyahu, *Origins of the Inquisition*, 158.

18. Baer, *History of the Jews*, 2:84.

19. Baer, *History of the Jews*, 2:105.

20. Sirat, *History of Jewish Philosophy*, 359–72.

21. Sachar, *Farewell España*, 46–47.

22. Baer, *History of the Jews*, 2:117.

23. Cantor, *In the Wake of the Plague*, 152.

24. Netanyahu, *Origins of the Inquisition*, 162–67.

15. The Church Campaign against the Jews

1. Baer, *History of the Jews*, 2:117.

2. Baer, *History of the Jews*, 2:111.

3. Baer, *History of the Jews*, 2: 132.

4. Keyserling, *Historia dos Judeus em Portugal*, 36–37.

5. Baer, *History of the Jews*, 2:134.

6. Baer, *History of the Jews*, 2:137.

7. Sachar, *Farewell España*, 50.

8. *Catholic Encyclopedia*, 15:438.

9. Gail, *Three Popes*, 186.

10. Baer, *History of the Jews*, 2:166.

11. Liss, *Isabel the Queen*, 37.

12. For an extensive discussion of this letter, see Gampel, "Letter to a Wayward Teacher."

13. Gampel, "Letter to a Wayward Teacher," 418.

14. Gampel, "Letter to a Wayward Teacher," 425.

15. Netanyahu, *Origins of the Inquisition*, 172.

16. Netanyahu, *Origins of the Inquisition*, 174.

17. Netanyahu, *Origins of the Inquisition*, 181.

18. Gail, *Three Popes*, 126.

19. Gail, *Three Popes*, 185.

20. Gail, *Three Popes*, 186.

21. Baer, *History of the Jews*, 2:167.

22. Netanyahu, *Origins of the Inquisition*, 192.

23. Netanyahu, *Origins of the Inquisition*, 193.

24. Amador de los Rios, quoted in Netanyahu, *Origins of the Inquisition*, 191.

25. C. Roth, *History of the Marranos*, 18.

26. Baer, *History of the Jews*, 2:175.

27. Gerber, *Jews of Spain*, 126.

28. Baer, *History of the Jews*, 2:175.

29. Gerber, *Jews of Spain*, 125.

30. Baer, *History of the Jews*, 2:181, 183.

31. Baer, *History of the Jews*, 2:203.

32. Baer, *History of the Jews*, 2:211.

33. Baer, *History of the Jews*, 2:224.

34. Baer, *History of the Jews*, 2:226.

35. Baer, *History of the Jews*, 2:230.

36. Baer, *History of the Jews*, 2:240.

37. Gail, *Three Popes*, 258.

38. Netanyahu, *Origins of the Inquisition*, 199–200.

16. New Christians

1. Netanyahu, *Origins of the Inquisition*, 1102.

2. Kaplan, "Inception of Limpieza de Sangre," 24n15.

3. Lea, *History of the Inquisition*, 1:120.

4. Netanyahu, *Origins of the Inquisition*, 424.

5. Netanyahu, *Origins of the Inquisition*, 526.

6. Netanyahu, *Marranos of Spain*, 59.

7. Baer, *History of the Jews*, 2:278.

8. Kamen, *Spanish Inquisition* (1965), 30.

9. Kamen, *Spanish Inquisition* (1997), 39.

10. Gitlitz, *Secrecy and Deceit*, 587.

11. Gitlitz, *Secrecy and Deceit*, 589.

12. Gitlitz, *Secrecy and Deceit*. 590.

13. Nirenberg, "Enmity and Assimilation," 137.

14. Gitlitz, *Secrecy and Deceit*, 135.

15. Gitlitz, *Secrecy and Deceit*, 428.

16. Kamen, *Spanish Inquisition* (1997), 5.

17. Kamen, *Spanish Inquisition* (1997), 39.

18. Peréz, *History of a Tragedy*, 71.

19. Peréz, *History of a Tragedy*, 72.

20. Gitlitz, *Secrecy and Deceit*, 627.

21. Malammed, *Heretics of Daughters of Israel*, 12.

22. Kamen, *Spanish Inquisition* (1997), 64.

23. Lazar, "Scorched Parchments and Tortured Memories," 180.

24. Gitlitz, *Secrecy and Deceit*, 77.

25. Netanyahu, *Origins of the Inquisition*, 849.

17. Converts and Castile

1. Hutcheston, "Desperately Seeking Sodom," 241.

2. Hutcheston, "Desperately Seeking Sodom," 227.

3. Hillgarth, *Spanish Kingdoms*, 2:301–2.

4. Netanyahu, *Origins of the Inquisition*, 387.

5. Round, *Greatest Man Uncrowned*, 170.

6. Baer, *History of the Jew*, 2:269–70.

7. Netanyahu, *Origins of the Inquisition*, 365.

8. Netanyahu, *Origins of the Inquisition*, 300.

9. Netanyahu, *Origins of the Inquisition*, 299–300.

10. Netanyahu, *Origins of the Inquisition*, 301.

11. Netanyahu, *Origins of the Inquisition*, 310.

12. Netanyahu, *Origins of the Inquisition*, 307–8.

13. Sicroff, *Los estatutos de Limpieza de Sangre*, 80, my translation.

14. Netanyahu, *Origins of the Inquisition*, 312.

15. Quoted in Netanyahu, *Origins of the Inquisition*, 316.

16. Netanyahu, *Origins of the Inquisition*, 317.

17. Netanyahu, *Origins of the Inquisition*, 317.

18. Netanyahu, *Origins of the Inquisition*, 353.

19. Netanyahu, *Origins of the Inquisition*, 354.

20. Netanyahu, *Origins of the Inquisition*, 355.

21. Netanyahu, *Origins of the Inquisition*, 355.

22. Netanyahu, *Origins of the Inquisition*, 356.

23. Netanyahu, *Origins of the Inquisition*, 376.

24. Netanyahu, *Origins of the Inquisition*, 381.

25. Netanyahu, *Origins of the Inquisition*, 382.

26. Netanyahu, *Origins of the Inquisition*, 330.

27. Netanyahu, *Origins of the Inquisition*, 473.

28. Netanyahu, *Origins of the Inquisition*, 336.

29. Netanyahu, *Origins of the Inquisition*, 337.

30. Netanyahu, *Origins of the Inquisition*, 338.

31. Netanyahu, *Origins of the Inquisition*, 333–35.

32. Netanyahu, *Origins of the Inquisition*, 341.

33. Round, *Greatest Man Uncrowned*, 40.

34. Round, *Greatest Man Uncrowned*, 42.

35. Round, *Greatest Man Uncrowned*, 234.

36. Round, *Greatest Man Uncrowned*, 72.

37. Round, *Greatest Man Uncrowned*, 213.

38. Netanyahu, *Origins of the Inquisition*, 710.

39. Marino, *Don Juan Pacheco*, 62.

40. Hillgarth, *Spanish Kingdoms*, 2:321.

41. Marino, *Don Juan Pacheco*, 18.

42. Netanyahu, *Origins of the Inquisition*, 416.

43. Marino, *Don Juan Pacheco*, 49.

44. Quoted in Hillgarth, *Spanish Kingdoms*, 2:327.

45. Lea, *History of the Inquisition*, 1:4.

46. Hillgarth, *Spanish Kingdoms*, 2:326.

47. Marino, *Don Juan Pacheco*, 1.

48. Netanyahu, *Origins of the Inquisition*, 733.

49. Netanyahu, *Origins of the Inquisition*, 892.

50. Netanyahu, *Origins of the Inquisition*, 891–92.

51. Netanyahu, *Origins of the Inquisition*, 894.

52. Netanyahu, *Origins of the Inquisition*, 740.

53. Netanyahu, *Origins of the Inquisition*, 741–42.

54. Netanyahu, *Origins of the Inquisition*, 761.

55. Netanyahu, *Origins of the Inquisition*, 761–62.

56. Netanyahu, *Origins of the Inquisition*, 772–83.

57. Netanyahu, *Origins of the Inquisition*, 783.

58. Netanyahu, *Origins of the Inquisition*, 786.

59. Netanyahu, *Origins of the Inquisition*, 798.

60. Edwards, *Christian Córdoba*, 183.

61. Netanyahu, *Origins of the Inquisition*, 801.

62. Netanyahu, *Origins of the Inquisition*, 80.

63. Edwards, *Christian Córdoba*, 183.

64. Netanyahu, *Origins of the Inquisition*, 80.

18. Anti- and Pro-Converso Writings

1. Netanyahu, *Origins of the Inquisition*, 727.

2. Netanyahu, *Origins of the Inquisition*, 817.

3. Netanyahu, *Origins of the Inquisition*, 829.

4. Netanyahu, *Origins of the Inquisition*, 821.

5. Netanyahu, *Origins of the Inquisition*, 742.

6. Netanyahu, *Origins of the Inquisition*, 831.

7. Netanyahu, *Origins of the Inquisition*, 820.

8. Netanyahu, *Origins of the Inquisition*, 829–30.

9. Netanyahu, *Origins of the Inquisition*, 835.

10. Netanyahu, *Origins of the Inquisition*, 837–38.

11. Netanyahu, *Origins of the Inquisition*, 839.

12. Villanueva, "Jewish 'Fools,'" 393.

13. Yovel, "Converso Dualities in the First Generation," 4–5.

14. Montoro, *Poesía completa*, poem 12.

15. Montoro, *Poesía completa*, poem 10.

16. Villanueva, "Jewish 'Fools,'" 403.

17. Montoro, *Poesía completa*, 23.

18. Montoro, *Poesía completa*, 29–30.

19. Yovel, "Converso Dualities in the First Generation," 5–6.

20. Weissberger "A Tierra, Puto!," 294.

21. Weissberger, "A Tierra, Puto!," 316.

22. Villanueva, "Jewish 'Fools,'" 397.

23. Wertheimer, "Converso 'Voices,'" 1:101.

24. López, "Lazarillo, Guzmán and Buffoon Literature," 237.

19. The Catholic Monarchy

1. Hillgarth, *Spanish Kingdoms*, 2:267–69.

2. Hillgarth *Spanish Kingdoms*, 2:273–74.

3. Liss, *Isabel the Queen*, 82.

4. Liss, *Isabel the Queen*, 70.

5. Liss, *Isabel the Queen*, 78.

6. Liss, *Isabel the Queen*, 79.

7. Hillgarth, *Spanish Kingdoms*, 2:351.

8. Hillgarth, *Spanish Kingdoms*, 2:354.

9. Hillgarth, *Spanish Kingdoms*, 2:340.

10. Netanyahu, *Origins of the Inquisition*, 1127–30.

11. Hillgarth, *Spanish Kingdoms*, 2:35.

12. Gutwirth, "Towards Expulsion," 69.

13. Liss, *Isabel the Queen*, 184.

14. Kamen, *Spanish Inquisition* (1997), 32.

15. N. Roth, *Conversos, Inquisition and the Expulsion*, 151.

16. Liss, *Isabel the Queen*, 165.

20. Origins of the Inquisition

1. Liss, *Isabel the Queen*, 16.

2. Liss, *Isabel the Queen*, 16.

3. N. Roth, *Conversos, Inquisition and the Expulsion*, 224.

4. Machiavelli, *Prince*, chapter 21.

5. Lea, *History of the Inquisition*, 1:155.

6. Liss, *Isabel the Queen*, 172.

7. Kamen, *Spanish Inquisition* (1997), 214.

8. Hillgarth, *Spanish Kingdoms*, 2:404.

9. Kamen, *Spanish Inquisition* (1997), 73.

10. Lea, *History of the Inquisition*, 1:154.

11. Liss, *Isabel the Queen*, 165.

12. Lea, *History of the Inquisition*, 2:315.

13. For *maravedis*, see N. Roth, *Conversos, Inquisition and the Expulsion*, 263; for ducats, see Lea, *History of the Inquisition*, 2:367.

14. Cantera Burgos, "Fernando del Pulgar," 343.

15. Beinart, *Conversos on Trial*, 29.

16. Vicens Yives, "Economy of Ferdinand and Isabella's Reign," 255–56.

17. Vicens Vives, "Economy of Ferdinand and Isabella's Reign," 260–61.

18. Alpert, *Crypto-Judaism and the Spanish Inquisition*, 24.

19. Liss, *Isabel the Queen*, 141.

20. Netanyahu, *Origins of the Inquisition*, 916.

21. Kamen, *Spanish Inquisition* (1997), 46.

21. The Inquisition

1. Netanyahu, *Origins of the Inquisition*, 1011.

2. Edwards, *Spanish Inquisition*, 74.

3. Kamen, *Inquisition and Society in Spain*, 31.

4. C. Roth, *Spanish Inquisition*, 45–46.

5. C. Roth, *Spanish Inquisition*, 46–47.

6. Kamen *Spanish Inquisition* (1997), 4.

7. Lea, *History of the Inquisition*, 1:164–65.

8. Sabatini, *Torquemada and the Spanish Inquisition*, 129.

9. Edwards, *Spanish Inquisition*, 75.

10. Kamen, *Spanish Inquisition* (1997), 203.

11. Lea, *History of the Inquisition*, 1:162.

12. Kamen, *Spanish Inquisition* (1997), 47.

13. Lea, *History of the Inquisition*, 1:161.

14. C. Roth, *Spanish Inquisition*, 47.

15. Lea, *History of the Inquisition*, 3:106.

16. Lea, *History of the Inquisition*, 2:108.

17. Lea, *History of the Inquisition*, 2:111.

18. Lea, *History of the Inquisition*, 1:164.

19. Edwards, *Inquisitors*, 14.

20. Sabatini, *Torquemada and the Spanish Inquisition*, 102.

21. Edwards, *Inquisitors*, 15.

22. Edwards, *Inquisitors*, 19.

23. Garcia Cárcel and Moreno Martínez, *Inquisicion*, 35.

24. Reston, *Dogs of God*, 39.

25. Netanyahu, *Origins of the Inquisition*, 431.

26. Netanyahu, *Origins of the Inquisition*, 1250.

27. Edwards, *Inquisitors*, 27.

28. Caro Baroja, *El senor inquisidor*, 20.

29. Edwards, *Inquisitors*, 13.

30. Lea, *History of the Inquisition*, 1:175.

31. Lea *History of the Inquisition*, 1:175.

32. Lea, *History of the Inquisition*, 1:174–75.

22. Arrest, Trial, and Punishment

1. Kamen, *Spanish Inquisition* (1997), 57.

2. Beinart, *Conversos on Trial*, 107–8.

3. Sabatini, *Torquemada and the Spanish Inquisition*, 150.

4. Lea, *History of the Inquisition*, 2:461.

5. Lea, *History of the Inquisition*, 2:460.

6. Beinart, *Conversos on Trial*, 109.

7. Beinart, *Conversos on Trial*, 97.

8. Lea, *History of the Inquisition*, 2:548.

9. Lea, *History of the Inquisition*, 2:538.

10. Lea, *History of the Inquisition*, 2:578.

11. Beinart, *Conversos on Trial*, 108.

12. Kamen *Spanish Inquisition* (1997), 176–77.

13. Lea, *A History of the Inquisition of Spain*, 2:510.

14. Lea, *History of the Inquisition*, 3:36.

15. Lea, *History of the Inquisition*, 3:42.

16. Sabatini, *Torquemada and the Spanish Inquisition*, 164.

17. Lea, *History of the Inquisition*, 3:4.

18. Lea, *History of the Inquisition*, 3:68.

19. Beinart, *Conversos on Trial*, 136.

20. Lea, *History of the Inquisition*, 3:17.

21. Lea, *History of the Inquisition*, 3:167.

22. Kamen, *Spanish Inquisition* (1997), 201.

23. Kamen, *Spanish Inquisition* (1997), 201.

24. Lea, *History of the Inquisition*, 3:186.

25. Lea, *History of the Inquisition*, 3:195–20.

26. Kamen, *Spanish Inquisition* (1997), 207–8.

27. Kamen, *Spanish Inquisition* (1997), 59.

28. Kamen, *Spanish Inquisition* (1997), 59.

29. Starr-LeBeau, *In the Shadow of the Virgin*, 177.

30. Starr-LeBeau, *In the Shadow of the Virgin*, 197.

31. Lea, *History of the Inquisition*, 3:220.

23. Inquisition Expansion

1. Lea, *History of the Inquisition*, 1:233.

2. Kamen, *Spanish Inquisition* (1997), 49.

3. Kamen, *Spanish Inquisition* (1997), 49–50.

4. Kamen, *Spanish Inquisition* (1997), 53.

5. Kamen, *Spanish Inquisition* (1997), 53.

6. Lea, *History of the Inquisition*, 1:251–52.

7. Peréz, *Spanish Inquisition*, 33.

8. Kamen, *Spanish Inquisition* (1997), 328.

9. Lea, *History of the Inquisition*, 1:252.

10. Lea, *History of the Inquisition*, 1:260.

11. Lea, *History of the Inquisition*, 1:256–57.

12. Kamen, *Spanish Inquisition* (1997), 56.

13. Netanyahu, *Origins of the Inquisition*, 1170.

14. Baer, *History of the Jews*, 2:40.

15. Baer, *A History of the Jews in Christian Spain*, 2:402–3.

16. Baer, *History of the Jews*, 2:404.

17. Baer, *History of the Jews*, 2:407.

18. Haliczer, "Jew as Witch," 152.

19. Lope de Vega, *Innocent Child*.

20. Caro Baroja, *Los judios en la España*, 187–88.

21. Hailczer, "Jew as Witch," 154.

24. Spain and Expulsion

1. Sachar, *Farewell España*, 58–59.

2. Meyerson, *Jewish Renaissance in Fifteenth-Century Spain*, 110.

3. Peréz, *History of a Tragedy*, 59.

4. Peréz, *History of a Tragedy*, 60.

5. Seed, "Origin of Modern Navigation," 80.

6. Sloan, *Sephardic Jews of Spain and Portugal*, 70.

7. Sachar, *Farewell España*, 333.

8. Lawee, *Isaac Abarbanel's Stance toward Tradition*, 36.

9. Baer, *History of the Jews*, 2: 315.

10. Gutwirth, "Towards Expulsion: 1391–1492," 69.

11. Baer, *History of the Jews*, 2:315.

12. Netanyahu, *Don Isaac Abravanel*, 10.

13. Lawee, *Isaac Abarbanel's Stance toward Tradition*, 10.

14. Lawee, *Isaac Abarbanel's Stance toward Tradition*, 31.

15. Lawee, *Isaac Abarbanel's Stance toward Tradition*, 28.

16. Lawee, *Isaac Abarbanel's Stance toward Tradition*, 12.

17. Netanyahu, *Don Isaac Abravanel*, 25.

18. Netanyahu, *Don Isaac Abravanel*, 27.

19. Lawee, *Isaac Abarbanel's Stance toward Tradition*, 9.

20. Netanyahu, *Don Isaac Abravanel*, 36.

21. Netanyahu, *Don Isaac Abravanel*, 38.

22. Lawee, *Isaac Abarbanel's Stance toward Tradition*, 16.

23. Netanyahu, *Don Isaac Abravanel*, 52, 53.

24. Kamen, *Spanish Inquisition* (1997), 21.

25. Raphael, *Expulsion 1492 Chronicles*, 190.

26. Netanyahu, *Don Isaac Abravanel*, 55–56.

27. Abravanel, "Introduction to the Former Prophets," 53.

28. Paramo, "On the Origins," 187.

29. Peréz, *History of a Tragedy*, 106.

30. Yerushalmi, "Exile and Expulsion in Jewish History," 21.

31. Yerushalmi, "Exile and Expulsion in Jewish History," 22.

32. Yerushalmi, "Exile and Expulsion in Jewish History," 22.

33. Kamen, "Mediterranean and the Expulsion," 53.

34. Peréz, *History of a Tragedy*, 86.

35. Capsali, "Minor Order of Elijah," 17.

36. Gerber, *Jews of Spain*, 141.

37. Lawee, *Isaac Abarbanel's Stance toward Tradition*, 18.
38. Kamen, "Expulsion," 79.
39. Bernáldez, "History of the Catholic Kings," 73.
40. Bernáldez, "History of the Catholic Kings," 74.
41. Baer, *History of the Jews*, 2:436.
42. Bernáldez, "History of the Catholic Kings," 75.
43. Cited in Kamen, "Mediterranean and the Expulsion," 32.
44. Baer, *History of the Jews*, 2:438.
45. Kamen, "Expulsion," 84–85.
46. Rosenberg, "Converso and the Spanish Picaresque Novel," 184.
47. Bernáldez, "History of the Catholic Kings," 77.
48. Hayyat, "Offering of Judah," 113–15.
49. Abraham ben Solomon, "Book of Tradition," 175.
50. Bernáldez, "History of the Catholic Kings," 78.
51. Netanyahu, *Don Isaac Abravanel*, 63.
52. Netanyahu, *Don Isaac Abravanel*, 218.
53. Netanyahu, *Don Isaac Abravanel*, 234.
54. Netanyahu, *Don Isaac Abravanel*, 205–41.
55. Lawee, *Isaac Abarbanel's Stance toward Tradition*, 45.
56. Goldman, "Abravanels Celebrate."

25. The Last Jews of Iberia

1. Soyer, *Persecution of the Jews*, 90.
2. Soyer, *Persecution of the Jews*, 100–101.
3. Soyer, *Persecution of the Jews*, 105.
4. Zacuto, "Book of Genealogies (*Sefer Yuhasin*)," 168.
5. Quoted in Soyer, *Persecution of the Jews*, 108.
6. Soyer, *Persecution of the Jews*, 109–10.
7. Soyer, *Persecution of the Jews*, 114–16.
8. Usque, "Consolation for the Tribulations of Israel," 140–41.
9. Garfield, "Public Christians, Secret Jews," 648.
10. Garfield, "Public Christians, Secret Jews," 650.
11. Soyer, *Persecution of the Jews*, 131.
12. Soyer, *Persecution of the Jews*, 159.
13. Soyer, *Persecution of the Jews*, 188.
14. Soyer, *Persecution of the Jews*, 195.
15. Soyer, *Persecution of the Jews*, 195.
16. Soyer, *Persecution of the Jews*, 194.
17. Soyer, *Persecution of the Jews*, 209.
18. Osório, "Of the Life and Deeds of King Manuel," 160.
19. Soyer, *Persecution of the Jews*, 213.
20. Soyer, *Persecution of the Jews*, 217.
21. Soyer, *Persecution of the Jews*, 220.
22. Ibn Faradj, "Family Origins," 123.
23. Soyer, *Persecution of the Jews*, 229.
24. C. Roth, *History of the Marranos*, 63.
25. Soyer, *Persecution of the Jews*, 185.
26. Yerushalmi, *Lisbon Massacre*, 8.
27. Yerushalmi, *Lisbon Massacre*, 10.
28. Yerushalmi, *Lisbon Massacre*, 11.
29. C. Roth, *History of the Marranos*, 65.
30. Yerushalmi, *Lisbon Massacre*, 30–31.
31. C. Roth, *History of the Marranos*, 220.
32. Gampel, *Last Jews on Iberian Soil*, 5.
33. Gampel, *Last Jews on Iberian Soil*, 20.
34. Gampel, *Last Jews on Iberian Soil*, 72.
35. Gampel, *Last Jews on Iberian Soil*, 78.
36. Gampel, *Last Jews on Iberian Soil*, 84.
37. Gampel, *Last Jews on Iberian Soil*, 105, 100.
38. Gampel, *Last Jews on Iberian Soil*, 106.
39. Regarding tax records, see Gampel, *Last Jews on Iberian Soil*, 111.
40. Hillgarth, *Spanish Kingdoms*, 2:541.
41. Gampel, *Last Jews on Iberian Soil*, 124.
42. Gampel, *Last Jews on Iberian Soil*, 126.
43. Gampel, *Last Jews on Iberian Soil*, 129.
44. Gampel, *Last Jews on Iberian Soil*, 132.
45. Gampel, *Last Jews on Iberian Soil*, 132.
46. Gampel, *Last Jews on Iberian Soil*, 130–31.

47. Gampel, *Last Jews on Iberian Soil*, 133.

26. Purity of Blood

1. Poliakov, *History of Anti-Semitism*, 2:221.
2. Sicroff, *Los estatutos de Limpieza de Sangre*, 87.
3. Caro Baroja, *Los judios en la España moderna*, 176–77.
4. Kamen, *Inquisition and Society in Spain*, 122.
5. Netanyahu, *Origins of the Inquisition*, 823.
6. Martonell and Galba, *Tirant lo Blanc*, 466–67.
7. Sicroff, *Los estatutos de Limpieza de Sangre*, 203–4.
8. Netanyahu, *Origins of the Inquisition*, 879.
9. Netanyahu, *Origins of the Inquisition*, 1104.
10. Siraisi, *Medieval and Early Renaissance Medicine*, 105–6.
11. Sicroff, *Los estatutos de Limpieza de Sangre*, 216.
12. Beusterien, "Jewish Male Menstruation," 451–52.
13. Beusterien, "Jewish Male Menstruation," 454.
14. Beusterien, "Jewish Male Menstruation," 454.
15. Kamen, *Inquisition and Society in Spain*, 117.
16. Netanyahu, *Origins of the Inquisition*, 1062.
17. Sicroff, *Los estatutos de Limpieza de Sangre*, 120.
18. Sicroff, *Los estatutos de Limpieza de Sangre*, 121.
19. Sicroff, *Los estatutos de Limpieza de Sangre*, 122.
20. Sicroff, *Los estatutos de Limpieza de Sangre*, 134.
21. Sicroff, *Los estatutos de Limpieza de Sangre*, 140.
22. Sicroff, *Los estatutos de Limpieza de Sangre*, 147.
23. Poliakov, *History of Anti-Semitism*, 225.
24. Netanyahu, *Origins of the Inquisition*, 1065.
25. Adolfo de Castro, *History of the Jews in Spain*.
26. Netanyahu, *Origins of the Inquisition*, 1066.
27. Sicroff, *Los estatutos de Limpieza de Sangre*, 167.
28. Donnelly, *Ignatius of Loyola*, 2.
29. Sicroff, *Los estatutos de Limpieza de Sangre*, 328.
30. Sicroff, *Los estatutos de Limpieza de Sangre*, 322.
31. Donnelly, *Ignatius of Loyola*, 149.
32. Sicroff, *Los estatutos de Limpieza de Sangre*, 325.
33. Kamen, *Spanish Inquisition* (1997), 246.
34. Kamen, *Inquisition and Society in Spain*, 126.
35. Sicroff, *Los estatutos de Limpieza de Sangre*, 218.
36. Kamen, *Spanish Inquisition* (1997), 32.
37. Kamen, *Spanish Inquisition* (1997), 32.
38. Lea, *History of the Inquisition*, 2:299.
39. Poliakov, *History of Anti-Semitism*, 289.
40. Sicroff, *Los estatutos de Limpieza de Sangre*, 216.
41. Kamen, *Spanish Inquisition* (1997), 239.
42. Martz, "Implementation of Pure Blood Statutes."
43. Kamen, *Spanish Inquisition* (1997), 240.
44. Lea, *History of the Inquisition of Spain*, 2:305.
45. Kamen, *Spanish Inquisition* (1997), 242.
46. Poliakov, *History of Anti-Semitism*, 229.
47. Kamen, *Spanish Inquisition* (1997), 243.
48. Poliakov, *History of Anti-Semitism*, 220–21.
49. Poliakov, *History of Anti-Semitism*, 220–21.

50. Kamen, "Limpieza and the Ghost of Americo Castro," 7.
51. Perednik, "Naïve Spanish Judeophobia."
52. Caro Baroja, *Los judios en la España moderna*, 31.

27. Jewish Blood, Black Blood

1. Ashtor, *Jews of Moslem Spain*, 1:28.
2. Wasserstein, *Rise and Fall*, 25.
3. Wasserstein, *Rise and Fall*, 59.
4. Davis, *Inhuman Bondage*, 49.
5. J. Sweet, "Iberian Roots," 16.
6. J. Sweet, "Iberian Roots," 163.
7. J. Sweet, "Iberian Roots," 164.
8. Schorsch, *Jews and Blacks*, 43.
9. Morner, *Race Mixture*, 17.
10. Schorsch, *Jews and Blacks*, 161.
11. Elliott, *Empires of the Atlantic World*, 51.
12. Martínez "Black Blood of New Spain."
13. Davis, *Inhuman Bondage*, 70.
14. Elliott, *Empires of the Atlantic World*, 171.
15. Morner, *Race Mixture*, 55–56.
16. Davis, *Inhuman Bondage*, 70.
17. Davis, *Inhuman Bondage*, 72.
18. For Mexico, see Martínez, "Black Blood of New Spain"; for Venezuela, see Lau, "Can Money Whiten?," 417; for Brazil, see Shepherd and Beckles, *Caribbean Slavery in the Atlantic World*, 29; Pijnigh, "New Christians," 488.
19. Israel, *Race, Class and Politics*, 93.
20. Spear, "Clean of Blood."
21. Nieto-Phillips, *Language of Blood*, 21, 25.
22. Xavier, "Purity of Blood and Caste," 143.
23. Elliott, *Empires of the Atlantic World*, 170.
24. Morner, *Race Mixture*.
25. Martínez, "Black Blood of New Spain."
26. Genesis 9:18–27, in Jewish Publication Society, *Tanakh*, 14–15.
27. Davis, *Inhuman Bondage*, 66.

28. J. Sweet, "Iberian Roots," 149.
29. J. Sweet, "Iberian Roots," 149.
30. Martínez, "Black Blood of New Spain."
31. Davis, *Inhuman Bondage*, 64–65.
32. Rout, *African Experience in Spanish America*, 127.
33. Rout, *African Experience in Spanish America*, 138.
34. Rout, *African Experience in Spanish America*, 146.
35. Elliott, *Empires of the Atlantic World*, 260.
36. Vaughan, *Roots of American Racism*, 145.
37. F. Sweet, *Legal History of the Color Line*, 122.
38. Smedley, *Race in North America*, 105.
39. Jordan, *White Man's Burden*, 61.
40. Miramon, "Invention of the Concept of Race," 204.
41. Nirenberg, "Was There Race before Modernity?," 249.
42. Smedley, *Race in North America*, 38–39.
43. Jordan, *White Man's Burden*, 166n67.
44. Fontaine, *Memoirs of a Huguenot Family*, 350.
45. Jordan, *White Man's Burden*, 547n5.
46. Jordan, *White Man's Burden*, 546.

28. Conversos and the Modern Novel

1. Gilman, *Spain of Fernando de Rojas*, 52.
2. Yovel, *Spinoza and Other Heretics*, 1:38.
3. Caro Baroja, *World of Witches*, 101.
4. Rojas, *La Celestina*, 17.
5. Rojas, *La Celestina*, 18.
6. Caro Baroja, *World of Witches*, 101.
7. Rojas, *La Celestina*, 110–11.
8. Costa Fontes, *Art of Subversion*, 84.
9. Costa Fontes, *Art of Subversion*, 251.
10. Quoted in Costa Fontes, *Art of Subversion*, 109.
11. Lea, *History of the Inquisition*, 3:546.
12. Gilman, *Spain of Fernando de Rojas*, 45.

13. Lea, *A History of the Inquisition of Spain*, 3:546.

14. Carpenter, "Converso Bestseller," 270–71.

15. Delicado, *Portrait of Lozana*, 1–2.

16. Delicado, *Portrait of Lozana*, 2.

17. Findlen, "Humanism, Politics and Pornography," 53.

18. Costa Fontes, *Art of Subversion*, 198.

19. Costa Fontes, *Art of Subversion*, 40.

20. Delicado, *Portrait of Lozana*, 23.

21. Delicado, *Portrait of Lozana*, 154.

22. Costa Fontes, *Art of Subversion*, 47.

23. Costa Fontes, *Art of Subversion*, 251.

24. Duran, "Picaresque Elements in Cervantes's Works," 226.

25. Mancing "Protean Picaresque," 283.

26. Hartveit, *Workings of the Picaresque*, 18.

27. Duran, "Picaresque Elements in Cervantes's Works," 229.

28. McGaha, "Is There a Hidden Jewish Meaning?," 173.

29. Duran, "Picaresque Elements in Cervantes's Works," 228.

30. Costa Fontes, *Art of Subversion*, 83.

31. Cervantes, *Interludes*, 144.

32. Cervantes, *Interludes*, 155.

33. Reed, *Exemplary History of the Novel*, 55.

34. Rothschild, "Falstaff and the Picaresque Tradition," 14.

35. Hartveit, *Workings of the Picaresque*, 18.

36. Reed, *Exemplary History of the Novel*, 140.

37. Reed, *Exemplary History of the Novel*, 143.

38. Regarding *Waverley*, see Reed, *Exemplary History of the Novel*, 167; for *Rob Roy*, see Hartveit, *Workings of the Picaresque*, 67.

39. Yovel, *Spinoza and Other Heretics*.

29. Coming to America

1. Katz, "Israel in America," 107.

2. Williams, "Atlantic Perspective," 373.

3. Israel, *Diasporas within a Diaspora*, 22.

4. Schama, *Embarrassment of Riches*, 590.

5. Sachar, *Farewell España*, 288.

6. Witnitzer, *Jews in Colonial Brazil*, 32.

7. Uchmany, "New Christians and Crypto-Jews," 197.

8. Israel, *Diasporas within a Diaspora*, 19, 29.

9. Pieroni, "Outcasts from the Kingdom," 345–46.

10. Witnitzer, *Jews in Colonial Brazil*, 10–11.

11. Boyajian, "New Christians and Jews," 475.

12. Emmer, "Jewish Moment," 510.

13. Emmer, "Jewish Moment," 511.

14. Witnitzer, *Jews in Colonial Brazil*, 49.

15. Witnitzer, *Jews in Colonial Brazil*, 49.

16. Witnitzer, *Jews in Colonial Brazil*, 59–60.

17. Feitler, "Jews and New Christians," 124–25.

18. Witnitzer, *Jews in Colonial Brazil*, 81.

19. Williams, "Atlantic Perspective," 375.

20. Israel, *Diasporas within a Diaspora*, 367.

21. Witnitzer, *Jews in Colonial Brazil*, 70.

22. Witnitzer, *Jews in Colonial Brazil*, 72.

23. Feitler, "Jews and New Christians," 126–27.

24. Witnitzer, *Jews in Colonial Brazil*, 136.

25. Witnitzer, *Jews in Colonial Brazil*, 174.

26. Witnitzer, *Jews in Colonial Brazil*, 171.

27. Witnitzer, *Jews in Colonial Brazil*, 82.

28. Witnitzer, *Jews in Colonial Brazil*, 95–96.

29. Israel, *Diasporas within a Diaspora*, 376–77.

30. Israel, *Diasporas within a Diaspora*, 369.

31. Witnitzer, *Jews in Colonial Brazil*, 97.

32. Israel, *Diasporas within a Diaspora*, 375.

33. Israel, *Diasporas within a Diaspora*, 379–80.

34. Witnitzer, *Jews in Colonial Brazil*, 101–2.

35. Witnitzer, *Jews in Colonial Brazil*, 141.

36. For population statistics, see Frankel, "Antecedents and Remnants of Jodensavanne," 397.

37. Frankel, "Antecedents and Remnants of Jodensavanne," 425.

38. Ben-Ur, "Matriarchal Matter," 154.

39. Israel, "Jews of Dutch America," 338.

40. Klooster, "Jews in Suriname and Curaçao," 356.

41. Arbell, "Jewish Settlement in the French Colonies," 300.

42. Klooster, "Networks of Colonial Entrepreneurs," 38.

43. Israel, "Jews of Dutch America," 336.

44. Witnitzer, *Jews in Colonial Brazil*, 142.

45. Williams, "Atlantic Perspective," 378.

46. Sachar, *Farewell España*, 362–63.

47. Williams, "Atlantic Perspective," 378.

48. Sachar, *Farewell España*, 360.

49. Williams, "Atlantic Perspective," 379.

50. Williams, "Atlantic Perspective," 379.

51. Williams, "Atlantic Perspective," 381.

52. Williams, "Atlantic Perspective," 386.

53. Snyder "English Markets, Jewish Merchants," 50.

54. Witnitzer, *Jews in Colonial Brazil*, 176.

55. Williams, "Atlantic Perspective," 387.

56. Kiron, "Mythologizing 1654," 583.

Conclusion

1. Gerber, *Jews of Spain*, 116–17.

Bibliography

Abravanel, Isaac. "Introduction to the Former Prophets." In Raphael, *Expulsion 1492 Chronicles*, 51–54.

Abu-Haidar, J. A. "Review of Abraham Ibn Ezra y su Tiempo." *Bulletin of the School of Oriental and African Studies* 55, no. 3 (1992): 549–52.

Alemán, Mateo. *The Rogue or the Life of Guzman el Alfarache*. Translated by James Mabbe. London: Constable, 1924.

Alpert, Michael. *Crypto-Judaism and the Spanish Inquisition*. New York: Palgrave Macmillan, 2001.

Amador de los Ríos, José. *Estudios históricos, políticos y literarios sobre los Judíos de España*. Madrid: D. M. Diaz, 1848.

Anonymous. *Lazarillo de Tormes and The Swindler: Two Spanish Picaresque Novels*. Translated by Michael Alpert. London: Penguin Classics, 2003.

Arbell, Mordechai. "Jewish Settlement in the French Colonies." In Bernardini and Fiering, *Jews and the Expansion*, 287–313.

Ashley, Benedict. *The Dominicans*. Eugene OR: Wipf & Stock, 2009.

Ashtor, Eliyah. *The Jews of Moslem Spain*. 3 vols. Philadelphia: Jewish Publication Society, 1973.

Assis, Yom Tov. *The Golden Age of Aragonese Jewry*. Oxford: Littman Library of Jewish Civilization, 1997.

Augustine. *The City of God*. London: Penguin, 1972.

Bachrach, Bernard. *Early Medieval Jewish Policy in Western Europe*. Minneapolis: University of Minnesota Press, 1977.

Baer, Yitzak. *A History of the Jews in Christian Spain*. 2 vols. Philadelphia: Jewish Publication Society of America, 1961.

Baron, Salo Wittmayer. *A Social and Religious History of the Jews*. Vol. 11. New York: Columbia University Press, 1967.

Barreto Xavier, Angel. "Purity of Blood and Caste: Identity Narratives among Early Modern Goan Elites." In *Race and Blood in the Iberian World*, edited by María Elena Martínez, David Nirenberg, and Max-Sebastián Hering, 125–50. Zürich: Lit Verlag, 2012.

Bat Ye'or. *The Dhimmi: Jews and Christians under Islam*. Translated from the French by David Maisel (author's text), Paul Fenton (document section), and David Littman. Rutherford NJ: Fairleigh Dickinson University Press; London: Associated University Presses, 1985.

Beinart, Haim. *Conversos on Trial*. Jerusalem: Magnes Press, 1981.

Ben Ezra, Moses. *Selected Poems of Moses Ibn Ezra*. Edited by Heinrich Brody. Translated by Solomon Solis-Cohen. Philadelphia: Jewish Publication Society of America, 1934.

Benjamin, Sandra. *The World of Benjamin of Tudela*. Madison NJ: Fairleigh Dickinson University Press, 1995.

Benjamin of Tudela. *The Itinerary of Benjamin of Tudela*. Translated by Marcus Nathan Adler. New York: Phillip Feldman, 1907.

Ben Solomon, Abraham. "The Book of Tradition." In Raphael, *Expulsion 1492 Chronicles*, 170–77.

Ben-Ur, Aviva. "A Matriarchal Matter: Slavery, Conversion, and Upward Mobility in Suriname's Jewish Community." In *Atlantic Diasporas: Jews, Conversos, and Crypto-Jews in the Age of Mercantilism*, edited by Richard L. Kagan and Philip D. Morgan, 152–69. Baltimore: Johns Hopkins University Press, 2009.

Bernáldez, Andrés. "History of the Catholic Kings Don Fernando and Dona Isabel." In Raphael, *Expulsion 1492 Chronicles*, 61–81.

Bernardini, Paolo, and Norman Fiering, eds. *The Jews and the Expansion of Europe to the West, 1450 to 1800*. New York: Berghahn Books, 2001.

Beusterien, John L. "Jewish Male Menstruation in Seventeenth-Century Spain." *Bulletin of the History of Medicine* 73, no. 3 (1999): 447–56.

Boonstra, Janrense, Hans Jansen, and Joke Kniesmeyer, eds. *Antisemitism: A History Portrayed*. Amsterdam: Anne Frank Foundation, 1993.

Boswell, John. *Christianity, Social Tolerance, and Homosexuality: Gay People in Western Europe from the Beginning of the Christian Era to the Fourteenth Century*. Chicago: University of Chicago Press, 1980.

Boyajian, James C. "New Christians and Jews in the Sugar Trade." In Bernardini and Fiering, *Jews and the Expansion*, 471–84.

Brann, Ross. *The Compunctious Poet: Cultural Ambiguity and Hebrew Poetry in Muslim Spain*. Baltimore: Johns Hopkins University Press, 1991.

———. *Power in the Portrayal: Representations of Jews and Muslims in Eleventh- and Twelfth-Century Islamic Spain*. Princeton NJ: Princeton University Press, 2002.

Burns, Robert I. *The Worlds of Alfonso the Learned and James the Conqueror*. Princeton NJ: Princeton University Press, 1986.

Cantera Burgos, Francisco. "Fernando del Pulgar and the Conversos." In *Spain in the Fifteenth Century*, edited by Roger Highfield, 296–353. London: Macmillan, 1972.

Cantor, Norman. *In the Wake of the Plague*. New York: Free Press, 2001.

Capsali, Elijah. "The Minor Order of Elijah." In Raphael, *Expulsion 1492 Chronicles*, 1–45.

Carmi, T. *The Penguin Book of Hebrew Verse*. New York: Viking Press, 1981.

Caro Baroja, Julio. *El señor inquisidor, y otras vidas por oficio*. Madrid: Alianza Editorial, 1983.

———. *Los judios en la España moderna y contemporánea*. Madrid: Ediciones Istmo, 1978.

———. *The World of Witches*. Translated by O. N. V. Glendinning. Chicago: University of Chicago Press, 1965.

Carpenter, Dwayne E. "A Converso Best-seller." In *Crisis and Creativity in the Sephardic World*, edited by Benjamin R. Gimpel, 267–81. New York: Columbia University Press, 1997.

Carroll, James. *Constantine's Sword*. Boston: Houghton Mifflin, 2001.

Castro, Adolfo de. *The History of the Jews in Spain*. Cambridge: J. Deighton, 1851.

Castro, Américo. *The Structure of Spanish History*. Translated by Edmund L. King. Princeton NJ: Princeton University Press, 1954.

The Catholic Encyclopedia. Edited by Charles G. Herbermann, Edward A. Pace, Condé Benoist Pallen, Thomas J. Shahan, and John J. Wynne. 16 vols. New York: Encyclopedia Press, 1913–14.

Cervantes Saavedra, Miguel de. *Don Quixote de la Mancha*. Translated by John Rutherford. New York: Penguin Press, 2003.

———. *The Interludes of Cervantes*. Translated by S. Griswold Moley. New York: Greenwood Press, 1968.

Chazan, Robert. *Barcelona and Beyond: The Disputation of 1263 and Its Aftermath*. Berkeley: University of California Press, 1992.

Cohen, Jeremy. *The Friars and the Jews*. Ithaca NY: Cornell University Press, 1982.

Cohen, Mark. *Under Crescent and Cross: The Jews in the Middle Ages*. Princeton NJ: Princeton University Press, 1994.

Cole, Peter. *The Dream of the Poem*. Princeton NJ: Princeton University Press, 2007.

Costa Fontes, Manuel da. *The Art of Subversion in Inquisitorial Spain*. West Lafayette IN: Purdue University Press, 2005.

Crompton, Louis. *Homosexuality and Civilization*. Cambridge MA: Harvard University Press, 2006.

Davis, David Brion. *Inhuman Bondage: The Rise and Fall of Slavery in the New World*. Oxford: Oxford University Press, 2006.

Delicado, Francisco. *Portrait of Lozana: The Lusty Andalusian Woman*. Translated by Bruno M. Damiani. Potomac MD: Scripta Humanistica, 1987.

Donnelly, John Patrick. *Ignatius of Loyola*. New York: Pearson/Longman, 2004.

Duran, Manuel. "Picaresque Elements in Cervantes's Works." In *The Picaresque: Tradition and Displacement*, edited by Giancarlo Maiorino, 226–47. Minneapolis: University of Minnesota Press, 1996.

Edwards, John. *Christian Córdoba: The City and Its Region in the Late Middle Ages*. Cambridge: Cambridge University Press, 1982.

———. *The Inquisitors*. Stroud, UK: Tempus, 2007.

———. *The Spanish Inquisition*. Stroud, UK: Tempus, 1999.

Elliott, J. H. *Empires of the Atlantic World*. New Haven CT: Yale University Press, 2007.

Emmer, Peter. "The Jewish Moment." In Bernardini and Fiering, *Jews and the Expansion*, 501–18.

Estow, Clara. *Pedro the Cruel of Castile*. Leiden: E. J. Brill, 1995.

Feitler, Bruno. "Jews and New Christians in Dutch Brazil, 1630–1654." In *Atlantic Diasporas: Jews, Conversos, and Crypto-Jews in the Age of Mercantilism*, edited by Richard L. Kagan and Philip D. Morgan, 123–51. Baltimore: Johns Hopkins University Press, 2009.

Fierro, Maribel. *Abd al-Rahman III: The First Cordoban Caliph*. Oxford: One World, 2005.

Findlen, Paula. "Humanism, Politics and Pornography in Renaissance Italy." In *The Invention of Pornography, 1500–1800: Obscenity and the Origins of Modernity*, edited by Lynn Hunt, 49–108. New York: Zone Books, 1996.

Fletcher, Richard. "The Early Middle Ages." In *Spain: A History*, edited by Raymond Carr, 63–89. New York: Oxford University Press, 2000.

———. *Moorish Spain*. New York: Henry Holt, 1992.

Fontaine, Peter. *Memoirs of a Huguenot Family*. Edited by Ann Maury. New York, 1853.

Frankel, Rachel. "Antecedents and Remnants of Jodensavanne." In Bernardini and Fiering, *Jews and the Expansion*, 394–437.

Gail, Marzieh. *The Three Popes*. New York: Simon and Schuster, 1969.

Gampel, Benjamin R. *The Last Jews on Iberian Soil*. Berkeley: University of California Press, 1989.

———. "A Letter to a Wayward Teacher: The Transformations of Sephardic Culture in Christian Iberia." In *Cultures of the Jews*, edited by David Biale, 2:87–146. New York: Schocken Books, 2002.

García Cárcel, Ricardo, and Doris Moreno Martínez. *Inquisición: Historia crítica*. Madrid: Ediciones Temas de Hoy, 2000.

Garfield, Robert. "Public Christians, Secret Jews: Religion and Political Conflict on São Tomé Island in the Sixteenth and Seventeenth Centuries." *Sixteenth Century Journal* 21, no. 4 (Winter 1990): 645–54.

Gerber, Jane. *The Jews of Spain*. New York: Free Press, 1992.

Gilman, Stephen. *The Spain of Fernando de Rojas*. Princeton NJ: Princeton University Press, 1972.

Gitlitz, David M. *Secrecy and Deceit: The Religion of the Crypto-Jews*. Philadelphia: Jewish Publication Society, 1996.

Glick, Thomas F. "Science in Medieval Spain: The Jewish Contribution in the Context of *Convivencia*." In *Convivencia: Jews, Muslims, and Christians in Medieval Spain*, edited by Vivian B. Mann, Thomas F. Glick, and Jerrilynn D. Dodds, 83–112. New York: Braziller, 1992.

Goldman, Ari L. "Abravanels Celebrate a Different Hero of 1492." *New York Times*, March 23, 1992, B3.

González-Salerno, Raúl. "Catholic Anti-Judaism in Visigothic Spain." In *The Visigoths Studies in Culture and Society*, edited by Alberto Ferreiro, 123–50. Leiden: Brill, 1999.

Green, Arthur. "The Zohar: Jewish Mysticism in Medieval Spain." In *Essential Papers on Kabbalah*, edited by Lawrence Fine, 27–66. New York: New York University Press, 1995.

Gutwirth, Eleazar. "Towards Expulsion: 1391–1492." In *Spain and the Jews*, edited by Elie Kedourie, 51–73. London: Thames and Hudson, 1992.

Halevi, Judah. *The Kuzari*. Translated by Hartwig Hirschfeld. New York: Schocken Books, 1974.

———. *Selected Poems of Jehudah Halevi*. Edited by Heinrich Brody. Translated by Nina Salaman. Philadelphia: Jewish Publication Society of America, 1974.

Haliczer, Stephen. "The Jew as Witch." In *Cultural Encounters*, edited by Mary Elizabeth Perry and Anne J. Cruz, 146–56. Berkeley: University of California Press, 1991.

Hartveit, Lars. *Workings of the Picaresque in the British Novel*. Oslo: Solum Forlag, 1987.

Hayyat, Judah ben Jacob. "The Offering of Judah." In Raphael, *Expulsion 1492 Chronicles*, 112–15.

Hillenbrand, Robert. "Medieval Cordoba as a Cultural Centre." In *The Legacy of Muslim Spain*, edited by Salma Khadra Jayyusi, 2 vols., 112–35. Leiden: E. J. Brill, 1994.

Hillgarth, J. N. *The Spanish Kingdoms*. 2 vols. Oxford: Clarendon Press, 1976–78.

Holmes, Jennifer S. *Terrorism and Democratic Stability Revisited*. Manchester: Manchester University Press, 2008.

Hutcheston, Gregory S. "Desperately Seeking Sodom: Queerness in the Chronicles of Alvaro de Luna." In *Queer Iberia*, edited by Josiah Blackmore and Gregory S. Hutcheson, 222–49. Durham NC: Duke University Press, 1999.

Ibn Faradj, Isaac. "The Family Origins of Isaac Ibn Faradj, the Pure Sephard." In Raphael, Expulsion 1492 Chronicles, 122–24.

Ibn Gabirol, Solomon. *Selected Religious Poems of Solomon ibn Gabirol*. Edited by Israel Davidson. Translated by Israel Zangwill. Philadelphia: Jewish Publication Society of America, 1974.

Idel, Moshe. *Kabbalah: New Perspectives*. New Haven CT: Yale University Press, 1988.

Israel, Jonathan I. *Diasporas within a Diaspora*. Leiden: Brill, 2002.

———. "Jews of Dutch America." In Bernardini and Fiering, *Jews and the Expansion*, 335–49.

———. *Race, Class and Politics in Colonial Mexico, 1610–1670*. London: Oxford University Press, 1975.

Jewish Publication Society. *Tanakh*. Philadelphia: Jewish Publication Society, 1985.

Jordan, Winthrop D. *The White Man's Burden: Historical Origins of Racism in the United States*. Oxford: Oxford University Press, 1974.

Kamen, Henry. *The Disinherited*. New York: HarperCollins, 2008.

———. "The Expulsion: Purpose and Consequence." In *Spain and the Jews*, edited by Elie Kecourie, 74–91. London: Thames and Hudson, 1992.

———. *Inquisition and Society in Spain in the Sixteenth and Seventeenth Centuries*. Bloomington: Indiana University Press, 1985.

———. "Limpieza and the Ghost of Americo Castro: Racism as a Tool of Literary Analysis." *Hispanic Review* 64, no. 1 (Winter 1996): 19–29.

———. "The Mediterranean and the Expulsion of Spanish Jews in 1492." *Past & Present*, no. 119 (May 1988): 30–55.

———. *The Spanish Inquisition*. New York: Mentor, 1965.

———. *The Spanish Inquisition: A Historical Revision*. London: Weidenfeld and Nicolson, 1997.

Kaplan, Gregory B. "The Inception of Limpieza de Sangre." In *Marginal Voices*, edited by Amy Aronson-Friedman and Gregory B. Kaplan, 19–42. Leiden: Brill, 2012.

Katz, David S. "Israel in America." In Bernardini and Fiering, *Jews and the Expansion of Europe to the West*, 107–23.

Keyserling, Meyer. *Historia dos Judeus em Portugal*. Translated by Abriele Borchardt Correa da Silva and Anita Novinsky. São Paulo: Livararia Pioneira Editora, 1971. Originally published in 1867 as *Geschichte der Juden in Portugal*.

Kiron, Arthur. "Mythologizing 1654." *Jewish Quarterly Review* (Fall 2005): 583–94.

Klein, Elka. *Jews, Christian Society, & Royal Power in Medieval Barcelona*. Ann Arbor: University of Michigan Press, 2006.

Klooster, Wim. "Jews in Suriname and Curaçao." In Bernardini and Fiering, *Jews and the Expansion*, 350–68.

———. "Networks of Colonial Entrepreneurs." In *Atlantic Diasporas: Jews, Conversos, and Crypto-Jews in the Age of Mercantilism*, edited by Richard L. Kagan and Philip D. Morgan, 33–49. Baltimore: Johns Hopkins University Press, 2009.

Koren, Sharon Faye. "A Christian Means to a Conversa End." *Namshim: A Journal of Jewish Women's Studies and Gender Issues* 9, no. 1 (2005): 27–61.

Kraemer, Joel. L. *Maimonides*. New York: Doubleday, 2008.

Lachter, Hartley. "Jews as Masters of Secrets in Late Thirteenth-Century Castile." In *The Jew in Medieval Iberia*, edited by Jonathan Ray, 286–308. Boston: Academic Studies Press, 2012.

Lau, Estelle T. "Can Money Whiten? Exploring Race Practice in Colonial Venezuela and Its Implications for Contemporary Race Discourse." *Michigan Journal of Race and Law* (Spring 1998): 417–69.

Lawee, Eric. *Isaac Abarbanel's Stance toward Tradition*. Albany: State University of New York Press, 2001.

Lazar, Moshe. "Scorched Parchments and Tortured Memories: The 'Jewishness' of the Anussim." In *Cultural Encounters*, edited by Mary Elizabeth Perry and Anne J. Cruz, 176–206. Berkeley: University of California Press, 1991.

Lea, Henry Charles. *A History of the Inquisition of Spain*. 4 vols. New York: Macmillan, 1906–7.

Lewis, Bernard. *Islam in History*. Chicago: Open Court, 1993.

Liss, Peggy K. *Isabel the Queen*. New York: Oxford University Press, 1992.

Lope de Vega, Félix. *The Innocent Child*. Translated by Michael Jacobs. London: Oberon Books, 1991.

Lowney, Chris. *A Vanished World*. New York: Free Press, 2005.

Machiavelli, Niccolò. *The Prince*. Translated by George Bull. London: Penguin Books, 2005.

Maimonides. *Guide for the Perplexed*. Translated by M. Friedlander. New York: Barnes and Noble, 2004.

Makki, Mahmoud. "The Political History of Al-andalus." In *The Legacy of Muslim Spain*, edited by Salma Khadra Jayyusi, 1:3–87. Leiden: E. J. Brill, 1994.

Malammed, Renee Levine. *Heretics of Daughters of Israel*. New York: Oxford University Press, 1999.

Mancing, Howard. "The Protean Picaresque." In *The Picaresque: Tradition and Displacement*, edited by Gancarlo Maiorino, 273–91. Minneapolis: University of Minnesota Press, 1996.

Mariana, Juan de. *Historia general de España*. Toledo, 1601.

Marías, Julián. *Understanding Spain*. Translated by Frances M. Lopez-Morillas. Ann Arbor: University of Michigan Press, 1990.

Marino, Nancy. *Don Juan Pacheco: Wealth and Power in Late Medieval Spain*. Tempe: Arizona Center for Medieval and Renaissance Studies, 2006.

Márquez Villanueva, Francisco. "Jewish 'Fools' of the Spanish Fifteenth Century." *Hispanic Review* 50, no. 4 (Autumn 1982): 385–409.

Martínez, María Elena. "The Black Blood of New Spain." *William and Mary Quarterly* 61, no. 3 (2004): 479–520.

Martonell, Joanot, and Martí Joan de Galba. *Tirant lo Blanc*. Translated by David H. Rosenthal. Baltimore: Johns Hopkins University Press, 1984.

Martz, Linda. "Implementation of Pure Blood Statutes in Sixteenth-Century Toledo." In *Iberia and Beyond: Hispanic Jews Between Cultures*, edited by Bernard Dov Cooperman, 245–72. Newark: University of Delaware Press, 1998.

McGaha, Michael. "Is There a Hidden Jewish Meaning in Don Quixote?" *Cervantes: Bulletin of the Cervantes Society of America* 24, no. 1 (2004): 173–88.

Melammed, Renée Levine. *Heretics or Daughters of Israel? The Crypto-Jewish Women of Castile*. New York: Oxford University Press, 1999.

Menocal, Maria Rosa. *The Ornament of the World*. Boston: Little Brown, 2002.

Meyerson, Mark D. *A Jewish Renaissance in Fifteenth-Century Spain*. Princeton NJ: Princeton University Press, 2004.

Miramon, Charles de. "The Invention of the Concept of Race." In *The Origins of Racism in the West*, edited by Miriam Eliav-Feldon, Benjamin H Isaac, and Joseph Ziegler, 200–216. Cambridge: Cambridge University Press, 2009.

Montoro, Antón de. *Poesía completa*. Edited by Marithelma Costa. Cleveland: Cleveland State University Press, 1990.

Morner, Magnus. *Race Mixture in the History of Latin America*. Boston: Little, Brown, 1967.

Morris, Colin. *The Papal Monarchy: The Western Church from 1250*. Oxford: Clarendon Press, 1989.

Moses de León. *Zohar: The Book of Splendor*. Edited by Gershom Scholem. New York: Schocken Books, 1977.

Murphy, Cullen. *God's Jury*. Boston: Houghton Mifflin Harcourt, 2012.

Nachmanides (Ramban). *Writings and Discourses*. Translated by Rabbi De. Charles Chavel. 2 vols. New York: Shilo, 1978.

Netanyahu, B. *Don Isaac Abravanel, Statesman and Philosopher*. 3rd ed. Philadelphia: Jewish Publication Society, 1972.

———. *The Marranos of Spain*. 3rd rev. ed. Ithaca NY: Cornell University Press, 1999.

———. *The Origins of the Inquisition in Fifteenth Century Spain*. New York: Random House, 1995.

Neuman, Abraham. *The Jews in Spain*. 2 vols. Philadelphia: Jewish Publication Society, 1944.

Nieto-Phillips, John M. *The Language of Blood*. Albuquerque: University of New Mexico Press, 2004.

Nirenberg, David. *Communities of Violence*. Princeton NJ: Princeton University Press, 1998.

———. "Enmity and Assimilation: Jews, Christians, and Converts in Medieval Spain." *Common Knowledge* 9, no.1 (2003): 137–55.

———. "Was There Race before Modernity?" In *The Origins of Racism in the West*, edited by Miriam Eliav-Feldon, Benjamin Isaac and Joseph Ziegler, 232–64. Cambridge: Cambridge University Press, 2009.

Nuland, Sherwin. *Maimonides*. New York: Schocken, 2005.

O'Callaghan, Joseph F. "Paths to Ruin: The Economic and Financial Policies of Alfonso the Learned." In *The Worlds of Alfonso the Learned and James the Conqueror*, edited by Robert I. Burns, 41–67. Princeton NJ: Princeton University, 1985.

Osório, Jerónimo. "Of the Life and Deeds of King Manuel." In Raphael, *Expulsion 1492 Chronicles*, 158–62.

Pagels, Elaine. *The Origin of Satan*. New York: Random House, 1995.

Pagis, Dan. *Hebrew Poetry of the Middle Ages and the Renaissance*. Berkeley: University of California Press, 1991.

Paramo, Luis de. "On the Origins and Advances of the Holy Office of the Inquisition." In Raphael, *Expulsion 1492 Chronicles*, 186–87.

Parkes, James. *The Conflict of the Church and the Synagogue*. Cleveland: Meridian Books, 1961.

Payne, Stanley. *A History of Spain and Portugal*. 2 vols. Madison: University of Wisconsin Press, 1976.

Perednik, Gustavo D. "Naïve Spanish Judeophobia." *Jewish Political Studies Review* 15, nos. 3–4 (Fall 2003): 87–110.

Peréz, Joseph. *History of a Tragedy*. Translated by Lysa Hochroth. Urbana: University of Illinois Press, 2007.

———. *The Spanish Inquisition*. Translated by Janet Lloyd. New Haven CT: Yale University Press, 2005.

Pieroni, Geraldo. "Outcasts from the Kingdom." In Bernardini and Fiering, *Jews and the Expansion*, 242–53.

Pijnigh, Ernst. "New Christians as Sugar Cultivators and Traders in the Portuguese Atlantic, 1450–1800." In Bernardini and Fiering, *Jews and the Expansion*, 485–500.

Poliakov, Leon. *The History of Anti-Semitism*. New York: Vanguard Press, 1965.

Raphael, David. *The Expulsion 1492 Chronicles*. North Hollywood CA: Carmi House Press, 1992.

Ray, Jonathan. *The Sephardic Frontier*. Ithaca NY: Cornell University Press, 2006.

Reed, Walter L. *An Exemplary History of the Novel*. Chicago: University of Chicago Press, 1981.

Reston, James, Jr. *The Dogs of God*. New York: Anchor, 2006.

Rohr, Isabelle. *The Spanish Right and the Jews*. Brighton: Sussex Academic Press, 2007.

Rojas, Fernando de. *La Celestina*. Translated by Lesley Byrd Simpson. Berkeley: University of California Press, 1966.

Roncero López, Victoriano. "Lazarillo, Guzmán and Buffoon Literature." *MLN* 116 (2001): 235–49.

Rosenberg, Deborah Skolnik. "The Converso and the Spanish Picaresque Novel." In *Marginal Voices*, edited by Amy Aronson-Friedman and Gregory B Kaplan, 183–206. Leiden: Brill, 2012.

Roth, Cecil. *A History of the Marranos*. New York: Meridian Books, 1959.

———. *The Spanish Inquisition*. New York: Norton, 1964.

Roth, Norman. *Conversos, Inquisition and the Expulsion of the Jews from Spain*. Madison: University of Wisconsin Press, 1995.

———. "'Deal Gently with the Young Man': Love of Boys in Medieval Hebrew Poetry of Spain." *Speculum* 57, no. 1 (1982): 20–51.

———. "Jewish Collaborators in Alfonso's Scientific Work." In *Emperor of Culture: Alfonso X the Learned of Castile and His Thirteenth-Century Renaissance*, edited by Robert I. Burns, 59–72. Philadelphia: University of Pennsylvania Press, 1990.

———. *Jews, Visigoths and Muslims in Medieval Spain*. Leiden: E. J. Brill, 1994.

Rothschild, Herbert B., Jr. "Falstaff and the Picaresque Tradition." *Modern Language Review* 68, no. 1 (January 1973): 14–21.

Round, Nicolas. *The Greatest Man Uncrowned*. London: Temesis Books, 1986.

Rout, Leslie B., Jr. *The African Experience in Spanish America*. Cambridge: Cambridge University Press, 1976.

Sabatini, Rafael. *Torquemada and the Spanish Inquisition*. Cambridge: Riverside Press.

Sachar, Howard. *Farewell España*. New York: Alfred A. Knopf, 1994.

Schama, Simon. *The Embarrassment of Riches*. New York: Alfred A. Knopf, 1987.

Scheindlin, Raymond, comp. and trans. *The Gazelle: Medieval Hebrew Poems on God, Israel, and the Soul*. New York: Oxford University Press, 1991.

———. *The Song of the Distant Dove: Judah Halevi's Pilgrimage*. New York: Oxford University Press, 2009.

———. *Wine, Women, and Death*. Philadelphia: Jewish Publication Society, 1986.

Scholem, Gershom. *Major Trends in Jewish Mysticism*. New York: Schocken Books, 1973.

———. *Origins of the Kabbalah*. Princeton NJ: Princeton University Press, 1962.

Schorsch, Jonathan. *Jews and Blacks in the Early Modern World*. New York: Cambridge University Press, 2004.

Schroeder, H. J. *Disciplinary Decrees of the General Councils: Text, Translation and Commentary*. St. Louis: B. Herder, 1937.

Seed, Patricia. "Origin of Modern Navigation." In Bernardini and Fiering, *Jews and the Expansion*, 73–85.

Shepherd, Verene A., and Hilary McDonald Beckles. *Caribbean Slavery in the Atlantic World*. Kingston, Jamaica: Ian Randle, 1999.

Sicroff, Albert. *Los estatutos de Limpieza de Sangre: Controversias entre los siglos XV y XVII*. Spanish translation by Mauro Armiño. Madrid: Taurus, 1985.

Siraisi, Nancy. *Medieval & Early Renaissance Medicine*. Chicago: University of Chicago Press, 1990.

Sirat, Colette. *A History of Jewish Philosophy in the Middle Ages*. Cambridge: Cambridge University Press, 1985.

Sloan, Dolores. *The Sephardic Jews of Spain and Portugal*. Jefferson NC: McFarland, 2009.

Smedley, Audrey. *Race in North America*. Boulder CO: Westview Press, 2007.

Snyder, Holly. "English Markets, Jewish Merchants, and Atlantic Endeavors." In *Atlantic Diasporas: Jews, Conversos, and Crypto-Jews in the Age of Mercantilism*, edited by Richard L. Kagan and Philip D. Morgan, 50–74. Baltimore: Johns Hopkins University Press, 2009.

Soyer, Francois. *The Persecution of the Jews and Muslims of Portugal*. Leiden: Brill, 2007.

Spear, Jennifer M. "Clean of Blood, without Stain or Mixture." In *A Centre of Wonders: The Body in Early America*, edited by Janet Moore Lindman and Michele Lise Tarter, 95–108. Ithaca NY: Cornell University Press, 2001.

Starr-LeBeau, Gretchen D. *In the Shadow of the Virgin: Inquisitors, Friars, and Conversos in Guadalupe, Spain*. Princeton NJ: Princeton University Press, 2003.

Sweet, Frank W. *Legal History of the Color Line*. Palm Coast FL: Backintyme, 2005.

Sweet, James H. "The Iberian Roots of American Racist Thought." *William and Mary Quarterly*, 3rd ser., 54 (January 1997): 143–66.

Uchmany, Eva Alexandra. "New Christians and Crypto-Jews in Spanish America." In Bernardini and Fiering, *Jews and the Expansion*, 186–202.

Usque, Samuel. "Consolation for the Tribulations of Israel." In Raphael, *Expulsion 1492 Chronicles*, 135–44.

Vaughan, Alden T. *Roots of American Racism: Essays on the Colonial Experience*. New York: Oxford University Press, 1995.

Vicens Vives, Jaime. "The Economy of Ferdinand and Isabella's Reign." In *Spain in the Fifteenth Century*, edited by Roger Highfield, 248–75. London: Macmillan, 1972.

Villanueva, Francisco Marquez. "Jewish 'Fools' of the Spanish Fifteenth Century." *Hispanic Review* 50, no. 4 (Autumn 1982): 393.

Wasserstein, David. *The Rise and Fall of the Party-Kings*. Princeton NJ: Princeton University Press, 1985.

Weinberger, Leon J., ed. *Twilight of a Golden Age: Selected Poems of Abraham Ibn Ezra*. Tuscaloosa: University of Alabama Press, 1997.

Weissberger, Barbara. "A Tierra, Puto!" In *Queer Iberia*, edited by Josiah Blackmore and Gregory S. Hutcheson, 291–324. Durham NC: Duke University Press, 1999.

Wertheimer, Elaine. "Converso 'Voices' in 15th and 16th Century Spanish Literature." In *The Conversos and Moriscos in Late Medieval Spain and Beyond*, edited by Kevin Ingram, 2 vols., 1:97–120. Leiden: Brill, 2009.

Williams, James Homer. "An Atlantic Perspective." In Bernardini and Fiering, *Jews and the Expansion of Europe*, 369–93.

Witnitzer, Arnold. *Jews in Colonial Brazil*. New York: Columbia University Press, 1960.

Yerushalmi, Yosef Hayim. "Exile and Expulsion in Jewish History." In *Crisis and Creativity in the Sephardic World, 1391–1648*, edited by Benjamin R. Gampel, 3–22. New York: Columbia University Press, 1997.

———. *The Lisbon Massacre of 1506 and the Royal Image in the Shebet Yehudah*. New York: Hebrew Union College, 1976.

Yovel, Yirmihayu. "Converso Dualities in the First Generation: The Cancioneros." *Jewish Social Studies* 4, no. 3 (1998): 1–28.

———. *Spinoza and Other Heretics: The Marrano of Reason*. Princeton NJ: Princeton University Press, 1989.

Zacuto, Abraham. "The Book of Genealogies (*Sefer Yuhasin*)." In Raphael, *Expulsion 1492 Chronicles*, 163–69.

Index

Suriname, 364
Susan, Susanna de, 235–37
Synagogue El Transito, 118

taifas, 52–54, 72, 83
Talavera, Hernando de, 225, 226
Talmud: attacks on, by the church, 105–12,
    148–53; and Disputation of Barcelona,
    106–11; and Disputation of Tortosa,
    148–53; and Kabbalah, 114, 115; and
    Karaites, 33; as legal system, 30; Mai-
    monides and, 45, 62, 63, 67; origin of,
    32, 36; Rashi and, 76; and the *Zohar*,
    88–91
tax farming, 74, 116, 152, 282, 360
Teruel, 264, 265, 289
Tirant lo Blanc, 313, 314
Toledo: and Alfonso X, 82; anti-Jewish riots
    in, 129, 134, 141; and conflict between
    Old and New Christians, 187, 196,
    197; Inquisition in, 247, 251, 256, 259,
    260, 270; Jewish origin in, 12; Jew-
    ish pietism in, 76; and Judah Halevi,
    38, 39; and Moorish conquest, 18; and
    Pedro the Cruel, 119; and purity of
    blood, 311, 312, 316, 318–20, 322, 326;
    and the rebellion of 1449, 172–84, 194,
    195, 226; and the reconquest, 71; and
    St. Vincent Ferrer, 141; and Synagogue
    El Transito, 117, 118

Torquemada, Tomás de: and Aragon, 264,
    265; and blood-libel trial, 270, 274;
    character and career of, 241–47; and
    expulsion decree, 283–85; and Inqui-
    sition, 239; instructions of, 254; and
    Isabella, 224, 225; and Juan de Torque-
    mada, 158; and purity of blood, 317
Torrejoncillo, Francisco de, 314, 315
Tortosa, 132, 148–53, 268, 308
torture, 18, 61, 82, 104, 116, 119, 145, 159,
    165, 173, 176, 226, 245, 251–53, 257,
    263, 268, 269, 271, 302

Umayyad, 19–21, 23, 24, 52

Valencia: anti-Jewish riots in, 127, 130–32
    136; and expulsion decree, 290, 293;
    Inquisition in, 244, 251, 263; and Jaume
    the Conqueror, 86; and Jews, 73, 137,
    277; and Pere the Ceremonious, 117; and
    Pope Benedict XIII, 191; and the recon-
    quest, 73, 84; and Solomon ibn Gabirol,
    46, 48; and St. Vincent Ferrer, 139, 140
Virginia, 336, 337, 339
Visigoths, 12–15, 18, 20, 26, 71, 179

West Indies Company (WIC), 359, 360,
    362, 363, 366, 367

Zacuto, Abraham, 278, 279, 286, 297
Zohar, 4, 88–93